isishweshwe

isishweshwe

A History of the Indigenisation of
Blueprint in Southern Africa

Juliette Leeb-du Toit

UNIVERSITY OF KwaZulu-Natal Press

Published in 2017 by University of KwaZulu-Natal Press
Private Bag X01, Scottsville, 3209
Pietermaritzburg, South Africa
E-mail: books@ukzn.ac.za
Website: www.uknpress.co.za

© 2017 Juliette Leeb-du Toit

All rights reserved. No part of this publication may be reproduced or transmitted in any form or by any means, electronic or mechanical, including photocopying, recording, or any information storage and retrieval system, without prior permission in writing from University of KwaZulu-Natal Press.

ISBN: 978 1 86914 314 5
eISBN: 978 1 86914 361 9

Managing editor: Sally Hines
Editor: Alison Lockhart
Proofreader: Cathy Munro
Design and layout: Marise Bauer, M Design
Indexer: Judith Shier

Cover photographs: A selection of *isishweshwe* cloth from Da Gama Textiles, 2006.
Photographs © J. Leeb-du Toit

Printed and bound in South Africa by Pinetown Printers

Contents

List of captions for full-page photographs vi
Acknowledgements viii
Introduction 1

1. Indigo Textiles in Context 11
2. Early Cape Dress in Context 35
3. Frontier, Voortrekker and Pioneer Dress 49
4. German Missionaries, *Blaudruck* and German Settlers 67
5. Modern European and American Blueprint in Context 85
6. Modern British Blueprint in Context 113
7. Da Gama Textiles and *isiShweshwe* 133
8. Traders and *isiShweshwe* 161
9. Cultural Usage of *isiShweshwe* in Lesotho and Swaziland 179
10. Cultural Usage of *isiShweshwe* in South Africa, Botswana and Namibia 205
11. *isiShweshwe* Dress and Its Modernities 237

Appendix: Naming *isiShweshwe* Designs 260
Notes 277
Select Bibliography 290
Index 296

Captions for full-page photographs

Bolts of *isishweshwe* in the Da Gama Textiles factory, c.2008.
Photograph © Kirsten Nieser ii

A selection of *isishweshwe* cloth from Da Gama Textiles, 2006.
Photograph © J. Leeb-du Toit x

Georg Stark in his blueprinter's studio in Jever, Germany, 2005.
Photograph © Kirsten Nieser 10

VOC plate, seventeenth century, Iziko Museums of South Africa............................ 34

Boer child's *kappie* (bonnet), late nineteenth century. National Museum, Bloemfontein.
Photograph © Kirsten Nieser 48

Replica of German settler dress, East London Museum.
Photograph © Kirsten Nieser 66

Perrotine rollers in the Kékfestö Múzeum, Pápa, Hungary, 2005.
Photograph © Kirsten Nieser 84

Wigan Printworks pattern book, c.1970, Da Gama Textiles achive 112

Discharge-printing machine, Da Gama Textiles, Zwelitsha, Eastern Cape, 2005.
Photograph © Kirsten Nieser.. 132

A selection of *isishweshwe* cloth from Da Gama Textiles, 2015.
Photograph © J. Leeb-du Toit 160

Swazi *amabutho* at the birthday celebrations of King Mswati III, 2005.
Photograph © J. Leeb-du Toit 178

BaPedi woman's marriage *diele* (or *semabajane*), Polokwane, 2005.
Photograph © J. Leeb-du Toit 204

Kaftan from Helen de Leeuw's collection, c.1980.
Photograph © J. Leeb-du Toit 236

Now looking back, things I took for granted come forward: for instance, what women wore. For decades every black woman in Southern Rhodesia and Northern Rhodesia and Nyasaland wore blue and white, indigo and white, patterned cotton stuff. Whose idea was it? At some point somebody must have said . . . 'We are going to manufacture this type of blue and white cloth for the women of Southern Africa.' The patterns look Indonesian. The cloth was manufactured in Manchester along with kenti [sic] cloth for North Africa and the kangas of Kenya. The great bales from England arrived in ships, were put onto trains, and the rolls of cloth, smelling of dye, found themselves on the shelves of hundreds of 'kaffir truck' shops. It was beautiful material, strong, good quality. The women looked beautiful. This cloth could not be worn by poor women now, for it is associated with a shameful past. Meanwhile, it is made up into luxury items for boutiques in the big cities of [South Africa], and bought by fashionable black women who may have never known its history. In Zimbabwe I saw it covering sofas and chairs in a farmhouse, and as curtains in Harare. Unwritten social history: in this case probably in the records of the great cotton manufacturers of the Midlands.

– Doris Lessing, *African Laughter: Four Visits to Zimbabwe*

Acknowledgements

Initially this book was meant to be no more than a segment of a project on the history of *isishweshwe* funded by the National Heritage Council. Its development led to several curated exhibitions. Two were in Pietermaritzburg and London in 2005, another was at the East London Museum in 2008, and a third was at the Slave Lodge (Iziko Museums of South Africa) in Cape Town in 2012. In the course of my research I also amassed a vast collection of images, dress items and recorded interviews (both audio and visual).

As my project advanced, what was to be a catalogue eventually became a book. I sincerely thank the National Heritage Council for their patience and understanding. As I progressed I often shifted publication deadlines and my work would never have been realised without their co-operation.

I am particularly indebted to the hundreds of people interviewed – too many to mention individually – who gave their time so freely and provided invaluable information that broadened my perspectives and deepened my research. I dedicate this text to them and to the many other informants and field assistants – archivists, librarians, traders, friends – who helped me on my way.

Special thanks to Helen Bester and her partner Marius. Helen supported this project from the outset and was unstinting in providing access to resources, informants and the archival collection at Da Gama Textiles. Her knowledge of the history and development of *isishweshwe* at Da Gama is phenomenal and her enthusiasm and dedication in sustaining its production and marketing, locally and internationally, are exceptional.

Particular thanks to Wieke van Delen for her sterling work on the Cape Town exhibition at the Slave Lodge and for finding one of the most important missing links in the project . . . a source on the turn of the century German provenance of the cloth in South Africa.

The late John Cowie and his family, notably his son Neil, gave me ongoing assistance and information during the compilation of this book. So did Chippy Bruce who patiently fielded endless questions and provided significant insights into the marketing of *isishweshwe*.

I am profoundly grateful to Kirsten Nieser, my colleague and friend, who supported every aspect of this research. She helped to write and edit initial funding proposals; was a frequent companion on field trips across South Africa and abroad; often provided her vehicle for extended trips and co-curated the first three *isishweshwe* exhibitions. An exceptional photographer, she also assisted in film and tape recordings and edited, transcribed and organised vast amounts of visual and audio data. She unstintingly provided accommodation in Pietermaritzburg and Hamburg (Germany) between field trips, and gave me endless moral support. In addition she eagerly conducted research on German *Blaudruck* and shared her knowledge with me when I asked her to help with this aspect of the project. Some of her excellent papers on *Blaudruck* and *isishweshwe* have enriched my project. Together we will develop this aspect for an exhibition in Dresden in the near future. My thanks to Hildegard, Kirsten's mother, who assisted in recovering histories of German *Blaudruck*, and contributed in many unspoken ways to this endeavour.

I thank my children, Alcuin, Christiane and Gregory, who patiently tolerated my absences from home and my obsession with *isishweshwe*. Their support and understanding are deeply appreciated.

I also thank my husband, Allan Botha, for his editing, proofreading and insightful contribution to this book.

To the publisher at UKZN Press, Debra Primo, who believed in the potential of the project, and to Sally Hines and Alison Lockhart, thank you for keeping the book on track.

Introduction

This book is an account of the history and indigenisation of blueprint or *isishweshwe*, a local blueprint cloth, which has permeated the dress of numerous South Africans, irrespective of race or culture, at one time or another. It is also an account of the deep-seated affinities of users of the cloth, affinities embedded in a fascinating history of national and international trade, coercion and the emergence of cross-culturalism and self-definition.

Earlier naming of *isishweshwe* in South Africa originated in its European prototypes, but the cloth was soon known in South Africa mainly as blueprint, *Duitse sis* or *bloudruk* (Afrikaans). In present-day Eastern Cape and KwaZulu-Natal, some of the first indigenous naming of blueprint appears to have occurred, possibly from the late nineteenth century, associated with German settler and mission dress and the cloth's later provenance – predominantly from Germany – resulting in the emergence of names such as *isijalmani* (among *isiXhosa* speakers). As shown in Chapter 9, the name *seshoeshoe* appears to have emerged in Lesotho by the early twentieth century, associated both with the name and deeds of Lesotho's founder, Moshoeshoe I. *seShoeshoe* later became more widely known throughout South Africa as *isishweshwe* (an *isiZulu* phonetic variant) (Leeb-du Toit 1995; Pheto-Moeti 2005: 39).

Internationally, however, as the precursor of *isishweshwe*, blueprint was known by various names – for example, *blauwdruk* (Holland), *Blaudruck* (Germany), blueprint (United Kingdom and United States), *kékfestö* (Hungary) and *modrotisk* (Czech Republic). In South Africa a number of vernacular names for *isishweshwe* emerged over time. They were coined by the cloth's users and often reflected its European origins. Hence 'German print' or blueprint (English), *Duitse sis*, *bloudruk* (Afrikaans), *ujamani*, *isijalmani*, *ujeremani*, *idark*, *iblu* (*isiZulu* and *isiXhosa*, as also used by the *amaBhaca*, *amaNtlangwini*, *amaMpondo*, *amaThembu* and *amaMfengu*). Consider also *amatoishi* (*sePedi*) and *ndoeitji* or *mateis* (*seTswana* or *otjiHerero*). Currently *isishweshwe* is the name most commonly used in South Africa, as well as its English equivalent, blueprint.

A knowledge of indigo production and indigo trade, dyeing and printing is indispensable for understanding and locating textiles such as blueprint in South Africa, as shown in Chapter 1. The cultural usage and colour preferences of *isishweshwe* in South Africa are likewise regionally variable. Three colours of the cloth still predominate – blue, brown and red – with other variants such as green, maroon and black. A combination of ochre with blue and brown, currently marketed as Fancy Prints by Da Gama Textiles of King William's Town, has also been used since the 1950s. More recently, *isishweshwe* has been produced by Da Gama in a range of colours – purple, turquoise, lime green, orange and pink, and in a myriad combinations of these – but indigo, blue and brown (and, to a lesser extent, red), retain their popularity and significance locally. Such preferences are, for the most part, culturally and historically derived and upheld.

Information on pre-colonial dress among the indigenous peoples in South Africa is scant, but what is available suggests they wore hide or other organic covering, depending on the availability of materials and the ingenuity of users. This distinctiveness was elaborated over the centuries by various groups – for example, in the use of beads derived from intercultural contact with other African, Asian and European peoples. In pre-colonial South Africa, as in most early African territories before 1700, dress functioned essentially as a form of protection against the elements and was aligned with cultural and ritual behaviours. As peoples elected to define themselves more distinctly, their dress gradually began to reflect a consensual cultural identity, distinguishing wearers both geographically and historically (Eicher 1995: 4).

Dress in South Africa, like culture, was attached to ideological and psychological boundaries calculated to individuate and identify its wearers after 1700 (Eicher 1995). It also designated heritage and other aspects of identity that reinforced its usage. In this way, dress often reflected desirable propriety and mores associated with gender, age and rites of passage; its social meaning later embracing wealth and status. Even though such encodings appeared fixed, they were essentially fluid, changing with the interplay of historical forces in which remnants of intercontinental trade and cross-cultural borrowing assumed collective expressions of identity in the colonial period.

Few peoples can claim to have remained uninfluenced by contact with others – multiculturalism and economic globalisation are not recent phenomena – and South Africa is no exception. Early trade conducted in the first century BC along the eastern seaboard by Arabs, Indians and Phoenicians established important routes for the dissemination of local and foreign goods. This interaction was dramatically affected by the influence of world trade as later European influence drew the subcontinent into the global economy. Portuguese expeditions, for example, initiated from the late fifteenth century, significantly interrupted the centuries-old canoe trade once plied by the Arabs along the eastern seaboard of Africa.

European trade in Africa soon surpassed other trade links in the region as new goods were gradually and selectively incorporated and adapted by indigenous

Introduction

groups. The expansion of European colonialism after the seventeenth century, and the ensuing resettlement and displacement of South Africa's peoples, changed the patterns of intercultural contact and absorption. New colonial centres, predominantly European, began to emulate prototypes of dress from their countries of origin, while variants flourished among European settlers in the more rural areas.

From the second half of the seventeenth century, as a result of growing European occupation in South Africa, dress at the Cape began to demarcate differences in terms of race, ethnicity and class. By the eighteenth century, many European preferences in dress were well represented in settlements such as the Cape, as shown in Chapter 2. Early trade activity in South Africa accelerated with increasing European settlement, especially from the nineteenth century, allowing hinterland dwellers greater access to European-manufactured goods.

Interaction between peoples and the exchange of the items they produce has a long history. Joanne B. Eicher's contention that dress functions as 'a history of contact with other peoples' (1995: 2) is an appropriate point from which to examine the cross-cultural associations and usage of blueprint in South Africa. Starting from the inception of contact with other peoples, intercultural borrowings in the form of trade from central Africa, from the continent's eastern and western seaboards and from Asia and Europe, gradually marked the embellishment of dress among local peoples. Late eighteenth-century trade provided a major source of items that could embellish prevailing dress or provide cheap alternatives, as shown in Chapter 3.

As suggested above, after centuries of exchange and indigenisation – involving cloth, beads, buttons, blankets and other embellishments – various encodings of indigenous South African dress evolved, becoming particularly distinctive in the late nineteenth century. Relations between European migrants and the indigenous population were often strained, based as they were on power exerted in various forms of coercion, control and displacement. When cultural interaction became more deeply established, however – in mission education, conversion, trade and migrant labour – further degrees of assimilation came about, based on the availability and accruing desirability of materials. Simultaneously, indigenous peoples on the colonial periphery began selectively to absorb Western cultural habits and products. They shaped the nature of goods and developed a marked cultural particularity in their attire. Consequently, dress conventions among black South Africans became identifiably more distinctive in their derivations from selectively acquired sources and bartered goods. In the process, the increasing use of colonial products was irrevocably modified or subverted in the nineteenth century.

Rather than merely denoting the economic and cultural imposition of European hegemony and control, the colonial usage of cloth, clothing and beads by black South Africans undeniably suggests the presence of individual and collective preferences and choices, despite European oppression and the invasiveness of trader holdings from the nineteenth century onwards. Thus the impact of European-derived dress can be said, partly at least, to reflect modernity, shifting economic mobility and personal aspirations among South Africa's indigenous peoples. The local adoption of Indian (and perhaps other East Asian) and European-derived cloth, such as blueprint, was also reinforced by its incorporation into significant rites of passage. These cultural practices stood for a condoned assimilation, synthesis or reinterpretation, in which cloth became aligned with important value systems among indigenous peoples (Hammond-Tooke 1974; Vilakazi 1973). The association could be implicit in colour choice, design and motifs – as located in clan totems – or even in the ideals of respect and decorum residing in acculturated wear and traditional cultural practices.

For South Africa's indigenous peoples, exposure to European dress codes was initially rare, except in strategic settlements or missionary contexts. Traders soon embarked into the interior, however, and established a selective market among the peoples there. This, as well as various forms of coercion, led to the replacement of indigenous dress items with goods the traders peddled as they criss-crossed familiar routes, as described in Chapter 8. Indigenous dress codes were reinforced or altered in this way as waves of industrially produced items accumulated on traders' wagons. What decided the choices of traders and customers was ultimately based on communication between traders and customers, on customers' preferences and on the availability of products that amplified or supplanted emergent dress encoding.

While colonialism established itself, indigenous groups gradually developed their cultural distinctiveness (often as a result of displacement, conflict and coercion), established their representations and perceived them as central to their world views (Buntman 1996: 3). But these encodings were seldom entirely fixed and remained subject to inflections over time. Cloth usage, for example, could only be assimilated, sustained and endowed if it conveyed, at least to some extent, associations implicit in dress, colour symbolism, mores and cultural practices. Hence, assimilated cloth, such as blueprint, represented a process of reinterpretation in which new items became aligned with familiar value sytems (Hammond-Tooke 1974; Winters 2015). After several years, even centuries, select items assumed collective acceptance in this way and over time acquired further associations, as with blueprint usage initiated on local mission stations, as considered in Chapter 4. These items could be regional, gendered, status-related or ceremonial, or they could be attached to age-grade rituals and practices. Other associations were linked to class or to cultural or political affinity or

Introduction

resistance, to nascent nationalism and to the later emergence of new states after independence and democratisation from the 1960s onwards, as in Swaziland, Lesotho and Botswana. Indigenisation thus resulted in specific preferences and their continuities. The naming of items in the vernacular, as happened with *isishweshwe*, possibly from the late 1950s onwards, or earlier, further conveyed cultural assimilation and relevance.

As I show later, historical and cultural developments, natural and man-made disasters and distinctive cultural events – the initial British (1820) and German (1858) settlements and the subsequent access of settlement in the nineteenth and twentieth century; the abolition of slavery (1834) and the start of the Trekboer exodus (1834); the Frontier Wars (1779–1879) and the Xhosa cattle-killing (1856); the Anglo-Zulu War (1879) and the Bambatha Rebellion (1906) – all generated changes in the use of trade items. The incorporation of specific items for sale was selective and considered, many pedlars asserting that they knew what could be traded in a particular region and to whom. Items such as cloth, for example, might be in demand only when the harvest had ended and customers were prepared to barter surplus produce.

Blueprint or *isishweshwe* has a long and complex history in South Africa. It may have reached these shores in the 1700s as a variant of indigo cloth – the term includes blueprint – which was produced in India from the eighth century onwards, as noted in Chapter 1. It was marked by white organic or abstract motifs on an indigo ground – a prototype of later blueprint – and was but one of the many Indian or East Asian cloth types used by the Portuguese for trade in Africa and Brazil. But, as I show later, it was also possibly rooted in the aesthetic of a fifteenth-century indigo slave-trade cloth produced on the Cape Verde islands off Africa by African weavers, dyers and slaves employed by the Portuguese. It probably reached South Africa as one of the many *indiennes*, a collective term used in Europe in the 1700s to denote printed or painted Indian cloth or emulated Indian cloth designs on European manufactured cloth. The Indian or East Asian prototype for *isishweshwe* was destined for eventual use in Holland and many other parts of Europe and was not initially a distinctive genre.

Blueprint was desirable because it was serviceable, hard-wearing and widely available. Another of its variants, certainly from India, was the indigo cloth widely used by slaves at the Cape in the seventeenth century. Indigo printed cloth (resist or painted) was also well known among eighteenth-century free burghers and nineteenth-century Trekboers and Boer pioneers' wives, as shown in Chapter 3.

In the 1800s other variants of indigo calico print – cotton print or *blou sis* – emerged in South Africa among traders' holdings. The cloth was also typified by a ground of indigo with motifs in white. Rural settlers and indigenous peoples identified it as a preferred cloth, together with plain indigo cloth, other cotton prints and plain and striped indigo *salempore*.[1] Thus by the 1900s *bloudruk*, *blou sis* or *Duitse sis* – all variants of blueprint – were meeting the accumulated dress-needs of diverse groups throughout South Africa (Whitham 1903: 42).

Blueprint was identifiable in particular among the *baSotho* from the late nineteenth century onwards. Printed calico settler dress was reinforced when German immigrants wore it as *Blaudruck* after the 1850s; settled on the seaboard of what is now the Eastern Cape and in KwaZulu-Natal and migrated as far afield as Mpumalanga. Many Christianised *amaMfengu*, *amaThembu* and *amaXhosa* from the Eastern Cape used blueprint, as did *baPedi*, *baTswana* and *baSotho* in their repective regions. Its usage also spread to present-day Zimbabwe, Mozambique, Angola and Namibia.

Blueprint or *isishweshwe* thus originated in various prototypes from Europe, the East and Africa. Its motifs and realisation were copied and its mass-production determined by various manufacturing centres, notably in Portugal, Holland, Germany, Britain and America (Leeb-du Toit 2005a; Nieser 2005). Its production was radically affected by technological development as when roller-printing emerged in the 1780s or when cloth dyed with synthetic aniline indigo flooded the world's textile markets in 1898. The widespread manufacture of blueprint resulted in its cheaper use in Europe and the British colonies, including many parts of South Africa by the nineteenth and early twentieth century, as shown in Chapter 3.

The production and distribution of *isishweshwe* in South Africa is substantial. Currently the cloth has assumed national associations and is sustained by widespread cultural, ritual and gendered associations prevailing in Swaziland, Lesotho and Botswana and among a wide range of other peoples in South Africa. Of late it has come to represent South Africanness and indigeneity and is currently associated with both alternate and mainstream fashion, which further emphasises its distinctive South African identity.

In 1994, on the eve of the first democratic elections in South Africa, I delivered a paper on *isishweshwe*. It was read at the first gender studies conference in South Africa and explored the cloth's usage as a marker of shifting identity among South African women (Leeb-du Toit 1994). It was a response to recollections of the early usage of *isishweshwe* by South African women from all cultures over

Introduction

the past 50 years and was prompted by personal preference and experience. I have used *isishweshwe* consistently since the late 1960s and was intrigued by its increased popularity in the 1980s. Since I was only vaguely aware then of the origins of the cloth and its cultural usage, I went on to initiate a documentation process in KwaZulu-Natal. I considered the cultural usage of *isishweshwe* and the motivation behind the proliferation of its many designs and current dress styles. I also located a number of traders, of Indian and European origin, involved in disseminating the cloth since the early twentieth century. Little did I know then that the complex history and cultural usage of indigo cloth – one of the precursors of *isishweshwe* – went back to India in the eighth century and later involved Portuguese, Dutch, German, British, American and many other international interventions.

As my research progressed, it became clear that *isishweshwe* was not merely a marker of identity among South African women and men, black and white, but was also esteemed in other areas of southern Africa – in Namibia and Botswana, Lesotho and Swaziland and (earlier) in Zimbabwe and Angola. Informants in some of these regions generously supplied me with information on the importance of *isishweshwe* as a marker of cultural identity and respect with regard to age grade, marriage and even funerary customs and ceremonies. They clarified the cloth's significance for gender and female beauty, in particular, as well as childbearing, propriety and morality and its appropriateness in *ukuhlonipha* or conventions of respect.

Subsequent investigations took my fellow researchers – in particular Kirsten Nieser – and me to national, provincial, private and mission archives throughout southern Africa. We were privileged to visit many wearers of *isishweshwe* in urban and rural areas, as well as seamstresses and tailors who predominantly used the cloth, and knowledgeable informants at various commercial outlets whose generosity and support were consistently encouraging. Subsequent travel to Germany, Hungary, the Czech Republic, Holland and Britain occurred whenever I was able to fund my visits to coincide with attendance at conferences.

By adumbrating the history of blueprint in context and then concentrating on the widespread local connotations of *isishweshwe*, this book will, I hope, add to an emerging body of research on the origins and use of textiles in southern Africa. Until the 1950s, writing on dress conventions among the colonised peoples in South Africa was located mainly in ethnographic texts, usually by white authors, coinciding with the rise of anthropology and ethnography as academic disciplines. These texts were largely informed by a Western modernist grammar, foregrounding Africans in terms of their origins and difference, and by the scrutiny of what were regarded as 'traditional' dress conventions. In early works by anthropologists – Eileen Krige, A.T. Bryant, A. Vilakazi and Hilda Kuper – and in the works of ethnologists such as N.J. van Warmelo and Max Kohler, some attention was paid to dress in terms of cultural practice, to the status of male and female users and to leaders and their entourages. But little information was provided on the dress of the ordinary citizen whose wear reflected the extent of cross-cultural influence and access to cloth trade items.

After the 1950s several writers and ethnographers in South Africa documented prominent cultural groups to foreground their distinctiveness. This emphasis was partly spurred by a grasp of the relevance of all peoples, their cultural practices and their emergent multiculturalism. Ironically many such texts emerged in the 1960s when the construction of a segregated South Africa was at its height, a process begun by the British in early colonial times. These texts on indigenous peoples and their material culture were the product of ongoing interest in ethnography and anthropology, but they were also inflected by preoccupations with difference that underscored segregation and the sinister agendas of marginalisation and white supremacy. Some of the books I have in mind here were written under the aegis of state ethnographic departments whose outlook was rooted in colonial, segregationist and racist practices.

Anthropological research, on the other hand, was complemented by popular texts, illustrated by authors such as Barbara Tyrrell and Alice Mertens, Aubrey Elliott and Jean Morris. Tyrrell and Mertens were inspired by ethnologist Killie Campbell, who pioneered the collecting of Africana, ethnographic documentation and indigenous material culture. The ethnographic detail provided by these individuals set important precedents and included striking illustrations by Tyrrell in her publications and field-based photographs by Mertens, Elliott and Morris in theirs.

One of the first texts to emerge on white South African dress conventions since European settlement in the seventeenth century was A.A. Telford's *Yesterday's Dress* (1972). This was followed by anthropologist Daphne Strutt's *Fashion in South Africa* (1975), a more informed text that centred on European-sourced clothing used by white South Africans. Strutt also provides invaluable data on early stylistic preferences among slaves, labourers, Trekboers, farmers and dissident settler groups and I rely closely on aspects of her findings in the early chapters of this book. Strutt, writing uncritically from a white colonial-Western perspective, identifies cross-cultural contact as a major influence on indigenous dress and on the development of clothing from hide and pelts to an 'elaboration', which she perceives as 'a first step towards civilisation' (Strutt 1975: ix).

More comprehensive research on dress and its embellishment in South Africa is called for. To date, authors have largely focused on beadwork and on other items that came into cultural usage – for example, blankets among the *baSotho*

Introduction

and heavy cotton sheeting among the *amaThembu* and *amaXhosa*. More recent texts have considered the cloth used by sangomas (Leeb-du Toit 2003); cloth and ornament from East Asian sources used mainly by *isiZulu* speakers and among Venda and Pedi peoples (in ongoing research by Sandra Klopper, Anitra Nettleton, Yvonne Winters, Victoria Rovine, Margrit Schulze, myself and many others); sartorial style in the new South Africa (Farber 2010; Koopman 2005a, 2005b; Rovine 2015; Leeb-du Toit 2005b); and Zulu hairstyles and dress conventions (Klopper 2005; Winters 2015). Cloth usage in South Africa, however, has yet to be extensively examined, although it has recently been treated in publications such as the *Berg Encyclopedia of World Dress and Fashion: Volume 1; Africa* (2010), edited by Joanne B. Eicher and Doran Ross.

Serendipity in my research has been keenly felt. Perplexing questions about *isishweshwe* have gradually been answered and details have emerged from the most obscure or unlikely sources. I have read extensively in a bid to contextualise the historical and cultural roots of *isishweshwe* over some 500 years. In the process I have hopefully reignited the need for deeper regional and culturally specific research on South African cloth and cloth usage. I cannot lay claim to more than that, although my work – with Kirsten Nieser as a major collaborator – has produced a wealth of data that needs to be applied and elaborated on in other publications. I recently donated some of the blueprint cloth and dress items collected in the field to the Iziko Museums of South Africa's social history collections. The rest of the collection in my possession is intended for similar bequest once exhibitions, both local and international, have taken place over the next few years.

In addition to the historical and cultural contextualising in this book, I have been keenly aware of the deep-seated affinities among most communities for *isishweshwe*. Poignant and nostalgic recollections of the usage of *isishweshwe* marked many an interview. Black South Africans have, in particular, been adamant that the cloth represents a salient part of their culture. Among many nostalgic affinities for the cloth was one from a friend, Liz Melville, now in England. Her father, Ricky Gaylard, owned a trading store in Natal near Melmoth in the 1960s. On attending a local quilters' biweekly meeting near Canterbury, she notes:

> A South African [Melville herself] in the group brought along a bag of *isishweshwe* offcuts and tipped them onto the table. One of the women scooped up the bundle of brightly patterned scraps, held it to her face, closed her eyes, breathed in deeply and then left the room as tears streamed down her cheeks. Returning a little later, she apologised and explained that she had nursed for many years in southern Africa [in the Eastern Cape] and the fabric, for her, embodied the memories of the warmth of Africa and of the women who wore the cloth.[2]

1
Indigo Textiles in Context

Dyed and printed indigo textiles in South Africa have a long history, starting in the earliest times. The role of indigo and indigo cloth in early South African dress and in textile furnishings bears testimony to a trade enterprise that involved the Portuguese from the 1400s and the Dutch from the 1640s onwards. The contact between these two maritime powers led to extensive intercontinental trade, primarily between Europe and India. Indigo – the currency of the day (Balfour-Paul 1998: 44–5) – became a major factor in their commerce. It may be said to have determined South African dress preferences – in terms of indigo cloth and its blueprint variants – at the entrepôt the Dutch established at the Cape in 1652. Indigo dyestuff and dress were also among the primary commodities that drove the Portuguese to sail around the Cape in search of safe and direct maritime access to the East. In 1498, when Vasco da Gama finally opened up the direct sea route to India – the source for most European indigo at the time – the Portuguese gained free access to China and Japan and escaped the dues imposed on Asian goods along the old route round the Arabian peninsula and overland routes via Turkey (Boyajian 2008: 14). Their initiative was followed, within the next two centuries, by the Dutch, English, French and Spanish, who created depots for themselves in India and plied the route around the Cape in their relentless search for indigo and the other valued commodities the East had to offer.

There are early precedents for indigo trade in Africa, but information about them is emerging very slowly. The Phoenicians under Necho II of Egypt, who circumnavigated Africa in approximately 700 BC, probably created the first contact between the peoples of southern Africa and other civilisations (Strutt 1975: x).[1] Perhaps indigo first reached these shores along ancient Phoenician trade routes, having been sourced in India or in North or West Africa, where it abounded and cloth-weaving and dyeing were well known. The dyeing of cloth has long been recorded in Egypt, but the Egyptians probably learnt their dyeing skills from

Indigenous South African species of indigo, *Indigofera frutescens* (river indigo, *rivierverfbos*). Photograph © Kirsten Nieser.

other areas in Africa, India or China (*HOCP* n.d.: 6).[2] African indigo, *Indigofera frutescens*, is widely known on the continent, but it appears that early trade in African indigo and cloth was limited regionally because of geographic restrictions on mobility. There are only a few records of early cloth dyed with indigenous indigo in southern Africa and we know very little about the original dyestuffs used here, even though *Indigofera frutescens* is indigenous to South Africa.

Alec Campbell, former head of the Botswana National Archive, interviewed in 2005, recounted that balls of indigo have been found intact at archaeological sites in central Botswana.[3] This discovery suggests the importation of indigo into the region, the presence of associated dyeing skills and even possibly the production of local dyestuffs from *Indigofera frutescens*. According to Campbell, there are historical records (and actual discoveries) showing that indigo cloth, as well as a black cloth, were used in Botswana by 1250 AD, as were black and dark-blue cotton skeins.[4] He says the cloth apparently came to the region 'down the east coast with

Indigo Textiles in Context

Swahili and Arab traders' via Sofala. It then reached inland through Mapungubwe and through Zimbabwe. Some indigo cloth has been located at Mapungubwe, but there is little evidence to show where it originated. Campbell suggests that the deep-blue cloth was worn by the 'upper echelons; black was probably worn by the next echelon down'. 'Spindle whorls', dating from 1200 onwards, have been found at many sites in Botswana, suggesting that people were spinning cotton as well, possibly also from India. Given speculation about trade with India, however, and finds of Egyptian amulets at Mapungubwe, the indigo cloth may well have come from Egypt or the Middle East. More recently, too, Professor Thomas Huffman from the University of the Witwatersrand has located cloth remnants in Mapungubwe, including indigo pieces, but their origins remain unknown.[5]

Jenny Balfour-Paul (1998: 18) remarks that India 'has exerted the greatest influence on the history of textiles worldwide'. Her extensive research confirms that the design, weaving and dyeing of cloth had reached exceptional heights in India as early as the second millennium BC. India was renowned for supremely gifted dyers and weavers in the textile arts; their skills crossed the trade routes of the world, exerting an enormous impact on Europe, and then were carried to remote corners of the globe, including the small Dutch settlement at the Cape.

The indigo dyestuff, which was so vital to Indian textiles, was probably used in the earliest cloth produced in India – no one can confirm this absolutely, however, since the resultant textiles are extolled primarily in literary texts – but the use of indigo has been established in later items important to the emergence of blueprint on the subcontinent.[6] Pieces of export fabric – Indian trade cloth – excavated from ancient refuse dumps in Cairo show small pale-blue patterns resist-printed by blocks on deep-blue cotton dating from 900 AD. These fragments constitute the earliest known examples of indigo-dyed cloth and may in fact be deemed one of the precursors of a generic 'blueprint' (Balfour-Paul 1998: 29–30).

Indigo dye blocks bound and wrapped with cotton thread in order to be able to detect theft. Photograph © Kirsten Nieser.

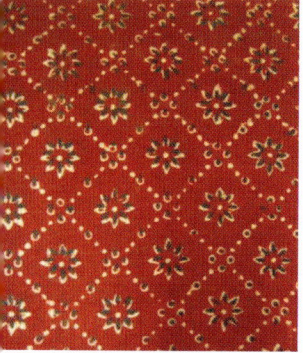

The natural indigo dyestuff used in Indian textile production before 1898, when aniline dyes emerged on the world's cloth markets, is grown today only in small areas of north-east and southern India. In its heyday, however, indigo grew prolifically in the wild, was farmed as a staple agricultural crop – alternating with food in annual rotation – or was cultivated in extensive plantations under strict supervision. Its production, which was highly labour-intensive, paid special attention to the yielding of seeds, which were vital to the quality of the dye and made exacting demands on indigo farmers (Balfour-Paul 1998: 97).

The earliest source of the indigo dyestuff and textiles that entered South Africa's eastern seaboard and the Cape of Good Hope was indubitably India. The records of voyagers and traders in Africa indicate that indigo textiles and dyestuff – termed *nila* (blue) in Sanskrit – originated from India as early as 2500 BC. Carl Linnaeus's generic botanical name for the indigo plant is *Indigofera*, showing its early origins in India (Greek *indikos* = Indian). There are more than 800 species of *Indigofera* worldwide, but only two are important in the history of the dye: *Indigofera tinctoria* (native to Asia) and *Indigofera suffruticosa* (native to Latin America). In South Africa, the cultivation of the indigenous *Indigofera frutescens* has been attempted several times; for example, by the so-called 'Cotton Germans' who endeavoured to grow it when they settled in Natal in the 1850s.

The main method of early indigo production in India and elsewhere in Asia took place in large wooden vats or in vats depressed into the ground, processes still in use today.[7] The *Indigofera tinctoria* – the leaves as well as the plant – was placed in a vat of alkali solution and left to ferment. When the dark liquid had hardened, it was cut into fist-sized bricks, also known as balls or pats, ready for the market. Indigo was transported on ships in wooden casks and very often served as ballast en route. Dyers ground the indigo balls into powder at their points of use and then dissolved and boiled them in water. Copperas and lime were added, producing a yellow liquid into which the items to be dyed were dipped several times, depending on the intensity of the blue required. When finally removed from the vat and exposed to oxygen, the dyed items turned from greenish-brown to blue as the indigo became insoluble.

Indian textiles dyed with indigo attracted European traders from the fourteenth century onwards. The colourfast Indian cloth and other bright Indian textiles that later entranced the European market proved desirable for a number of reasons. Only a handful of Europeans had access to imported organic dyes, which were extremely costly in the seventeenth century. Thus Europe developed its own organic dyes, which produced golden yellows and oranges, violets, pinks and greens. Centres located in Amsterdam even created black and brown, the predominant underclass colours of the day, especially in Dutch and English wear. Given the cost and time involved in dyeing, however, the peasant classes avoided

Indigo Textiles in Context

saturated colours – they could not easily realise these hues in the absence of the necessary dyestuffs and technical knowledge. They regarded purple and red, for example, as expensive colours reserved for the wealthy. Blue, however, which derived from indigenous woad (*Isatis tinctoria*) and cheaper indigo imports, became widely used. Woad was grown extensively in England and especially in Germany where it had been a thriving industry in Thüringen since the thirteenth century. But its production was expensive, both in time and labour, and the shades of blue it produced were not remotely as colourfast or attractive as those of indigo (Nieser 2005).[8]

As contact between Europeans and other peoples increased at the close of the seventeenth century, so too did the desire for vividly coloured textiles and dyestuffs, especially of the kind sourced in India. The Crusades had already contributed, by the turn of the fifteenth century, to changing preferences in European dress. New textiles and ornaments from the East were already familiar to European consumers. India was regarded as a major source of textiles and dyestuffs and attracted European traders irresistibly to its shores (Nieser 2005).

In 1498 Portuguese navigator Vasco da Gama, filled with the zeal expressed by his prince, Henry the Navigator, for travel to the East, 'for the glory of God and the profit of Portugal', opened up the direct sea-route to India (Strutt 1975: x).[9] This initiative marked a crucial turning point in indigo's fortunes (Balfour-Paul 1998). Indigo and the Indian textiles associated with it, including variants of plain indigo-dyed and printed cloth – the source of so much of Europe's future dress – soon became major aspects of the commerce of the day (Vogt 1975).[10] The Portuguese took the lead in international cloth and indigo trade at a time when the dyestuff was at the centre of the widest economic interest.[11] They retained this place until their monopoly began to decline in the face of fierce competition, notably from the Dutch and English, who went on to become the leading actors in world blueprint production in the seventeenth century.

The Portuguese were not well received when they arrived in India in the early 1500s, but they soon forged significant trade links with East Bengal and the Tamil Nadu coast, colonising Malabar and obtaining cloth from Chittagong and Coromandel on the south-west coast of India, both important centres of Muslim and Levantine trade (Boyajian 2008: 17). The Portuguese were the first to import indigo into Europe in the early 1500s and they established a trend by shipping their cargoes back to Lisbon and then re-exporting them, especially to Amsterdam. They also initiated the practice of copying the designs of the Asian textiles in their

Opposite page:
1. Indian cotton print, nineteenth century. Victoria and Albert Museum, London.
2. Indigo cloth from India, nineteenth century. Victoria and Albert Museum, London.
3. Indigo trade cloth from India (possibly *salempore*), nineteenth century. Victoria and Albert Museum, London.
4. Indigo trade cloth from India, nineteenth century. Victoria and Albert Museum, London.

ladings. The Dutch, whose desire for textiles was growing steadily in the 1500s, usurped this practice and were Europe's most accomplished emulators by the 1670s. Their achievements in textile design climaxed in the concepts of *Hollands* and *het oostindische manier*, which identified their specific styles of emulation. This aspect of their legacy intrigued their trading competitors. The English and the Germans also pursued their own emulation of Indian textile design in London and Hamburg in the 1700s, exerting a profound influence at the same time on the tradition of blueprint as peasant dress. The imitative textiles produced by this intervention soon became loosely known as *indiennes* throughout Europe, but the term also still applied to painted and printed patterned cloth imported en masse from India.

Portuguese East Indiamen, meanwhile, plied the waters around the tip of southern Africa on their way to Asia, using their entrepôt at Delagoa Bay (now Maputo Bay) on the east coast to gain access to the African interior. It is from here that early variants of blueprint and other painted or printed cottons may well have entered the Cape. The Portuguese continued to trade with Asia well into the 1700s (Strutt 1974: x), retaining Goa as their Indian station until 1961. Textiles and indigo, spices, precious stones, gold and ivory formed the bulk cargo of their ships from 1500 onwards. By the early 1600s, however, *indiennes* made up about 60 per cent of Portuguese ladings. This coincided with a fashion revolution in Europe where the demand for brightly coloured cottons and silks among the elite increased enormously (Nieser 2005).

Cargoes of colour-saturated Asian cottons in the ladings of Portuguese ships circumnavigating the Cape are well documented. Cheaper cloth types were meant for barter, both at the Cape and especially in West Africa, where the Portuguese supplemented their vast indigo and dyed cloth supplies. There is also evidence of a West African demand for Asian luxury products, including cloth (Boyajian 2008: 15). The India-derived cloth trade encouraged interaction between the Portuguese and Africans who inhabited the Indian and Atlantic seaboards. The two peoples traded selectively with each other and cloth and indigo were among the items traded.

Thanks to their maritime skills and entrepreneurial acumen, the Portuguese soon eclipsed the ongoing trade with West Africa and Morocco, Guinea and the Saharan coast. They wrested this enterprise from Muslim traders between 1480 and 1540, trading enormous quantities of cloth in a system of barter devised to meet African preferences. They not only acquired Indian cloth for this purpose, but also later produced and dyed their own equivalents, using the cloth to obtain African slave-labour for their Cape Verde colonies where indigo plantations were established. The cloth was also intended for colonial Brazil's sugar plantations (Balfour-Paul 1998: 61).

Indigo Textiles in Context

The Portuguese had long admired West African indigo-dyed cloth and for some time much of the indigo 'slave cloth' was African-produced under the auspices of Portuguese entrepreneurs and slavers. The Portuguese had 'discovered' the fertile but deserted Cape Verde islands (off the coat of Senegal) in 1456. By 1462 African slaves and skilled weavers were brought to these islands by the Portuguese to cultivate cotton and indigo for use in cloth types based on existing and admired African traditions. Ironically this cloth was used for procuring slaves. The *pano preta*, a deep, almost black, indigo cloth is said to have originated from the Cape Verde islands, as with the *barafula* indigo cloth, which was widely used as currency by the Cape Verde Portuguese and African settlers, slavers and traders.

Indigo cloth produced in the Cape Verde islands appears to have included a white and blue variant realised by crumpling (similar to tie-dyeing using small stones, seeds or rice) or starch-resist, both well-known African resist-techniques to create blue and white contrasts. These contrasts may well have been precedents for blue and white patterned cloth in many regions along the African Atlantic seaboard from which both slaves and slavers hailed. The techniques may have originated in the coastal (Cape Verde) region of Senegal, and may have been spread through West Africa by the Soninke and Manding peoples.[12] This might also explain why blueprint as a product of Indian and subsequent European origin was later well received – it supplemented an 'existing industry' and preference (Thomas 1997: 317–20). As there was too little African-made indigo cloth available for use as trade cloth in the lucrative slave trade, Indian and later European cloth variants were attractive alternatives. According to Balfour-Paul, this would also explain the mystery of colonial indigo resist-fabrics and the ready acceptance and desirability that correlate with the blue and white fabric for commercial purposes formerly used by slavers and Africans alike.[13] It is therefore tempting to situate *isishweshwe* preferences within this historical matrix.

The Portuguese continued to use their India-derived indigo cloth in West Africa for barter since it was desirable for local users where a tradition of weaving, dyeing and indigo cloth usage was centuries old. The indigo cloth was certainly used extensively in the slave trade until that was abolished in the nineteenth century. John Vogt (1979) writes that the Portuguese traded at least 102 types of cloth in Africa. Most of it came from India, but a good deal was later sourced in Germany, Belgium and France – it may well have resembled blueprint – countries where indigo cloth was by now manufactured and printed in large amounts for use by the peasant classes. Throughout these developments, from 1600 to 1800, India remained 'the greatest exporter of textiles the world has ever known' (Balfour-Paul 1998: 48).

The textile districts of India – the south-east and the north-west – produced different qualities of cloth during Portugal's monopoly over trade around the Cape

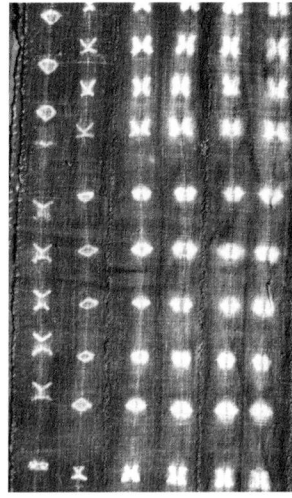

Tie-dyed fabric from West Africa, possibly Ghana. Photograph © J. Leeb-du Toit.

Pano de obra bicho, indigo-woven textile from the Cape Verde islands, mid-twentieth century. Private collection, London.

in the seventeenth century. The poorer India-derived Portuguese textiles, *baftas*, *guineas* and *mouris*, were cheap and served as trade cloth (Jacobs 2000: 80) and were often in indigo. *Guinea*, a cloth with checks and stripes, was also to become popular as dress in West Africa. In Asia, again, Indian cottons and calico in vivid colours and floral designs – the *indiennes* mentioned above – were widely prized. Chintz, called *sits* in Holland, *zitz* in Germany and *sis* in South Africa, was among the many valued cloth types. A genre of *indiennes*, it cost 12 guilders per measure of 90 centimetres square in the eighteenth century.

Other textiles the Portuguese exchanged in Africa were *niquanias* and the ubiquitous *salempore*, their staple trade cloth. It is also important for the history of blueprint to reiterate that the Portuguese obtained vast quantities of dyed cloth, as mentioned above, well before the abolition of slavery in the nineteenth century. They also bartered a deep-blue *salempore* prolifically in Africa.[14] Another *salempore* variant that emerged later had interspersed stripes of red, yellow, light-blue and green. It was central to the trade from the Portuguese entrepôt at Delagoa Bay in the eighteenth century and is still culturally important in South Africa today. Portuguese India-derived textiles designated for the West African market were colour-saturated, achieved by the long-standing expertise of Indian dyers. This suggests that contemporary West and East African preferences, despite Portugal's links with the Dutch textile trade, did not include blueprint, which was widely established in Europe by this time.

The Portuguese also initiated trade links with the Far East in indigo cloth and dyestuff early in the sixteenth century.[15] They reached Canton in 1513 and Tanegashima in 1543.[16] They acquired Chinese and Japanese cotton cloth (probably early variants of indigo paste-resist *shibori* cloth or the peasant indigo *noragi* cloth) and no doubt emulated many textile designs sourced in the Far East (Boyajian 2008: 69).[17] Many designs derived from East Asia are still reflected in blueprint designs from Britain and especially in South African-manufactured blueprint. It is unlikely, however, that the Portuguese traded much Chinese and Japanese cloth in South Africa, although the cheaper India-derived cloths – *salempore* and the more costly, finer *indienne* chintz – were widely available in this country.

Left and centre:
Chinese indigo print cloth, nineteenth century. Private collection.

Right:
Contemporary Chinese indigo cloth, c.2001. Photograph © J. Leeb-du Toit.

Indigo Textiles in Context

Left to right in rows:

1. Japanese *boro* cloth, late nineteenth century. ©Jim Austen, https://www.kimonoboy.com/.
2. Japanese-influenced motif on fabric for export from British blueprinters, 1827. The circular shape is similar to those located in China and South Africa. © Jim Austen, https://www.kimonoboy.com/.
3–9. Japanese *katazome* cloth, *c*.1900. © Jim Austen, https://www.kimonoboy.com/.
10. Japanese *katazome* jacket, early 1900s. © Jim Austen, https://www.kimonoboy.com/.
11. Japanese *katazome* pattern book, nineteenth century. http://rivergardenstudio.tumblr.com/.

Increased maritime trade around the Cape resulted in Portuguese shipwrecks, most of them meticulously documented. Records disclose large amounts of blue and white porcelain on board, destined for Europe, but sourced in the Far East. Cloth designs rendered in the Dutch technique of 'China Blue' or 'Pencil Blue' reflected patterns sourced in Chinese-East Asian ceramic designs. Painted onto cloth with indigo dyestuff, they can, in part, be regarded as establishing precedents for blueprint designs (Balfour-Paul 1998: 149). This practice certainly revealed the encroaching Dutch hold on Portuguese trade along the teeming sea route to India that Vasco da Gama had opened.

To this day, blueprint is still used by farmers' wives and especially among the older generations in Spain and Portugal, as well as in select traditional wear in these countries. This usage reflects both early trade prototypes and the ongoing production of blueprint in these regions.

The Dutch decision to conduct maritime trade in the East was prompted by their dependence on Portuguese imports. They were also aware of the wealth the Portuguese had acquired from maritime trade, although this trade had saturated European markets by 1618 (Boyajian 2008: 144). Holland had traded indigo dyestuff and cloth with Portugal for much of the sixteenth and early seventeenth century and the Vereenigde Oost-Indische Compagnie – the Dutch East India Company, the VOC, abbreviated throughout this book as the Vereenigde Oostindische Compagnie – was determined to challenge the Portuguese monopoly over these valuable commodities in the East.

From 1640, when they entered the Indian Ocean to trade, the Dutch were intent on making their presence felt in East Asia. They soon became Europe's pre-eminent importers of cloth and indigo dyestuff from India. The Cape sea route was vital to their enterprise, as it had been for the Portuguese, and intrigued the British East India Company – the EIC – which had entered Table Bay in 1601 for the first time. The new passage to India also gave the Dutch access to Africa's eastern and western seaboards, to India and Indonesia, China and Japan. Their maritime skills further enabled them to intensify their exploration of the East and, acting under the auspices of the VOC, which they had established in 1602, they commandeered the Cape as their permanent entrepôt en route to India in 1652.[18]

The textiles acquired by the Dutch in India were intended for European clothing, military wear (indigo melton cloth among others) and a range of domestic uses – ever the domain of cheap and durable cloth. Vast amounts of Dutch textile acquisitions were also used as trade cloth to procure slaves and to barter for gold,

Indigo Textiles in Context

ivory, precious stones, spices and indigo on Africa's eastern and western seaboards. Thus, from the seventeenth century onwards, the Dutch, like the Portuguese, identified specific textile preferences in parts of Africa, including their entrepôt at the Cape. Many of the textiles they imported – VOC records prove – were cottons and calicoes dyed with indigo and some with resist-paste white patterns. This indigo cloth preference was in keeping with aspects of Africa's own production and use of indigo in dyeing cloth, particularly in West Africa where the Dutch were perennially active and indigo abounded. Both the Dutch and the British had tried to occupy the Cape Verde islands, well known for the production and marketing of indigo and slave cloth.

By the eighteenth century, Coromandel Coast, formerly a Portuguese trade centre in India, had become Holland's most important emporium for indigo and textiles.[19] The Dutch exported 1 500 000 guilders' worth of indigo from there as early as 1640. They also stationed some 500–800 soldiers there to protect their trade interests against European rivals. Furthermore, they anchored a number of ships there on permanent standby, ostensibly for trade with India and Indonesia. Clearly commerce in indigo dyestuff and Indian cloth was highly profitable for the Dutch, especially in the Indonesian archipelago, where it was important in rites of passage, making it a rich source of income. Batavia (now Jakarta), in Java, where the VOC had established itself in 1619, received the bulk of Dutch goods by far, with over 2 000 000 guilders' worth for the period 1751 to 1753. Java remained the centre of Holland's presence in the East for the next 200 years (Jacobs 2000: 253).

In the seventeenth century indigo was still the major trade commodity for the Dutch and the English in Asia (Mattson 2005: 1). The dyestuff was so affordable and widespread and posed such a threat to European woad-growers that its importation was intermittently prohibited in England, France and Germany after

From left:

Part of an image from a calendar, the Calendario Fideiria, Spain, 2015.

Woman in Portomarín, Spain, wearing locally produced aniline indigo cotton print working dress, 2015. Photograph © J. Leeb-du Toit.

Portuguese blueprint with border. Sourced originally at Pretoria Textile Wholesalers in 2007, produced and imported to South Africa c.1970. Photograph © J. Leeb-du Toit.

Chintz cloth in garments worn by Hindeloopen mother and daughter, late nineteenth century. Kling collection, German National Museum, Nuremberg, Germany.

1670.[20] By the late seventeenth century *indiennes* – the Indian cottons mentioned above – and various types of plain indigo cotton cloth identified by Portuguese traders were widely used for clothing in Holland.[21] The indigo cloth was cheap, durable and colourfast and the Dutch wore wool underneath it for warmth (Jacobs 2000: 74). It became standard peasant wear throughout Holland by the eighteenth century. At the same time, however, *indiennes* were in such demand in Europe, both as clothing and as textile furnishings – including a popular genre produced as *blauwdruk* – that France and England banned *indiennes* outright to protect their markets in wool, hemp and linen. Significantly, too, *indiennes* intended for Holland now became generally available to Dutch settlers at the Cape, together with indigo cloth for the Khoisan, the region's first inhabitants. The growing number of slaves at the Cape, as shown in Chapter 2, also preferred indigo cloth as their dress. The Iziko Museums of South Africa in Cape Town has an example of Indian chintz – a variety of *indienne* – in the form of a petticoat with a painted dark and light-blue pattern on a white ground imported into the Cape in the eighteenth century. Chintz reached the Cape in large quantities in the early eighteenth century to cater for an elite segment of the market and was extremely popular in Europe (Abbott 1999).

Chintz designs from pattern sheets, eighteenth century. Rijksmuseum, Netherlands.

Toile peinte or chintz from India, eighteenth century. Iziko Museums of South Africa.

Indigo Textiles in Context

The Dutch ladings of indigo cloth and *indiennes* destined for the Cape and Holland in the eighteenth century comprised textiles traded and recorded by the VOC offices in Asia. A shipping list from 1790 (Jacobs 2000: 130) indicates that commodities worth about 1 000 000 guilders per year were imported into Holland by the VOC from 1711 to 1713. Cloth imports into the Cape at this time were valued at 18 900 guilders. They were worth more than cloth imports into Holland itself, which were valued at 15 000 guilders. Most of the textiles shipped into the Cape were probably meant for slave dress and for use as trade cloth, but some would have been used by local residents and farmers. Thus the average textile ladings probably consisted of *indiennes*, trade cloth of various kinds and indigo cloth types, including India-derived variants of what later became known as blueprint. The VOC archives refer to 'hundreds of thousands of indigo-dyed cotton pieces, hundreds of thousands of mordant red, and many thousands of superior pieces of chintz or floral-motif pieces' traded at the Cape *c.*1790 (Abbott 1999).

The continuing demand for *indiennes* in Holland in the eighteenth century made them the most important Indian textiles shipped into that country (Jacobs 2000: 74). By 1790 *indiennes* and indigo cloth (plain and resist-printed) were mass-produced in Europe and on a much larger scale in Britain. Both cloth types were an inextricable part of rural dress and, thanks to their variety and quality, even the humblest servant girl could now afford to buy herself a print dress of one type or another.

Once the Portuguese had introduced indigo into Europe in the fifteenth century, Holland, and especially Haarlem, continued to import the dyestuff so abundantly that it remained the country's most lucrative commodity. Indigo was cheap at its source, often serving as ballast on VOC ships, and was in huge demand as dyestuff for the navy-blue uniforms of thousands of European soldiers, including the Dutch contingent at the Cape. Cloth was now mass-produced in Holland and, with the advent of fabric-printing in Amsterdam *c.*1790 – a skill at which the Dutch excelled – textiles meant for local consumption soon also became trade cloth in Africa and the East. The Dutch used their vast textile acquisitions to stockpile indigo to such an extent that its importation into France, Germany and England was again banned early in the eighteenth century to protect local woad production.

Given the Dutch contact with South Africa from 1650 onwards, and their occupation of the Cape as a VOC entrepôt on the trade route to India, the primary sources of South African blueprint after 1650 must indubitably go back to Holland. In the seventeenth century, Amsterdam became the site of hundreds of blueprint workshops where the production of indigo cloth with small white motifs – Dutch *blauwdruk*, as I shall now term it – was carried out not only to meet the needs of local peasants, but also to provide trade cloth (together with other cloth types) for barter in Africa and the East. With this initiative, enhanced by the export of

Top: *Druk overleg* at a Staphort auction held in 2014. Photograph © Berthi Smith-Saunders.

Middle: Scarves at a Staphort auction held in 2014. Photograph © Berthi Smith-Saunders.

Bottom: Staphorst *stipwerk* on mourning cloth, c.1964.

mass-produced *blauwdruk* around the world, the Dutch maintained the trade in indigo textiles and dyestuff their forebears had initiated in the sixteenth century.[22] They also confirmed the status of *blauwdruk* as an independent cloth type in the growing tradition of European blueprint (Hartkamp-Jonxis 1995: 189–98).[23]

A historical residue of this tradition may still be seen at Staphorst in Friesland where fishermen's wives wear indigo-patterned cloth – *Staphorster doekjes* – on their bodices with a *borstrip* of dark-blue indigo cloth. The patterns on these items are usually floral and derive from hand-carved wooden printing blocks. The blocks are dipped (to a depth of less than 1 millimetre) into a paste that has been infused with a fixative and are hand-pressed onto *undyed* cloth where the pattern is *resist-printed*, that is, it emerges as an impression on the cloth once the cloth has been dipped into indigo vats and the paste subsequently removed. The patterns may also be *discharge-printed*, that is, the cloth is dipped into indigo infused with a mordant, then the pattern is imprinted with a bleaching paste and is hand-pressed onto *dyed* cloth where the indigo is bleached out and the pattern realised. These techniques were used throughout the blueprint workshops of Europe from the earliest history of the cloth until they were replaced in the 1780s by mechanised rollers of wood and etched copper.

In the 1790s bright European copies of Asian *indiennes* were first mass-produced in Holland, Germany and France. These innovative textiles brought about a reversal of fortunes in the East. The new European *indiennes*, as they became known, overpowered the Indian market and a number of textile economies on the subcontinent collapsed under the impact of their popularity (Lunde 2005a; Boyajian 2008: 140). The new European *indiennes* were accurate reproductions of the Asian originals, showing floral patterns with delicate leaves and tendrils in the Indian manner. Over time many East Asian designs became indigenised as European, such as the clam, the mango (later known as paisley) and the many variants of floral motifs.

In the eighteenth century, indigo cotton resist-printed in Germany with small white floral motifs – the design prototype of *Blaudruck* – became increasingly popular, locally and across Europe, as working-class wear. The unassuming patterns, discharge-printed on cheap, durable

Indigo Textiles in Context

Young girls dancing at Scheessel, Germany, 2005. Photograph © Kirsten Nieser.

calico, much of it still sourced in India, heralded an attractive and affordable product for use by the peasant classes (Nieser 2005).

The rapid spread of early *Blaudruck* across German-speaking regions, and indeed throughout Europe, originated mainly from the proliferation of blueprint workshops in places where the older block-printing methods and later the mechanised perrotine, which could hold several printing blocks at once, greatly increased *Blaudruck* output. It may also be attributed to the competition between the VOC and the EIC in the late 1670s. They had begun experimenting with chemical agents – resist and discharge pastes – in an attempt to perfect the ideals of *Hollands* and *het oostindische manier* mentioned earlier (Koch 1984: 33).

It is not surprising that the Dutch and the English, within a few years of each other, had established cotton factories in Amsterdam and London to pursue colour research and to produce blueprint at the same time.[24] Thus, even in the early seventeenth century, the dyeing of colourful calicoes promised to become the predominant influence on future European textile production, on the history of *Blaudruck* and on the textile markets of the East. The German port city of Hamburg established its own cotton factory in 1690 – it was intent on producing multicoloured textiles (Koch 1984: 122) – and became one of the textile industry's great emporia, with Amsterdam and London, in a flourishing textile industry where *Blaudruck* assumed a prominent place (Koch 1984: 119; Nieser 2005).

Woman at Scheessel, Germany, 2005. Photograph © Kirsten Nieser.

Dyeing technology in the cotton factories concentrated on the new *indiennes*, which were also called *toiles peintes* or *toiles printes*: painted or printed cloths. Indian indigo was still the primary dyestuff used to colour these fabrics, but as inorganic Indian indigo was cheap and Indian homespun calico widely available, the vogue for colour extended to the German peasant classes as well. The whole of Europe was intent on doing away with the dull monochromes, in particular from locally sourced woad and madder, which had showed so disappointingly on peasant wool and linen since medieval times (Nieser 2005).

German *Blaudruck*, initially a hand-printed indigo cloth with small white patterns, emerged from an imbroglio of political, social and financial interaction in seventeenth-century Europe. It arose concurrently with Dutch *blauwdruk* in Amsterdam, but its usage was spread less by mass-production than by guilds of individual blueprinters who migrated across German-speaking Europe late in the eighteenth century (Nieser 2005).

German blueprinters were skilled in the techniques of indigo dyeing, which were acclaimed as an art in the East from earliest times. The dyers were also masters at using the wooden blocks first devised in India to create (by the resist-paste method) patterns resembling blueprint. The Germans initially carved their own blocks, moreover, and later enhanced and refined them with metal strips and pins affixed to the face in order to create more intricate patterns showing the dots and lines so typical of *Blaudruck* (Nieser 2005).

Interchange between printers who brought their skills with them from workshop to workshop as they migrated, exchanging knowledge and even the blocks, which they sold among themselves, resulted in repositories of thousands of designs accessible to European clientele. German farmhands and labourers brought their homespun linen to local blueprint workshops for dyeing, printing, finishing and upgrading. Upgrading involved the calendering of *Blaudruck*, that is, its translation from everyday peasant wear into items suitable for important occasions such as market days, weddings and church services. This practice lent the cloth its long-standing associations with religion (Bell 1993: 58). Calendering resulted from passing the cloth through heavy rollers, often heated, making the cloth thinner, smoother and more lustrous.

Blaudruck aprons, which Kirsten Nieser (2005) refers to, emerged in approximately 1750. They are a special genre of German blueprint and occupy their own niche in the process of upgrading. An apron could effectively distract attention from a worn dress and, at the same time, was small enough to be lavishly enhanced at minimal cost. In this manner *Blaudruck* became suitable attire for formal occasions in peasant life: it was no longer merely working wear. The popularity of upgrading caused *Blaudruck* manufacturers to embellish the cloth more decoratively at production. It was elaborated with Asian patterns showing floral motifs, leaves and tendrils in the Oriental manner. Larger designs, which included biblical narratives, were used for textile furnishings such as curtains, covers and drapes, which were popular in rural interiors.

Examples of German textile patterns, including those used in *Blaudruck*, were incorporated into pattern books in the 1750s (Nieser 2005). Some books contained up to 3 000 designs, displayed in full colour. The books were distributed from Westphalia in northern Germany to Spain, Portugal, Poland, Hungary and the United States by *Blaudruck* printers and salesmen, middlemen and agents. The German textile workshops producing large quantities of *Blaudruck* – there were a number of them by this point – had to work at full capacity to meet the ensuing demand for the *Blaudruck* advertised in German pattern books (Koch 1984: 50; Nieser 2005).

◆ ◆ ◆

The EIC, as noted above, visited Table Bay for the first time in 1601 – the Company had been established the year before – but the VOC pre-empted any political ambitions the English might have had by commandeering the Cape as an entrepôt in 1652. Within the next twelve years they established a Dutch colony at the Cape – with the Fish River to the east as a later frontier – by introducing Dutch settlers into the region. Simon van der Stel arrived as commander in 1679, bringing the settlers with him.

When France invaded the Netherlands in 1795, the British occupied the Cape in a show of anticipated resistance, but withdrew following the Treaty of Amiens, in 1803. The Cape reverted to Dutch rule – it now fell under the Batavian Republic, as the Netherlands was known – until 1806 when hostilities with France were renewed. At this juncture, while the Cape lay exposed and unclaimed, the British revived their earlier interest in an entrepôt that had provided direct access to indigo supplies in the East since 1498. They entrenched their occupation of the Cape by planting their first South African colony there in 1815 and by confirming the Fish River as their eastern frontier.

Britain's early textile industry, located in Manchester and Scotland, initially obtained its indigo from Europe. The best dyestuff was sourced in India, however, and was exported from there to London and then re-exported to various parts of Europe. This procedure was simply a complex method, followed throughout Europe, of avoiding dues and taxes and exerting economic control. In Britain at the time there was a growing demand for indigo dyestuff and textiles, which led to the establishment of the EIC in 1600. Its headquarters were located in Calcutta where the British were allowed to settle in the eighteenth century and which they soon transformed 'from a swampy village into a thriving city' (Balfour-Paul 1998: 48).

The British were determined to outmanoeuvre the other great shipping companies – notably the Dutch, French and Spanish – for control of the trade with north-west India, monopolised primarily by the Dutch, and to obtain a share of the exceptional indigo traded there.[25] European competition for the best indigo was frenzied at the time and it was a coup for the EIC when it forged trade links with Surat, a major indigo centre, and began to re-export luxury textiles from north-west India to Holland, the Mediterranean and the Levant in the mid-1650s, just as the Portuguese had done before them. The EIC also gained access to ports along the Coromandel Coast where indigo supplies were plentiful (Balfour-Paul 1998: 48). The Company occupied Bengal in 1757 – which presently became the world's greatest indigo supplier – and outstripped the other East India companies, monopolising the indigo dyestuff and textile trade from Bombay to Madras (Jacobs 2000: 106). When the Dutch lost control over trade with India in the 1750s, moreover, the EIC reacted quickly and began to export Indian cottons and calicoes to Holland and France, from where they were distributed to Germany and Switzerland (*HOCP* n.d.: 16). 'Wiles' such as these, as Balfour-Paul terms them, offer a plausible explanation for the presence of the German *Blaudruck* that swamped the South African market in the latter half of the 1800s. German textile scholars attribute some of the cloth's importation here to 'ambiguous' transactions (Nieser 2005).

A large quantity of the textiles involved in the EIC's initial trading, as with the Portuguese and the Dutch before them, were *indiennes*, which were intermittently banned in Britain and Europe to protect the local textile industry, as mentioned earlier. For the most part, however, the British ignored these prohibitions and allowed *indiennes* to flood the English market, not merely as cloth intended for clothing, but also in the form of counterpanes and curtains.

From 1600 to 1800, India was the world's greatest exporter of textiles. The EIC traded with India in indigo dyestuff and textiles because England was crying

Indigo Textiles in Context

out for for dress commodities. By the eighteenth century, however, an increasingly competent dyeing and printing industry had emerged in Britain, although local texile designers were initially unable to emulate the colour and precision of Asian *indiennes* (*HOCP* n.d.: 17; Jacobs 2000: 91).[26] Thus the British lagged behind the Europeans in dyeing and printing and even further behind the Indians in vision and artistry. They sought to improve their standards by interacting with textile craftsmen from Holland, Germany and France who visited England to exchange knowledge and skills. The outcome of this interaction enhanced British cloth production in a tradition characteristic of blueprint manufacture from its earliest days.

By the mid-eighteenth century the English had emerged as good dyers, the Dutch as good finishers. France and Germany had also competed fiercely, but English textiles, it seems, surpassed any work from Europe, and had the capacity to produce vast competitively priced volumes of cloth (*HOCP* n.d.: 18). Thus the advent of industrialism in Britain in the eighteenth century facilitated the replication of Indian chintzes, first on Indian-derived calico and later on English-woven cottons. These local textiles, together with large amounts of plain and resist-printed indigo cloth, were exported around the world to serve as dress and trade cloth. The concomitant demand for British calico increased from 30 000 yards in 1712 to more than 600 000 yards in 1719 – a growth of 220 per cent (*HOCP* n.d.: 103).

Large-scale blueprint production, which was initiated in Lancashire, came to the fore at this time, when indigo was cheap and home-produced British cloth abundant. The process was modified by the introduction of stormont-based designs in 1785. These are realised by affixing metal strips and pins to the face of handblocks to create typical dot-and-line blueprint patterns, as noted above.

Above and overleaf: Pattern books of fabric for export from unidentified British blueprinters from the Calico Printers' Association, c.1847. ABC archive, Manchester.

N° 2 7/8 Prints

N° 2 7/8 Prints

N° 13 is a very good
13 it is here used for half
    = mourning

14 very good, if the dots were
    left out, and the white
    leaves green

    very good sized stripe

The British perrotine introduced in 1834 (as in Holland and Germany) was a mechanised printer that could hold several printing blocks at the same time – allowing large quantities of English blueprint to be manufactured quickly and easily. The profitability of this enterprise is evident in the dramatic increase in the number of looms in Britain – from 22 000 in 1813 to 85 000 in 1823 (*HOCP* n.d.: 28). The British never developed guilds of blueprinters who travelled the country, as in Holland and Germany, but encouraged the mass-production of blueprint in localities where mechanisation facilitated a profitable enterprise, just as the Dutch did in Amsterdam.

In the eighteenth century, the British textile industry was strong and viable, far outstripping the gains of its competitors.[27] But the British were convinced that the prior success of *indiennes* and indigo trade cloth in Holland and Germany, where the cloths were imported from Asia and then re-exported to other markets, would repeat itself if British replications of the same items – including poor-quality blueprint – were manufactured and finished at home, marketed to the working classes in Britain and also exported to places such as South Africa where, the producers believed, the colonial market would accept an inferior product that nevertheless suited local conditions. The British textile industry devised these tactics in the 1850s. The scheme involved discharge-printing indigo cloth to imitate genuine resist-printed *Blaudruck*. The cloth was intended for sale to the German and Dutch settlers in South Africa and would also be used to clothe naked *amaXhosa* and *amaZulu* on the country's mission stations and in the workplace (Balfour-Paul 1998: 162–3).

Pattern book of fabric for export from the Calico Printers' Association, mid-nineteenth century. ABC archive, Manchester.

The EIC, meanwhile, continued to ply the Indian coastline in search of indigo. The need for it had reached a new peak in the eighteenth century with the advent of industrialism in Britain. Bengal was firmly in the Company's sights as a major supplier of indigo (Balfour-Paul 1998). The EIC promoted the production of the dyestuff in Bengal by establishing efficient factories on the coast and disposing of the dyestuff quickly to experienced profiteers. This policy proved highly successful and Bengal's ladings of indigo to London amounted to 4 368 000 pounds in 1795 (3 tons) and to 7 650 000 pounds in 1815 (5 tons). India itself exported a total of 10 000 tons of indigo in 1896, Bengal probably accounting for the lion's share (Balfour-Paul 1998: 76). These figures give some idea of the impact on the indigo trade and its Indian producers when Adolf von Baeyer's synthetic indigo was discovered and radically affected the world's textile markets from 1898.

At the end of the nineteenth century, British textile factories prepared to increase the export of blueprint and other cloth to South Africa. This country was destined to become one of Britain's major consumers of blueprint and other textiles. What Britain's potential customers really wanted, however, and the repercussions of what they actually got, are revealing:

> In these markets it was useless to offer the fine quality demanded by the home trade, *and the primitive desires of the people had to be catered for, not only in the quality of the material but also in the type of the design*. They required cheap and economical production to come in at a cheap price, and the English printer, with the advantages which he possessed, was able to meet the demand. At the same time, it must be recognized that this low quality production would have a tendency towards lowering the taste in the home trade (*HOCP* n.d.: 142; emphasis added).

Perhaps the most problematic aspect of this quotation is its patronising tone. It implies that a supposed lack of discernment among local black peoples – their ignorance of blueprint and other textiles – justifies the export of an inferior commodity to South Africa. This attitude became a major stumbling block for British cloth-makers in the nineteenth century and soon their competitors from the United States and Europe – Germany above all – monopolised the export of blueprint to South Africa by producing a better product at a more competitive price.

Importantly the British had overlooked the discernment and accruing economic capacities of a demanding black female clientele, who, through their support for vastly superior European and American cloth, were to contribute to the decline in British indigo prints in South Africa for most of the late nineteenth and early twentieth century. As will be shown below, it was only when British blueprinters were encouraged to realise a better product that their blueprint could again challenge that of European and American manufacture.

Thanks to the calico printers' flawed marketing strategy, British blueprint sales declined drastically in South Africa. The Germans, their main competitors, were not only becoming increasingly industrialised, but were also determined to locate and establish markets for their goods in South Africa. Thus British textiles in this country were constantly impugned in the late nineteenth century by European exports, which were often cheaper and of better quality, especially in the case of mass-produced cottons such as *Blaudruck*.

Britain took steps to challenge German *Blaudruck* in 1903 when S.W. Whitham, a British textile commissioner, visited South Africa after the Second

Anglo-Boer War (1899–1902) at the invitation of the British-dominated and influential South African Trade Committee. The date of his arrival was auspicious and heralded the onset of Anglophile domination of South African trade and business, coupled with British capitalist-imperialist strategies. Whitham's task was to assess the local textile market, to identify European competition and to discern market preferences in order to encourage profitable ranges for Britain's textile manufacturers. In identifying new outlets, Whitham (1903: 8, 12, 16) observed that a 'considerable portion' of trade was being conducted locally by German firms, especially in Port Elizabeth where he traced imports from Germany, Belgium and France.[28] American textiles too, he learnt, were becoming increasingly competitive in South Africa, especially in blueprint used as working wear. He urged the British to regain the South African textile and blueprint market in order to challenge their German and American competitors and the German trading houses in this country.[29] In Port Elizabeth he observed:

> Although there is here an influential body of importers of the British type, birth and sympathy, there is also a strong body of German importers, of German birth and sympathy. These two sections work, I am told, amicably side by side. The Germans have full access to our Chamber of Commerce, and are members of it (Whitham 1903: 45).

Whitham wished to visit the city's 'German houses', but was refused permission. He was convinced that he would find there 'other goods of Continental manufacture . . . which reach the consumer, but . . . are not found in the depôts of the British importing firms'. Whitham goes on to identify the widespread use of aniline-dyed *Blaudruck* by the Boers and the local black population.

Blueprint production improved in places such as Manchester as a result of Whitham's report. The British continued to ply South Africa with their cloth, especially after the Second World War – when *Blaudruck* importation all but disappeared – despite opposition from locally established competitors such as the United States, Hungary and Czechoslovakia, as shown in Chapter 5. Until the early 1970s, however, British indigo prints were often preferred and enjoyed a special status in South Africa.

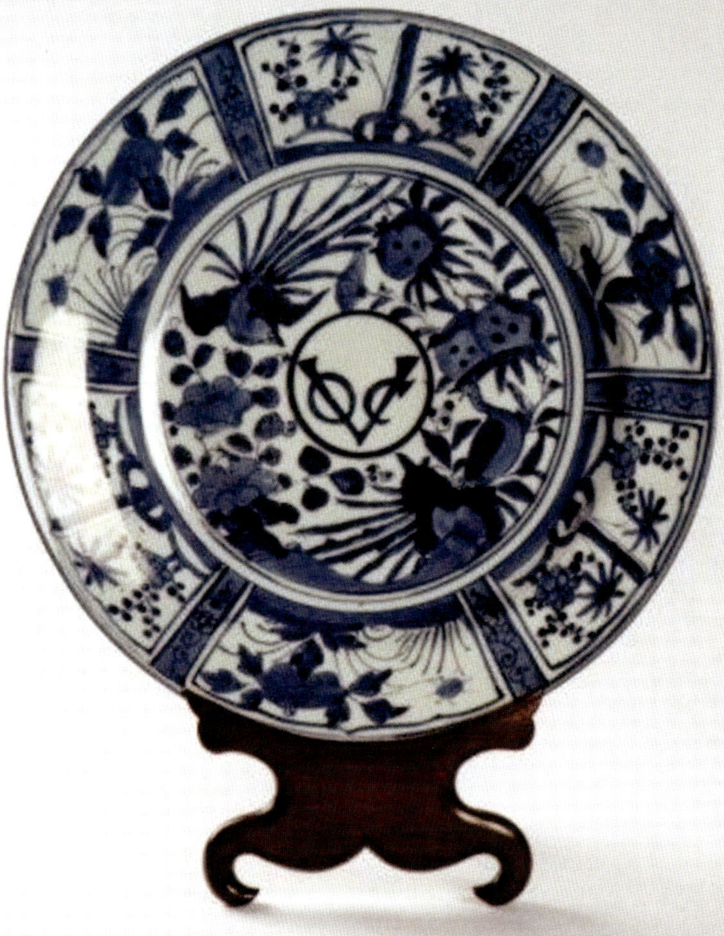

2
Early Cape Dress in Context

Early dress codes in South Africa must be evaluated against the backdrop of trade and military settlement. The Dutch mercantile and military presence at the Cape, which marked the onset of colonialism in South Africa, initially protected the trade route to the East, but later defended the boundaries imposed by expanding settlement, which extended as far as the Fish River to the east from 1785 (Crais 1992: 2). Tension between Europeans and the indigenous Khoisan arose at the Cape soon after Jan van Riebeeck established a settler presence there in 1652. The Khoisan were pastoralists and hunters and they traded with the Dutch. Their land and cattle were precious commodities (Newton-King 1999: 11), however, and they resisted trade as well as exchange in the face of relentless Dutch encroachment. They also contracted disease in the wake of trade. Contaminated linen from a passing fleet washed up in 1713, for example, and hundreds of Khoisan died of smallpox.

Very few employees of the Vereenigde Oostindische Compagnie, the VOC, who were mainly soldiers and sailors, left Europe in 1652 intending to settle permanently at the Cape. Supplies of water, fresh produce and meat had been traded there with the indigenous Khoisan since the 1590s, but the VOC decided in 1657 that some of its servants should be released from Company contracts to grow their own produce, farm cattle and save the VOC expense and possible conflict with the Khoisan (Newton-King 1999: 1). Included among these new free burghers – as the former VOC employees were known – were some of Van Riebeeck's company. They numbered 156 French Huguenots and a few Germans from Saxony and Westphalia, all of whom would have been familiar with blueprint, which was well known as workwear throughout France and Germany by this time.

The population at the Cape was duly increased in 1679 by additional European arrivals, now immigrants, under Simon van der Stel as commander. Dutch and French, German and British, all of them familiar with blueprint, they sought economic benefits, escape from persecution, and trade and adventure in South Africa. Moravian missionaries arrived in 1737 – they were a main source of blueprint – and many of them laboured at the Cape and in the eastern hinterland, initially under the aegis of the Reform Church and later alongside the London Missionary Society. Many of them, like the settlers, traded with the Khoisan to earn a livelihood. Generally, however, the early European immigrants were loosely affiliated in their association. Their clothing not only defined them, historically and nationally, as distinct from the colonised other, but also demarcated the boundaries between them as distinct groups (see Chapman 1995: 16). Their allotments at the Cape, moreover, assigned by Van der Stel in 1679, invested their varied European wear with moral attitudes and cultural vestiges, with assertions of colonial authority, whiteness and cultural superiority. For revisionist historians, indeed, the settlers – and often the missionaries – stood out as the acquisitive torchbearers of European hegemony.

The Moravians, again, for all the criticism directed against mission work by modern commentators, stood at the heart of the frontier zone in the encounter between the local people, the Colony, its social stratifications and Christian missionary endeavour (Phillips in Keegan 2004: vii–ix). Clothing was, of course, de rigeur on the local missions and throughout colonial society. Thus the widespread use of *Blaudruck* in the eastern Cape later provided valuable insights into the social advancement of missionised black people, as shown in Chapter 4.

The perception of ethnicity at the Cape, then, initially based on linguistic and cultural differences, especially between Khoisan and settler, was soon complicated by colonial contact. The catalyst was located in mission work, trade and economic exchange. Before long, facets of indigenous dress emerged under cross-cultural influence. They may have denoted difference, but they also signified proximity and exchange. This development reinforces Malcolm Chapman's (1995) reminder that changes in dress move from the centre to the periphery. Pedlars and traders contributed significantly to these changes and tendered cloth, dress items and preferences shared by coloniser and colonised. Early preferences based on cost and functionality prevailed. As shown in Chapter 3, Boer and pioneer dress reinforced these preferences.

❖ ❖ ❖

The extent to which indigo dyestuff and textiles first reached the Cape and other areas of the southern African seaboard is only now being closely researched. After the Dutch rounded the Cape in 1652, they were motivated particularly by the need to establish a victualling station *in situ* – they were losing hundreds of sailors annually to scurvy en route to India. They also wished to support the garrison that Van Riebeeck had built in 1655 to protect the station and the handful of new settlers he had brought with him (Strutt 1975: 30). Thus the Cape of Good Hope, a key entrepôt, enabled the VOC to stabilise its trade with the East and to outmanoeuvre its Portuguese, British and French competitors in the endless quest for indigo and other trade goods. The earliest VOC ships were so laden with Bengal indigo, believed to be the best in the world, that the crews used the boxes in which the dye was shipped as ballast en route. The early significance of this indigo for the Cape was that it was used for dyeing cotton and flax – from which linen was made – and indigo trade cloth and other items of European manufacture served as barter with the Khoisan for meat and victuals. The desire for indigo so obsessed the Dutch that they attempted to grow it, without success, as one of their first crops at the Cape in 1727.

Dress at the Cape was a clear marker of status and occupation (Strutt 1975: 30). Most Dutch men and women, who were pre-eminently Calvinists, wore black as formal attire. The military and sailors, VOC servants and the working classes – including slaves, whom Van Riebeeck and Simon van der Stel imported from East and West Africa, from Angola and Mozambique, and from Coromandel in India – were given the indigo dress items associated with their status. Initially the Dutch at the Cape consisted of company officials and their entourages. Van Riebeeck and Van der Stel, who arrived as commander at the Cape with a number of settlers in 1679, consolidated the station's colonial status by releasing additional VOC servants who became farmers. As free burghers, they were allowed to settle the eastern hinterland and provide the Company with produce and meat. This arrangement dealt the Khoisan pastoralists, who had rendered produce to visiting ships since at least the 1590s, a heavy blow. The free burghers, who wore the varied European fashions of the day, devised or imported their own clothing – many merchants and traders later sprang from their ranks – and gradually adapted their dress to suit the climate and their own expanding needs and tastes (Strutt 1975: xi). It was not by accident that Van der Stel and his son, Willem Adriaan, became wealthy farmers at the Cape, to the chagrin of the VOC.

Indigo cloth is mentioned in many early accounts of the Cape as being worn predominantly by workers and sailors, travellers and labourers. In Europe, too, it was the cloth of preference for employees and the working classes. Daphne Strutt refers to an image of a man by Dawid Teniers in the William Humphreys Art Gallery, Kimberley, which she perceives as displaying typical working-class dress at the Cape. The man wears the blue cap favoured by hunters and travellers, a blue coat and blue stockings (Strutt 1975: 16). Henry de Meillon depicted similar dress in his sketches, c.1830.

Shortly after his arrival at the Cape in 1652, when he brought the VOC's first group of settlers to the colony, Van Riebeeck listed the cloth requirements for his men. Their needs included several of the Portuguese textiles mentioned in Chapter 1 as sourced in north-west and south-east India, the major textile regions of the subcontinent. Van Riebeeck specifies *mouris* – a cheap watered cotton – various grades of the ubiquitous *salempore* and fine gingham in stripes, checks or plaid as 'outside wear' (Strutt 1975: 13). He goes on to say that trade items were plentiful at the Cape – perhaps he is referring to the established barter in iron and copper for use as weaponry and personal adornment – and adds that a package of cloth from the VOC included inferior coloured chintz – probably *indiennes* on dyed and painted calico – and two packets of *negros*, used in Guinea and West Africa for barter and slave clothing, as shown in Chapter 1 (Strutt 1975: 402).

Desirable cloth at the Cape was imported mainly from India or re-exported from Europe in smaller amounts. By 1659 the local VOC stores held Irish and Guinean linen, English sheets, striped cloth and calico, possibly printed. They also held serge (a strong twilled material), *bafta* (Indian cotton) and plain muslin (also cotton). Initially muslin was grey and brown, but later became white and coloured (Strutt 1975: 400). It was used mainly for barter and was often indigo-dyed to heighten its desirability. In addition, the VOC stores kept cheap 'fancy articles' for trading, including 'some textiles and items of clothing' (Strutt 1975: 13). These supplies contained strips of *negros*, various types of *salempore* and chintz and *niquanias* in red and blue variants. There was also *betbilla*, a muslin-like cloth figured or with checks. Sometimes the cloth used for trade was worn by the local and Dutch working class. Guinean linen, for example, was used for shirts for Van Riebeeck's men (Strutt 1975: 15).

As early as 1654 Van Riebeeck and Van der Stel brought slaves to the Cape, who were used as unpaid labour, since the enslavement of indigenous peoples was expressly forbidden by the VOC. The slaves were sourced in the regions mentioned above, notably Coromandel (Strutt 1975: 143; Maclennan 1986: 20). There were 891 slaves at the Cape in 1700, 5 327 by the mid-1750s, 26 000 in 1798 and 29 286 upon enforced emancipation in 1834 (Newton-King 1999: 77). Slaves from Coromandel were prized and were adept at learning new skills. Their continued

Romance or Reality, or Hotentots as they are said to be and are, hand-coloured lithography, by Frederick l'Ons. Parliament Collection, Cape Town.

Early Cape Dress in Context

importation, recommended by the VOC in 1717, suggests that the Dutch were intent on establishing a caste system in Cape society (Davenport 1987: 23). Female slaves, in particular, had a desirable reputation as seamstresses and sewed for their owners and for themselves (Strutt 1975: 143). Most of them originated from areas that produced indigo, such as West and East Africa or East Asia. Their later dress preferences commonly included indigo cloth, some of which may well have resembled blueprint. Their owners were obliged to clothe them under Roman-Dutch law, the legal system applying at the Cape. Early images of slaves at the Cape, dating from the eighteenth century, show them in jackets, trousers and even robes of plain blue cloth.

The VOC slaves, whose number seldom increased above 600 (Davenport 1987: 22), were kept under poor conditions, but were provided with a blue jacket, vest and trousers. Strutt notes that their women 'wore loose gowns or caftans made up from six ells of coarse cotton cloth'; they also received veils or headcloths (Strutt 1975: 143). Influenced by Dutch habits and their own preferences, the VOC slaves from the East and Madagascar – from where Van der Stel preferred his slaves to come – continued to wear indigo cloth at the Cape.

The German-born VOC official Joachim Nicholas von Dessin confirms this tendency among local slaves. He adds that his male slaves wore blue *cursai* (or kersey) jackets with brass buttons, blue shirts and scarves. The latter were widely used as trade items in the East and Africa (Strutt 1975: 143). Von Dessin's female slaves wore white shirts, brightly coloured skirts and patterned jackets, probably *indiennes*. In 1754, Von Dessin claims, they preferred striped baize petticoats and blue-flowered jackets – again probably *indiennes* – and in 1756 eight of them received 'blue jackets and skirts' (Strutt 1975: 145). Images by De Meillon around 1830 depict continuities in these preferences.

1. *Slave at the Cape*, watercolour by Henry de Meillon, c.1850. Brenthurst Library, Johannesburg.
2. *Slaves and Farmer at the Cape*, W. Huntly, 1830. Brenthurst Library, Johannesburg.
3. *Slaves at the Cape*, watercolour by Henry de Meillon, c.1850. Brenthurst Library, Johannesburg.

Slaves at the Cape, watercolour by W. Huntly, 1830. Brenthurst Library, Johannesburg.

As Von Dessin's affiliations were German-Dutch, it is not suprising that he sanctioned indigo and the floral designs (*indiennes*) associated with Europe's working classes in the eighteenth century. The origins of the cloth used by his women slaves must remain speculation, but seeing that the Dutch strictly controlled all trade items at the Cape, and that the VOC was the most influential trading organisation in the Netherlands, the women slaves' attire was probably sourced in India. The men's jackets may have been of German cloth, for indigo jackets had emerged in Germany by 1750 (Nieser 2005). One of the rare descriptions of Cape slave dress, Von Dessin's account again reinforces slave preferences at the Cape for indigo cloth – some of it possibly blueprint – and for

Early Cape Dress in Context

plain cotton. Blue was so closely associated with slave dress in the Colony, Ben Maclennan notes, that when an important British official visited the Cape and his regiment was offered blue jackets with red facings, he disdained the blue jackets, declaring that they 'disgusted' his men who associated them with the Dutch, whom they detested, and 'with the generality of slaves at the Cape' (Maclennan 1986: 29).

This curt British dismissal of slaves reinforces the fact that as a class they were inhumanely treated at the Cape, notwithstanding their depiction in local art, which verges on the romantic. Some local historians believe that they were trapped in 'a closed and rigid slave society' (Davenport 1987: 24). They could be punished within those confines, depending on the offence, by breaking on the wheel or physical mutilation and by scourging. Despite these sanctions and the large number of personal slaves, there were only two slave rebellions at the Cape, both when it was under British rule. Slaves were clearly subject to the most rigorous forms of control. The distinctive uniformity of their dress in society at large supports this conclusion.

Many Indian and Indonesian political prisoners were exiled to the Cape. They can be seen in an image by Charles Davidson Bell wearing long indigo robes and woven conical hats. Many of them became 'free blacks' with the privilege of trade

Malay and Malay Priests, mixed media, mid-nineteenth century, by Charles Davidson Bell. Bell Heritage Trust, Cape Town.

and land ownership. Their dress preference and its influence remain unidentified, but, as they certainly participated in regional trade, they may well have promoted the use of indigo cloth.

Slaves in the farming districts were less smartly dressed. Those from Guinea were used as agricultural labour, like the Khoisan from the 1680s, and their need for clothing was minimal. Their owners often gave them the second-hand clothing of guests who had failed to pay for their stay at hostelries (Strutt 1975: 145). The importation of discarded clothing from Europe later augmented this practice. Much imported clothing included discarded military wear, such as indigo jackets and pants. Emancipation was enforced at the Cape around 1834 (Maclennan 1986: 49) and newly freed slaves went in search of clothing. Even when enslaved, they were still allowed to earn money by sewing and many made their own clothes. Freedwomen wore blouse-like garments, skirts, petticoats and kerchiefs over the shoulder, which together with turbans, comprised their common attire.

By 1660 the white immigrant population of the Cape was still small – only some 346 persons – with a few women among them (Strutt 1975: 30). In 1679 Van der Stel had been intent on replicating Amsterdam at the Cape, his critics assert, and had increased the number of European settlers there (Strutt 1975: 43). Perhaps there *was* a need to reinvigorate a social milieu that allowed only VOC imports to be bought at the Cape, forbade ladings of unapproved textiles and permitted only one ship per year to transport chintzes, plain calicoes, linens and muslins to the Cape for sale to the colonists (Newton-King 1999: 163). In defiance of Company regulations, illegal trade overcame the shortfall in desirable clothing and Dutch seamen smuggled items inside their own trunks (Newton-King 1999: 164). Dissemination of these goods was clandestine, making the *smous* (pedlar) a feature of the Colony in the exchange of illicit goods for cattle and sheep (Newton-King 1999: 170).

French and Dutch fashions and cloth preferences prevailed among the more cosmopolitan Cape immigrants after 1679 and British arrivals began to prefer the Cape-French or Dutch style after their arrival. The farming and working classes, however, the poorer and more conservative inhabitants, continued to wear serviceable dress, what Strutt (1975: 48) terms 'French peasant elegance'. Working women's wear influenced Huguenot fashions, for example, with aprons and gowns tucked up at the hemline, head-kerchiefs and loose hoods. According to Strutt, colours at the time were darker and richer. 'India cottons' – the familiar *indiennes* – previously used for furnishings, were converted into aprons and dressing gowns, underskirts and flowing *banyans* (Strutt 1975: 51, 402). *Indiennes* painted and dyed on export cottons, many in the indigo floral variants popular during the seventeenth and eighteenth century, entered the Cape regularly at this time (Strutt 1975: 51). As the colony was the entrepôt on the direct route to India, some

Early Cape Dress in Context

of the best examples of *indiennes* were displayed there, especially by visiting dignitaries and their wives (Strutt 1975: 52). Dress became so lavish at the Cape that a sumptuary law, inspired perhaps by Calvinist persuasions, was introduced to enhance the existing dress restrictions.

The free burghers had gradually usurped the Khoisan's trade with the Cape in meat and produce. Although they were mostly self-sufficient pastoralists, the Khoisan were reliant on basic items, 'which could only be procured by trade' (Newton-King 1999: 20). Some of these items were textiles that were controlled by the VOC. The *vendu rollen* (auction or estate lists) at the National Archives in Cape Town refer to a few of the germane cloth types, showing that textiles were expensive and valued. Indian cloth, plain and printed – the *indiennes* widely used by free burgher women in the interior – cost three-and-a-half sheep per measure in 1781. A single ell (27 inches) of *laken* or sheeting, from which men's short blue jackets and women's black mourning dress were made, cost 14 *schellingen*, or two sheep (Newton-King 1999: 24). Women's clothing could cost less than men's if Indian cottons were used instead of linen or *laken*. Lining or *voerschitz* 'came in pieces large enough to make a dress and several kerchiefs', but was very expensive (Newton-King 1999: 187, 190).

For the Khoisan to clothe themselves, then, even in the emergent free burghers' humblest wear, would usually have been an unattainable goal, the more so as they were no longer able to trade productively with visiting ships as they had done since the sixteenth century. Thus many of the wealthier Khoisan found themselves trapped, in their very first encounter with European hegemony, by a capitalist settler economy that rendered their stock almost worthless and compelled them to turn to local free burghers for contractual employment as labourers. This must have initiated painful reflection on their part over a society where they were incorporated on a par with slaves as exploitable labour. As their plight worsened steadily, their subsequent reliance on shipments of old clothing from Europe, handed out on the missions where dress was imperative, emphasised their wretchedness as a social underclass at the Cape.

The first free burghers at the Cape in the seventeenth century married 'simple countrywomen' (Strutt 1975: 223). Their women wore white or coloured linen or cotton hoods and bonnets typical of Dutch and German peasantry – headwear that suited the harsh Cape climate. In addition they donned cotton aprons, printed or plain, and Indian shawls with paisley – known as the mango in India – and other floral designs (Strutt 1975: 239). For the working classes, materials used were twill or ribbed cotton, linen and ticking, or striped cotton. Linings were of brown or blue glazed cotton or *holland*, a fine linen in brown, blue, buff or black (Strutt 1975: 64). Most of this cloth came from India, especially the *indiennes* on green, white or yellow grounds. Most big floral patterns were no doubt *indiennes*, too, as seen in Jürgen Leeuwenberg's *Wreck of the Visch* (1740), now in the National Library in Cape Town (Strutt 1975: 78).

Dress was so varied and elegant in the eighteenth century at the Cape that the entrepôt was wittily called 'Little Paris' (Strutt 1975: 85). In 1795, however, a significant event overtook the Cape. France invaded the Netherlands in a prelude to the Napoleonic Wars and overthrew the Dutch monarchy, replacing it with the Batavian Republic – the united Netherlands – and the British, ever ready to defend the EIC's lucrative trade links with India, occupied the Cape for the first time. The Dutch entrepôt, they argued, was under potential threat from the foreign (French) satellites now ruling the Netherlands. The EIC promptly commandeered Holland's faltering trade with India – by the eighteenth century, the VOC's financial position was tenuous – and dress at the Cape, populated now by some 22 000 settlers, 25 000 slaves and a large assortment of local people, continued to reflect the elegance of the former VOC period. The EIC astutely lifted the Dutch restrictions on the textile trade. The large-scale importation of cloth, including *indiennes* and blueprint sourced in Europe and India, driven by the new fashion-consciousness in Britain and France, resumed in Europe – from where prized commodities were re-exported to the Cape.

The enlightenment of the Colony was entrenched by the second British occupation. The Batavian Republic returned to the Cape from 1803 – under the Treaty of Amiens – but Napoleon attacked Holland again in 1805 and the treaty fell into abeyance. The British, alert to the EIC's profits during their first occupation, adopted a firmer stance and regained the Cape in 1806. They obtained it by treaty from the Dutch and planted their first South African colony there in 1815. The mercantile VOC had finally bowed before the imperialist EIC (Crais 1992: 22).

❖ ❖ ❖

Land was not plentiful in the western Cape and some 600 farmers opted to trek to the eastern hinterland in 1770. They were called Trekboers – stock farmers or graziers – and also acted as traders and hunters. They provided the colony with meat and, as they established themselves, their demand for pasturage brought them into direct conflict with the Khoisan and later the Nguni *amaXhosa* (Crais 1992: 36).

The free burghers in the interior openly defied the British. Their clothing, which was markedly different from that at the Cape, distinguished them as an independent group. A navy-blue silk *banyan*, lined with Indian cotton, has been identified as belonging to a free burgher (Strutt 1975: 128). Other popular free burgher materials included flimsy *indiennes* and embroidered muslins; French

Early Cape Dress in Context

lawn – a silky cotton – and seersucker, a fine linen with alternating puckered stripes (Strutt 1975: 133). Later in the 1780s the *caraço*, a long Indian jacket of painted and dyed cotton, became popular with the free burghers (Strutt 1975: 114, 401). Indian muslins with or without stripes and chintzes for the wealthier free burgher – of whom there were many – were also prominent, as were Indian cottons and indigo *salempore*. Blue and undyed sailcloth and dimity, or fustian, have also been identified as common fabrics used by this class. Many of these preferred cloths were in indigo with designs sourced in India and elsewhere in the East. They set important precedents for subsequent emulation by local wearers and European producers of peasant dress, whether German, Dutch or English. Furthermore, as more traders penetrated the interior, this working-class indigo cloth, much of it undoubtedly blueprint, would have been prominent among the wares selected for the pioneers and local indigenous people in the hinterland.

Free burghers who visited the Cape to trade were easily identified by what they wore: a blue cloth jacket ending just below the waist, usually single-breasted, the trousers of a working man, usually of the same blue as the coat, lined with brown or blue glazed cotton or linen (Strutt 1975: 139). Wine and corn farmers wore blue calico shirts, often with a cotton kerchief around the neck (Strutt 1975: 101). Such was the proliferation of indigo cloth at the Cape that in 1797 Lady Anne Barnard, Governor Earl Macartney's hostess, remarked: 'I hope all this blue cloth is coming from Britain' (Strutt 1975: 139). Lady Anne's hopes were fulfilled. Much of the cloth was indeed from Britain, but the indigo was indubitably from the East.

The Old Cape Town Fish Market at Roggebay, 1898, Cecil Schott, oil on canvas, William Fehr Collection, Iziko Museums of South Africa. Photograph © Pam Warne.

Boors Returning from Hunting, Samuel Daniell, 1804. Iziko Museums of South Africa.

By the eighteenth century the free burghers opted increasingly for farming although some, when permitted, moved further into the eastern hinterland to become cattle traders or Trekboers. C.G. Botha (1970) says the free burgher's wife was identified as wearing 'a plain close cap and a coarse cotton gown' and as seeing 'virtue and good housewifery' as adornment enough for her person (in Strutt 1975: 122). The wives of free burghers and Trekboers wore brown or blue skirts with a printed or plain shoulder-scarf of cotton, often from indigo patterned cloth. The women were able to make their own clothes and they trained slaves and servants to assist them. The dress of the free burgher's wife soon became standardised. The daughter wore simple high-waisted muslin or cotton frocks and, as a matron, draped herself in a blue or brown petticoat, over which she wore a loose cotton gown, figured or plain, short and reaching between the waist and the knee – a petenlair or *caraço*, in fact – and sometimes drawn in at a medium-high waistline (Strutt 1975: 141). The gown was high-necked and her shoulders were covered by 'a mock shawl, a square of printed or plain cotton cloth or silk for best, pinned high at the neck'.

Early Cape Dress in Context

Strutt (1975: 142) also distinguishes Trekboers who, she observes, were often on the move and had few possessions. The men wore hide clothing and their wives had simple attire that suited their life in a small wagon or dwelling. They made their own clothing of 'strong serviceable materials (even leather), in strong serviceable colours. Plain brown or blue dresses covered by dark bibbed aprons and the usual shoulder-shawl were general wear, topped by the cap and hood of the countrywoman.' The most frivolous cloth worn by the Trekboer's wife was of printed cotton and not the lighter muslins worn in the towns. Cloth was available to all, but considerations of durability and context influenced the preferences of farmers and Trekboers, both men and women.

An image by Charles Bell shows a farmer's wife wearing a plain indigo dress with blue hooded cap, a skirt and shawl. Her female slave wears a cotton dress of blue floral design on a white ground – possibly blueprint or a cheap *indienne* – dress conventions that were, in all probability, typical of the time. The usual free burgher or Trekboer family, finally, was probably of mixed European origin – Dutch, French or German – and farming workwear had emerged in their homelands, much of it in coarse indigo cottons, blueprint or cheaper *indiennes*.

The Schoolmaster Reading De Zuid-Afrikaan, water colour, by Charles Davidson Bell, 1850. Iziko Museums of South Africa.

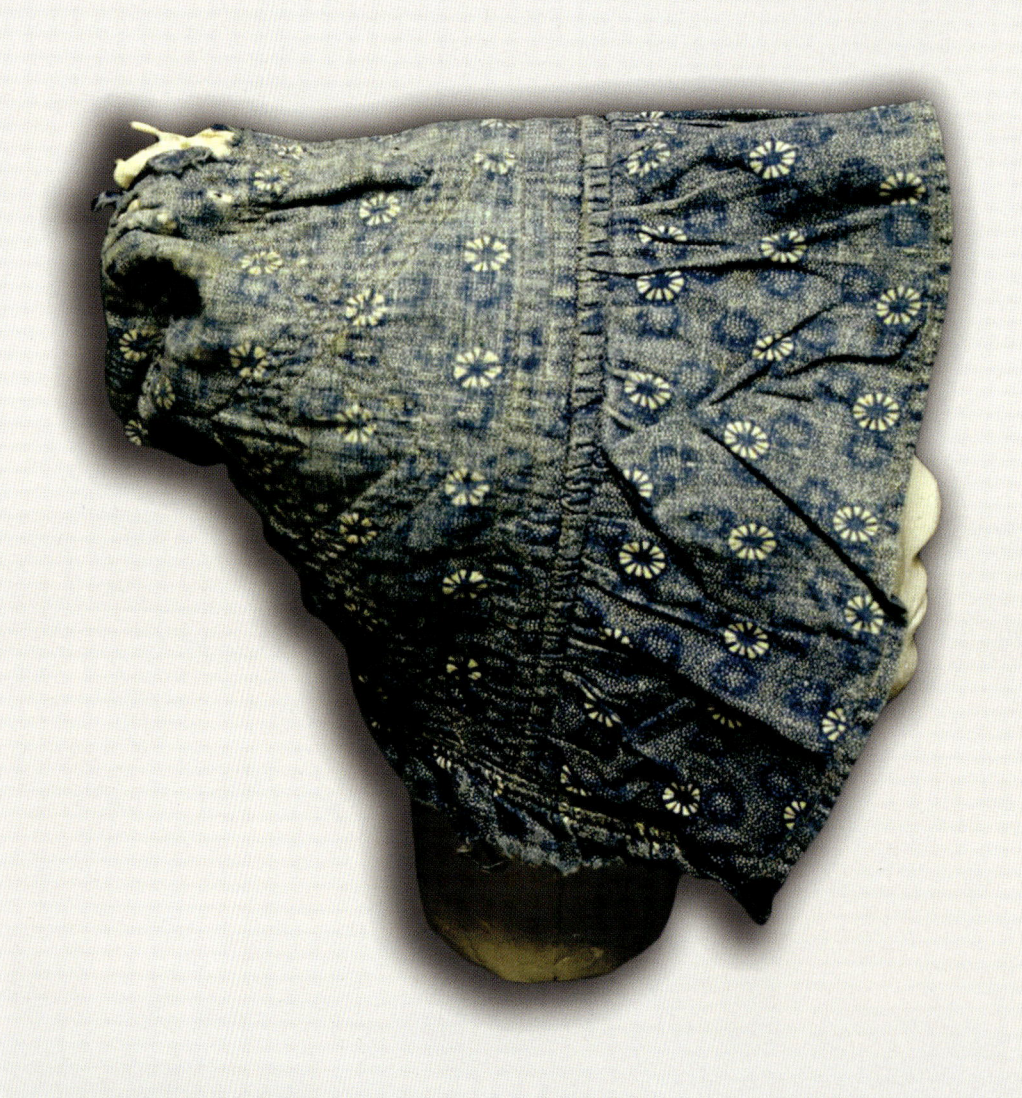

3
Frontier, Voortrekker and Pioneer Dress

In eighteenth-century South Africa, the British presence was initially concentrated in the western and eastern Cape and on the Natal Indian Ocean seaboard. It only shifted northwards in the nineteenth century to regions such as modern Gauteng. The arrival of the British at the Cape in 1795, like that of their Dutch counterparts in 1652, was connected to trade and their resolve to retain the sea route to the East. British trade in textiles resembled that of other East Indian companies and their interest intensified in the shadow of the Napoleonic Wars (1803–15), resulting in the second British occupancy of the Cape in 1806, overthrowing the Dutch. By this time, many of the preferred cloth types in South Africa derived not only from India, but also from a growing textile industry in the British industrial north.

Under British rule, 'imperial free trade' applied at the Cape, since the Colony was of direct benefit to the mother country. Traders, who penetrated the interior along explorers' routes and wagon paths from the beginning of the eighteenth century, formed alliances with remote Xhosa chiefdoms, settlers and white merchants, extending beyond the Fish River, which was declared the Colony's eastern border in 1875. A degree of franchise ensued, but settler capitalism remained entrenched (Crais 1992: 193).

The British introduced new legislation in South Africa with the advent of colonialism, basing their power on imperial sovereignty, on the hegemony of the 'rule of law' and on the conviction that 'unfree labour' caused instability and impeded progress (Crais 1992: 2). To these notions they added the idea of legitimate trade and a clarion call to spread Christianity, ideals that henceforth underpinned colonialism, the missionary endeavour and racial capitalism in South Africa.

To expand their presence and develop agriculture in the eastern Cape and to create a buffer against local people who crossed the Fish River – the 'natural border' of the Colony – the British, under Lord Charles Somerset, attracted immigrants from abroad in 1820 with glowing reports of the eastern Cape. The settlers were keen to leave Britain, impoverished by the Napoleonic Wars, and settled around Port Elizabeth and East London and occupied Albany, an area suited to mixed farming with Grahamstown at its centre. They numbered almost 5 000 and the territory they settled was occupied mostly by Khoisan, by small groups of *amaXhosa*, *amaMfengu* and *amaThembu* and by free burghers and traders. Each settler received 100 acres to farm (Strutt 1975: 168; Rivett-Carnac 1961: 8). The settlers reflected changing economic fortunes and dwindling privilege in Britain. They were unemployed tradesmen, failed artisans and inexperienced or unsuccessful farmers who had fallen victim to industrialism in the British economy. Other settlers were parish gentry or simply struggling indigents. Most of them hailed from working-class backgrounds and were familiar with the blueprint widely used by the poor in Britain. They were protected by contingents of British dragoons in blue jackets and by infantrymen in scarlet.

On arrival, many of them stared in disbelief at the local farmers clad in short blue coats, veldskoens and suede trousers – dress they would soon adopt. Clothes in the region were always at a premium and calico or cotton cloth, which included blueprint or cheaper *indiennes*, was sought after when supplies arrived. Women even made use of tent canvas to produce garments for themselves (Rivett-Carnac 1961: 72). Reverend William Shaw later notes a change in clothing among the settlers: 'The taste and skill of the females were displayed in contriving for themselves gowns and other articles of dress out of the coarser kind of cotton stuff from India called *voerschitz* (cheap cotton chintz lining) . . . and in addition they were sent clothing and funds from England' (Rivett-Carnac 1961: 73). *Voerschitz* referred to striped, patterned or plain cotton cloth, and indigo and other variants were widespread at the Cape.

The British settlers, many unsuited to or ignorant of the demands of farming, lived under harsh conditions. Frontier farmers rejected British restrictions on self-defence in the face

Trekboer and His Wife, Lady Anne Barnard, pencil sketch. *The Cape Diaries of Lady Anne Barnard, 1799–1800*, edited by M. Lenta and B. le Cordeur, Cape Town: Van Riebeeck Society, 1999.

of tribal raids. Britain was at war with France and the Cape remained important to both countries. Shipping declined in the area between 1750 and 1794 and the First Xhosa-Cape Frontier War raged from 1779 to 1781. Early traders, such as Margaret Salt, travelled by wagon deep into the interior. There was also a strong Jewish presence in the person of Joshua Norden, an early municipal commissioner (Rivett-Carnac 1961: 112). Farming advanced with the importation of sheep, fruit trees and vines. Perhaps the summit of the shift was Robert Bradshaw's establishment of a textile mill near Bathurst in 1821, producing woollen blankets and coarse cloth. The mill was destroyed by fire in 1835 (Rivett-Carnac 1961: 87). Some British settlers endured poverty in the eastern Cape for years and then migrated to surrounding towns. Others maintained links with their home country and acquired goods such as indigo cloth, which they used for trade and barter with African communities. Goods were scarce in the eastern Cape and still other settlers resumed their erstwhile trades and became tailors, seamstresses or cobblers. Frontier women, who were far from commercial centres and shops, relied on 'itinerant pedlars' – *smouse* – to obtain cotton prints for their clothing and leather for their men's wear (Strutt 1975: 168). W.J. Burchel (1953) describes the wagon holdings as including blue check handkerchiefs used as neckwear and blue check cottons (in Strutt 1975: 168). J.W.D. Moodie (1835) describes how many frontiersmen wore indigo greatcoats, which were the vogue in Westphalia at the time (in Strutt 1975: 168; Nieser 2005).

The 1820 settlers' plight was aggravated by their small allotments, by drought, blight and bad weather, their lack of experience and crop failures. Many of them persisted in their choice of trading as an alternative to agriculture and many resorted to selling cloth, which included large amounts of blueprint, doubtless from Germany, Holland and Britain (Strutt 1975: 170). Albany, where many of the settlers were located, was thus translated from a farming into a trading community (Rivett-Carnac 1961: 78). Traders from Grahamstown, in particular, saw the enormous potential of the eastern Cape hinterland. Until 1826 double dues were payable on goods landing in Cape Town, but Port Elizabeth and Port Alfred remained free ports. This contributed to a steady influx of cheaper goods at these entries and attracted African trade to Grahamstown. Most of the transactions there were done by barter with farmers and local people in the hinterland across the Fish River (Rivett-Carnac 1961: 84).

Trading between colonists and indigenous people, especially the pastoralist *amaXhosa*, was initially prohibited by the authorities, but was allowed after 1824, resulting in an unprecedented upsurge of exchange in the hinterland (Crais 1992: 48). Xhosa peasant farmers at first controlled this trade, for numbers of them were rich in cattle and produce. Trade was conducted at Fort Willshire and showed that indigenous preferences were for 'brightly-coloured handkerchiefs, blankets, cotton-stuffs and European clothing' (Rivett-Carnac 1961: 85). Africans were said to be awkward customers, very selective in their choices and with vacillating preferences. Having recognised that their main trade would be with local people beyond the Fish River, traders retained assiduous contact with these groups. As a result, their enterprise was so successful that it contributed to a major shift in the economy of Grahamstown. Even widows became itinerant traders, shopkeepers and dealers, and worked as seamstresses and bonnet-makers or ran small schools (Rivett-Carnac 1961: 112). As Clifton Crais (1992: 50) points out, however, 'the penetration of merchant capital on the frontier . . . spawned both indebtedness and coerced labour'. In 1834 a major conflict erupted in Albany. Stock, clothes and furniture were plundered, farmhouses were razed and all trade brought to a halt. The manumission of slaves at the Cape in the early 1830s and growing discontent among a number of local farmers, including British settlers, initiated the Great Trek, which took place from 1834 to 1842.

◈ ◈ ◈

Sir Benjamin D'Urban was sent to the Cape to oversee the abolition of slavery. A group of dissident farmers from landed communities, later called Voortrekkers, expressed their opposition to English constraints and lamented the poor compensation paid to them for their freed slaves. Prompted further by the British Colonial Office's failure to understand their plight and their desperate need for labour and forced to surrender their land to local indigenous peoples in Queen Adelaide province, the dissidents trekked to the interior in search of farmland. They remained under British jurisdiction, however, as extended by official proclamation (Rosenthal 1967: 22–3).

By 1837, approximately 2 000 Voortrekkers had left the Cape. They lost contact with the Colony and struggled to conserve their meagre possessions. They mended cloth and reused material from one item to the next, whether on clothing, patchwork garments or quilts (Strutt 1975: 190). A painting by Frederick I'Ons, of women in workday browns (1836), shows the prevailing wear among Voortrekker wives.

The Voortrekkers were mostly dissident farmers, but their ranks included Trekboers and British settlers. They stocked up for the trek, loading bolts of cloth and leather into their wagons (Strutt 1975: 212). Waistcoats for trekker men were of cotton or linen; silk and satin were reserved for best. For everyday wear, women wore ordinary cottons, usually printed cottons resembling blueprint or cheap chintz, with small floral designs, checks or stripes in muted colours (Strutt 1975: 221). Silks and brocade were kept for best and shawls made from *indiennes* or wool served for everyday wear (Strutt 1975: 239).

Frontier, Voortrekker and Pioneer Dress

Diorama of Voortrekkers. Hartenbos Museum, Western Cape.

Given their diasporic origins, their isolation and their dependence on pedlars, the Voortrekkers were compelled to use serviceable, long-lasting fabric for clothing. In the Hartenbos Museum in the Western Cape, which concentrates on the Great Trek – and on the symbolic re-enactment, the Ox-wagon Trek of 1938 – a diorama built in 1982 shows a Zulu impi attacking a Voortrekker family. All the women wear plain, blue cotton dresses and *kappies* – bonnets – and a man wears a blueprint scarf. The items for this museum display were collected from all over the country under the auspices of the Afrikaanse Taal- en Kultuurvereniging (ATKV). The display shows the dress preferences of the time and challenges later perceptions of Voortrekker women's wear.

Voortrekker quilts, which were usually made from cloth remnants and discarded clothing, provide a significant source to determine contemporary preferences and the availability of cloth. Older quilts include a range of fabric choices and many in museum collections include indigo- and white-patterned cloth. They testify clearly to the use of these cloth types by Voortrekker women for their clothing. Patchwork quilts from the Msunduzi Museum in Pietermaritzburg also reveal coexistent linen blueprint as well as mass-produced blueprint or *bloudruk*. Other cloth samples of thinner cotton in quilts may have been sourced in dresses or in the popular indigo scarves worn by men and women. Some of the best examples of quilts in local collections occur in the Anglo-Boer War Museum in Bloemfontein.

54 isiShweshwe

Quilt, late nineteenth century. Anglo-Boer War Museum, Bloemfontein.

Detail of Boer quilt, late nineteenth century. Anglo-Boer War Museum, Bloemfontein.

Detail of Boer quilt, late nineteenth century. Anglo-Boer War Museum, Bloemfontein.

Details from Boer quilts of blueprint, late nineteenth century. Anglo-Boer War Museum, Bloemfontein.

Frontier, Voortrekker and Pioneer Dress 55

Details from Boer quilts, late nineteenth century. Anglo-Boer War Museum, Bloemfontein.

Details from Boer quilts, late nineteenth or early twentieth century. Anglo-Boer War Museum, Bloemfontein.

Details of pioneer quilts, late nineteenth century. Msunduzi Museum, Pietermaritzburg.

Detail of Boer quilt, nineteenth century. Iziko Museums of South Africa.

Settler quilt, late nineteenth century. Albany collection, Port Elizabeth Museum/Bayworld, Port Elizabeth.

1. *Kappie* donated by G. Kleingeld from Bloemfontein in 1968. The *kappie* was worn at the Bloemfontein concentration camp c.1902. Anglo-Boer War Museum, Bloemfontein. 2. *Kappie* donated by Rose Potgieter in 1954. It was worn by Martha H. Raubenheimer (née Van Wyk) in the Kimberley concentration camp during the Anglo-Boer War. Anglo-Boer War Museum, Bloemfontein. 3. *Kappie* donated by Trudie Kestell from Bloemfontein in 1959. This *kappie* comes from Franschhoek, Western Cape, early twentieth century.

1. *Kappie* donated by Engela Odendaal in 1959. It was worn by Engela van Rensburg. c.1902. Anglo-Boer War Museum, Bloemfontein. 2. *Kappie* donated by W.P. Kotze from Clocolan in 1975. It belonged to Alida Uys from Kranskop, Vrede, Natal. Anglo-Boer War Museum, Bloemfontein. 3. *Kappie*, early twentieth century, National Museum, Bloemfontein.

Examples of authentic Voortrekker dress are rare. Handmade white *kappies* in museum collections reinforce the perception that the white cotton *kappie* was de rigeur in Voortrekker dress. Annemarie Carelsen, curator of textiles at the National Cultural History Museum in Pretoria, is convinced that Voortrekker women would not have used blueprint for their dresses or *kappies*.[1] Increasing evidence suggests, however, that some of their garments and *kappies* were made of blueprint. Their preference for the cloth probably derived from their heritage as farmers, from their dress at the Cape and from the availability and durability of the fabric. Carelsen's qualms were based, in part, on current debates about the meaning of 'Voortrekker'. The term has come to denote the actual Voortrekker community from 1834 to 1838 who, once they had settled, became known as 'pioneers' or 'Boers'. This change in naming coincides with the advantages of settlement. The profits derived from a stable livelihood such as farming enabled pioneers to trade with indigenous peoples and to purchase items such as blueprint from the pedlars who followed specific routes into the interior to encounter the settled communities living there.

Thus some of the machine-sewn *kappies* located at the Msunduzi Museum, the Anglo-Boer War Museum and the National Cultural History Museum are called *Boer-* or *smouskappies*. But the very fact that the *smous* – often a Jew or Muslim – may have machine-sewn these *bloudruk* or *blou sis* items to sell in local communities suggests their widespread dissemination and acceptability across cultural and racial divides. To this day, Coloured[2] women in the north-western Cape still make and wear similar *kappies*, though seldom in *bloudruk*. Their preference for blueprint was clearly expressed, but they currently find the cost of the fabric to be prohibitive. A photograph located in the Amathole Museum in King William's Town shows an African woman wearing settler-cum-Boer garments and a *kappie* probably of *bloudruk*. In the same museum, I discovered a *kappie* that showed *bloudruk* was used by settler women of German lineage.

Boer Life: Sammy. Postcard by H. Egersdorfer, 1885. McGregor Memorial Museum, Kimberley.

I found more evidence of *bloudruk* usage at the Msunduzi Museum Complex in the form of a machine-made *kappie*, the fabric design comprising small, white, interlinked circles and probably dating from 1890 to 1900 (Strutt 1975: 382). In 2007 I again visited the National Cultural History Museum in Bloemfontein in search of remnant *bloudruk* in quilts or dress items. Sudré Havenga, the curator of the section, suggested that we visit the quilts first. On our way to the collection, she showed me a child's *kappie.* It was clearly of *bloudruk* and was probably a *smouskappie,* as it was machine-stitched. Havenga later identified its origins from a Boer family, but it may not have been a Voortrekker *kappie*, but rather a later Boer *kappie*.

In 2009 I discovered six *kappies* in the National Cultural History Museum. One of them, donated by Rina van Graan, was in blue and its embellished head and shape closely resembled a Voortrekker *kappie*. According to Erica Erasmus, Van Graan's sister, Van Graan clearly remembers her grandmother referring to *blou sis* or *bloudruk* clothing and recalls that both these cloth types were again popular among the white youth in Pretoria in the late 1970s and early 1980s.[3] Interestingly, Erasmus recalled that her brother was made to wear a *blou sis kappie* when playing outside on hot summer days, mortified that he was obliged to wear a girl's *blou sis* bonnet! Such was his loathing of this obligatory wear that he used to fling his *kappie* on a nail affixed to the verandah wall, hoping that it would rip the item to shreds and save him from embarrassment. The remaining *kappies* at the National Cultural History Museum were in brown or maroon, with one in red, and were all of European or English blueprint.

A large mural in the Mutual Building (now converted to apartments), just off the Parade in Cape Town, reinforces the perception that trekker and Boer women wore *bloudruk*. Painted by Le Roux Smith Le Roux, the mural includes three panels. One depicts trekkers on the move defending themselves against Africans; the other shows trekkers engaged in farmwork on virgin soil; and the third shows Boer progress and early urbanisation. In several portrayals of women in the mural, both dress and *kappie* are unmistakably *bloudruk*. The artist may have known Boer women's *bloudruk* preferences, but he may also have heeded oral tradition.

There is ample photographic evidence at the National Archives in Bloemfontein showing women in cotton-print *kappies* and clothing in the Boer concentration camps. This material enabled me to locate several *kappies* in *bloudruk* at the Anglo-Boer War Museum, a section of the Women's Monument or Vrouemonument. Their collection reflects the extensive usage of *bloudruk* and white *kappies* at the turn of the nineteenth century. This find was prompted in particular by my reading of *Emily Hobhouse: Boer War Letters*, edited by Rykie van Reenen (Hobhouse 1984), where I came across a moving description of

Frontier, Voortrekker and Pioneer Dress

Detail of mural of Boer men and women by Le Roux Smith Le Roux, 1942. Mutual Building, Cape Town. Photograph © J. Leeb-du Toit.

Opposite page:

1. *Kappie* in blue and white *bloudruk*, 1910–1920. Worn by Van Graan children. Donated by Rina de Villiers, Pretoria. Ditsong: National Museum of Cultural History, Pretoria.

2. *Kappie* in blue and white *bloudruk*, c.1900. Ditsong: National Museum of Cultural History, Pretoria.

3. *Kappie* in brown and white *bloudruk*, c.1900. Donated by Mrs Nortje. Ditsong: National Museum of Cultural History, Pretoria.

4. *Kappie* in brown and white *bloudruk*, 1908. Worn by Anna Susanna Kruger (b. Eloff) (1886–1910), donated by A.S. van Dyk in Pretoria. Ditsong: National Museum of Cultural History, Pretoria.

Top left: Boer women in the Bloemfontein concentration camp, late nineteenth or early twentieth century. Anglo-Boer War Museum, Bloemfontein.

Centre left: The Camp Committee, Bloemfontein concentration camp, c.1901. Free State Provincial Archives Repository, Bloemfontein.

Bottom left: Boer children at the Bloemfontein concentration camp, c.1901. Free State Provincial Archives Repository, Bloemfontein.

Top right: Detail of the Steyl family in the Boer concentration camp, late nineteenth or early twentieth century. Anglo-Boer War Museum, Bloemfontein.

Frontier, Voortrekker and Pioneer Dress

Emily Hobhouse (centre), with Johanna (in blueprint) and Marie, at left, and other companions, at right, in South Africa, c.1901. Free State Provincial Archives Repository, Bloemfontein.

a twelve-year-old Boer girl whom Hobhouse encountered in 1903 some fifteen miles from Lindley in the Orange Free State. Ironically, this date coincides with the Whitham report cited in Chapter 1. The girl is riding some distance behind her father, a prisoner of war from Ceylon, judging by his green trousers. Hobhouse describes her: 'She was neatly dressed in a blue print frock and kapje, and she was riding a creature which must by courtesy be called a horse' (Hobhouse 1984: 254). In conversation with the girl, Hobhouse ascertained that her family lived frugally on a few mealies. When asked, 'And how are you off for clothes?' the girl replied: 'It goes scarce with clothes.' After giving her a loaf of bread, Hobhouse concluded: 'Then silently she turned and hugging the loaf trotted away over the veld, a solitary blue speck in the vast brown expanse' (Hobhouse 1984: 255).

Not only does Hobhouse's book support the idea that Boer women and children wore *bloudruk*, it also reinforces that she often pleaded with her British supporters, benefactors and family to collect cloth and discarded clothing and send it to the Boer women who were so adept at making their own clothing. In many instances she describes how threadbare their clothing was and how urgently it needed to be supplemented by donations. An employee at the Anglo-Boer War Museum mentioned that he had read in a novel that Boer women were sometimes displeased with the clothing they received. They took it without complaint, however, because they were grateful and loath to offend their beloved Hobhouse. The employee was not able to recall where this anecdote appeared and whether it was based on fact.

❖ ❖ ❖

My most reliable and informative source on *bloudruk* and Boer women in the nineteenth century is S.W. Whitham's Report on the Textile and Soft Goods Trades of South Africa (1903), which Wieke van Delen, then Iziko Museums of South Africa's curator of textiles, unearthed for me at the National Library in Cape Town. Identifying the presence of Dutch and German blueprint in South Africa in 1902, Whitham advised British manufacturers to heed his plea for the production of blankets and 'a printed cotton worn by Boer women and children and also by natives'. He added:

> This cotton is woven, dyed and printed in Germany or Belgium; it is of great weight, which constitutes its value. And it is entirely fast both in dye and in print. I am told it will wash, and wash, and wash so long as the threads remain together, and retain its colour and print to the very end. Here, again, those importers who are truly desirous of having only British-made goods have done all in their power, on many occasions, to get this cloth produced at home; but so far without success. One importer went so far as to tell me he had interviewed the Calico Printers' Association of Manchester and Glasgow on the subject, but had failed to obtain a satisfactory answer as to whether or not these cotton goods could be made at home (Whitham 1903: 15–16).

Whitham emphasised that the production of blueprint, and of a white blanket with 'a narrow coloured bordered heading', was 'entirely in the hands of German, Dutch or Belgian manufacturers'. He reported that 'immense quantities are imported into our Colonies' (1903: 16) and went on to say that blankets and cloth 'are in the stores of every importer, and through them sent to the retailer in every town, great or small, throughout South Africa'. On his visit to the major centres in South Africa, Whitham noted that in King William's Town there was a shared preference among Boer and African peoples: 'For the most part the Boer and the Kaffir, each in his own way, buy strong, serviceable articles in textiles and soft goods for wear and domestic use. In these lines British goods are preferred; the Kaffir buys them from choice and the Boer from policy to his pocket' (Whitham 1903: 42).

The coarse cloth in holdings was British, Whitham notes, as were the shawls and rugs, but the blankets were European. As for the shops he visited:

> Here again is the German and Dutch print in various qualities, but always heavy, and in a bewildering number of designs. This I now look for by intuition, and from a feeling that it must be there. I am never disappointed, nor slow to recognise it; and those in whose care I may for the time be, little knowing how often I have been introduced to this article, appear somewhat astonished when I say: 'This is a German print', and traders invariably add: 'Yes, I was about to call your attention to it.' They listen again to the story that the Boer woman and the Kaffir will have nothing else; and hear statements of its lasting properties and its immense sale. Usually I am asked why this cannot be made in England. I know this story well by now, and it will not be my fault if the Britisher does not learn to make it. I must in honour admit that the article is good; the very hold it has obtained here in South Africa is ample guarantee of this, and the test of years is indisputable (Whitham 1903: 42–3).

Whitham (1903: 47) ascertained that *Blaudruck* for Boer women and children also derived from Holland. Furthermore, speaking to a 'foreign' importer of general goods in Johannesburg, he determined that the importer stocked British goods, even in preference to foreign goods, but never compromised the Boer market and retained only the best possible stock: 'H1 quality *deutsche Blaudruck*, and the best quality of Dutch print, for which I have not as yet found a good substitute amongst English prints.'

Having encountered this *Blaudruck* everywhere in South Africa, Whitham commended the enterprising foreign manufacturer:

> [He] makes preparations to supply an article widely used. He goes out and ascertains on the spot the requirements of the community, carefully and without haste. He studies their habits and customs; watches them in their work and in their pleasures; notes the effect of sun, rain, and dust on their dress, and its appearance after being washed a few times. In a word, he learns by observation and enquiry *what these people want*, and when he has gathered all the information necessary he comes home and makes the thing to fit them. I would draw attention to the fact that what he goes to look into and afterwards makes is for use by the multitude; he does not go abroad to find out the wants of the few; those he can see at home. The big trade is what he goes for (Whitham 1903: 47–8; emphasis added).

Having learnt the Boer woman's preferences, Whitham continues, the manufacturer proceeds as follows:

> What does he learn, and what does he make? He learns, first, that the great bulk of the Boer women work either in the homestead, the field or

the dairy, and they need something strong, from which the mud stains or grease spots can be washed. He learns that neither sun nor rain must affect the colour; that the pattern on the cloth must be neat and pleasing to the eye; and that this must not be liable to disappear the first time the garment is washed, in whatever kind of water (Whitham 1903: 48).

The manufacturer then ensures that the quality of the cloth meets the requirements of the situation:

[He] makes a cotton cloth, heavy and strong, so that it will wear well and wash well; he dyes it with pure indigo, that it may withstand the action of the powerful sun; he prints upon it a neat and pleasing pattern in such a way that no amount of washing can remove it or spoil the effect. He then offers it for sale in qualities, widths, and the prices to suit every one (Whitham 1903: 48).

Not surprisingly, Whitham stresses that European machinery was always running. The manufacturer does not seek a new outlet, therefore, or make a new cloth every year, but rather 'meets the demand which lasts and increases. *He tends to create the demand himself*' (Whitham 1903: 48; emphasis added). Whitham goes on to say that the manufacturer defies competition – he perfects the cotton-print article, introduces economical alterations, increases production. Whitham then concludes: 'In this way have been produced the German and Dutch prints which have such a hold on the people of every Colony of South Africa.'

Whitham points out that the German and Dutch monopoly over blueprint, for which the two peoples were so well known that the cloth was named after them – *Blaudruck* (German) and *blauwdruck* (Dutch) – meant that future British manufacturers would struggle to capture the market. 'In view of the enormous trade in these prints,' he says, 'surely they will not rest content to be beaten. They have this advantage – they have not to create; they can see, touch and handle what they have come to compete against, which is more than half the battle' (Whitham 1903: 48). Thus British items should embody the same qualities as German and Dutch cloth – strength, weight and durability, use of pure indigo and attractive detailed print, with small motifs. All of this, Whitham believed, could be achieved in Lancashire, although wages and machinery might create problems for the rapid and economically competitive production of blueprint.

Whitham was convinced about the prospective significance of blueprint production for Lancashire, where there was no lack of knowledge, enterprise or labour. His proposals interested entrepreneurs, makers of spinning and weaving machinery and the Calico Printers' Association of Manchester and Glasgow (Whitham 1903: 49–50). It was up to British manufacturers to explore the matter and to overcome the stumbling blocks to their competition with foreign manufacturers (Whitham 1903: 16). Whitham also noted that the very lowest class of ready-made clothing – low in material, linings and make – was intended solely for blacks, who, when they approached towns or 'civilisation', were compelled by law to wear European dress (Whitham 1903: 21).

To motivate British manufacturers, Whitham brought home with him samples of 'H1 quality *deutsche Blaudruck*' and the best Dutch print (Whitham 1903: 50). He was disconcerted to learn on his return to Britain that the yarn and some of the woven cotton cloth used to produce *Blaudruck* emanated from the Lancashire mills and was sent to Germany for dyeing.

❖ ❖ ❖

Whitham's report conclusively identifies the position and origin of German and Dutch blueprint produced for Boer and African wear, whether among Trekboers or pioneers, *amaXhosa* or *amaZulu*, probably throughout the 1800s. The report provides no details of precise sources for the cloth, but Whitham's research on the subject is nevertheless admirable. The fact that he reinforces the preferences of local African wearers signifies one of the earliest instances of shared textile choices in South Africa. It also suggests that Boers and Africans were able to afford cheap but durable blueprint and may have had shared preferences in dress style. It proves, too, that in all the regions Whitham visited, blueprint was everywhere to be seen and that vast quantities of the cloth were sold locally. British manufacturers should attempt to capture this huge market, Whitham insisted, and, while replicating the quality of German and Dutch blueprint, should involve themselves in careful research and sharpen their competitiveness. This would not only entail borrowing from established trends and design preferences, but would also demand adherence to cost-effectiveness and high quality.

It took all of four decades, however, before Lancashire broke Europe's stranglehold on the sale of blueprint in South Africa. Eventually British production of blueprint was carried over from Manchester to Da Gama Textiles near King William's Town in the Eastern Cape in the 1970s, a development outlined in Chapter 7. Da Gama Textiles began to produce its own blueprint – *isishweshwe* – in 1975 and British control over blueprint manufacture in South Africa, which had been initiated in the 1950s, finally came to an end in the 1980s.

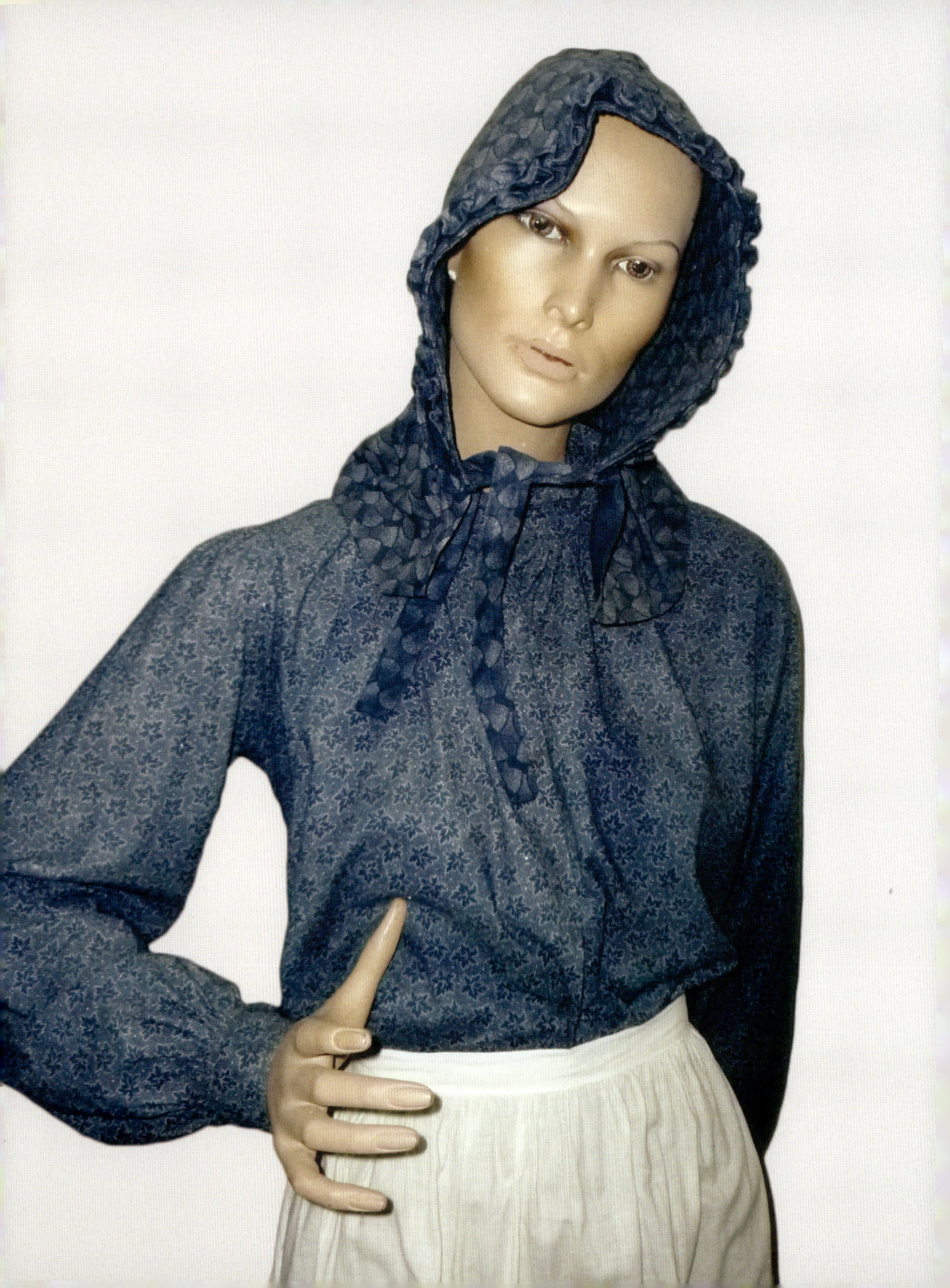

4
German Missionaries, *Blaudruck* and German Settlers

A German presence in South Africa can be identified from the country's earliest written records. German-speaking members of the Vereenigde Oostindische Compagnie, the VOC, were included among the first Dutch and European settlers at the Cape in 1652, when Jan van Riebeeck established the church in this country. Some of the VOC employees were single men who were accepted by the Dutch and married into the community. Others were assimilated into the British community – but less often and much later – and married English women (Schnell 1954: 14).

Later German arrivals at the Cape included the Moravian Missionary Society – also called the Moravian Brethren – among the most inconspicuous yet significant missionaries to work in this country. Their organisation was revived in the Lutheran Church in 1722 by the great Pietist, Count von Zinzendorf, of Herrnhut in Saxony. The Moravians reached Baviaanskloof, east of Cape Town, in 1737, but withdrew in 1744 when the VOC expelled their leader, Georg Schmidt, who had already suffered Catholic persecution in Germany. The Reform Church at the Cape, which initially oversaw the Moravians' work in the Colony, branded Schmidt a heretic for baptising five Khoisan when he was only a layman (Keegan 2004: xix).

The Dutch initially disallowed German trade and maritime traffic at the Cape (Schnell 1954: 20). They also prohibited the establishment of a Lutheran Church there, severing the early German settlers from their religious and cultural background. Catholic worship was also disallowed until 1820 (Mukuka 2008: 2). A unified Germany only emerged in the 1870s, however, after the Franco-Prussian War (1870–1), which was part of a religious struggle against the Catholic Habsburgs. Thus missionary endeavours in the Colony after the arrival of the Moravians were launched by diverse German organisations – for example, the Rhenish Mission Society (1833), the Berlin Mission Society (1833) and the Hanoverian Free Church Missions (1850).

Three of Georg Schmidt's followers returned to the Cape in 1792. They resumed their work at Genadendal – as Baviaanskloof was later known – where they found their former Khoi followers starving and reliant on Dutch farmers for contract labour. The rejuvenated Moravians, however, restarting their enterprise from what is now the oldest mission in South Africa, flourished from the enlightened Batavian era onwards.

The authorities welcomed the Moravians, whose return coincided with the first British occupation of the Cape (1795–1803). The London Missionary Society (LMS) initially worked alongside them. The redoubtable Dr John Philip was the superintendent of the LMS at the Cape from 1819 to 1851. He was fiercely critical of aspects of British colonial policy, which aimed to subjugate the local people in order to secure their entry into the colonial economy as a compliant Christian labour force.

One wonders to what extent the Moravians, who seldom expressed themselves politically, were influenced by a firebrand such as Philip. Their relationship with the Colony remained stable throughout his 30-year term as superintendent of the LMS. The Moravians had no ambitions to make converts of their congregants or avid believers of their followers. Their objective was to establish self-sufficient Christian communities in the Colony – integrated ecumenical and non-denominational settlements – and to avoid political controversy and theological dispute by preaching the Gospel within these structures as dispassionate laymen, helped by groups of indigenous catechists.

Du Pré Alexander, the second Earl of Caledon and the first governor of the Colony (1807–11), welcomed the Moravians in person. Despite his misgivings about missionary settlement among the *amaXhosa*, he invited the Moravians to help investigate an outbreak of Khoisan dissent on the eastern frontier in 1809 (Keegan 2004: xix). Although the Moravians never engaged the Colony politically, they henceforth found themselves in the vanguard of its two most urgent problems – free-burgher control over land and the labour of the local inhabitants (Davenport 1987: 41).

The Moravians were well received even by the intransigent governor, Lord Charles Somerset (1814–26), who often coloured his political speeches with expedient evangelical rhetoric. Within 50 years of their return, they had established outstations at Enon (1815), Elim (1824) and Shiloh (1828), their prospective mission to the *isiXhosa*-speaking people beyond the frontier.

Two events of importance to Moravian missionary endeavour occurred at this time. Following the interaction with the Khoi in 1809, two Xhosa refugees visited the Moravians at Genadendal – they brought a letter from the British commander who had brutally driven their people beyond the border – and the missionaries accepted the pair into their community. This not only changed the racial composition of Genadendal, but also stimulated the Moravians' interest in a mission to the eastern frontier. After a meeting with the Thembu chiefdom – personally initiated by Governor Richard Bourke, Somerset's successor – they established Shiloh beyond the Fish River in 1828 (Keegan 2004: xxii).

German Missionaries, *Blaudruck* and German Settlers

The second event, extraordinary in its scope and character, followed the Moravians' establishment of a number of Pietist missions in various corners of the globe before their return to Genadendal in 1792 (Keegan 2004: xvii). Their reappearance at the Cape was followed by an influx of Nonconformist missionary organisations into the Colony, which began with the arrival of the LMS in 1799. This wave of evangelicalism was the harbinger of a vigorous campaign to bring Christianity to the Africans before it was too late, that is, before the Second Coming and the end of the world (Davenport 1987: 177). Unmistakable signs of Christian millenarianism, or belief in the Second Coming, can be traced in several apocalyptic events, which were soon to occur in the eastern Cape during this period. These included the Xhosa cattle-killing of 1856 and the flood of local Christian conversions that followed in its wake (Keegan 2004: xvii, xxix).

Early paintings of Genadendal, and later photographs, suggest that Moravian dress on the mission was black and dour, but converts wore white cotton garments during religious ceremonies, notably baptism, to proclaim the purity of their rebirth as Christians. By the nineteenth century, however, most of the women at Genadendal — they were predominantly Khoisan with an admixture of Africans — wore *Blaudruck* as their working dress and may well have done so earlier as well. Perhaps they were emulating the missionaries or the free-burgher wives and working-class women on the outlying farms and settlements. An informant from the Genadendal Museum, drawing on a long-standing oral tradition at the mission, confirmed that *Blaudruck* was the predominant dress there throughout the 1800s. Relying on the same source, he assured me that the Genadendal Trading Store had carried large *Blaudruck* holdings well into the 1950s.

The Moravians, as noted above, founded several missions in the nineteenth century. There were doubtless trading stores on these stations that resembled the outlet at Genadendal. As the by-products of pastoral endeavour, these shops played an important role in the spread of blueprint dress types and personal accessories. Sometimes the impropriety of the owners, however, either evangelists or traders, embarrassed the Moravians so deeply that they pressed for the segregation of traders from their stations on the eastern frontier (Davenport 1997: 178). On the other hand, as an integral part of the evangelical process, the Moravian trading store catered for the everyday needs of the surrounding people — and not only for the Christian community — by selling cloth, domestic items, food, small luxuries and sewing materials. *Blaudruck* was indisputably a part of the holdings, as stated by my informant at Genadendal, and the presence of British blueprint is suggested by the revisionist historian Nosipho Majeke (Dora Taylor) quoted below. The export of British and German cloth types to South Africa — both mass-produced in England and Europe by this time — grew throughout the 1800s (Nieser 2005). Perhaps it was exploitation by a grasping minority, either missionaries or

Genadendal, hand-coloured lithograph, by George French Angas, 1849.
Iziko Museums of South Africa.

traders, which led Majeke to discredit the evangelical movement as 'a revolution in social taste for the benefit of the producers of Manchester cotton-piece goods' (Davenport 1987: 179). The only way to evaluate her criticism is carefully to balance the Moravians' intentions against the degree to which they fulfilled the fundamental needs of their followers at Genadendal (see Bate in Mukuka 2008: 3). Only when the community was satisfied would the mission be successful. This is especially true, Stuart Bate continues, of the role of culture as a determinant of priority in mission work (see Mukuka 2008: 3).

Adults were the bearers of culture and tradition on South Africa's mission fields. Preserving culture – 'an exceptionally important medium in which human beings engage and interact' (Mukuka 2008: 15) – was not solely a woman's prerogative in local indigenous society. Both men and women could uphold continuity – and thus ultimately attain modernity – by selectively foregrounding aspects of their own traditions and culture. This was how women accommodated the vicissitudes of cultural change in long-standing dress codes, which they located in *Blaudruck*, for example, as an emblem of age grades, marital status and cultural traditions of respect on the missions.

Cultural confrontation over rites of passage such as circumcision, bride price and polygamy could engage two contrasting cultures – it could stir the resolute mindsets of the missionaries and their dissident followers – but the interface between the protagonists might eventually bring about mediated cultural accommodation. Dress conventions, colours and combinations could play their own esoteric role in this process. Adaptations of dress could be widely – and often problematically – associated with dissident groups and ideologies. *Blaudruck* and European-derived Mfengu wear on Moravian mission land c.1830, for example, in comparison with 'red' unschooled Xhosa wear on the colonial periphery, are only two examples of oppositional dress adaptation.[1]

The use of *Blaudruck* at Genadendal, like the later Mfengu dress on some of the Moravian mission fields, could accentuate cultural difference within the divided Xhosa community and thus impart a unified sense of Western superiority or nascent modernity to mission-dwellers. The increasing value and popularity of imported beads to unschooled *amaXhosa*, especially when their use was heightened by exploitative trading, could accentuate any resultant dress modifications. For the *amaMfengu*, the use of *Blaudruck* could signify their entry into the colonial sphere, secured by their mission-inspired proximity. Perhaps their use of *Blaudruck* could also designate the onset of voluntary cultural change, an awakening of modernity or the emulation of the mission's piety and compassion. It is responses such as these, which reside at the core of the missionary enterprise, that have been critically analysed by modern revisionist historians and socio-political commentators. The only way to evaluate their opinions is to weigh them up against the extent to which the Moravians, for argument's sake, fulfilled the needs of the missionary community at Genadendal where *Blaudruck*, it seems, was standard dress.

The Moravians came from the rural areas of Saxony in northern Germany. As country people, they were not class conscious and, unlike members of the LMS, they shunned the elite circles of colonial society (Keegan 2004). They kept diligently to the New Testament precepts of simplicity, honesty, humility and forgiveness. They encouraged their adherents to follow their example

Detail of *Genadendal*, hand-coloured lithograph, by George French Angas, 1849. Iziko Museums of South Africa.

Detail of *Genadendal*, hand-coloured lithograph, by George French Angas, 1849. Iziko Museums of South Africa.

Top left: Genadendal missionaries in the forest, mid-nineteenth century. © Moravian Missionary Society Archive, Herrnhut, Germany.

Top right: Detail of woman with blueprint blouse, Moravian Mission, Genadendal, Western Cape, mid-nineteenth century. © Moravian Missionary Society Archive, Herrnhut, Germany.

Bottom left: Two women at Genadendal, c.1910. © Moravian Missionary Society Archive, Herrnhut, Germany.

Bottom centre: Old woman at Genadendal, c.1910. © Moravian Missionary Society Archive, Herrnhut, Germany.

Bottom right: Women parishioners at Genadendal, late twentieth century. Genadendal Mission archive.

German Missionaries, *Blaudruck* and German Settlers

Top: Osman family in Greyton, near Genadendal, eary twentieth century. © Osman family.
Bottom left : Moravian store, c.1910, Western Cape. © Moravian Missionary Society Archive, Herrnhut, Germany.
Bottom right: Detail from Moravian store, c.1910, Western Cape. © Moravian Missionary Society Archive, Herrnhut, Germany.

– the Moravians and their indigenous catechists were the exemplars of Christianity on their own missions – and treated the shortcomings of their followers with insight and compassion. They worked at the heart of the missionary process and seldom declared themselves on politics, which they relegated to the periphery (Keegan 2004: xxiii).

The mission stations established by the Moravians became models for the other evangelical societies at the Cape (Keegan 2004: xxiv). They were self-sufficient, industrious and unified communities – they replicated the village life of central Europe (Keegan 2004) – in which the mission-dwellers led fruitful lives committed to the Gospel. Ultimately they improved their livestock, increased crop production and secured admission to the emergent colonial economy. The basic material aspects of the Moravian endeavour – clothing and the plough, the hoe and the mill, a clean dwelling, soil and water, basic healthcare – were accessible to all who occupied the mission, abided by its rules and paid the nominal rent (Keegan 2004: xxiv).

The men had to produce food and support their families by hard work – the need for labour, in keeping with ancient monastic codes, was central to mission life – as agriculture underpinned the mission's existence and ensured its adherents' survival in an essentially pastoral milieu. Mission wives learnt to sew and knit, looked after the children, carried out domestic chores and kept their surroundings and families clean to combat disease. Within this medieval framework, Moravian education, as one might expect, was basic and practical. It involved manual, agricultural and artisanal training and differed markedly from the literary and academic programmes advocated by the British missionaries (Keegan 2004: xxiv).

The colonial authorities favoured the Moravian missions above their own, perhaps because the stations were popular with the local people. At least three British governors – Caledon, Somerset and Bourke – obliquely declared their preference. The Moravians' popularity with the Colony might suggest that they belonged to the type of early missionary criticised by the revisionist historians and social commentators referred to above. The nineteenth-century missionaries were generally accused of focusing all their attention on the country's indigenous people in order to convert them to Christianity for exploitation as labourers in a system of colonial capitalism.

I now briefly review the theories of three of the social commentators I have mentioned, with reference to a few tenets of Moravian and British evangelism. The essence of my review contains aspects of the Moravians' use of *Blaudruck* at Genadendal. The cloth is rich in meanings, values and beliefs and one must ponder its functionality by determining to what extent it satisfied its users' basic needs on the mission.

George Mukuka, a proponent of the rights of black priests in the Catholic Church, has briefly expounded the transactional theories advocated by James

Blaut (1995) and John Comaroff and Jean Comaroff (Mukuka 2008: 11–19). He introduces Blaut's ideas of diffusion with reference to the American geographer's hypothesis that the early missionaries in South Africa were convinced that the West was far superior to the non-West, that is, that 'the core innovated and the periphery imitated' (Mukuka 2008: 10).

As applied to Genadendal, Blaut's theory makes the Moravians the core of the mission. Their adherents, I suggest, also form part of the core. The periphery constitutes interaction outside the mission, beyond the integrated pastoral community. On the periphery the mission-dwellers – who sustain the core in voluntary submission to its demands – forfeit all their privileges. They lose their rights to an agrarian lifestyle, their access to education and primary healthcare. For the Moravians, these aspects of their pastoral endeavour were especially important. They integrated and unified the core by their own example – ecumenical and non-denominational – and by supporting their adherents in a joint endeavour, which, in theory at least, was distinguished primarily by its spiritual unity.

The large-scale use of *Blaudruck* in this process, as affirmed by the long oral tradition at Genadendal, does not entirely, in my view, suggest compulsory entry into the colonial sphere. The Moravians deliberately kept the Colony on the periphery and their early use of *Blaudruck* at Genadendal did not accentuate cultural difference or encourage Western emulation. The missionary perspective at Genadendal, rather, was pastoral and evangelical, not political. The early use of *Blaudruck* served to clad the mission-dwellers – covering dress was de rigeur throughout the Colony – who shared the evangelical core with the missionaries in a process of personal renewal, mediated cultural adaptation and prospective conversion to Christianity. Colonial politicians, on the other hand, and perhaps some mission-dwellers themselves, tended to superimpose ideas of superiority and cultural modification on commodities such as *Blaudruck*, which later became receptacles of ideology (Comaroff and Comaroff 1997a, 1997b).

When I visited Genadendal in 2005, many of my informants told me that they and their parents and grandparents before them had always worn *bloudruk* – Afrikaans for blueprint – on the mission and that, in their opinion, the cloth they used was sourced in Germany. One male informant insisted that he was familiar with *bloudruk* that was distinguished by a *swart steweltjie* – a small black logo of a boot – on the reverse side of the cloth. My collaborator and co-researcher Kirsten Nieser scoured the Web in search of the logo and its source. She translated *stewel* into *Stiefel*, German for 'boot' and discovered that the logo belonged to Stifel, an American company. I found several swatches of Stifel at the Iziko Museums of South Africa in Cape Town in 2012. Many of the designs were identical to those still produced by Da Gama Textiles today. The Stifel swatches were presented to Iziko by Cyril Ovens, who wrote a book about his experiences as a textile intermediary in South Africa. He was well aware of Stifel blueprint and of attempts by local wholesalers to corner its lucrative niche in the South African textile market (Ovens 1954).

Stifel was a unique cloth distinguished later in South Africa by a single vernacular name, *mericani*, which set it apart from widespread blueprint such as *Blaudruck*, which had several vernacular names. I cannot believe that Stifel was ever used extensively at Genadendal – its wearers always vaunt the exclusive logo – and my informant, Ernie Lennert, never distinguished the cloth as a hand-me-down or recalled it as compulsory wear for early mission-dwellers. Stifel, moreover, only reached South Africa's shores late in the nineteenth century – though it was exported here from the United States in small quantities from the mid-nineteenth century – and John Cowie, the largest *isishweshwe* wholesaler in South Africa, claimed that Stifel only became a desirable cloth around 1948.

Clothing, one should never forget, was the greatest need on South Africa's mission fields in the 1850s (Peires 1982). *Blaudruck*, Dutch *blauwdruk* and British blueprint, moreover, were cheap and durable – they were mass-produced at the time and were preferred throughout the Colony and on its fringes. All these factors, borne out in S.W. Whitham's report (1903), contributed jointly to make these cloth types ideal wear, practically if not ideologically, at Genadendal where the cost of clothing was largely borne by the missionaries. Perhaps Stifel blueprint, then, was selectively worn at a later stage by a particular group, or by a handful of individuals at Genadendal. To my mind, its usage there would denote a measure of freedom in later mission dress, which, like the varied blueprint shown in pictorial and photographic evidence of early life at Genadendal, suggests a process of personal selection and mediated acculturation. This would challenge Comaroff and Comaroff's reference to 'the unspoken authority of habit' as 'the most violent coercion in directing thought and action' at least in a milieu such as the one I surmise at Genadendal (see Mukuka 2008: 16).

Mukuka (2008: 15) goes on to describe the evangelisation of the *baTswana* in South Africa as a process in which 'a group of British missionaries thought they were going to make history for an African community and help them on the road towards civilisation'. Comaroff and Comaroff (1997b: 15), rightly in my view, contradict Mukuka when they describe the mission to the *baTswana* as part of 'the cultural and social revolution that accompanied the rise of industrial capitalism' and refer to the endeavour as 'an expression of expansive universalism that marked the dawn of modernity'. Mukuka, it seems, reaffirms Blaut's theory of diffusion in his perception of the Tswana mission. He translates the capacity to make history – the resistance eventually provoked among local Africans by the British missionary enterprise – into a dynamic reaction on the periphery of localised social involvement. He also underestimates the evangelical work of the

LMS, although, like other British missionary societies, the LMS held that African culture was incompatible with Christianity (Keegan 2004: xxii). The eastern Cape chiefdoms, the Colony and some of its missionaries argued, should be replaced by white rulers (the core) and the indigenous people (the periphery) should function contentedly on the mission fields as exploitable Christian labour.

Similar ideas underpinned British colonial hegemony in the Colony and gave revisionist commentators justified reason to suspect that the early British missionaries had played an active role in conquest (Davenport 1987: 177). Thus the LMS, for example, as an agent of colonial history, invariably overshadowed the Moravians, who relegated politics to the periphery (Keegan 2004: xv). The Moravians originated from rural Germany and their life-world – to oversimplify its nature greatly – was based on a system of medieval pastoralism. The core of their missionary enterprise remained an essentially spiritual and evangelical process, obedient to the unequivocal command to go forth and preach the Gospel. Moravian adherents accordingly resisted diffusion to the periphery and took no meaningful part in the radical developments – the cultural and historical revolution and the attendant emergence of modernity – which Comaroff and Comaroff rightly emphasise as by-products of the British evangelical process among the *baTswana* and which, in my view, culminated later as a historical continuum in the eventual emergence of contemporary South Africa.

The LMS and its affiliated societies, which sprang from the industrial heart of Britain where growth and development were the driving forces (Keegan 2004), encouraged diffusion from the core of their mission to the colonial periphery where their adherents participated in the 'industrial capitalism' and 'expansive universalism' of emergent modernity. The schooled *amaXhosa* beyond the Fish River in particular were highly responsive to this development – their later adaptation of dress, including blueprint, denotes as much.

Throughout my review of transactional theory, British colonial hegemony has been the salient theme, even though its presence has remained latent or has been internalised as social or political convention in many of the interactions I describe (see Mukuka 2008: 16). I have referred in places to cultural adaptation, however, which, as Comaroff and Comaroff (1997b: 23) rightly argue, challenges convention and translates it into ideology – 'the worldview of any social grouping'. Unlike power and hegemony, however, ideology is open to debate: 'Hegemony homogenises,' Comaroff and Comaroff (1997b: 23–5) observe, 'ideology articulates'. This is the context in which I conclude my discussion of *Blaudruck* at Genadendal.

Despite the wealth of evidence, oral and photographic, showing its widespread early use on the mission, I found no trace of *Blaudruck* when I visited Genadendal in 2005. Several informants explained that they had stopped using *bloudruk* – which became known as *isishweshwe* after 1950 – decades before. They had later found it 'unsuitable' because it was linked to 'black persons'. This explanation suggests that the *early* use of *Blaudruck* at Genadendal was never compulsory, that it never drew people into the colonial sphere, that it never asserted a state of cultural difference on the mission. At the same time, however, the explanation implies that the *later* use of *Blaudruck* became an ideology at Genadendal, an 'articulated system of meanings, values and beliefs' – to use Comaroff and Comaroff's phrase – which was exclusively based and communally debated and which accentuated cultural difference and a sense of group superiority among the core of Moravian adherents on the mission and its outstations.

I found that the very same explanation for abandoning *Blaudruck* was common among many Coloureds in the Eastern Cape – use of the cloth persists in the Western Cape to this day – and that the time of decisive rejection was around 1960 when apartheid had diffused widely from the core of South Africa's National Party government to the provincial periphery of the Western Cape. The people of Genadendal were 'homogenised' by the power of separatism and articulated the new ideology on the periphery of their own enterprise, supplanting the old dress code once accepted and lived out by the early Moravian adherents on the mission.

❖ ❖ ❖

In Germany *Blaudruck* was worn by farm women, but it never officially became national dress. One can readily understand that new settler women in South Africa should wear this cloth, for many second-wave German immigrants to this country were tradesmen whose families were familiar with *Blaudruck*. The chemical indigo dyestuff developed by Adolf von Baeyer in 1895 was widely available on the world textile markets, having been patented in 1898, and had made mass-produced *Blaudruck* much cheaper. Traders could market the cloth to German settlers and to local whites and blacks, as Whitham's 1903 report emphasises. The *Blaudruck* reaching South Africa as printed fabric was made into clothing by settler women and African seamstresses initially taught to sew on the missions.

The arrival of German settlers persisted over several centuries at the Cape, but no deliberate attempt was made to attract them until the 1850s. Invitations issued at that time coincided with a pressing need for well-trained industrious settlers and for soldiers who could form a buffer against the *amaXhosa* on the Colony's eastern frontier. A contingent of some 2 000 German-speaking volunteers found themselves at a loss when hostilities ceased before they could get involved in the Crimean War (Schnell 1954: 51). The British decided that these disengaged men were ideally suited for immigration to the eastern Cape, where they settled early in 1857 for periods coincident with their military function. Their stay entailed promises of permanent settlement and land ownership. Some of these men were accompanied by their wives – voluntary Irish brides – and Lady Kennaway introduced others to local women in the hope that the newly-weds would settle in South Africa. Very few marriages took place, however, but the Irish women brought their dress traditions with them.

Some of the German soldiers – members of the British German Legion and the German Military Settlers – were from noble backgrounds. Most of them were military adventurers, however, and their stay at the Cape under Baron Richard von Stutterheim was short-lived. Their farming enterprises failed, mainly because they were not agriculturalists, but the few soldiers who remained turned into respected settlers. They supplemented their income by becoming traders in the flourishing market for cloth and blankets, later singled out in Whitham's report. They also derived benefit from the pressing need for Western goods, which arose after the Xhosa cattle-killing of 1856. By the following year, clothing was widely needed to replace the traditional hides used by the *amaXhosa*. Thus a drastic change in local dress occurred in the eastern Cape in the late nineteenth century in which traders played a central role.

Undaunted by the flaws of the first German settler project, Sir George Grey – as governor of the Cape – initiated a second venture for German settlers in 1858. A new group of settlers, most of them agriculturalists accompanied by their wives and children, arrived in South Africa from the German states adjacent to Poland and Czechoslovakia – Überwarck and Pomerania – where they had been virtual serfs working in subjection to their landlords for meagre wages with no land of their own (Schnell 1954: 177). The prospect of freedom and land ownership in South Africa attracted them strongly, but informants suggest that they were ill equipped for local farming. Furthermore, the Colony's promises to them never materialised and they became desperately poor and verged on starvation and were often assisted by *isiXhosa* speakers. The Colony eventually alleviated their plight by granting supplies and loans.

German settler family, c.1900. Amathole Museum, King William's Town.

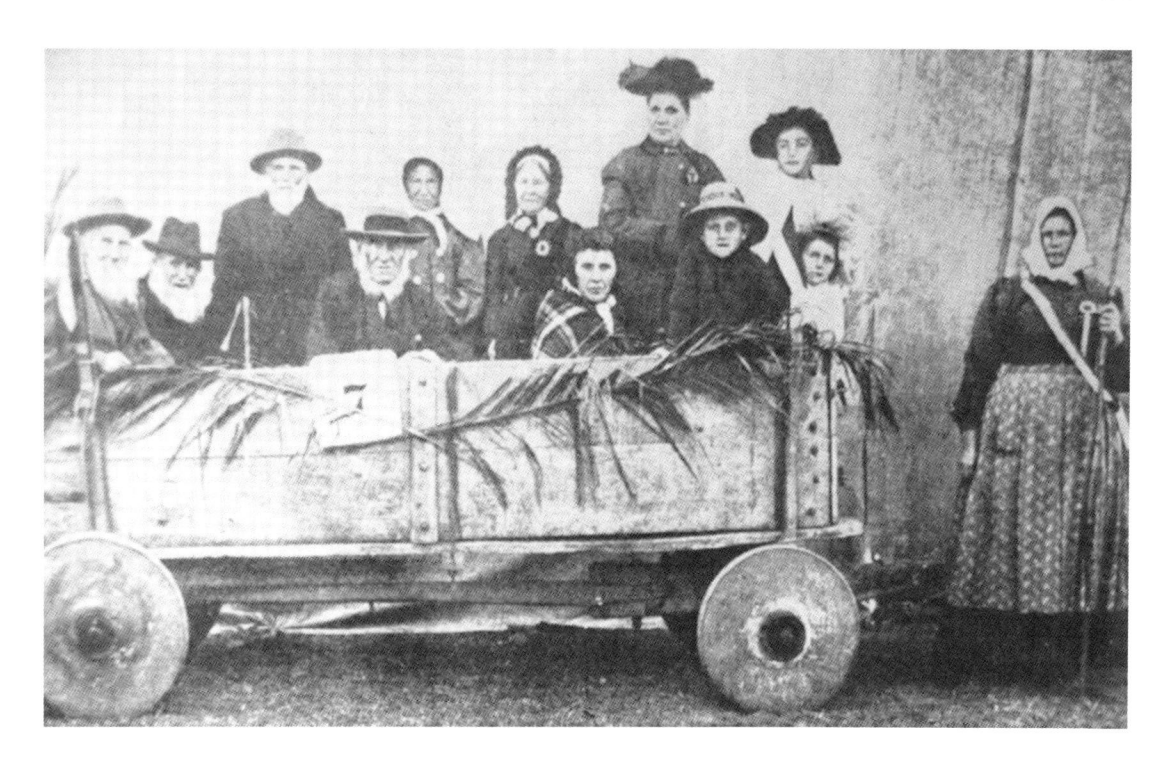

Trudelwagen (block-wheeled wagon) built by Mr Ziegenhagen from Berlin, Eastern Cape. It was used again as part of the 1908 German Settler Jubilee parade in King William's Town. The wagon is drawn by a team of oxen owned and driven by widow Alwine Salzwedel (far right) of Berlin, South Africa. Amathole Museum Archive, King William's Town.

Oral history recounts that many German settler wives wore *Blaudruck* and that, in order to continue the tradition, they imported more of this cloth from their home areas or from those regions where it was manufactured. Local families, the Schwedhelms and Schultzes of Keiskammahoek, recall that their forefathers used and traded in *Blaudruck* (Nieser 2005). One of the oldest photographs available, appearing on the cover of E.L.G. Schnell's book, *For Men Must Work: An Account of German Immigration to the Cape* (1954) and also in the *German Settlers' Jubilee Souvenir Booklet* (1908), shows a German settler family in their Sunday best. They are clad mostly in black, but at right is a portly matron at one end of a *Trudelwagen* – an open wooden cart – wearing a *Blaudruck* apron over a dark underskirt. One cannot tell whether the apron is machine- or block-printed, but the photograph is a significant image of a German settler woman's working wear.

In the districts from which the 1858 settlers hailed, handprinted *Blaudruck* was still well known in the nineteenth century. Did these settlers arrive here with *Blaudruck* garments – the few available images show them in black – or did they wear *Blaudruck* to reinforce their cultural distinctiveness? An image from the early twentieth century of a German widow with her block-wagon, a display to coincide with the 1908 German Settlers' Jubilee, shows her wearing a blueprint apron, reflecting a tradition no doubt widely identifiable in the eastern Cape among

German Missionaries, *Blaudruck* and German Settlers

German farming immigrants. Thus the questions I pose above cannot be briefly answered, but the settlers' wives, once solvent, would surely have obtained the Dutch and German blueprint preferred in South Africa at the turn of the century, as Whitham's 1903 report proves. Archival photographs in South Africa show blueprint attire among African staff and pupils on the European mission stations of various organisations and from different European countries – for example, at Genadendal in the western Cape, at Morija in Lesotho and at Lovedale in

Left: Replica of German settler dress. Amathole Museum, King William's Town.

Top right: Replica of German settler child's dress. Amathole Museum, King William's Town.

Bottom right: German settler *kappie* (bonnet), early twentieth century. The *kappie* belonged to the Tessendorf family of Braunschweig, near King William's Town. Donated by Hilda Bottcher (neé Tessendorf). Amathole Museum, King William's Town.

German woman and child, late nineteenth century. Hermannsburg Museum near Greytown.

the eastern Cape. Most of South Africa's blueprint continued to emanate from Germany and was preferred locally by white as well as black inhabitants. Photographs taken in the East London Museum in 2005 show a German settler woman with her child, the latter wearing *Blaudruck*.

◆ ◆ ◆

When the British occupied the Cape for the second time in 1806, they surveyed the eastern seaboard of South Africa from 1822 to 1823. They identified a port, known as Durban today, and the new harbour, called Port Natal at that time, functioned as a major trading entrepôt along the eastern Indian Ocean seaboard. Negotiations with the Zulu monarch Shaka resulted in the cession of the port as a trading depot. Wagons from Port Natal brought goods to all parts of South Africa, initiating major interlinked trade (Strutt 1975: 242). With the increased presence of new settlers and migrants, blueprint from Germany, Holland and England was among the traded cloth in constant demand and traders holding the cloth criss-crossed the territory. The British settled Natal in 1824 and opened up trade with the hinterland. They facilitated the Transvaal Republic (1837), the Free State Republic (1854) and the South African Republic (1856) – products of the Great Trek earlier that century – stimulating further trade in Natal and ending the isolation of communities in the interior. Merchants had called persistently for increased trade and the British annexed Natal in 1843.

A new allotment of immigrants reached Durban in 1846, having been recruited in Hamburg by Jonas Bergtheil, who moved from Bavaria to Natal in 1843. He started a cotton-growing industry, but the venture failed. Most of the 'Cotton Germans', – *die Baumwolldeutschen*, as they were called, remained in Natal and many became traders and businessmen. One cannot establish how much they contributed to dress preferences in the area, but it is certainly reasonable to assume that they wore the widely available *Blaudruck* that had been associated with their farming background for so long. I discuss these settlers in more detail in Chapter 9.

German Missionaries, *Blaudruck* and German Settlers

Indigo vat near Pinetown. Photograph Hazel England, Pinetown Museum.

Indigenous Africans who entered towns in Natal after 1854 were obliged by law to cover themselves. The British had introduced neck-to-knee legislation throughout South Africa, which led to a greater demand for cloth and to the arrival of shipments of discarded European clothing sent by benefactors from abroad (Strutt 1975: 250). The modesty legislation applicable in Natal was promulgated in 1854 by Lieutenant-Governor Sir Benjamin Chilley Pine and required all indigenes residing in or visiting Durban, Pietermaritzburg or Ladysmith to wear prescribed covering (Strutt 1975: 271). Plain or printed calico and second-hand clothing were soon called for in large amounts to facilitate entry into the labour market. Daphne Strutt observes that in the early 1850s a survey of cloth in Natal showed that 'the ordinary South African woman made good use of the pretty printed cottons [*indiennes* or blueprint] and muslins that were readily available and were being imported in large quantities for the country *and the African trade*' (Strutt 1975: 269; emphasis added). Cotton prints from Holland and Germany were clearly being used by settler immigrants, as well as local Africans, reinforcing the probability that cloth preferences existed between the two groups. Various cotton cloth types, especially *salempore*, were particularly favoured by the *amaZulu*. Beads were also popularised by the 1850s (Strutt 1975: 290). It is remarkable that no museum display in KwaZulu-Natal includes any reference to blueprint dress among its exhibits of settlers, *amaZulu* or other groups familiar with the cloth.

Top right: Pig slaughter, eastern Cape, late nineteenth century. © Moravian Missionary Society Archive, Herrnhut, Germany.

Bottom: Children on a picnic outing, Greytown area. Hermannsburg Museum, Greytown.

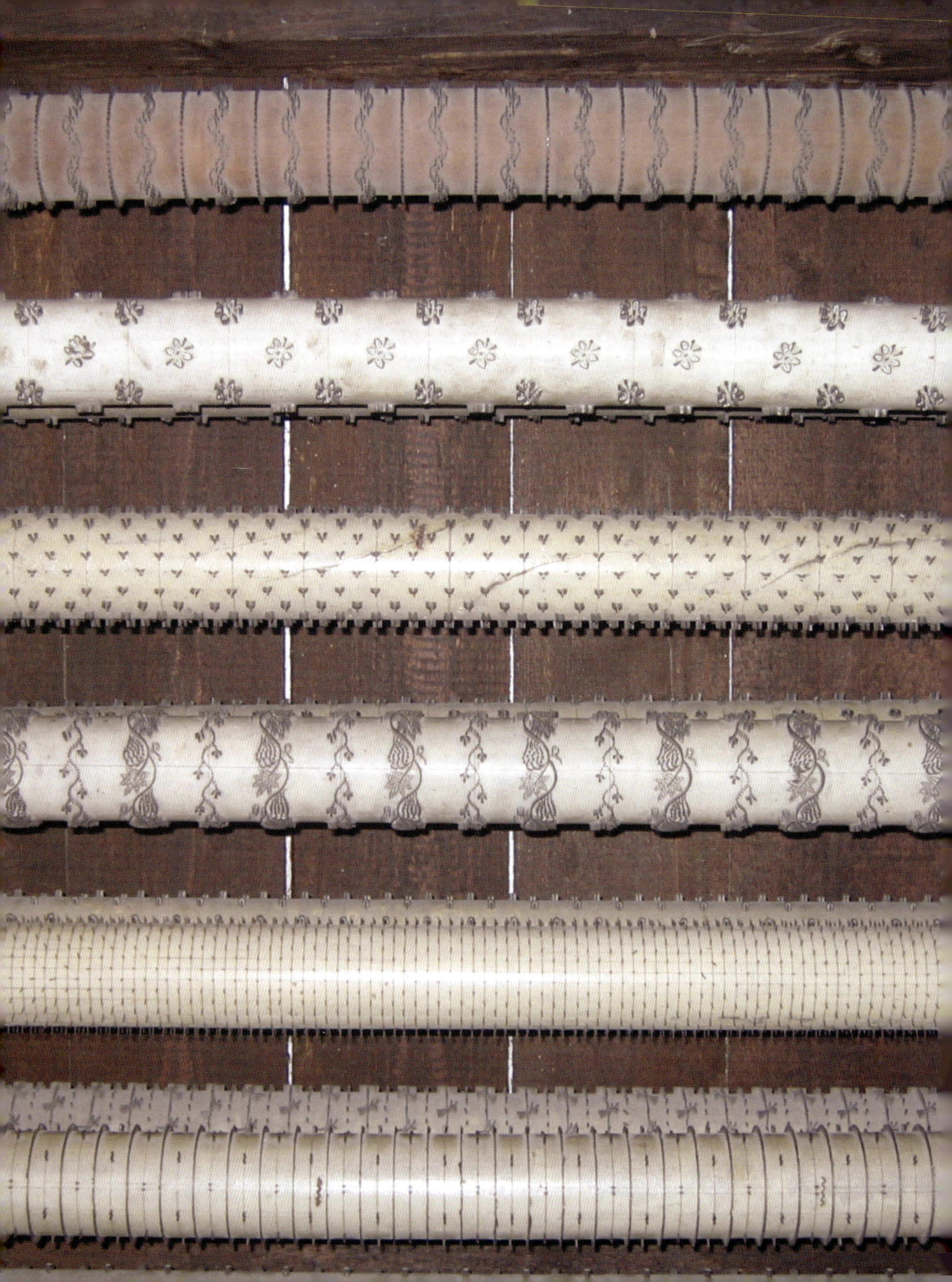

5
Modern European and American Blueprint in Context

The manufacture of modern blueprint in Europe has declined considerably, except for some studios and a few small factories in various countries, though the cloth still maintains its links to rural and peasant wear and is still associated with agriculture, national and political events and important periods of history. It also retains its regional affinities and domestic usage, despite threats to its continuity, which have loomed for more than a century.

Several informants in South Africa provided me with a wealth of information about the production of modern blueprint in parts of Europe and America. They also explained the sourcing of the blueprint enterprise, which was linked to and was acquired – and extensively developed – by Da Gama Textiles in King Willam's Town in the mid-1970s when English blueprint became known as *isishweshwe* in South Africa. Some older traders, moreover, reminisced about their imports of blueprint from Portugal, Holland and Belgium, from Hungary, Czechoslovakia (now the Czech Republic), Poland and the United States. I was lucky enough to visit some of those countries during my research to access archives and to see modern blueprint production *in situ*. I travelled to Germany and Britain for the same purpose. I hope that the discoveries I made on those journeys, and what I learnt from my reading about American blueprint, will serve to elaborate and further contextualise the earlier history of blueprint sketched in Chapters 1 to 4 of this book. I also hope that my findings will illuminate the events that led to the eventual genesis of *isishweshwe* at Da Gama Textiles c.1975, a process discussed in Chapters 5 to 7.

◆ ◆ ◆

I visited Holland in 1995 to interview the director of Vlisco Cotton Company in Helmond in the eastern Netherlands – Frans van Rood – who confirmed that the Dutch use of *blauwdruk* and its manufacture in Holland originated from that country's centuries-old trade with India, Indonesia and Africa. Initially Vlisco

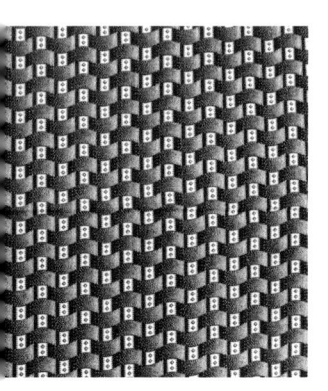

Bloudruk, c.1960, from Vlisco produced under the Three Fish logo for export to South Africa. Vlisco Archives, Helmond, Netherlands.

produced textiles in the west of Holland, Van Rood explained, because of that locality's advanced industrial development and proximity to major ports. But production costs proved too high and forced Vlisco to move to eastern Holland, close to the German border, where Helmond is located. Vlisco began at Helmond around 1846 by emulating various designs sourced in the East, notably Javanese batik patterns. The company used its own designers to produce this cloth type and employed some 50 to 60 of them from 1910 to 1920.[1]

Vlisco began exporting various cloth types to South Africa again after the Second World War, despite competition from Britain and the high cost of production and shipping. The company even questioned whether it should enter the South African market at all. Vlisco was well aware of the demand for *blauwdruk* in South Africa, but recognised that the motifs found on South African blueprint were often larger than the Dutch equivalents, though the designs were typically floral or geometric. Perhaps Vlisco had large blueprint patterns from Germany, Britain or the United States in mind. Van Rood conceded that Vlisco produced cheaper *blauwdruk* especially for South Africa after the Second World War. Additional prototypes for Vlisco's cloth were sought in Hungary, Czechoslovakia and Austria, where blueprint was still resist-printed by hand and by perrotine. There was also a home industry in *blauwdruk* in the eastern Netherlands, Van Rood observed, but he was unable to say whether the patterns were sourced in Europe or the East. Perhaps he was referring here partly to the Staphorster items mentioned in Chapter 1.

Van Rood showed me examples of the *blauwdruk* headscarves Vlisco had mass-produced for more than a century. He stressed that these were exported to South Africa from their earliest production in Holland in the eighteenth century. Unable to compete with Manchester, however, Vlisco stopped exporting *blauwdruk* to South Africa around 1960. This move was also prompted by the international embargo on trade with apartheid South Africa imposed at that time. Although Vlisco no longer produced *blauwdruk* for South Africa, it nonetheless allowed Da Gama Textiles in the Eastern Cape to retain several popular Vlisco designs under licence. These appeared as Da Gama Textiles' Three Fish range and the designs are still highly desirable today. Although Da Gama has discontinued the Three Fish range per se, royalties continue to be payable to Vlisco whenever Three Fish patterns are used.[2]

Vlisco returned to South Africa after the trade boycott ended in 1991, coincident with the abolition of apartheid, and targeted the new high-earning black middle class. Vlisco saw its role as developing a distinctive South African identity in cloth. The company rejected Western cloth preferences in favour of an emergent pan-African code in the political and official spheres of the day. Vlisco South Africa opened a business in Small Street, Johannesburg, with franchises across the country, and received a favourable reception despite the high cost of their products.[3] Vlisco plied

Modern European and American Blueprint in Context 87

the South African market with cloth from their Batik and other long-established ranges, some of it created especially for South Africa in the African National Congress (ANC) colours, green, yellow and black.[4] The future identification of *isishweshwe* with political idealism was perhaps reinforced by this development. Many Vlisco designs, moreover, reflect aspects of *blauwdruk* patterns used by Da Gama Textiles to this day, and vice versa.

◆ ◆ ◆

German *Blaudruck* reached South African shores mostly from northern Germany, which produced 'H1 quality *deutsche Blaudruck*' for consumption by black and white South Africans throughout the nineteenth century (Whitham 1903: 50). The arrival of *Blaudruck* in South Africa through Eastern Europe – one of the many ploys to avoid dues and taxes – was not serendipitous. Slovenia had exported beads to South Africa for many years, through German middlemen, and these desirable items, shipped here with ladings of cloth, including *Blaudruck*, continued to reach the local market until the 1960s. John Cowie, South Africa's leading blueprint wholesaler at the time, believed that both *Blaudruck* and beads were intended for use mainly in the Eastern Cape.

My research collaborator, Kirsten Nieser, who lives in Hamburg for most of the year, has already done exceptional work on *Blaudruck* in Germany. The section on Germany in Chapter 1 is largely based on her research and outlines the situation of *Blaudruck* in Germany today. Nieser points out, as noted in Chapter 1, that *Blaudruck* flourished in Germany in the late 1700s. She adds that the cloth retained its associations with durability and practicality in Germany throughout the eighteenth century. Its qualities bound it to the farmlands of Europe and to hosts of peasant wearers – hence the well-known remark that indigo, the 'king of colours', had become 'the most important colour in peasant culture' in Germany by the 1890s (Sandberg 1989: 16; Nieser 2005).

Museum exhibits in Thüringen, Nieser points out, confirm that *Blaudruck* predominated as peasant wear in Germany

Top: Women from Queck, Germany, in summer everyday *Blaudruck tracht*, 1992.

Bottom: *Tracht* (traditional dress) wearers from the Aula valley, Germany, in 1984. Both images located in the remnants of a 2005 exhibition held at the Supa-Ngwao Museum, Francistown, Botswana.

throughout the nineteenth century. The Museum für Thüringer Volkskunde in Erfurt, for example, exhibits a number of peasant dolls against the expansive backdrop of German regional dress and costume. Each doll is dressed in *Blaudruck*.

Nieser's remarks, as quoted in Chapter 1, emphasise that *indiennes* were initially intended for the elite in Europe, but also became readily accessible to the German peasant classes. Indigo was widely available in the nineteenth century and German mass-produced cloth was cheap. She also mentions the early cotton factories in Holland, Britain and Germany, created in the 1800s, which served as colour laboratories and produced large amounts of blueprint at the same time. Amsterdam, London and Hamburg, the three cities at the heart of this enterprise, became vast emporia for the European textile industry in the nineteenth century and exported their own blueprint vigorously.

At this juncture I have to emphasise S.W. Whitham's identification of the phenomenal increase – 260 per cent – in British textile production in the late nineteenth century. One must also consider the German chemist Adolf von Baeyer's discovery of aniline indigo, which flooded the world's textile markets from 1898 onwards. The chemical dye led to the collapse of organic indigo production in Asia within a decade, just as woad production collapsed in Thüringen in the seventeenth century when organic indigo arrived in Germany from India.

Although *Blaudruck* came to fruition in Germany, then, it was no long-term match for mass-produced British cloth, which cornered world blueprint markets from 1850 to 1870, when English textile production reached its apex. The Germans had no answer to the cheaper aniline dyes that embellished the ubiquitous *indiennes* manufactured in Holland and Britain from cheaper cloth and by cheaper means. In addition, the perrotine was no longer a match for the later etched copper cylinders, which produced hundreds of thousands of metres of discharge-printed cloth in a single day. *Blaudruck* had slowly toppled from its niche in the world market by the outbreak of the Second World War and had all but disappeared from the mainstream of German textile production by the mid-twentieth century.

Nieser's findings on the demise of *Blaudruck* propose an earlier date for the cloth's decline than my investigations of its continuity do. John Cowie, the former doyen of *isishweshwe* traders in South Africa, assured me that the importation of *Blaudruck* continued until at least 1965. Nieser, however, following her German sources closely, stresses the vagueness of lading bills from Westphalia to Africa in support of her dating of *c.*1955 (Nieser 2005; Bindewald and Kaspar 1950: 154). She rightly concludes that the matter calls for more research.

After the cessation of *Blaudruck* imports into South Africa – at whatever date – only a localised antiquarian interest in blueprint remained in Germany. Nieser observes that the continuing allure of *Blaudruck* was based on romantic memories of bygone peasant culture in a prevailing age of depersonalisation and

Modern European and American Blueprint in Context

Top left and right: Participants in the Festival of the Scheessel Shepherds, Germany, 2005. Photograph © Kirsten Nieser.

Bottom left: Couple from Scheessel, woman wearing a burnished calendered skirt and apron from the late nineteenth century, Germany, 2005. Photograph © Kirsten Nieser.

Bottom right: Participants in the Festival of the Scheessel Shepherds, Germany, 2005. Photograph © Kirsten Nieser.

Top: German house interior, reconstruction in diorama in Thüringen Museum, Germany. Photograph © Kirsten Nieser.

Bottom left: German work apron. Thüringen Museum, Germany. Photograph © Kirsten Nieser.

Bottom right: Child in blueprint for everyday wear, Schaumburg-Lippe region, Germany. Diorama in the Lippische Landesmuseum, 2014. Photograph © J. Leeb-du Toit.

industrialism. The cloth's enduring ethos, she asserts, was no more than nostalgia. She confirms her belief by describing the annual celebration of *Blaudruck* at Scheessel, a village some 70 kilometres south of Hamburg. Participants in the Festival of the Scheessel Shepherds – *die Scheesseler Beekscheepers* – wear rare and beautiful *Blaudruck* aprons and garments and, meandering through the village in song and dance, celebrate the cloth once worn by rustic peasants in the verdant rural surroundings. The dancers pay homage to the beauty of *Blaudruck* and its rich, deep-blue indigo patterns created by the printing blocks so deftly wielded by their forebears. As they dance and sing, accompanied by children dressed in *Blaudruck*, they ponder indigo, the blue sky and sparkling waters in the region as timeless archetypes of German peasant life.

Nieser shows that in 1900 there were only a handful of textile manufacturers left in Germany who printed *Blaudruck* by machine – perrotine – and employed more than 500 workers. She mentions Firma Harbig, which printed with indigo until 1914 and continued in business until 1945 (Bell 1993: 63). She adds that Franz Becker used indigo and perrotine machines until 1952 – the cloth intended especially for export to Africa – and that *Afrikadrucke* (African prints) were a tradition in Westphalia until 1955.

During a visit to Germany in 2012, I was allowed access to the Costume Archive of the German National Museum in Nuremberg, which houses a collection of garments from rural Germany. The clothing was gathered from 1890 to 1905 by Dr Oscar Kling, who died in 1926. He wished to document the threat posed to rural dress by the consolidation of Germany in 1871 and by the rapid industrialisation that followed. The collection covers some 400 regions and includes the finest *Blaudruck*, as well as German beadwork resembling Nguni designs from today. Most of the *Blaudruck*, a thick linen weave, is handprinted. Given its sourcing from 1890 to 1905, and Whitham's confirmation of 'H1 quality *deutsche Blaudruck*' imported into South Africa in the 1800s, the cloth may well represent a dress type shared by native Germans, by German settlers in South Africa and by financially advantaged Africans, as stated in Whitham's 1903 report. The ethos of

Modern European and American Blueprint in Context

From left: 1. *Blaudruck* attire, Wipp valley, late nineteenth century. Kling collection, German National Museum, Nuremberg, Germany; 2. *Blaudruck* attire from Sticht Kr Stade (left), Gegend Buxtehude, Kr Stade (right). Kling collection, German National Museum, Nuremberg, Germany; 3. *Blaudruck* attire from the village of Tiers in the Eisack valley, *c*.1847. Kling collection, German National Museum, Nuremberg, Germany; 4. Women in their Sunday best and workwear (left to right) from various regions in Germany. Lippisches Landesmuseum, Detmold, Germany. **5. Woman in her Sunday best.** Lippisches Landesmuseum, Detmold, Germany.

nostalgia, emergent nationalism and cultural pride in Kling's collection evokes corresponding sentiments linked later to *isishweshwe* – and to other South African dress, such as rural, culturally specific wear – as discussed in detail in Chapter 9.

Nieser refers to *Blaudruck* exports to Africa from the 1950s (Nieser 2005; Bindewald and Kaspar 1950: 154). When I revisited Germany in 2014, she and I saw numerous variants of *westfalische Stoffe* in indigo, which was meterage intended for contemporary export. Clearly a continuity of *Duitse sis* or *blou sis,* the cloth could be traced to 'discharge blueprint meterage on cotton from Westphalia . . . where many [eastern Cape] settlers originated' (Nieser 2005; Krostewitz 1938: 226). Whitham's affirmation of extensive *Blaudruck* imports into South Africa (1903) and Jenny Balfour-Paul's explanation (1998) of inferior *Blaudruck* in South Africa, both outlined in Chapter 1 of this book, provide invaluable sources of information in speculative puzzles such as this.

◆ ◆ ◆

isiShweshwe

Two major sources of local blueprint in South Africa, besides Holland, Germany and Britain, were Hungary and Czechoslovakia. Hungarian blueprint (*kékfestö*) was first imported into South Africa in the late nineteenth century. The cloth probably reached these shores through German middlemen. My visits to Hungary in 2005 and again in 2012 showed that early Hungarian textile exports to South Africa were in all probability derived from large-production factories and not from small home-based bluepint enterprises.

Several informants in South Africa confirmed that mass-produced *kékfestö* imports into South Africa began before the Second World War and continued into the 1970s. Cyril Ovens, a South African commercial traveller who worked for several major distributors, noted that East European textile manufacturers were keen to enter the South African market when their own production ground to a halt during the war (Ovens 1954). They faced considerable competition, however, and their imports merely trickled in. By the late 1960s there was little mass-produced *kékfestö* in Hungary. Its current production, as pointed out below, is restricted to family workshops in rural areas where it is printed with hand-blocks and resist paste in the time-honoured tradition. John Cowie, mentioned above, reinforced Ovens' remarks on the importation of *kékfestö* into South Africa. Noting that trade with Hungary increased before and after the Second World War, Cowie added that *kékfestö*, because it was relatively inexpensive and was often the only blueprint available for export after the war, was imported into South Africa in large quantities in the mid-1940s.[5]

Mr Naren Kala and his wife, of Pretoria Textile Wholesalers, recall that they acquired Hungarian *kékfestö* in the late 1960s.[6] In 2010, generously aided by the Kalas, I located several of the only remaining bolts of *kékfestö* with geometric patterns at their premises in Pretoria. One of the motifs comprised pale-blue, pinhead dots regularly spaced on a plain, darker indigo ground. Another showed adjacent 1 millimetre lines, set 2–3 millimetres apart. The *kékfestö* was loosely woven and diaphanous and after washing resembled colourfast linen. It was dyed with aniline indigo, but it was impossible to tell whether it was resist- or

Left: Hungarotex samples, mid-twentieth century. Cyril Ovens' collection, Iziko Museums of South Africa.

Top right: Hungarian kékfestö dress, Kékfestö Múzeum, Pápa, Hungary, 2005.

discharge-printed. A label indicated that it was made in Hungary, but there was no manufacturer's name.

Cyril Ovens donated samples of *kékfestö* to the Iziko Museums of South Africa in Cape Town. The cloth derived from Hungarotex, a commercial producer and distributor, which is still functioning in Hungary today, but no longer manufactures *kékfestö*. The patterns on the Hungarotex samples were mainly geometric, in dark blue and white, with insertions in orange. Lucotrope orange was especially popular from 1960 to 1970 in *kékfestö* entering South Africa. The dye also featured in designs from ABC at Hyde in Manchester and in *isishweshwe* made by Da Gama Textiles after 1975.[7] Many of the designs I saw on the *kékfestö* in Hungary were similar, even at times identical, to the designs I knew from South Africa in the late 1970s.

The *kékfestö* tradition in Hungary is directly linked to the exchange of preferences and skills among European and German blueprinters subject to Habsburg rule in the sixteenth century. Nieser's description of the process is outlined in Chapter 1 – its continuities persist to this day – and shows how it facilitated the dissemination of blueprint, accelerated textile production, increased manufacturing expertise across Europe and developed trade in blueprint through middlemen in various countries (Nieser 2005).

Dr Katalin Földi-Dózsa, former curator of textiles and a director at the National Museum in Budapest, provided me with valuable information on the history and significance of *kékfestö*.[8] I use some of the material here to discuss the continuity and usage of *isishweshwe* in South Africa after the 1950s when blueprint first became locally known by that name.

In the 1850s extensive agricultural development took place in Hungary, Földi-Dózsa pointed out, and vast fields of maize, wheat and barley blanketed the landscape. The Danube separated Buda and Pest at the exact geographical centre of Hungary. Buda, a small town of 50 000 inhabitants, was home to working-class people, small farmers and artisans, many of them German-speaking. Pest, a city of 200 000 inhabitants, bustled with merchants, businessmen and traders, mainly in agricultural produce. However, *kékfestö*, in its traditional associations with agriculture and pastoralism as cheap and durable workwear, drew the divided city together. The cloth had been worn for centuries by farmers and their wives in Hungary, by artisans and the bourgeoisie on both sides of the Danube.

The division of Budapest, as Földi-Dózsa recalled it, echoed early *Blaudruck* in Germany – its significant place in peasant culture, its pervasive ethos in the agricultural environment – and reminded me too of the cloth's unifying influence among the German settlers in the eastern Cape in 1858. They also wore *Blaudruck* to distinguish their enterprise and to demarcate and link the timeless parameters of their rural lives.

Logo of the Kékfestö Múzeum, Pápa, Hungary. Photograph © J. Leeb-du Toit.

Indigo vat, Kékfestö Múzeum, Pápa, Hungary. Photograph © J. Leeb-du Toit.

Calendering machine, 2014. Tolnai Kékfestö Mühely, Tolna, Hungary. Photograph © J. Leeb-du Toit.

Sales outlet at the Tolnai Kékfestö Mühely, Tolna, Hungary. Photograph © J. Leeb-du Toit.

The term *kékfestö* applies to all printed indigo-dyed cloth in Hungary, but local blueprinters are identified by their personalised techniques of manufacture and production. They print their cloth with hand-blocks and visit other parts of Europe to learn more about their trade, to augment their skills, to exchange or sell their designs and to market their cloth. By the nineteenth century more refined designs were realised in Hungary when brass or copper ribbons and pins were driven into the wooden blocks instead of intaglio carving, resulting in the achievement of far more detailed designs marked by fine dots and thin lines. These metal insertions also prolonged the life of designs almost indefinitely and could be easily repaired should damage occur. It is therefore not surprising, even today, to find that metal-implanted blocks well over a century old are still being used in Hungary and elsewhere in Europe. The positioning of the design for repeat patterns was realised by four protruding pins at each corner of the metal-implanted blocks, so that the design could be positioned to coincide with two corner pins of the previously printed section. This was observed in the printing in Tolna in the Kovacs' workshop, as well as in Pápa.

By the late nineteenth century, Földi-Dózsa added, *kékfestö* produced by mechanised printing in Hungary had widely replaced the handprinted equivalent, much of it for the export market. Today the perrotine, which is capable of holding several printing-blocks at the same time, is still used by families of blueprinters such as the Kovacs near Szentendre and the Horvaths in Tolna, who continue the centuries-old tradition of blueprinting once pursued by their forefathers.

In 2005 I visited the Kovacs' commercial outlet in Szentendre. Their *kékfestö* included complex blueprint designs, abstract motifs and modern references. This latter aspect of their production, they confessed, drew little attention from the traditional *kékfestö* market. The Kovacs also produced conventional items for their shop where I bought a few pieces. Their *kékfestö* closely

Modern European and American Blueprint in Context

Left: Hungarian blueprint, Szentendre, near Budapest, Hungary, 2014. Photograph © J. Leeb-du Toit.
Centre and right: Hungarian blueprinters Kovacks' commercial outlet in Szentendre, near Budapest, Hungary, c.2012. Photographs © J. Leeb-du Toit.

resembled some designs popular in South Africa from 1960 to 1970, the very period when *kékfestö* was imported into this country. I recall one pattern in particular, a repeat diamond motif, which has two variants in current *isishweshwe*. The well-known *isitebe* (shield) design, and the smaller version called *libete* (rice), were both identified at the Kovacs' *kékfestö* outlet. Their dresses on sale at Szentendre were mostly conservative – with elbow-length puffed sleeves, high necklines, hemlines below the knee – and thus echoed continuities in style from mission contexts in South Africa.

While I was in Szentendre in 2005, I purchased an antique skirt from the 1940s and its matching apron from a Russian trader in vintage dress. The black pleated skirt (resembling the Zulu pleated hide *isidwaba*) included a band of mass-produced *kékfestö* around the waist. The fine pleated apron was also of *kékfestö* and, when worn over the skirt, reproduced a matching attire common in *Blaudruck* and in *isishweshwe* in many parts of southern Africa.

At a second *kékfestö* outlet in Szentendre called Blue Land Folklor, owned by Toth Kona, much of the *kékfestö* was from the Horvaths in Tolna. The cloth sold was narrow – only 80 centimetres wide – a measure equal to South African *isishweshwe*. I subsequently met the Horvaths in Tolna in 2012. Some of the patterns in their shop were regional designs created by different blueprinters, after the Hungarian manner, and were based on motifs sourced in local fauna and flora. Irene Body, among the best-known *kékfestö* designers in Hungary, also lives in Tolna, but I was unable to locate her there. The Horvaths' stock, which I was allowed to peruse, showed preferences and continuities similar to the Kovacs', as revealed by the dress type worn by an elderly woman I spoke to

Bottom left: Woman at a market in Pest, Hungary, 2011. Photograph © Jacquie Sarsby.

Bottom centre: Woman selling herbs at a market near Pest, Hungary, 2011. Photograph © Jacquie Sarsby.

Bottom right: Woman selling walnuts and flowers, near Tolna, Hungary, 2012. Photograph © J. Leeb-du Toit.

in a nearby village. *Kékfestö* dress was not as widespread in Tolna as I thought it might be, neither was it common in the other parts of Hungary I visited.

I noted, finally, that there were several other *kékfestö* centres in the vicinity of Szentendre and Tolna: Udvarhelyi and Gyöngyvér, Veszprém and Bolalu, all renowned for their *kékfestö* tradition. Földi-Dózsa remarked later that the geographical location and distribution of these small outlets helped make *kékfestö* among the most affordable dress for the peasant classes in Hungary.

The cost and durability of blueprint has always been a crucial factor for its users – wherever the cloth was made – but this does not seem to have been central to the production of *isishweshwe* by Da Gama Textiles after 1975. Perhaps a twofold identification has evolved there, undetected by researchers, between the quality of yesterday's blueprint imports and today's South African *isishweshwe*, which seems to be upgraded at manufacture for use as best, perhaps because of the expense of subsequent modifications, and has therefore lost some of its associations with rurality, rusticity and pastoralism. An anonymous source, who formerly worked at the social history section of the Iziko Museums of South Africa, was adamant that *isishweshwe* was a problematic cloth. To her it had come to be associated with female oppression and expected subservience to male dominance. She also regarded it as signifying rurality and even ignorance.

According to Földi-Dózsa, many wearers of *kékfestö*, at least until the late 1980s, frequented fairs and markets in the Hungarian countryside where blueprinters also sold their wares. Currently, many of the blueprinters sell at national and international markets, reviving an interest in *kékfestö*. In 2012 fellow blueprint researchers from Britain, Hillary Burns and Jacqueline Sarsby, sent me two photographs of an old Hungarian woman in a rural setting dressed in a spotted *kékfestö* garment. In the same year I was lucky enough to see an elderly rural inhabitant wearing a floral and geometric *kékfestö* dress in a Hungarian village square where she sold produce from her garden.

Initially *kékfestö* was distinguished by resist-paste designs on white cloth that was subsequently dyed indigo, but by the late eighteenth century, the patterns included red and yellow, pale-blue and green. They may well have been the prototypes for the later mass-produced cloth type that Cyril Ovens donated to the Iziko Museums of South Africa, as noted above. Multicolours were also to be seen in the Néprajzi Múzeum in Budapest. The same genre appeared later in South Africa at Da Gama Textiles in 1975 under the Fancy Prints logo, as shown in Chapter 7.

Kékfestö served not only as clothing in Hungary, but also as wallpaper, an adaptation related to the use of *Blaudruck* as interior furnishing in rural homes in Germany and South Africa. Földi-Dózsa identified *kékfestö* as wallpaper in the staff living-quarters of the royal palace in Budapest during restorations in 2005.

Földi-Dózsa noted that by 1844 *kékfestö* had become highly significant in Hungary as an adjunct to *Heimatliebe*, a patriotic signifier of love for one's country. This trend was instigated by various reforms – political and economic – proposed by the fiery Hungarian leader Lajos Kossuth. His ideals emerged from the 1830s as aspirations to national freedom and as demands for the franchise and other equalities. Under the apartheid regime in South Africa, both black and white women wore *isishweshwe* for the very reasons set forth by Földi-Dózsa. Recent revivals in the use of *isishweshwe* have disclosed similar patriotic overtones. White wearers, for example, often identify with the cause of oppressed African women – who wore *isishweshwe* precisely to denote their oppression – and declare themselves in their widely recognisable 'African' wear, a category of cross-cultural dressing discussed in detail in Chapter 11.

Kossuth's support for the rights of peasants and the abolition of peasant dues and services resulted in partisan expressions of support, such as donning and upholding local peasant dress preferences, mainly in *kékfestö*, and the continued production of such cloth.[9] Not surprisingly, the wearing of *kékfestö* soon became attached to nationalism and resistance to Austrian hegemony. In 1844, Kossuth initiated the *Vèdegylet,* a protection society that upheld and protected Hungarian culture and vigorously promoted Hungarian-manufactured products.

In a gesture of national support and resistance in 1844, patrons from the upper classes attending society balls elected to wear *kékfestö* cotton prints instead of their batiste, in a partisan gesture, but also to foreground their support of local manufacture and of Kossuth's national reform movement. Although Kossuth's rise was temporary (he was forced to flee Hungary in 1849), his defiance and revolutionary ideals and patriotism have remained partly attached to the wearing and retention of *kékfestö* and to subsequent associations with Magyar-Hungarian identity and the upholding of Hungarian autonomy and nationalism.[10]

The wearing of *kékfestö*, Földi-Dózsa told me, thus evolved as an expression of nationalism and opposition to Austrian rule in Hungary. The wearing of *isishweshwe* by dignitaries and even royalty in southern Africa on public occasions can, in part, also be regarded as a partisan gesture to demonstrate empathy with their followers at large – those who wear *isishweshwe* as their hard-earned best – and to promote the dignitaries' political aspirations through their shared dress. However, wearers may also be acting out of patriotic nationalism, as *isishweshwe* began to acquire associations with emergent cross-cultural nationhood especially after 1990, as shown in Chapters 9 and 10 of this book.

According to Földi-Dózsa, *kékfestö* was prominent again in Hungary in the 1960s. This time it functioned primarily as a signifier of resistance and national folk dress to protest against Russia's plans to make Hungary a predominantly industrial state. Stirrings of opposition to Russian Communist control saw widespread protests that were harshly suppressed. This again saw the popularising of *kékfestö* cloth as a form of dress embedded with associations of independence and nationalism. The protests caused an upsurge in Hungarian textile production and exports and led to the adoption of *kékfestö* motifs by the likes of Laura Ashley in London. Within the next ten years, *kékfestö* was transformed. It became widely associated in the West with peasantry and rural origins, with national dress and trampled political aspirations.

Nieser mentioned to Földi-Dózsa that a German settler's descendant in the Eastern Cape in South Africa denied wearing German print during the 1940s, due to its association by then with black South African wearers. In response Földi-Dózsa noted that *kékfestö* had at times also acquired similar ostensibly negative associations, but this had occurred only briefly when its association with the much-maligned Romanians in Hungary was identified.[11]

The wearing of *isishweshwe* as oppositional dress in a foreign country – many white South Africans adopted this protest in the 1960s when apartheid was approaching its legislative zenith – shows a spirit of solidarity against oppression similar to the Hungarian protests against Russia. The same nationalist ethos imbues *Blaudruck* portraits of Frederick the Great exported from Westphalia to Prussia c. 1870 and the patriotic fervour attached to Kling's German costume collection of 1890 to 1905. In South Africa this continuity extends irresistibly to Da Gama Textiles' Madiba range – an essentially positive representation – from the 1990s, which proved highly

Dr Monika Lackner showing a *kékfestö* apron, Néprajzi Múzeum, Budapest, 2005. Photograph © J. Leeb-du Toit.

Modern European and American Blueprint in Context

popular and is now a collector's item. The former president's smiling countenance transcends the nation's internecine conflict and emotion at the time – resentment and anger, mistrust and fear – and his composed demeanour portends peace and prosperity. Positive emotions also fill the continuing use and identity of *isishweshwe* in Lesotho, Swaziland and Botswana, as described in Chapter 9.

A visit to the Hungarian Museum of Ethnography – the Néprajzi Múzeum – disclosed further links between *kékfestö* and South African *isishweshwe*. The current curator of textiles, Dr Monika Lackner, gave Nieser and me access to the *kékfestö* holdings in the museum archive – drawers full of samples and hundreds of pieces of old and new *kékfestö* cloth and dress. The *kékfestö*, with few exceptions, was a very dark saturated blue. Most of it was resist-printed with hand-blocks and displayed a distinctive sheen resembling upgraded *Blaudruck* that had been subject to calendering. A few of the designs I saw were replicated in South Africa and many showed the small white floral motifs typical of the twentieth-century mass-produced *kékfestö* exported to this country from Eastern Europe.

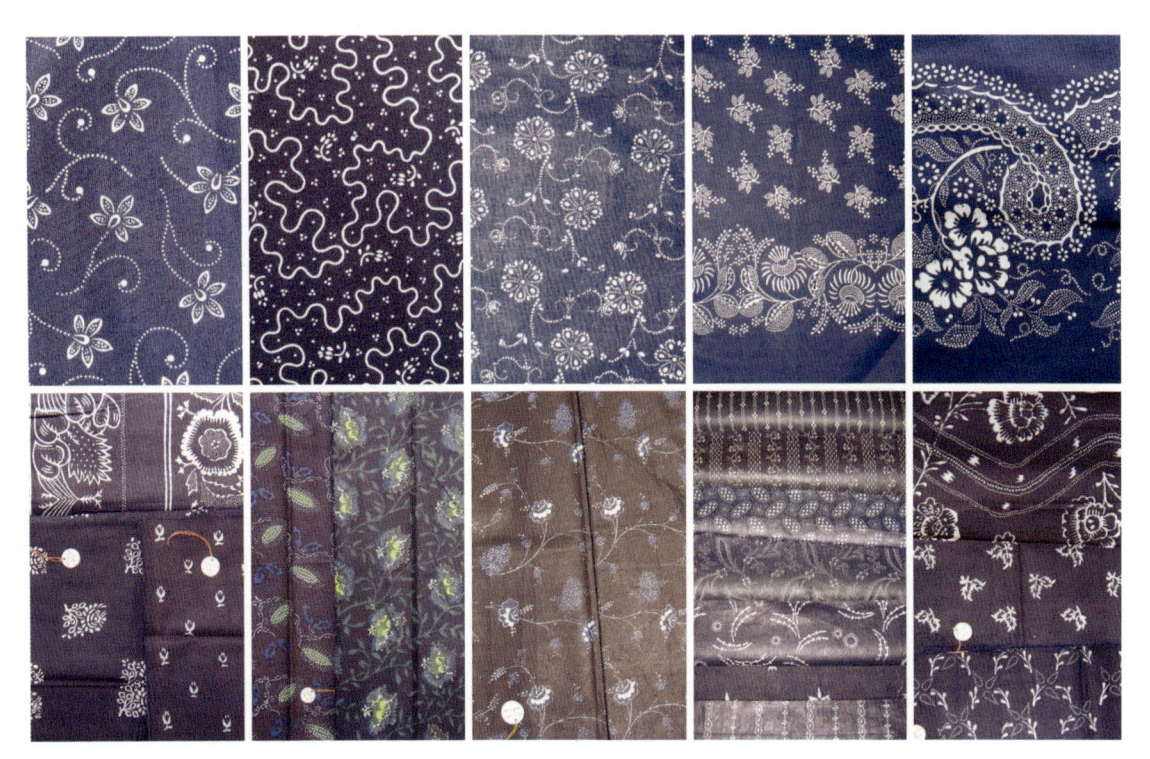

Top row: 1. Hungarian *kékfestö*, 2014. Photograph © J. Leeb-du Toit; 2. Hungarian *kékfestö*, 2012. Photograph © J. Leeb-du Toit; 3.–5. Hungarian *kékfestö*, 2014. Photographs © J. Leeb-du Toit.

Bottom row: Hungarian kékfestö, Museum of Ethnography (Néprajzi Múzeum), Budapest. Photographs © Kirsten Nieser.

Top: Diorama of a *kékfestö* market stall by the Kluge blueprinters, late nineteenth century. Museum of Ethnography (Néprajzi Múzeum), Budapest. Photograph © J. Leeb-du Toit.

Middle and bottom: Hungarian pattern book, mid-nineteenth century. Tolnai Kékfestö Mühely, Tolna, Hungary. Photographs © Kirsten Nieser.

More attention needs to be paid to pattern books as an influence in creating continuities such as these across the world of blueprint design. The dissemination of pattern books exerted a much greater influence than the travels of blueprinters, which are so often invoked to explain the continuity of *isishweshwe* designs in South Africa. Nieser alludes to pattern books from Westphalia c. 1750 in Chapter 1 of this book. A few of the pattern books contained some 3 000 colour images and were sent from *Blaudruck* centres in Germany to places across the world, including Stifel in America (Nieser 2005). I have seen many British and German pattern books, both early and late editions, being used by South African *isishweshwe* dealers. They consult the books to make recommendations to the designers at Da Gama Textiles – I describe the process in Chapter 6 – and they identify this usage as a perpetuation of the old practice of travelling from place to place to share information.

The *kékfestö* I found at Pretoria Textile Wholesalers, with the Kalas' help, had simple dot-and-line discharge-printed designs on a dark indigo ground, but its texture and weave were different from that seen at the Néprajzi Múzeum. Hungary was part of the Austro-Hungarian Empire and it is not surprising that skills and designs associated with *kékfestö* were disseminated across the country by blueprinters of German and Austrian origin.

Lackner regards *kékfestö* as associated mainly with workday wear.[12] She ascribed the decrease in wearers and blueprinters to the fact that most of the older blueprinters had died, taking their expertise with them. She pointed out that after the Second World War *kékfestö* dress was restricted to small numbers of elderly women who wore it on traditional occasions or to impress tourists. As in Scheessel, Lackner added, a nostalgic evocation of *kékfestö* took place periodically in Hungary, but, in her view, it sprang from ongoing political dissent and not from any sentimental feeling for the cloth.

Lackner also pointed out that *kékfestö* was regarded as Christian wear in Hungary and as festive wear with secular overtones. The cloth's Christian and religious associations linked it to modesty – the high neckline, long sleeves and hemline well below the knee – a trend peculiar to blueprint in many parts of Europe. The same tendency is found in mission contexts in South Africa, as mentioned above – at Genadendal, Lovedale and Morija – and is discussed in detail in Chapter 9.

Modern European and American Blueprint in Context

Earlier in Hungary, Lackner said, brides wore handprinted *kékfestö* linen garments – the linen deriving from former Czechoslovakia or even Russia – just as some Zulu, Sotho and Xhosa brides wear *isishweshwe* in the rite of dress-change during marriage and, more recently, as a preferred marriage garment. Lackner said that when these special or elaborate garments were faded and worn, they were modified for use as everyday workwear. *Kékfestö* was also worn by women after bereavement. Initially the woman wore black as a sign of her widowhood and thereafter garments of dark-blue *kékfestö*, signifying an extension of her mourning and vulnerability. This is of significance in South Africa, where many rural women (in the northern and eastern Cape, in KwaZulu-Natal and Lesotho) wear *isishweshwe* as mourning apparel and for long periods, as discussed in Chapter 10.

I visited the Goldberger Museum in Budapest in 2005, which was originally part of the Goldbergers' home and lay adjacent to their textile factory. Goldberger, an Austrian Jew, became a Hungarian citizen in 1784. His son Ernst, who hailed from Vienna, created a vast textile industry in Budapest, becoming one of the biggest *kékfestö* manufacturers in the country, noted for his production of cottons. Lackner believes that Goldberger traded *kékfestö* with the United States, Switzerland and France at least until the 1930s. The family's control of their textile empire subsequently collapsed, however, although other companies absorbed their enterprise after the Second World War. But by 2012 most of their buildings were deserted and dilapidated. Archivists at the Goldberger Museum showed me the pattern books from the remnant Goldberger *kékfestö* range, many identical to those used in South Africa.

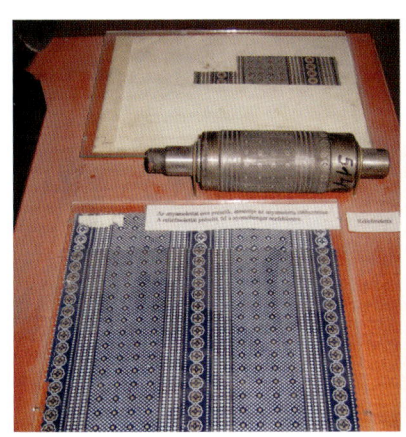

Left: Goldberger *kékfestö*, early twentieth century. Goldberger Museum of Textile and Clothing Industry, Budapest, Hungary, 2008. Photograph © J. Leeb-du Toit.

Right: Interior of Goldberger Museum of Textile and Clothing Industry, Budapest, Hungary, 2008. Photograph © J. Leeb-du Toit.

Many Goldberger *kékfestö* designs had a defining border, like some Hungarian blueprint, and showed a logo fixed to the reverse. Goldberger had at least fifteen factories in Hungary that mass-produced *kékfestö* and were linked to other textile undertakings. It is feasible – but still not certain – that his empire traded directly with South Africa. Perhaps it used intermediaries such as Czechoslovakia or even Germany. No further details were available on my second visit to Budapest in 2012, as the museum was under repair. In fact, the archivists and historians I met there were surprised to learn that *kékfestö* had ever been exported to South Africa from Hungary in the twentieth century.

In 2005 I also visited the town of Pápa and its textile museum. The Kékfestö Múzeum is dedicated to *kékfestö* – the only one in Hungary – and I was able to see the original dyeing and printing workshops and a range of items on display, including large dyeing vats. The Múzeum holds dyeing workshops intermittently, using organic indigo, but is not involved in the commercial production of *kékfestö*. The few remaining printing shops and dyeworks in the area perform this role on a small scale.

Hungarian handprinted *kékfestö* was still relatively cheap in 2005 and again in 2012 compared to Da Gama Textiles' *isishweshwe*. The cotton weave is closer and of better quality, moreover, and the range of blues varies considerably. Some of the tones are lighter; others appear as royal-blue indantrine. These are the hues, it seems, which please the Magyars today. Some of the cloth has a distinctive lustrous finish due to calendering, and its desirable stiffness is enhanced by starching. This practice, common since the earliest days of *Blaudruck*, remains a salient preference in Da Gama Textiles' *isishweshwe*.

◈ ◈ ◈

Trade links between the Czech Republic and South Africa have existed for more than a century. Initially, as already shown, they involved the importation of glass beads into this country from Czechoslovakia via Germany in the late nineteenth century (Ovens 1954: 23). The availability of cheap glass beads generated lucrative trade and transformed personal bead adornment and conventions of dress among indigenous groups in South Africa. Trade links with Czechoslovakia persisted throughout the twentieth century and continued to be brokered by middlemen in Germany. The same brokerage applied to the importation of factory-produced Czech blueprint, or *modrotisk*, into South Africa.

South African traders, such as the Kalas in Pretoria, indicate that middlemen brought samples of *modrotisk* with them from Czechoslovakia. Once the *modrotisk* became popular in South Africa, Czech variants entered the local

Modern European and American Blueprint in Context

market. When this took place is uncertain, but informants suggest the period from 1930 to 1950. Ovens (1954: 23) points out that by the 1950s Eastern European countries had tried to break into the South African market. He adds, however, that consumers here were particular and that other manufacturers supplying the local market resolved to retain their stronghold in South Africa. Eastern Europeans faced an uphill battle, Ovens observes, and their products were soon eclipsed by their British competitors.

In 2012 I visited several museums, archives and *modrotisk* blueprinters in the Czech Republic to establish their traditions and to identify the source of imports to South Africa from 1930 to 1950. As in Hungary, dyeing by hand and block-printing still prevails in small family-owned businesses in the Czech Republic. All the *modrotisk* I saw in local workshops was resist-printed and then dried, after which it was dyed in wooden vats of aniline indigo. I visited the Danzinger family of blueprinters at Olešnice. Many of their products are sold in the Manufactura commercial outlets of Prague and other major centres of the Czech Republic and include serviettes, tablecloths, clothing and tourist items such as rag dolls. The Danzinger blueprint workshop opened in 1816, when the elder (grandfather) Danzinger travelled from Germany to Czechoslovakia to learn pattern-making and dyeing. In Olešnice he met and married the local blueprinter's daughter and remained in the very workshop where his family continues production today. A few of their designs are akin to some in Britain and South Africa, but the Danzingers have never exported to South Africa.

Left: The Joch brothers in their studio in Strážnice, Czech Republic, 2012. Photograph © J. Leeb-du Toit.

Right: Dyed cloth emerging from the Joch brothers' vats at their workshop, Strážnice, Czech Republic, 2012. Photograph © J. Leeb-du Toit.

The renowned Joch brothers from Strážnice produce block-printed *modrotisk* from a vast range of extremely old metal blocks impregnated with indigo. Some of their motifs bear an uncanny resemblance to the mass-produced *isishweshwe* made in South Africa by Da Gama Textiles. One such local motif is the *seSotho*-named *diphororo*, 'rippling river', another is an undulating design called 'brains' in *seSotho*. None of the designs in the Strážnice workshop are named, but their similarity to Da Gama's *isishweshwe* idiom suggests to what extent motifs were disseminated by interaction and pattern books and later by mass-production in textile factories.

The Joch's *modrotisk* workshop is at the back of their large factory building. The brothers continued production throughout the Communist era, although they were nationalised, and were allowed to repurchase their factory in the 1990s when the Iron Curtain collapsed. Currently their main clientele is local, but they

Left: Hand-blocks for printing with paste. Textile Museum, Česká Skalice, Czech Republic.

Centre: Joch brothers' wave-like design, Czechoslovakian *modrotisk*, 2014. Photograph © J. Leeb-du Toit.

Top right: Hand-block with metal inserts, Joch brothers' workshop, Strážnice, Czech Republic, 2012. Photograph © J. Leeb-du Toit.

Bottom right: Da Gama Textiles *isishweshwe* with wave-like motif known as *diphororo* (rippling river). Photograph © J. Leeb-du Toit.

Modern European and American Blueprint in Context

also export to Europe, the United States and Britain. I was their first-ever South African visitor and they were certain that their products were never exported to South Africa.

Czech cottons and cloth were highly desirable in Europe, the United States and South Africa in the twentieth century. I remained intent on locating Czech *modrotisk* mass-produced in factories, which was imported to South Africa, and not only the workshop-produced cloth described above. In the country's only museum of textile production, the Textile Museum in Česká Skalice – in the north-east Czech Republic – I was fortunate enough to identify one likely manufacturer of *modrotisk*. The museum contains samples in pattern books and the manufacturer's name was identified by a poster on the museum wall. I also discovered a Kolora pattern

Left: Perrotine printing machine. Textile Museum, Česká Skalice, Czech Republic.

Right from the top: *Modrotisk* pattern book. Textile Museum, Česká Skalice, Czech Republic, 2012; Display of Kolora factory information in the Textile Museum, Česká Skalice, Czech Republic, 2012; Samples of copper and chromed etched rollers for discharge-printing. Textile Museum, Česká Skalice, Czech Republic. Photographs © J. Leeb-du Toit.

isiShweshwe

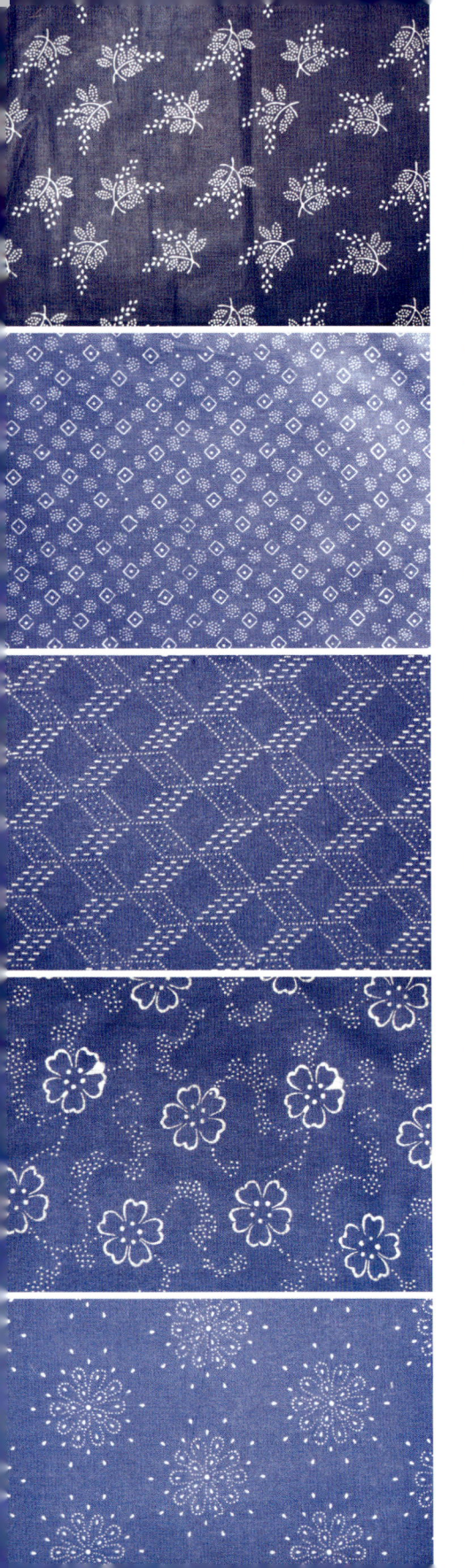

book of blueprint with patterns very similar to those produced later in South Africa. Kolora was a Jewish-owned factory mass-producing commercial *modrotisk*. Their *modrotisk* was of the kind that entered South Africa and it closely resembled the cloth that Hungarotex exported here from 1950 to 1960. It was also similar to cloth produced in Britain during the same period and copied at Da Gama Textiles in the Eastern Cape in the 1970s. I located three more pattern books in the Česká Skalice Textile Museum, but was unable to gain access to the display cases in the museum to identify the manufacturers. Traders and importers of Czech blueprint in South Africa have not been able to recall the names of any of the manufacturers. Thus my research into which Czech manufacturers exported to South Africa on a large scale from 1930 to 1950 must remain speculation. As in Hungary, many of the textile factories in Czechoslovakia were Jewish-owned and their proprietors were obliged to relinquish control before or during the German occupation and after the inception of the Communist regime.

In the Czech Republic *modrotisk* is still associated with national, cultural and rural origins, particularly in the agricultural population. The centuries-old patterns used by the few handprinting workshops left still testify to the referencing of rural designs – wheat, pomegranates and wild flowers – and to a selection of geometric patterns, as noted in Hungary. The Czech mass-production blueprinters, while producing *modrotisk* for South Africa, would certainly have responded to preferences in this country conveyed to them by middlemen or salesmen, so that their handprinted patterns in effect partly persist in local mass-produced variants.

In the early 1990s, when the Iron Curtain had fallen, however, many of the larger mechanised textile factories in the Czech Republic closed down. Production was no longer cost-effective, they faced competition from East Asian exports and the state failed to protect the local textile industry. These circumstances caused further closures from 2005 to 2008, according to a student I met en route from Česká Skalice. There

Left: Czechoslovakian *modrotisk*, 2014. Photographs © J. Leeb-du Toit.

were now only a handful of textile manufacturers left in the Czech Republic, he said, and the country no longer produced *modrotisk* or any of its variants in significant amounts. In fact, a bolt of *modrotisk* found in a store in Česká Skalice was produced in Hungary.

❖ ❖ ❖

The British tacitly supported the American South in the American Civil War (1861–5), recognising the United States as a major producer of cotton and indigo. In the eighteenth century most American cotton was exported for manufacture in Britain's industrial centres where it was spun, woven, printed and dyed – later mostly with American indigo. The yardage was then shipped back to the United States for use by American consumers. The British were very protective of their textile industry and initially banned the export of their machinery and intellectual property to the colonies and the New World. Attempts to initiate a textile industry in the United States were at first unsuccessful, but after the American War of Independence (1775–83), printmaking industries developed rapidly in the northern and eastern states of America. Production skills were attracted from Europe and led to a drastic reduction in American textile imports. American production progressed rapidly and the British finally sought other markets for their blueprint, looking especially to the colonies and South Africa. As a result of its expansion, the American textile industry made enough affordable cloth, especially cotton print, and grew enough indigo to satisfy local needs by the 1830s. American manufacturers became increasingly adept at dyeing and used excellent mineral-based dyestuffs. Many new blueprint producers immigrated to the United States from Europe, Germany in particular. They perpetuated the long-established tradition of exchanging knowledge and skills in blueprint manufacture.

The United States has a diverse immigrant population and represents one of the largest diasporic settlements in the world. In the pioneering era (late eighteenth and nineteenth century) the dress of European settlers in the United States was clearly distinguished by urban and rural preferences. The development of certain durable and hardwearing textiles was prompted by the character of the settlers – many came from German, Dutch and Nordic stock – and by their strenuous way of life. Their countries of origin produced and wore blueprint, which was widely used by their rural populations. In the nineteenth century one of the preferable cloth types among American immigrants was blueprint, the serviceable indigo and brown variants being preferred. The settlers themselves first brought this cloth to the United States and further supplies were acquired from their countries of origin until such time as the United States produced enough cloth to meet its own needs.

Stifel commercial blueprint exported from the United States to South Africa. Cyril Ovens' collection, Iziko Museums of South Africa. **Centre:** Stifel boot brand logo. Iziko Museums of South Africa.

Modern European and American Blueprint in Context

109

The production of blueprint in the United States was realised by, among others, Johann L. Stifel, or Johan Louis as he was known. An entrepreneur, he had trained as a dyer and calico printer in Germany. He settled in Baltimore, Maryland, in 1833 and established his own printing works in Wheeling, West Virginia, specialising in blueprint for use by local clientele and for trade with the American West and Northwest. He produced Wheeling Prints, as they were known, which were highly regarded for their quality. His factory made indigo prints exclusively, buying the cotton direct from local mills and importing the dye from Calcutta (Kiplinger 2011). The calico was block-printed until 1866 and the early designs consisted mainly of floral motifs with leaves and geometric shapes in the traditional blueprint manner.

In 1866 Stifel switched to mechanical roller-printing in wood and then copper (Kiplinger 2011). By 1874 the company was the largest calico printer in the United States and the first to produce yard-wide blue calico, which was shipped to all parts of the world. Stifel also began to discharge-print cloth at this time. It produced drills and denims, which became household names, for example, Bulldog denim and Miss Stifel cloth, a lighter, less dense version of denim.

In 1903 the Stifel trademark – *Stiefel* means 'boot' in German – was patented and printed with a boot on the reverse side (US Patent Office #210849). Large quantities of Stifel cloth were shipped abroad to Latin America and India, the Phillippines, Canada and Africa. Stifel blueprint was so popular in export countries that the locals wore it inside-out in order to display the boot as a symbol of prestige (Kiplinger 2011). This trend is also found in South Africa today where prestige logos, such as Three Cats (now

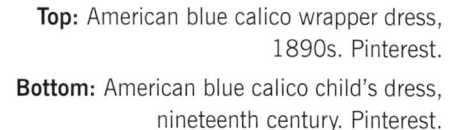

Top: American blue calico wrapper dress, 1890s. Pinterest.
Bottom: American blue calico child's dress, nineteenth century. Pinterest.

exclusive to Da Gama) often appear on the collar, cuffs, hem or pocket of a dress item to identify it as authentic and also to convey the wearer's financial capacities.

Indigo cloth is still used to produce quilting in the United States. By 1929, however, the production of indigo cloth at Stifel began to decline. Trends and tastes in fabric changed and synthetic fibres were introduced c.1957 (Kiplinger 2011). The decline finally resulted in the closure of Stifel after 122 years of manufacture and trading. Ironically some of the blueprint available in the United States today is South African *isishweshwe*, produced by Da Gama Textiles and exported increasingly to the United States as an African cloth for quilting and dress.

By the 1850s the missionary enterprise in South Africa (and in former Natal and Zululand in particular) constituted one of the largest evangelical ventures in the world (Leeb-du Toit 1989; Strutt 1975: 242). One of the first endeavours on the eastern seaboard of Natal – today KwaZulu-Natal – was launched by the American Board of Missionaries at Umlaas in 1835. I have identified very little blueprint in images from their stations, but, seeing that blueprint flooded the United States in large quantities, where it was worn by rural settlers and by African Americans, it would be interesting to locate any sources of the cloth among the Board's adherents in the United States and South Africa.

John Cowie recalled the presence of Stifel-derived blueprint in South Africa, noting that the product was the best-known cloth available here around 1948. American producers of Stifel doubtless benefited from the disruptions in Europe caused by the Second World War and identified gaps in the market previously dominated by Britain and Europe. Cowie was well aware that Stifel was backstamped with a boot, which potential buyers found essential. Another informant indicated that in a trading store in Germiston late in 1949, African customers referred to various types of blueprint cloth as *mericani*, clearly a vernacular description of Stifel-derived (or other) American imports. The development of this terminology for Stifel blueprint could only have emerged with time, indicating that its continuity in South Africa was considerable.

As Stifel's blueprint sales began to decline in the late 1920s, the manufacturers were only too grateful to meet the demand from South Africa from 1930 to 1955 before finally closing down in 1957. The closure coincided with the emergence of Da Gama Textiles in King William's Town, where blueprint production only began in earnest in South Africa after 1975, a process traced in Chapter 7.

Of the many missions in South Africa, the Swedish Evangelical Lutheran Church in Natal was one of the earliest. The missionaries may well have worn blueprint, which was well known among Nordic communities, but could also have derived their cloth from pedlars who plied the area for the Boer and African market. In the Nordic countries blueprint was a well-known rural convention reflected in interior usage as well as dress. Reverence for handmade items and for the irregularity associated with them was a prominent feature of blueprint dyeing in the twentieth century (Sandberg 1989: 113).

◆ ◆ ◆

After a visit to the United Kingdom in 2005, I decided that the story of the British sourcing of *isishweshwe* in South Africa was so compelling and relevant locally that it warranted a chapter of its own. Chapter 6, which deals with aspects of modern British blueprint in context, is thus a prelude to the genesis of South African *isishweshwe* on the looms of Da Gama Textiles in 1975, which I recount in Chapter 7.

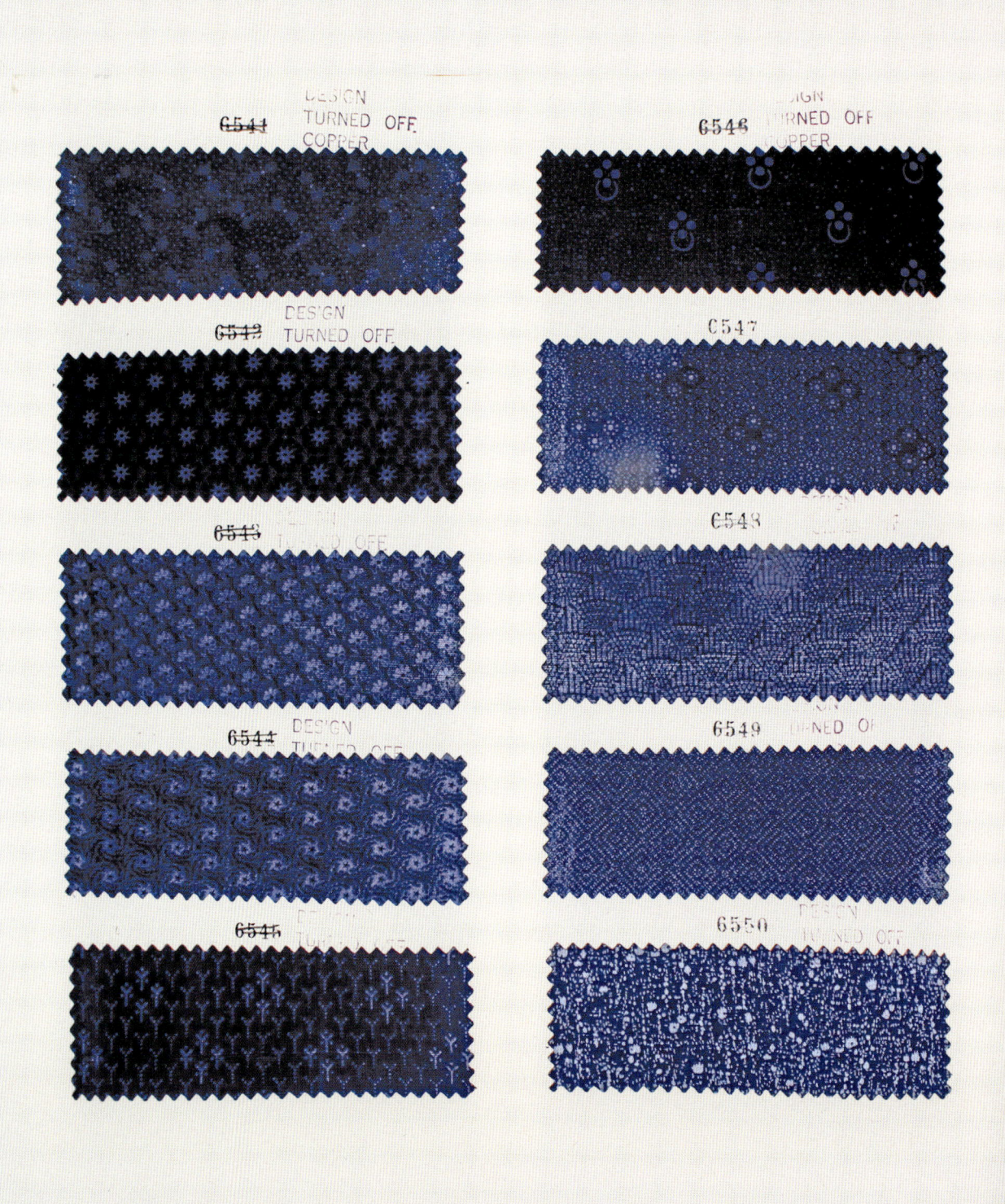

6541 DESIGN TURNED OFF. COPPER	6546 DESIGN TURNED OFF COPPER
6542 DESIGN TURNED OFF	6547
6543 DESIGN TURNED OFF	6548 DESIGN TURNED OFF
6544 DESIGN TURNED OFF	6549 DESIGN TURNED OFF
6545 DESIGN TURNED OFF	6550 DESIGN TURNED OFF

6
Modern British Blueprint in Context

Textile printing is relatively new in England. It was introduced in 1676 by a French immigrant who established a printing works in Richmond on the banks of the Thames. By the eighteenth century Britain was one of the world's main importers and users of indigo. The English cornered the indigo market and trade in indigo cloth in the 1850s and again from the 1960s to the 1970s. These developments created markets in the colonies for mass-produced British blueprint, which grew to include South Africa and other parts of the continent, as well as the Americas and the Caribbean, India and the East.

In Britain in the 1850s blueprint, with cheaper *indiennes* and other print cloth, was used mostly by the working classes and the rural and urban poor. The British met the needs of these markets until the early twentieth century. According to David Bradley, former head of ABC Textiles in Manchester and author of the company's history, the London poor at that time wore black, blue or brown print. The designs on the cloth were, in his opinion, from Germany or the East.[1]

Far left: British blue calico winter day dress, late nineteenth century. Pinterest.

Left: Maid's dress in blueprint with white dot motif, late nineteenth century. Gallery of Costume, Platt Hall, Manchester.

As a result of the Industrial Revolution, printed cloth became one of the main products of the Manchester textile mills in the early 1800s.[2] The mass-production of printed cloth in Europe was accelerated by the perrotine, which facilitated faster and more precise printing. In Britain the use of roller-printing – also called cylinder- or machine-printing – was patented and developed in 1785. The process was further developed by Adam Parkinson of Manchester and refined by Livesey, Hargreaves and Company of Bamber Bridge.[3] Copper rollers could print more than six colours on 12 000 yards of cloth in a few hours. This capacity, which was also highly accurate, led to widespread preferences for British cloth both at home and abroad.

The blueprint that first reached South Africa from Britain, which became *isishweshwe* here after 1950 and on the looms of Da Gama Textiles after 1975, was discharge-printed by roller. By 1899 various printers in Manchester had amalgamated to form the Calico Printers Association (CPA). This body had members from 85 per cent of all British calico printing companies by 1850 and

Late eighteenth-century samples of blue and brown printed cloth. ABC archive, Manchester. Photographs © J. Leeb-du Toit.

Modern British Blueprint in Context

brooked little opposition in the printing industry. At the end of the First World War, however, trade in Britain came to a virtual standstill. Countries such as Brazil, Japan and the United States emerged as competitors. China also entered the fray and Britain, by the late 1930s, appeared to have lost the monopoly over cotton goods, which it had once held as a result of its earlier industrial development.[4]

The design and printing of British blueprint was centred in Manchester and surrounding villages, which became the heart of the English textile trade. The production of cloth and other textiles for the colonial market was so large that in Manchester each important colonial centre had its own 'house' in Whitworth Street where export fabric was first documented. A number of printing houses manufactured blueprint in particular – Spruce, Strines, Brotherton – and in Stockburn near Manchester the Ashton family monopolised the textile industry. Benjamin Ashton, son of Samuel, built the Newton Bank Print Works in 1816 with his brothers as partners. The venture produced its own cloth in black, purple and chocolate hues. The annual production in the early years was more than two million yards, all for home consumption. Newton Bank joined the CPA in 1899 (*HOCP* n.d.: 27).

Alfred Brunnschweiler started a small printing company – later known as ABC – at Hyde outside Manchester in the late 1800s. Gustav Deutsch, a Swiss national, obtained permission for Britain to utilise and copy blueprint designs from Germany at this time. Brunnschweiler, who had moved to Britain because printing was cheaper there, traded in Manchester as F.W. Ashton and Company, producing madras cottons and blueprint, the latter developed from a range of designs, including those on *Blaudruck* facilitated by Deutsch.

ABC was a member of the CPA and in its heyday could produce six million yards of fabric per year. By 2005, however, when ABC catered for Ghana and Nigeria in African wax prints, production had diminished to some three million yards a year. In 2008 ABC imported undyed cotton cloth from China and was soon taken over by Cha Chi Ming. The main design studio moved to China soon after.[5]

ABC abandoned its blueprint trade with South Africa around 1990, just before the new political dispensation. Craig McCann, head of design at ABC, has provided a thorough account of ABC's history.

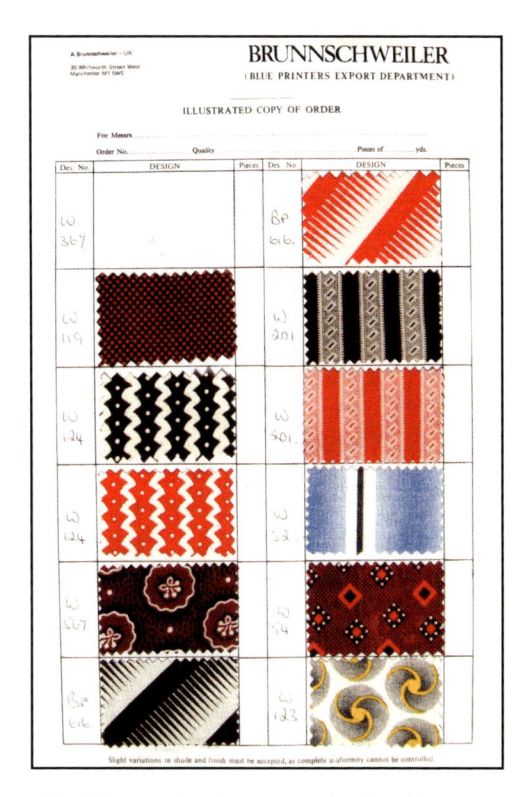

Alfred Brunnschweiler pattern book, mid-twentieth century. Da Gama Textiles archive, Zwelitsha, Eastern Cape.

ABC now falls under a major textile group known as CHA, owned by a Hong Kong-based Chinese citizen, Cha Chi Ming, who bought ABC from Coates Viyella in 1992. Prior to that ABC was owned by Tootal, which Coates Viyella took over in the late 1980s.

Cha Chi Ming started his career in textiles by acquiring factories and properties worldwide. He opened businesses in West Africa in the 1950s, including a factory in Ghana, his first African enterprise. When ABC became part of CHA in 1992, it was the only group in CHA with a design section. ABC exploited this advantage within the group by accessing its own archive. When I visited ABC in 1995 and again in 2005 the archive was still used to develop designs – under ABC's Group Design Centre – specifically for the African wax range and market. The archive contained a large number of Three Cats, Toto and other blueprint design books and textile samples that ABC had developed over the years exclusively for South Africa.

The training of designers and the development of design at ABC have a fascinating history. Both programmes have been associated with South African *isishweshwe* from the 1950s and have not been studied previously. This aspect of British blueprint calls for detailed treatment, but I confine myself to input by the 'invisible designer' who is invariably overlooked in the mass-production of blueprint.

Exterior of ABC, Hyde, near Manchester, 2004. Photograph © J. Leeb-du Toit.

◈ ◈ ◈

Most blueprint producers in Britain had closed when I first initiated my research on ABC in 1989 and first visited there in 1995. The company was one of the last suppliers of British blueprint to the South African market. After they ceased production in 1990, all their metal rollers were shipped to Da Gama Textiles near King William's Town in the Eastern Cape. I deal with this development in detail in Chapter 8. In its heyday ABC accepted trainee apprentices in design and engaged several women to produce blueprint patterns. The intricate designs called for skill and patience and, once created, were hand-engraved onto copper rollers and printed by discharge process. From the late 1980s designs were replicated or directly drawn on computer. They were then developed electronically before being placed on rollers for engraving. Later, as technology advanced, designs were transferred to rotary screens.[6]

Designers from ABC were significant in mediating themes destined for South Africa. In 1995 and 2005 I interviewed Margaret Hickson and her colleague Ann Shaw. They were the last two blueprint designers from ABC and both had retired when I interviewed them in 2005. From 1963 Hickson and Shaw had worked

Modern British Blueprint in Context 117

British Calico Printers Association pattern books, mid-twentieth century. ABC archive, Manchester, 2005. Photographs © J. Leeb-du Toit.

Wigan Blue Printers' export pattern book, *c.*1960. Da Gama Textiles archive, Zwelitsha, Eastern Cape. Photographs © J. Leeb-du Toit.

Modern British Blueprint in Context

as textile designers – including blueprint – for other British companies. In 1972 they decided to join forces and moved to ABC where they worked together until they retired in the 1990s. Hickson had done blueprint designs for the CPA, but Shaw's experience had not extended that far. Hickson turned to the ABC archive to realise new designs. Both women had considerable impact on designs emanating from ABC. They were responsive to the suggestions and requirements mediated by sales representatives from South Africa who visited ABC in search of desirable blueprint.

Until the 1980s all ABC blueprint designs were handmade. Blueprint demarcates pattern and detail with fine lines and minute dots, the representation of which demands a mastery of technique as well as design. Initial designs were made on paper prepared with a brown (black mixed with havana lake) or blue (black mixed with ultramarine) Winsor & Newton gouache. Hickson recounts that the blue base she used tended to be brighter than the blue printed onto the textile, which made the white-on-blue design more visible for working on. The line-and-dot pattern of the image was applied using a fine brush, sometimes consisting of a single bristle, to render the smallest dots. Also the scale was tiny, sometimes little more than the size of a large postage stamp. Hickson notes: 'One had to keep the ground clean as you could not rub things out, any errors requiring overpainting, or you would have to start over again from the beginning.'[7] The design was transferred to acetate, a task undertaken by Shaw, and then to copper, where it was engraved electronically, a process done by hand in the past. In her last years at ABC, Hickson notes, when she worked on other

Margaret Hickson, former textile designer, including blueprint, ABC, Manchester, 2005. Photograph © J. Leeb-du Toit.

Ann Shaw, formerly of ABC, Manchester, 2005. Photograph © J. Leeb-du Toit.

Above: Margaret Hickson's design notebook, late 1980s. **Below:** Her designs (not used). Margaret Hickson collection. Photographs © J. Leeb-du Toit.

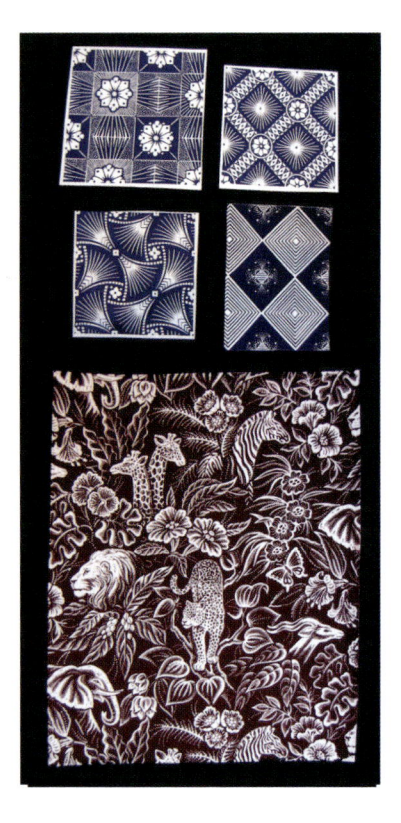

cloth types as well as blueprint, the line-and-dot design for Java print became digitised, though the designs for blueprint were still manually rendered.

The input of designers and the nature of blueprint design at ABC involve a personal dimension, which generally, Shaw notes, 'is not taken into account'.[8] When Hickson and Shaw worked at ABC there were at one stage about sixteen designers, many of whom produced blueprint designs. In the 1970s, twice a year, always on a Monday, Mr Knotts, who was in charge of the studio, would announce: 'It's blueprints!' This would evoke a plaintive response, the 'Monday morning groan'.[9] Shaw continues: 'That was rock bottom . . . because we'd all be doing it, and we'd all end up with bad shoulders, stiff necks, bad tempers.' Both Shaw and Hickson emphasised that realising the blueprint designs was exacting, even frustrating, because of the precision required. Hickson added: 'They were quite awkward designs to do . . . you'd end up tearing your hair sometimes.' What made blueprint design so taxing was that neither woman had specialised in the genre. Previously they had both worked in African prints, notably 'fancy prints', that is, predominantly floral designs. To produce a range of meticulous

Modern British Blueprint in Context

blueprint designs twice a year was 'laborious, painstaking and you'd have to be absolutely spot on'. Shaw adds: 'There was quite a lot of swearing because we were fed up to the back teeth with it.' Hickson agrees: 'It was hard work, it was . . . you built up the tension with sitting so cramped over the design . . . and working with a magnifying glass on a stand'. In the early 1990s I saw Hickson working on blueprint designs under a large magnifying glass. According to Hickson, the blueprint designs were difficult to do:

> You had to stay focused on what section you were painting up. And with it being so small, the little white pin ends that came off the end of your brush . . . you'd have to, what we called 'keep your eye in' to make sure that they were a similar size and the space in between and you could see something wrong there because you could see that one pin was a little different.[10]

The corrections were made by overpainting with the original blue or brown ground. Often there was so much overpainting that the faulty area appeared raised in relation to the ground. As a result the design was frequently redone from scratch when undulations on the surface became noticeable and detracted from the uniformity required.[11]

Blueprint designs were done 'by eye', rather than being 'technically spaced' as with Java or Africa wax print. Thus the designer filled the space between or within the motifs by gauging the spaces between the dots by eye. The entire field was demarcated by dots and the spaces in between them were almost the size of the dots themselves. Hickson describes the precision imposed by this peculiarity:

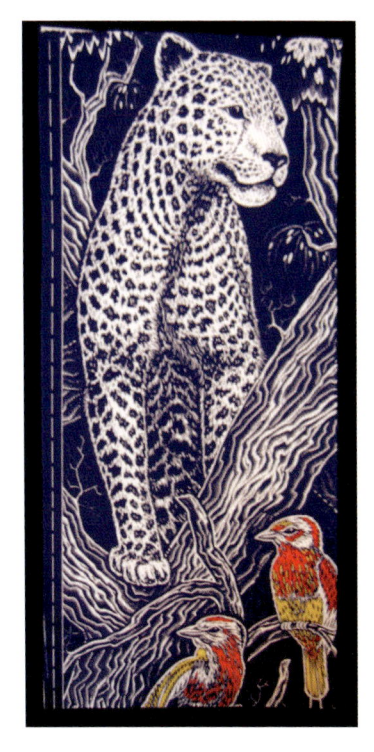

> If you were trying to replicate it you had to count those dots as well because if the pressure on your brush or the paint that you were using was a bit more liquid you'd get a bigger or smaller dot in which case you'd get more spots within that line.[12]

Panel design in gouache, destined for the South African market, by Margaret Hickson, late 1980s, Manchester. Margaret Hickson collection. Photograph © J. Leeb-du Toit.

The resulting precision of their designs betokens care, skill and pride in their work – despite the grumbling.

Hickson and Shaw designed blueprint twice a year for a fortnight. Once the design was realised, Shaw would screenprint it onto paper. The designs were then presented to Ted Lowe, the marketing manager at ABC, who took them to South Africa and showed them to specific traders and wholesalers who were 'large-volume buyers'. The traders were familiar with clientele preferences and discussed the marketability of the designs with Lowe. Traders such as John Cowie and Jock Morrison and Sons, the Kala family, Peers Brothers and Fleur Rourke, among many others, thus made important contributions to the design realisations of blueprint and to the preferences of African clientele, about which they kept themselves well informed. Fleur Rourke from Lesotho, as shown later, made especially important design contributions to ABC blueprint destined for South Africa.

After his meetings in South Africa, Lowe would return to Manchester and negotiate any suggested changes with ABC, which would be carried out by Hickson and Shaw. Only rarely did marketing mediators such as Lowe, who were in direct contact with the clientele base, suggest alternative designs. Hickson notes that 'nine times out of ten' their original designs were accepted with very few changes.[13] Finally, when agreement was reached about what would be printed, orders were placed and production of the cloth began at ABC.

❖ ❖ ❖

The geometric and organic designs of blueprint were based on established conventions and on the designer's imagination and inventiveness. Neither Hickson nor Shaw felt constrained to create a particular design or pictorial subject. There was pressure on both of them, however, to execute and realise blueprint designs rapidly. They had to be familiar with the idiom and repertoire of centuries-old patterns and be versatile and inventive in realising fresh designs. The whole new range had to be achieved within two weeks, but some of the prototypes – especially those for repeat designs – were only 2 inches square. Thus the designers had to be certain that the replication was feasible and that the dots matched internally when the replication occurred.

Knowing that they would have to produce designs under pressure at least twice a year, designers such as Hickson drew on a range of ideas they had envisioned and pondered throughout the year. This can be seen in Hickson's sketchbooks. She regularly recorded motifs and images encountered on her travels and at work, the practice providing her with a range of potential designs to draw on. In one of her sketchbooks, which I saw in 2005, many of the motifs were organically sourced, but could easily be reduced to dot-and-line patterns.

While the two designers prepared and developed their work autonomously, the designs became a closely kept secret once they were realised. No designer from other printworks was allowed to visit the studios. This was in keeping with the policy of the CPA to protect printwork designs. Despite this incipient

Modern British Blueprint in Context

copyright, however, there were continuities based on the designers' knowledge of obsolete patterns, some from other printworks. Hickson said it was difficult to pin down designs and that, in effect, there was little new subject matter in the blueprint repertoire, at least while she worked at ABC.[14]

Soon only a few designers pursued blueprint designs at ABC. Hickson and Shaw remembered the time when only four designers were left, one of whom was Mr Knotts himself, the head of design. Knotts was trained in design and originally came from Elson and Neill, a West African printworks in Manchester.

In between major blueprint projects, designers worked on other types of cloth. From the 1970s designers at ABC were involved with West African textiles and worked on cloth called African wax print. Even in these designs, produced as late as 2008, aspects of blueprint were included as background or fillers in blue, white or other colours. These inclusions were called 'pin-spot ground fillers'.[15] The clam-design filler was one of the most frequently used motifs I saw at ABC in 1995 and again in 2005.

In the late 1960s the concept of skirt panels was presented to Hickson and Shaw. It was mediated by Ted Lowe of ABC and Rodney Breetzke, a South African commercial traveller. Hickson was one of the first designers to realise and develop designs for the panels, but the concept seems to have been suggested by an Indian trader in Durban in 1965 or thereabouts.[16] The development of the skirt panels is a salient example of trader intervention in design preference.

Pattern book located at Da Gama Textiles, 2015.

Retailers noted that local black women (not only *amaZulu*) made partly flared skirts with tucks (*liteke*) or ric-rac braid as embellishment at the hemline. The imitation ric-rac trim and stitching-line on the panels emerged in the 1960s and proved desirable from the outset. Some of the skirts made by rural women, with the ric-rac stitched on, were brought to Hickson and Shaw from South Africa by Lowe and Breetzke. Hickson introduced the broad stitch-line markers, which often appear horizontally above and below the ric-rac braid. She did this to create a 'hand-crafted effect', the stitching also providing areas for the addition of beadwork or tucks. The replica-stitched areas resemble the *liteke* popular among Sotho, Tswana and Xhosa wearers. But as they now appeared on the cloth in printed form, they were no longer 'tucked' and sewn by seamstresses, but were left merely to denote the tradition. The replica ric-rac braid facilitates precision in the applying of detail to the skirts and provides a clear register of the points of juncture when making up the skirt. The seamstress is thus able to align the pattern and design as a whole. Bearing in mind that the panels were situated top-to-end on the meterage on which they were printed, and were cut for realignment top-to-bottom, it becomes clear that precision in design, ric-rac and stitching was crucial.

In addition, the A-shaped panels included a range of motifs in the lower register that allowed for more inventiveness in narrative or decorative motifs. Hickson noted that these motifs were done to scale, that is, the size of the designs was the actual size of the motif to be used above the register hemline.[17]

isiShweshwe panels outside a Durban store, 1995. Photograph © J. Leeb-du Toit.

The motifs included Dürer's praying hands, a mineshaft with workers, Sotho hats, a tailor and soccer player, leopards and various other animals, including an eagle and guineafowl and a range of indigenous feline motifs. The motifs were drawn from diverse sources such as promotional adverts and coffee-table books on South Africa provided by Lowe and Breetzke.

Hickson felt she could be more inventive in her designs for the pictorial motifs of the panels. She was given more flexibility in their realisation, displaying her representational and interpretive skills. Many of her designs from 1970 to 1980 have been retained and are still produced at Da Gama Textiles in South Africa – for example, the Sotho horse and rider, Dürer's praying hands, sheaves of corn, the lion and leopard (all adapted by recent designs) and the rhino. Other motifs Hickson is known to have designed include a tailor at a sewing machine in front of a trading store, schoolboy soccer players and boys on bicycles. Lowe also suggested some of the themes. Hickson recalls his requesting some designs of a diamond mine and a gold mine and others of cranes. But she was aware too of popular preferences such as soccer in South Africa.[18]

Hickson's and Shaw's input into the development of *isishweshwe* motifs reflects their dedicated and meticulous training, their mediated interpretation of African motifs, and the market for blueprint. They brokered ideas and perceptions about the market and South Africa, which were conveyed to them by traders and the marketing arm of ABC. Their insights reflect an interpretive process that ended in the 1990s when they both retired from ABC. Neither of them ever visited South Africa, or indeed any part of Africa, while they worked on blueprint or skirt panels. Instead they relied on tourist brochures, promotional publications and postcards brought to them by importers associated with Da Gama Textiles. They also received a regular supply of South African journals, including *Panorama* and the *South African Digest*, which they kept for years as reference sources. An article on Hendrik Pierneef in *Panorama* pricked their interest and they were attracted to his work. One would like to think that Pierneef's reductive images of trees and mountains were inspirational in the women's narrative panels.

Hickson and Shaw were well aware that the wearers of Da Gama Textiles' blueprint were predominantly rural African women. They reinforced what they took to be these women's interests, cultural particularities and labour. Given the stereotypical images they were plied with, predominantly of rural dwellers and settings, they attempted to highlight clearly identifiable features of ethnic groups such as the *amaZulu*, *amaXhosa*, *baSotho* and North Sotho. Thus the skirt panels show stereotypical images of tribal figures and cultural dress, indigenous animals and national symbols. The women's early motifs from 1960 to 1970, such as mineworkers and boys on bicycles, have since been discontinued as the

Left: Sotho male on horseback, panel design for *isishweshwe*, Da Gama Textiles archive, Zwelitsha, Eastern Cape. Photograph © J. Leeb-du Toit.

Right: Malawian tailor, design for *isishweshwe* panel, c.1960s. Da Gama Textiles archive, Zwelitsha, Eastern Cape. Photograph © J. Leeb-du Toit.

aspirational and contextual motifs formerly deemed appropriate have changed. In the main, Hickson, Shaw and other designers engaged in a dialogue of perception and misconception. They seldom saw their motifs in real life, or on the *isishweshwe* they themselves designed, although Lowe brought some of the cloth in from time to time.

Rather than being isolated in their studios, African wax print designers at ABC engaged with their clients. 'Designers did the paperwork, went on trips and did the colourways.'[19] Thus in 1988 Hickson and Shaw were offered their first trip to Africa, but it was cancelled at the last minute. From 1992 they began to interact directly with customers, a role previously monopolised by intermediaries such as Lowe and Breetzke.

◆ ◆ ◆

Besides the work of designers, technical knowledge was crucial in realising blueprint at ABC and at the many other English blueprinters still in operation. One of the key technical staff at ABC was Jeff Wood. He was trained in colour chemistry under the 'day release' system, that is, he trained for one day a week at college and then worked in the factory for four days. He studied at the local

Modern British Blueprint in Context

technical college and did his advanced training at John Doulton College in Manchester. He became a specialist in colour chemistry, worked in Watford for several years and came to ABC in 1967. Wood described discharge-printing as follows:

> The basic concept is you dye the fabric indigo and then print discharge acid on it, to white in some instances and to orange in others. The orange or white depends on the chemical combination of the print paste. One would turn the indigo from a solid blue dyestuff into a soluble product that you then wash away and the other application then converts it into an insoluble golden-yellow product instead of white.[20]

This process, Wood explains, is why the print colours were restricted, for example, to blue and orange, brown and red – it depended on the print paste. ABC also printed on brown fabric called chrysodene brown.

Wood notes that they would initially test the design by placing plain cloth on a table. They used a roller to print a table-sized piece of the cloth as a test sample, without discharge, and then back-printed with white paste to simulate the discharge. He added that they would print the logo on the back, 'but this too was in white paste and not discharge-printed'. Indigo aniline dye had been used at ABC and in the cloth-printing industry in Britain for more than 100 years. The product used at ABC was manufactured in Elsmere Port, Liverpool, which, Wood says, has since closed down.

Peter Barton, one of the last 'traditional' British roller-engravers, decided to join the textile industry when at school.[21] He had two choices – to become a painter-decorator or to do 'armbench work' at Watford. He chose to train at Watford in hand-engraving and photo-engraving and became a highly skilled master, one of the last specialist engravers at ABC. He explained that the designs for blueprint were realised as follows: 'You started the process with a plain copper roll. In the old days you drew the design onto the roll and then engraved with chisels by hand. You would tap the dots out with a fine chisel and that would gather the discharge in. Each engraver would have his set of chisels.'[22]

Barton has an assortment of chisels dating from the eighteenth century and others from modern times. He honed them for use and

Peter Barton, one of the last remaining hand-engravers at ABC, Hyde, in 2005. Photograph © J. Leeb-du Toit.

Top: Small hand rollers for engraving cylinders at ABC, Hyde, in 1995. Peter Barton collection. Photograph © J. Leeb-du Toit.

Middle: Small hand-punches for engraving cylinders at ABC, Hyde, in 1995. Peter Barton collection. Photograph © J. Leeb-du Toit.

Bottom: Test pieces for engraving, ABC, Hyde, in 1995. Peter Barton collection. Photograph © J. Leeb-du Toit.

Top right: Small hand rollers for engraving cylinders at ABC, Hyde, in 1995. Peter Barton collection. Photograph © J. Leeb-du Toit.

had formerly applied needle-sharp pins for dots. The engraver's finesse and dexterity were of utmost importance in mill-engraved and hand-engraved designs.[23] Barton was the last roller-printer at ABC experienced in engraving by hand, a process now no longer used. Within his time the process had advanced to the use of film: 'You paint the chemical-resist ink onto the roll or now use a film and then expose the film you want to resist, wash off the remainder of the ink, and then etch the copper away in acid.' Although there are still skilled etchers such as Peter Barton in the cloth-printing industry, their function today is limited and he is now only called on to do repairs.

Some designs were done with hand-punches on solid copper rollers in the 1820s, but were later etched on plates and then transferred to a mill. The girth size of the mill determined the width of the cloth, initially set at 36 inches,

Modern British Blueprint in Context 129

British blueprint logos, *c*.1950. Margaret Hickson collection. Photographs © J. Leeb-du Toit.

but varying today from 38 to 88 inches (for rotary-screen printing). Designs could also be copied using a pentagraph, which transferred the image from a zinc plate onto the roller. The pentagraph had a sharp diamond tip, which facilitated transfer of the design. Pentagraph copying onto a roller was like for like, but designs could be rescaled. Once the roller bore the engraved design, it was thinly chrome-plated to increase its longevity and protect the design.[24]

While working at Watford, before his move to ABC, Barton did a large amount of blueprint engraving for customers, including Da Gama Textiles. The cloth was printed at other blueprinters and textile works. Watford closed in 1970, having centralised three engraving works concentrated in Levenshulme, which became a significant centre for roller- and flat-bed screen engraving, photographic engraving and orthodox and pentagraphic engraving. At one time Levenshulme was the largest engraver in Europe, on the process side, engraving about 30 rollers a day.[25] According to Barton, printing by copper roller was started by a man called John Potts who had worked in the potteries at New Mills where transfers for cups and plates suggested an application in textiles to him.

The chromed copper roller, once etched, caused the engraving to lose some of its resolution. The roller was always checked for flaws and plugged with copper when necessary, even in the chromed area, after which printing commenced. After running off several thousand metres of cloth, the roller might become obsolete due to the wearing of the chrome and the number of repairs. Barton emphasised, however, that virtually all roller-printing ceased at ABC and in the United Kingdom around 1995.[26] By 2016, Da Gama Textiles itself had turned to rotary-screen printing, as explained in Chapter 9.

Barton described several processes used in copper etching, one of which was roller-screen printing, or the realisation of a fine abrush or 'smoky' gradation by applying various techniques. Today such processes are more easily – but not as effectively – achieved via computerised design and rotary-screen printing. Barton recalled having worked with an etcher at Watford in the 1960s called George (he could not recall his surname). 'He sprayed the fine detail with a little cup on an airbrush. This would be sprayed onto the roller with this very fine detail, and this would then be etched, washed off and resprayed in order to build up a tonal effect to realise the most detailed graduation.'[27] He saw George realise this effect in some very intricate designs of roses that were so detailed that they looked as they did in real life. The same process was used in some blueprint designs.

Barton was well aware of continuities and sources in blueprint design, identifying the peacock feather, sourced in the East, as one of the oldest designs. He noted that it was printed on copper rollers and later reproduced photographically. Many ABC designs were unique to the company, but its staff and other mass-production blueprinters copied designs and drew on the blueprinting tradition in Europe and the East to renew and invigorate their designs.

◆ ◆ ◆

As one textile printer after another closed down in Britain, many of the design holdings and pattern books in their archives were simply discarded. Jennifer Harris, acting director of the Whitworth Art Gallery at the University of Manchester, noted that many archives and sample collections had been 'sent to the tip' in the past, simply placed in skips and thrown into landfills.[28] As a result of this archival limitation, the sale of pattern books on auction in Britain had soared. At a recent auction, she said, size A4 pattern books had sold for £800 each. This price put the collecting of these books out of reach of the average museum or archive, further inhibiting research. She added that one of the most serious criticisms of the textile industry was that so much of its history had disappeared, largely due to the fact that the value of the material was not recognised until the 1980s. The Museum of Science and Industry in Manchester, however, had formulated a collecting policy, though it only covered Manchester materials and pattern books. Harris added that sadly there was no central archive or printworks in Manchester. The Gallery of English Costume at Manchester Art Gallery holds some sample books, however, and has also one of the only examples of a working-class dress in blueprint.

Harris added that she was aware that many printworks and their skilled employees had moved to South Africa in the late 1960s. David Whitehead and Tootal were good examples. I visited the archives at ABC several times in 2005, establishing that many of the earlier blueprint designs emanated from Tootal. The fate of ABC itself is currently under consideration. David Bradley, head of design at the company and within the CHA group as a whole, noted that since ABC was a part of CHA, a global company, its prospects were entirely in the hands of CHA. In 2009 I received a disconcerting e-mail from Craig McCann, who had since become head of design at ABC. He noted that Cha Chi Ming, the owner of CHA, had decided to shut ABC from the end of 2009. It appears that the archive will move to mainland China. I wrote to McCann in 2012 and he replied that most of the ABC plant had indeed shut down, but the archive was still *in situ*. In ongoing research in 2016 I am tracing the East Asian sources of blueprint design used in the West and in Africa.

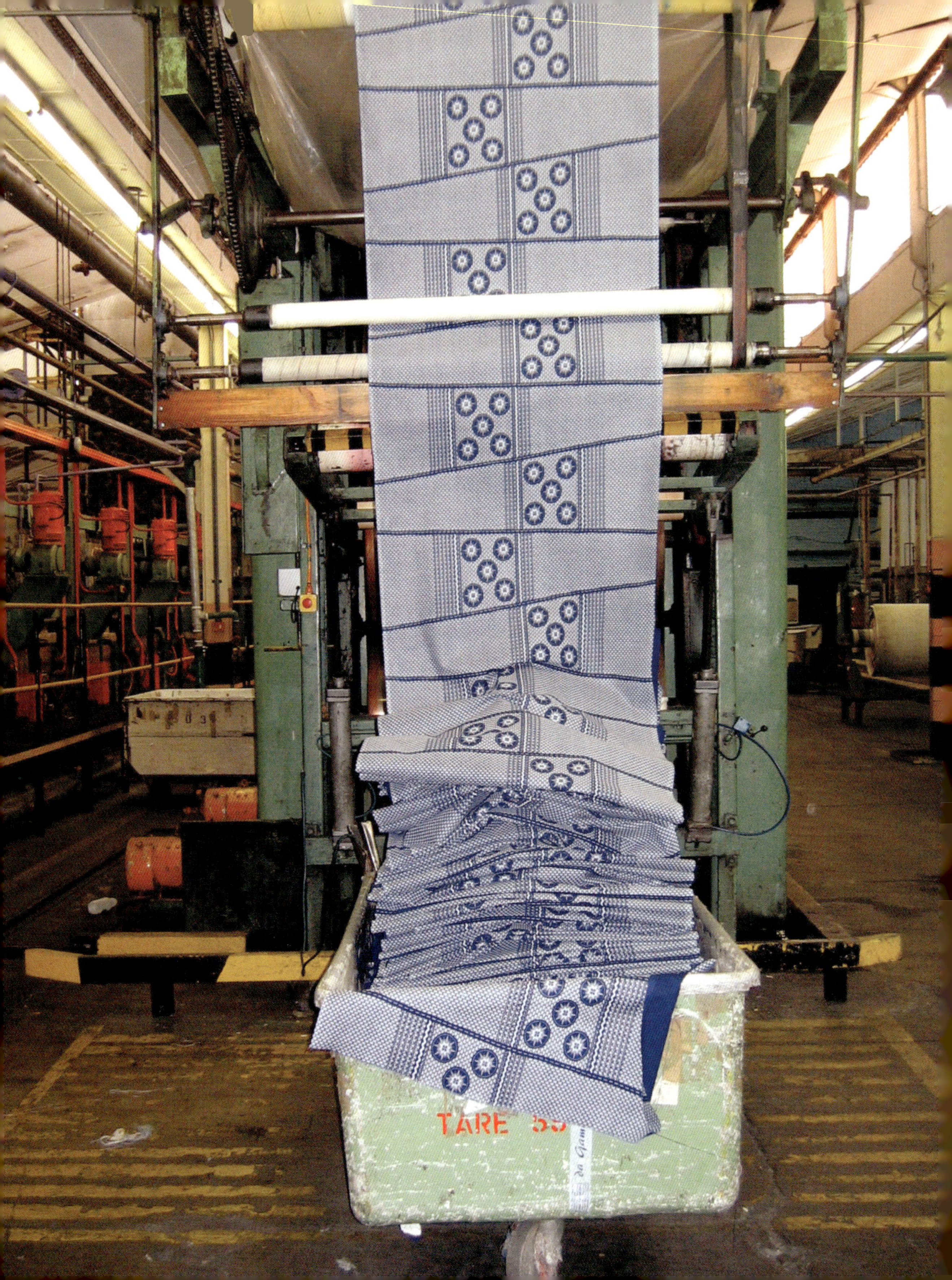
TARE

7
Da Gama Textiles and *isiShweshwe*

The migration of textile-printing expertise from Britain to South Africa from the 1950s onwards can be directly linked to the development of South Africa's textile industry. The emergence of Da Gama Textiles near King William's Town in the Eastern Cape in 1961 created a significant continuity in the production and dissemination of blueprint. Known in the Eastern Cape (by *amaMfengu*, *amaThembu* and *amaXhosa*) as *ujamani*, *isijalmani* or *ujeremani* – names I have already mentioned – blueprint or *isishweshwe*, as it was called locally from the 1950s, was widely sourced in many parts of South Africa and throughout the Eastern Cape.

The location of Good Hope Textiles (later Da Gama Textiles) near King William's Town in 1958 was sheer serendipity. The catalyst was the start of cotton production in the Eastern Cape by Vernon King – the 'cotton king' himself – who dreamed of a viable milling industry in the region. He also recognised the pressing need for employment around King William's Town, which, in turn, reinforced the emergent National Party government's vision of an apartheid homeland in the Eastern Cape.

The British dominions, moreover, were eager at this time to grow their economies by developing secondary industries abroad (CPA 1949: 41). Thus dominion policy welcomed British textile manufacturers who established themselves in colonial territories, bringing employment opportunities and investment with them. The policy had already seen the growth of large British textile factories in localities such as China. At this juncture John Cowie intervenes in my account to provide more invaluable information about *isishweshwe* in South Africa and its links to Britain, Europe and East Asia.

According to Cowie, by the 1940s the Calico Printers Association (CPA) had relocated some of its textile production from Manchester to the Shanghai Printing and Finishing Works (SPFW) in China, which employed an enormous Chinese workforce.[1] When the Communists came to power in China after the Cultural Revolution, they demanded 50 per cent of the SPFW's profits for the previous year. As the company was privately owned and the profits were distributed to shareholders, with a small amount retained in company coffers, this request was unacceptable to the SPFW, which would be unable to buy stock without profits.

The SPFW refused to comply, whereupon the company was ordered to close down in the mid-1940s and thus prepared at once to ship all its assets back to Britain.

In South Africa at this time, the South African Party (SAP) – later the United Party (UP) – a benign government with a patriarchal attitude to black people, was about to topple. The SAP government, however, was still intent on developing industry in South Africa and maintaining a productive black labour force. It was acutely aware of the widespread unemployment throughout the country and of the concomitant need for industrial consolidation and development. Dr D.L. Smit, a UP parliamentarian from the Eastern Cape, who was aware of the SPFW's plight in China, approached the newly elected South African government – the National Party (NP) had come to power in 1948 – and proposed that South Africa should acquire all the SPFW's machinery from China, initiate a major textile industry near King William's Town and employ the SPFW's management to oversee the local enterprise. Smit's proposal was not only in line with British post-war development in the former dominions and Third World countries, but also resonated with the nationalist government's apartheid vision of preventing mass black migration to urban areas and confining local people to the areas of their birth – what was to become the Ciskei homeland in this case.

Having previously set up a worsted spinning and weaving factory in China, the CPA suggested a new partnership with Africa in the form of the Good Hope Textile Corporation (Pty) Ltd (GHT), near King William's Town once the preliminary arrangements had been finalised.[2] Cheap black labour was amply available *in situ*, newly built townships could provide modern housing and there was a large indigenous market in the hinterland. The CPA built a model village known as Zwelitsha near King William's Town and provided good housing, sanitation and electricity for its workforce. GHT was established in 1948, the year in which the nationalist government came to power in South Africa.

The SPFW transferred an entire textile works, including all the printing and weaving equipment, from Shanghai to King William's Town around 1945. No workforce came with the move, but Chinese preferences in design must have influenced some of GHT's later production in South Africa. In Shanghai the SPFW had marketed its textiles both locally and in remoter parts of East Asia. GHT also catered for a range of preferences from Zwelitsha, but initially no indigo cloth or prints were produced.[3] It took South Africa years to realise the benefits of owning its own textile industry. Local cloth traders gladly welcomed the increased business, but were disconcerted by the government's attitude to dues and taxes and often had to appeal to the state to place or increase dues on imported goods for GHT's protection. The problem was often addressed, but never fully resolved.[4]

GHT's first cloth, produced in 1950 – a bleached calico called First Line –

was popular and sold about 500 000 metres annually. The local African clientele used it extensively for headscarves, aprons, funeral wear and shrouds. GHT continued to manufacture calicoes throughout the 1950s. Production included popular variants dyed in a selection of basic colours. There was also a calico from late in the decade called Ox, which was 27 inches wide and showed an ox-head logo. GHT's first printed textiles – they were not blueprint – were marketed as Daydawn in the early 1960s, but were initially 'killed by the Far East trade'.[5]

From 1950 to 1965 GHT imported blueprint into South Africa from Manchester – and from ABC in Hyde in particular, which Tootal still owned – but in 1965 GHT began producing some Toto and Three Cats blueprint under licence from Cyril Lord, a subsidiary of Tootal, who allowed GHT to borrow designs for production in South Africa. GHT had the same machines as ABC, but lacked their expertise and finesse. For a while GHT tried to compete with British imports, to acquire full rights to the Three Cats range and to master the skills associated with its production. GHT also started its own quality Falcon and Trigg lines, but was unable to attain the finish achieved by ABC. When Tootal bought GHT in the early 1960s, however, thereby giving GHT access to all its facilities, GHT finally mastered the full gamut of discharge technology that formed the basis of *isishweshwe* as reflected in the Three Cats range.

Tootal blueprinting folded in Britain in 1961 – although technically it still owned GHT and ABC – and GHT became Da Gama Textiles in 1962. This major coup heralded an independent and uniquely South African industry that could

Da Gama Textiles factory, Zwelitsha, Eastern Cape, 2005. Photograph © Kirsten Nieser.

develop without constraint. Many of Da Gama's designs, however, were still produced at the design studio of ABC. Some even came from Holland – from Vlisco in Helmond, as shown in Chapter 5 – and were produced by Da Gama under licence for the Three Fish range. When Da Gama first created Fancy Prints – multicolours on cotton, including *isishweshwe* – Rodney Bell, a Da Gama executive, took the designs to ABC in Manchester to be realised and brought them back to South Africa. This design input can still be seen on the inverse of *isishweshwe* cloth from the early 1960s which may read: 'Three Cats designed in Britain for Da Gama' or 'Designed by ABC for Da Gama'.

Top left: Copper and chromed cylinders, Da Gama Textiles, Zwelitsha, Eastern Cape, 2005. Photograph © J. Leeb-du Toit.

Right: Chromed cylinder, with Transkei panel motif, Da Gama Textiles, Zwelitsha, Eastern Cape, 2005. Photograph © J. Leeb-du Toit.

Bottom left: Chromed cylinders, Da Gama Textiles, Zwelitsha, Eastern Cape, 2005. Photograph © J. Leeb-du Toit.

As the British textile industry declined and cloth printers closed, Bell arranged for the purchase of all the copper cylinders at ABC in Manchester for Da Gama's Three Cats range. Some of the chromed cylinders were lost at sea in the late 1980s, but were replicated onto new rollers by computer, using the many pattern books in Da Gama's archive. South Africa's own textile company, thanks to its blueprint and other cloth types, was finally able to 'squeeze out Lancashire'.[6]

Sadly since I began this research, all Da Gama's discharge-printing machines that used copper rollers have ceased to exist. Da Gama still has a vast collection of chrome copper cylinders from ABC, but these too are to be scrapped. Some have been retained for museum display, but new spatial and organisational arrangements have had to be made. Furthermore, the value of the copper in each roller is such that the Da Gama executive has decided that most of the rollers will not be kept.

◆ ◆ ◆

From the early 1960s Da Gama Textiles recognised the economic potential of producing cottons for use by the local African community. In particular, Da Gama was well aware of the accruing use of blueprint. Da Gama was able to copy Tootal's blueprint designs from Manchester and produce a local blueprint that came to be known as *isishweshwe*. Mr Naren Kala of Pretoria Wholesale Textiles noted that in his view Da Gama's *isishweshwe* was first marketed as Three Falcons, then as Sweetwaters and after that as Three Leopards. Only dyed and printed cotton – not *isishweshwe* – was produced at GHT in the early 1960s as well as a light-blue aniline cloth.[7]

Da Gama Textiles was well aware of the need to retain and emulate the quality of the blueprint formerly imported from ABC. This precedent was set by the preferences of customers and wholesalers alike. One of the British cloth's distinguishing features was its salty taste and stiffness. This was ascribed by some to its exposure to saline air on long voyages from Britain and to the waves lapping against the wooden crates in which it was stored on board ship.[8] The stiffness of the fabric was also important and was said to reflect its desirable strength. Many older African female customers, if in doubt about the fabric's authenticity, would taste or lick it. They would also test its smell and feel: the smell – a musty chemical odour – being especially important.[9]

Rodney Breetzke claims that the smell and feel of *isishweshwe* derived from its wrapping for export. It came in bales wrapped in waxed paper and covered with hessian. When a bale was opened the smell was intense and would remain attached to the cloth until it was washed out. Trading stores are fondly remembered by many informants for the familiar, if overwhelming, smell of newly arrived cloth.[10]

The distinctive smell and salty taste of *isishweshwe* derive, in fact, from the application of sulphuric acid used after drying to neutralise the lime from the bath and to affix the colour, enabling the cloth to stand up to rubbing.[11] Helen Bester, former head of apparel at Da Gama, later head of marketing, now head of development at Da Gama, maintains that the fabric's touch and smell were also the result of the starch applied at manufacture in England to protect the cloth while it was being transported by sea.[12] She points out that the cloth was still sized and starched before printing, adding that Da Gama 'have to starch now just as part of a tradition. If you had to export to the UK today you would not need to go through this [process].' Da Gama's American patchwork customers also asked Bester why the cloth was starched. She noted that if exports abroad increased, starching for this market might cease altogether. Manchester University has a website on textiles that clarifies this point. The starch is used in the finishing process when lucatrope orange dye has been used: 'The saltiness in the cloth is a soapy flourish derived from a wheat starch (cellulose) but the end product is a closely guarded secret which Baeyer imported from Germany.'

Breetzke heard from customers and traders that *isishweshwe* needed to be so saturated with indigo that the dye would show in the first wash and leave a desirable blue behind it as an authenticating feature. This information came from a missionary source in the Eastern Cape, which provided converts with blueprint in the interests of modesty and conversion. The saturated indigo would rub off onto the proselytes' bodies and leave a blue sheen, which was so desirable among them that they were loath to wash it off. They associated the blueness with conversion and acculturation. Blue is sacred to the Nguni people, however, who associate it with their nation, or with God's realm in the sky. These references may well relate to the wearing of and preference for blue *isishweshwe* among Nguni people to this day. Brown and blue variants are preferred in the Eastern Cape, but blue *isishweshwe* predominates in KwaZulu-Natal.

The undyed cotton cloth used by Da Gama Textiles was initially imported from Britain and later from China. More recently Da Gama produced its own cotton fabric coincident with the rise of cotton production in South Africa since the 1950s. In 2008 it was suggested that Da Gama Textiles might initiate a localised cotton-growing scheme.[13] This ambition was not realised, however, and Da Gama no longer spins or weaves its own cloth and today imports its cotton cloth from the East.[14]

Da Gama's process of realising *isishweshwe* is almost identical to the process formerly used by ABC and other British blueprinters. The machines Da Gama used until recently are the roller-printers from the erstwhile SPFW in China. Apparently some of these were later replaced by parts and substitutes from Eastern Europe. As indicated earlier, roller discharge-printing has given way to rotary-screen discharge-printing. Da Gama also employs other machines, which

Da Gama Textiles and *isiShweshwe*

came from ABC in the late 1980s. The roller-printing capability of these machines matches that of Russian and Czech equivalents, but in view of the massive decline in textile production in those regions, most of Da Gama's future machines might well derive from the East. In late 2015 two Chinese mechanics were helping to install some of the new Chinese-manufactured rotary-screen printers.

In the discharge-printing process, good quality cotton cloth is dyed with aniline indigo. Then the designs are realised by printing with discharge acid, which bleaches the indigo to realise the desired pattern. The designs appear as orange paste on the cloth – the colour of the discharge acid or mordant. The cloth then undergoes additional heating and washing, which eliminates the orange paste and reveals the pattern underneath in white on an indigo ground. To realise a design in a combination of orange and blue – a popular blend in the 1970s and still to be found today on Fancy Prints – the appropriate heating and washing processes are eliminated and the orange hue remains on the cloth as a colour.[15]

Designs at Da Gama may reveal a slight shift in tone and resolution, depending on the pressure of the rollers. This occurred only when the older machines were used and is no longer applicable in rotary-screen discharge printing. During the print run the team takes sample cuttings, knowing that printing is lighter at the back of the machine. After this process the cloth goes to another machine where the logos are printed on the obverse in printing ink – not by resist-based bleaching, since the logo must not bleed through the cloth. The cloth is then dried, folded into bolts and shelved for marketing and bulk orders to wholesalers.

Most of Da Gama's *isishweshwe* designs are discharge-printed on cotton, but there are also polyester versions and ink-printed versions. Initially requested by church groups in Butterworth, the polyester variants are a response to the fake *isishweshwe* that has swamped the market since the early 1990s. Most fakes emanate from Pakistan and China, but cheaper variants are also being produced locally in Durban and Johannesburg. More recently,

Top right: William Tini Msondeze at the original discharge-printing roller machines (scrapped in 2015), Da Gama Textiles, Zwelitsha, Eastern Cape, 2005. Photograph © Kirsten Nieser.

Bottom right: Discharge-printing roller machine, Da Gama Textiles, Zwelitsha, Eastern Cape, 2005. Photograph © Kirsten Nieser.

Fake *isishweshwe* design. Photograph © J. Leeb-du Toit.

around 2005, competitors from the Netherlands even entered the market for a while. Da Gama itself experiments with fakes from time to time by producing polycotton, viscose and other fabric as *isishweshwe*. In 2015 I noted that a range known as Kwanobantu had been produced since 2010 in China exclusively for Cowie Trading, the cheaper range intended to challenge fake *isishweshwe* imports, as well as to offer a cloth that was cheaper than the original Da Gama *isishweshwe*. It is still being produced, now for Cowie-owned Da Gama, but the designs, although in the *isishweshwe* idiom, are smaller, often more cluttered or 'busy', but nonetheless very appealing. Kwanobantu is mostly manufactured as a polyester variant and at times as a cotton mix. The designs differ from those of Da Gama's Three Cats range, but there is sufficient similarity in detail and concept to make the cheaper cloth an acceptable alternative. Often a design realised by the Da Gama studio will be regarded as too remote from the motifs sourced in the Three Cats range and will be included in the Kwanobantu range.[16]

Helen Bester has provided me with invaluable information about the standard of design and Da Gama's resolution of problems such as definition and cloth quality.[17] When Three Cats was first obtained from ABC, the Three Cats pattern book became what Bester calls the 'Da Gama Bible', constituting a vital part of the company's design archive. Many of the rollers lost at sea bore designs Da Gama wished to copy. Da Gama was thus initially unable to realise ABC's meticulous standards and had to emulate the simpler designs at first. Da Gama realised then that it needed advanced technical skills. This changed later when the company acquired a waxjet machine, which facilitated intricate designs and textures in stipples and blurs. The waxjet allows for 'smokies', which include halation or shading that can only be produced on a copper roller and not on a rotary screen, although halation realisation was being improved in rotary printing by 2016. On the copper roller the ink or discharge paste is picked up and transferred onto the cloth. The smaller the design, the more essential copper rollers were originally for precision and detail.

Da Gama Textiles has attracted highly skilled individuals who are committed to the perfection of design. This has enabled the company to sustain the market for *isishweshwe* throughout southern Africa. One such individual is Adrie Landsman, an artist in his own right, who joined Da Gama in 1994. A specialist

Da Gama Textiles and *isiShweshwe*

Left: Lizo Somhlahlo, designer at Da Gama Textiles, 2011. Photograph © J. Leeb-du Toit.

Right: British blueprinter's pattern book, mid-twentieth century. Da Gama Textiles archive, Zwelitsha, Eastern Cape. Photograph © J. Leeb-du Toit.

in etching, he previously employed copper roll engraving and wax sheet printing. The latter is quicker, allowing for finer tonal work and 'smoky' designs, such as Mandela's portrait in the Madiba range produced by Da Gama in the 1990s. Special permission was obtained for this reproduction, but it was not a particularly successful transcription of a photographic image. In 2015 new technical staff worked on the rotary screens in close co-operation with newer designers such as Lizo Somhlahlo.

When most of the blueprint in South Africa was still produced at ABC, it was issued under closely guarded patented logos. Marked with specific motifs to alert buyers to the manufacturer, these logos became distinctive markers at ABC. Many of them were retained by Da Gama Textiles. Early ABC logos were sourced in the CPA's Star motif, for example, Six Star Toto. The Three Cats range, however, persisted for blueprint at ABC until the 1990s when Da Gama bought the last copper rollers on which the designs were inscribed with the copyright vested in them. I have located a range of early logos, many of which derive from defunct printers such as Richard Brotherton and Spruce. Some were specific in targeting their market, as noted in finds at local retailers and trading stores, at the ABC archive and in examples shown to me by Margaret Hickson. The logos included African women, a Zulu warrior and images of local fauna. There is no information on how these early logos were selected, but they clearly targeted an African clientele in their referencing of local contexts.

Da Gama Textiles' *isishweshwe* has for decades utilised logos printed in white paste on the obverse of the cloth. These logos have also been replicated in different colour combinations on adhesive paper affixed to the rolls of fabric. The logos printed on *isishweshwe* have acquired a distinctive status and are often shown on the obverse side of home-sewn garments as a sign of authenticity.

Selections from the 'Da Gama Bible', which originated from ABC. Da Gama Textiles archive, Zwelitsha, Eastern Cape, 2015. Photographs © J. Leeb-du Toit.

Over the years Da Gama has developed specific design ranges realised and marketed under different logos. The ranges are designed and released to particular clients and markets, so that a measure of exclusivity and status attach to the logos. Some ranges are only released to 'closed panels', that is, the cloth is made available only to selected traders. Other ranges are released to wider markets or sold in wholesale stores such as Jacksons, the former Da Gama outlets, now owned by Neil Cowie, John Cowie's son. Most of the Da Gama buyers today are large wholesalers or major trading companies such as those belonging to Neil Cowie. Bulk buyers of Da Gama ranges pay cheaper prices. They have a closing date to submit orders and a delivery date to collect them. This arrangement is necessary, as Da Gama cannot keep all its designs in stock, since it produces for a selling period only. A lot of clients fail to grasp this and request a piece of one or other design not in store. Ideally Da Gama would like to stock the full design range, but production and storage are too expensive to enable this.

Many traders still buy from Da Gama and from wholesalers such as Jacksons under the impetus of customer demand. Rising local prices, however, have prompted some traders to buy cheaper ranges made locally or in India or Pakistan. This cheaper stock is not discharge-printed, but is mostly paste on polyester. However, even the poorest customers prefer original Da Gama print. More recently Chinese textile printers have copied Da Gama designs, some almost exactly, and are producing discharge-printed variants that threaten Da Gama's production. Wholesalers compete among themselves and add small mark-ups. One of Da Gama's largest customers only adds 12 per cent to his stock, claiming that his ancestors have blessed the growth of his trade and that he cannot exceed a nominal profit.[18]

Three Cats was a design range initiated, produced and developed at ABC under Tootal and Cyril Lord. It was largely designed by Margaret Hickson in the 1980s. The sources for the patterns, however, reside in design emulation from the East and include adaptations by the West over at least three centuries. Panel members of Three Cats, which is a closed range, are obliged to purchase a minimum of 1 000 metres of the cloth. Access is by invitation only and the criteria for entry are strict. Purchasers must be identified as honest, reliable customers approved by the area manager, who must verify their calibre and marketing practice. If one wished to join the panel, one would apply to Da Gama, but would usually gain admission only if there were a vacancy. This system was inherited from Britain, but Da Gama has maintained its exclusivity. Wholesalers such as the Cowies, who trade extensively in the Eastern Cape, Lesotho and Botswana and buy tremendous volumes of *isishweshwe* from Da Gama, and other dealers such as the major wholesaler Dadabhay's of Johannesburg, are among those who benefit from the exclusive arrangement. Significantly, when Da

Left: Chippy Bruce and John Cowie at the former Cowie Trading warehouse, near Fort Jackson and Zwelitsha, Eastern Cape, 2005. Photograph © Kirsten Nieser.

Right: Steven Freeman, former printing manager, with Helen Bester, then marketing executive, Home Sewing Division, now design manager at Da Gama Textiles, checking the quality of the Madiba range, 2005. Photograph © J. Leeb-du Toit.

Gama was experiencing some logistical difficulties in 2014, Neil Cowie agreed to purchase Da Gama from its then German owners. His passion for the cloth and his 'hands-on' approach to his company augur well for the future of cloth and company. A textile archive and museum might be realised in the near future at the Da Gama premises.

The Three Cats range is an example of how a closed range of designs is distributed. A new range of older design combinations, or (rarely) entirely new Three Cats designs, appear twice a year and comprise some 30 examples. Based mainly on the Three Cats book of designs – the 'Da Gama Bible', originating from ABC – this range seldom has new designs. Rather, designers innovate based on extant designs. Designers currently develop two ranges per annum, each comprising 25–30 designs. Helen Bester and her team choose the most successful designs in terms of sales and add others from the core book of designs. Copies of the original Three Cats book of designs are held only by Da Gama and Neil Cowie of Cowie Trading. From 2005 to 2008 new designs were executed mainly by Mandy Rudolph with recent input (from 2011) by Lizo Somhlahlo. If asked to realise a design panel with wave-like motifs, for example, the designer innovates and renews the design by combining it with other Three Cats motifs. Specific designs are developed for specific traders; for example, Neil Cowie requires many variants of Sotho horseman designs for his substantial market in Lesotho.

An open range at Da Gama is Three Leopards, essentially the equivalent of what the company has been producing since the 1960s. This was the first line manufactured by Da Gama before the company acquired the rights to Three Cats. It came out in blue, brown and red. The Three Leopards logo, in effect, indigenised the Three Cats logo. The leopards as substitutes for the cats firmly locate the cloth's provenance in South Africa. As Three Leopards is an open range, it is generally sold on the open market to any-volume customers.[19] It is a much smaller and less popular range than Three Cats, however, which over the years has acquired considerable status as a desirable quality product with exciting designs.

Some designs are only made in the Three Leopards range and many skirt panels appear under this logo. Currently the Three Leopards range is the same quality as other Da Gama ranges, but popular perception holds otherwise. Three Leopards has a new range twice a year with 25–30 new designs, Da Gama retaining the top six sellers. It then introduces new designs to make up numbers for the following range.[20]

Toto is an even smaller open range distinguished by a logo of a small African boy with a protruding belly in profile. The image appears in several logos adapted over the years. The logo originated in Britain in the 1950s, at Spruce and ABC, and was designed in keeping with blueprint's association with the African market. At one point Toto designs were also produced as Six Star and as Five Star.[21] By 2013 the production of Toto became limited. The advantage of this classification is that potential buyers can order a minimum of 500 metres of the range. Many Toto designs are similar to the branded designs, but there are variants as well.

Another open range is Three Fish, initiated in Holland and Britain. There are often overlaps in design between Toto and Three Fish emblems. Three Fish

Toto logo, Da Gama Textiles. Photographs © J. Leeb-du Toit.

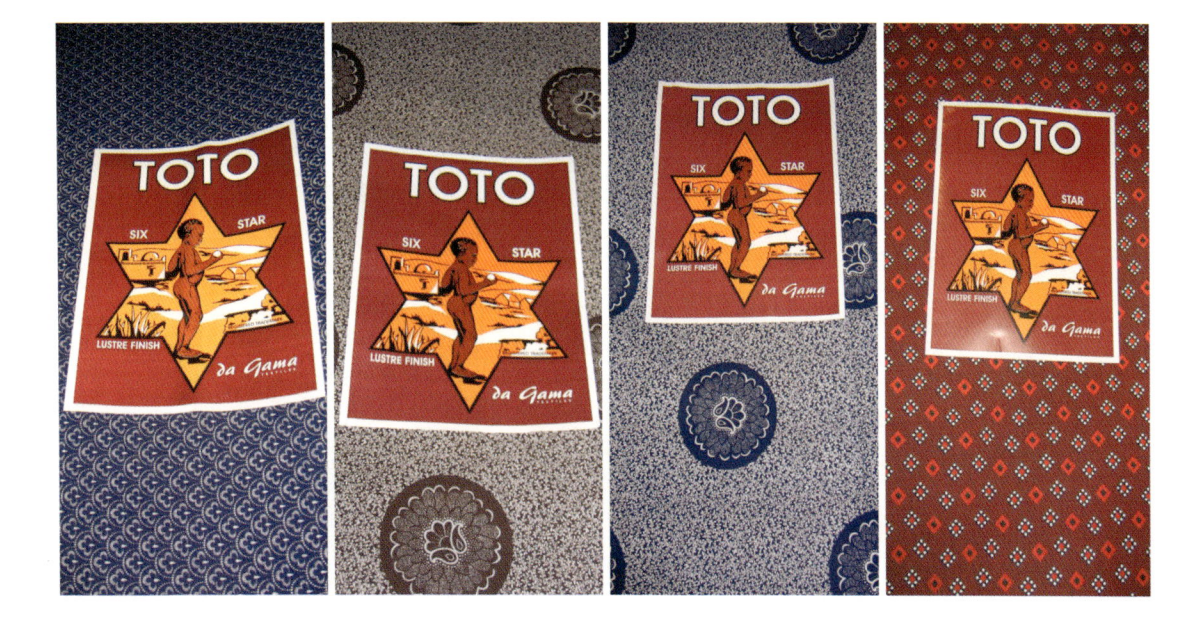

designs do not belong to Da Gama, as indicated earlier, but originated from Vlisco in Holland, which once produced large quantities of *blauwdruk* for South Africa, as shown in Chapter 5. This is a significant link in that Vlisco's designs derived from earlier Dutch preferences for indigo cloth and from cloth produced for their vast international and African markets. I visited Vlisco in 1995 and have since received images of some of its early *blauwdruk* destined for local Dutch and African markets.

In Da Gama's Fancy Prints open range the colours are not achieved by discharge-printing, but by using combined processes involving affixed pastes. This range increased in popularity in 2011 when Bester and the design team developed a range of saturated colours in the designs. These included purples and greens, turquoise, midnight blue, ochre and a vibrant cerise. In this range a significant degree of experimentation is allowed and the market is tested on an ongoing basis to sound out the popularity of the experiments. In items from 2013 there were combinations of cerise and orange, of blue, brown, green and turquoise and of red and orange.

Soon after South Africa's first democratic elections in 1994, President Nelson Rolihlahla Mandela endeared himself to the nation with his wisdom, reconcilitiation, integrity and acclaimed governance. He was fondly referred to as 'Tata Madiba', a name reflecting the esteem of his people and political adherents. Mandela is a Thembu from Qunu in the former Transkei and Da Gama was approached by the Mandela Trust to develop an *isishweshwe* fabric to include his portrait. In 1999 it was agreed to produce a Madiba range that displayed the motif of Mandela's head as a central feature on *isishweshwe*. Da Gama acquired the copyright for this exclusive range from the Mandela Trust. The proceeds of the copyright go to the Nelson Mandela Children's Fund. The cloth first appeared in 2003, but once Da Gama closes this range there will be no repeat of the designs. In fact, the cloth became a collector's item with Madiba's death on 5 December 2013.

Fancy Prints logo, Da Gama Textiles. Photograph © J. Leeb-du Toit.

The Mandela motif is set against various decorative grounds. The design was not very popular in 2005 and a variant with a border of Mandela heads was preferred.

In Port Elizabeth the local civic authority, known as the Nelson Mandela Metropolitan Municipality, used Madiba-range cloth for uniforms. In 2005 the former Eastern Cape premier, Mrs Balintulo, was seen in a Mandela-print dress at the opening of Parliament. She appeared on several other occasions wearing *isishweshwe* variants combined with Thembu or Xhosa dress items. By late 2006 the Madiba range was doing so well that Bester looked into

Da Gama *isishweshwe* cloth with portrait of Nelson Rolihlahla Mandela, former president of South Africa. Photograph © J. Leeb-du Toit.

the possibility of developing similar ranges featuring the Lesotho monarch Letsie III and the Zulu king Goodwill Zwelithini. The Letsie III motif appeared in 2009, but was never popular.

In 2012 it was decided that cloth with the head of Albertina Sisulu – MaSisulu, struggle veteran and late wife of former African National Congress (ANC) president Walter Sisulu – would be produced to celebrate her part as an activist and exemplary role model for South African women. She hailed from the Eastern Cape and the incentive to include her in a new design came from local politicians and residents. The design was executed by Da Gama's designer Lizo Somhlahlo, who comes from Zwelitsha. This was the first time that an iconic woman appeared on *isishweshwe*. Unlike the Madiba range, the MaSisulu head was realised partly in the more conventional handpainted dots that amplified the photographic image, resulting in a much better resolution in detail.

From time to time Da Gama brokers would meet to discuss anticipated discontinuities in design. In 2005 former Da Gama executive Rodney Breetzke mentioned that while 'allover designs' were flourishing, dress panels had decreased in popularity. John Cowie identified the same trend. Wholesalers and traders were aware that the panels were still seasonally popular, mostly before Easter and Christmas, when sales soared and demand increased for motifs of animals, organically sourced patterns and cultural emblems. This seasonal popularity was prompted by the coincidence of cultural festivals with religious holidays or other forms of celebration.

When popular ranges such as Three Cats 'move slowly' due to market oversupply, decisions are taken to complement the traditional brown (chocolate), indigo and red by adding ochre or multicoloured designs for innovation and to awaken new interest.[22] The significance of this is that manufacturers and traders are vital components of production at Da Gama Textiles. As a result, the views and suggestions of bulk customers on design preferences, colour changes and sales

Top left: King Letsie III of Lesotho on cloth produced by Da Gama Textiles. Photograph © J. Leeb-du Toit.

Middle: MaSisulu design on skirt panels produced by Da Gama Textiles. Photograph © J. Leeb-du Toit.

Bottom: Lizo Somhlahlo from Da Gama Textiles with MaSisulu design. Photograph © J. Leeb-du Toit.

become vital to sustaining production. In addition, Da Gama is well aware of the invaluable input of staff members in the orders section. They often advise and add their perceptions to current trends at Zwelitsha and more recently to fashion design. Individuals at Da Gama contribute to vetting designs and a significant input also derives from staff members on the factory floor. Many of the workers at Da Gama come from several generations of employees who have worked at the factory since it started as GHT in 1948. They have a vested interest in the production of *isishweshwe*, as many women from Zwelitsha have become highly regarded seamstresses in their own right. This valuable insider perspective and input occurs in several ways, from reviewing designs to encouraging the traditions of wearing *isishweshwe*.

Changes in design, like suggestions for new patterns or colours, derive from a range of sources. Trusted and knowledgeable wholesalers and traders are at times asked to evaluate in the printing trials to ensure that quality, finish and design are acceptable. John Cowie's perception of *isishweshwe* designs and their popularity indicates the extent to which traders are aware of local preferences. Both John and his son Neil developed many of the designs themselves. One of Cowie's main salespeople, Chippy Bruce, who travelled the length and breadth of South Africa, centring on Botswana, was quick to point out that specific designs were not selling. In 2005, certain designs, such as the 'rice' motif (*libete*) – *isitebe* (shield) in *isiZulu* – and small designs on a dark ground, such as Design 463, were especially popular in Botswana. During the same period no designs containing a lot of white were popular in either Botswana or South Africa. In 2008, as occurred in the 1970s, blue and brown *isishweshwe* included orange and proved highly popular after 2012. By late 2015 it was noted that this popularity had waned. The shift in these preferences is seldom explained, but may be based merely on the need for new motifs or combinations.

Cowie Trading owns some of the original Spruce pattern books from Manchester. John Cowie was known to select designs from these books for Da Gama Textiles to produce for his clientele. Some of the designs perhaps appeared too often, until Cowie's clients told him that they were *gatetsi* or *gatvol* – sick and tired – of the patterns. Their input quickly led Cowie's salespeople to request new designs from Da Gama.[23]

Big, bold designs come and go. In 2005 they were not particularly popular. Cowie ascribed this to the fact that likes and dislikes were informed by current fashion. Design 2478, a bland geometric, sold very well, as did Design 2465, an original used for decades. The 'Hitler Print', an inverse swastika originating in ancient Hindu mythography, was also widely popular.

Preferences in *isishweshwe* design are often associated with the preferences of people from political, royal or cultural spheres. If the queen of Lesotho, for example, wears a new design at the National Day celebrations on 11 March, as discussed in Chapter 9, there is bound to be a mass demand for the design. Recently the red rice (*libete*) or shield design (*isitebe*) and in 2005 the saw design (*isage*), in white and blue, were the queen's established preferences.

Anecdotal information from John Cowie provides a fascinating account of trade interventions. Cowie notes that when customers identified particular designs as essential, traders became intent on getting manufacturers to reproduce those designs, even when their distinctiveness was problematic. He recalled one such instance:

> In the 1960s, on the road between Pitseng and Leribe, there was a small black trader who occasionally bought pieces, five or so. One day his wife showed me a minute sample of cloth with the 'Hitler' design and asked whether I had a print like this. She had asked every intermediary for this pattern, to no avail, and she claimed that it would be a good seller.[24]

As Cowie himself had none of this design in stock, he sent the cloth fragment to Manchester and asked for it to be engraved. Within a week of marketing the new stock, all Cowie's supplies were sold – to his surprise and Manchester's. 'Hitler' designs are all produced under the Toto logo. The *isishweshwe* 'Hitler' motif resembles the Hindu swastika – the sun-chariot's wheel – and not the infamous Nazi symbol. But there was also a potentially positive association with National Socialism, as during the Second World War many black South Africans were

Top and right: 'Hitler' designs for Toto, in various colourways.
Bottom: Designs for the Swazi market. Photographs © J. Leeb-du Toit.

persuaded that should Hitler come to dominate Europe, blacks would be better off. Further, the motif could also be emblematic of victory over the Nazi enemy, in keeping with Hildi Hendrickson's (1996) contentions about the embrace of colonial dress by the *ovaHerero*, noted in Chapter 10.

Images associated with soccer balls and soccer players appeared as early as the 1960s, many developed at ABC by Margaret Hickson. In 2004 the interest in soccer motifs re-emerged, no doubt in anticipation of the forthcoming 2010 World Cup in South Africa. In most new ranges from 2010 to 2013, variants of soccer balls have appeared, often modified to abstraction. Mandy Rudolph, with Lizo Somhlahlo, innovated the design by splicing it into four and creating a motif with segments, the ball now resembling a flower or wheel.

Helen Bester has been instrumental in foregrounding and marketing *isishweshwe* nationally and internationally since the 1990s. Bester's mother, Margie Anderson, worked at Da Gama Textiles from the 1980s. Mike Donegan and other executives from the company asked Bester to take over the apparel section in 1999, as Breetzke had only a year until retirement. Da Gama felt that apparel needed to be foregrounded. Bester noted an increased demand for *isishweshwe* as wearers and African designers returned to its use in contemporary designs. 'Their forefathers had used it,' Bester said. 'They knew its

Soccer motifs on Three Leopards panels. Photograph © J. Leeb-du Toit.

strength and wanted to employ the designs and the cloth their forefathers had used before them.'[25] I also became aware of the enormous increase in the wearing of the cloth from the mid-1980s, coincident with a recovery of tradition and perceived Africanness typical of nations in transition in the years prior to independence. With the emergence of a new democratic dispensation in South Africa, *isishweshwe* has assumed national association and identification. However, as shown earlier, aspects of gender discrimination and oppression, as well as rurality, still attach to the cloth for some South Africans.

Bester organised a local fashion show using *isishweshwe* in the 1980s and introduced new colours, acknowledging that preferences for colours were regionally specific. It is only since 1994, however, that real foregrounding of contemporary South African clothing designs in *isishweshwe* has emerged. Bester notes that in 2005 Da Gama was asked to support designers at South African Fashion Week (SAFW) in Johannesburg. As a result of this show, Da Gama's meterage sales doubled in less than a year. Da Gama was unprepared for this sudden increase in demand for *isishweshwe* and competitors developed similar alternative products that came onto the market as substitutes. Hence the emergence of, among others, Five Star and Windmolen as initial competitors. Many of these substitutes have remained on the market as cheaper but less desirable alternatives to Da Gama's authentic and more costly *isishweshwe*. The authenticity of Da Gama's *isishweshwe* lay in the fact that it was one of the only blueprints in the world discharge-printed initially by a copper roller operation. By 2015 Da Gama had opted to discharge-print using rotary machines. The quality of the discharge process was retained, if not improved.

Bester has contributed extensively to South Africa's contemporary clothing design in *isishweshwe* by organising Da Gama's sponsorship of emergent and established designers at SAFW and at the Cape Town Fashion Week, supporting, among others, Bongiwe Walaza and Amanda Laird-Cherry. Da Gama's association with Laird-Cherry and Walaza, for example, has been important in that both the designers and Da Gama have benefited by promoting designs, by foregrounding *isishweshwe* and by disseminating and marketing their products. As a result the two designers' names have become associated with *isishweshwe* since 2003, when Laird-Cherry and Bester met for the first time. The designers produce quite different ranges that change annually, but each returns to *isishweshwe* from time to time, particularly when clients request it.[26] More recently the two designers have proposed a children's range and a men's range. Dion Chang, well-known South African designer and columnist, was also for a time keen to make *isishweshwe* caps and wraparounds. Others have suggested jewellery, shoes, purses and bags, which have been realised on a small scale in many home industries.

The traditionalist market is the main market for *isishweshwe*, but there are others that cater for the demand in developing contemporary fashion. One cannot corrupt *isishweshwe* production, however, as Bester points out: 'Traditionalists walk into a shop and say, "We want *isishweshwe* in Three Cats" and if Da Gama suddenly produces a 150-width cloth or produces cloth in a different colour, it will lose its clientele.'[27] However, Bester later revised this view and by 2015 a wider-width *isishweshwe* range was produced, intended for duvet covers, tablecloths and the like. By 2012 the new Da Gama ranges in Fancy Prints were testing the market with vibrant colours and combinations of older designs and colourways. Continuities are very important to the buyer and Da Gama ensures, via its bulk buyers, that it is attuned to its client base. Mike Donegan and Paul van Schouten, both former Da Gama executives, regarded anything that is profitable as the most important aspect of textile production. On the other hand, as Bester and her design team have a better understanding of the history of the whole process, their input becomes vital in sustaining designs and quality. They prevent *isishweshwe* from flooding the market, as they believe this would reduce its desirability and value.

Phil Staunton, a former CEO at Da Gama, was convinced that they had not exhausted *isishweshwe* production and ranges.[28] He recognised the need for change and new ideas, however, and trials took place to attain a 'new look' from time to time. An example is what Staunton calls the Rainbow range, which introduced more colour in 2006. Developments in finish are also being mooted. By 2016 a vast range of new colourways and motifs had emerged from Da Gama.

◈ ◈ ◈

Da Gama drew on ABC's copper rollers for their designs for decades, as did Tootal before them, and it is not surprising that these designs replicated and innovated a tradition that emerged from Britain and indirectly from European and East Asian sources. This emergence in turn derived from centuries of design copying and development in the East and elsewhere, as shown in Chapter 1. Copyright issues in blueprint were major factors in Britain and Europe for centuries. Printers were keen to protect the exclusivity of their designs. Copyright over blueprint designs thus remains a constant concern for Da Gama Textiles and other manufacturers. In South Africa Da Gama bought the copyright for designs from ABC when the latter's cylinders were imported to South Africa in the 1980s. Given the increased demand for *isishweshwe*, fake cloth and replicated motifs abound in South Africa, where they are copied the moment the real cloth appears.

Lawyers acting for Da Gama Textiles indicate that it is all but impossible to prove the origin of *isishweshwe* designs. More recently, however, Da Gama has developed unique designs and has issued stern warnings about copyright infringement. In 2012, on the other hand, it was noted in King William's Town that a Da Gama design printed less than two months before had already been replicated exactly and was being marketed as ready-made garments at a Chinese-owned apparel outlet in town. Often a textile design will be copied with slight adjustments in scale or detail. This suffices for the copyist to avoid infringement and in such instances nothing can be done. Chinese-owned stores throughout South Africa reflect the extent to which *isishweshwe* and contemporary South African fashion are copied. Until recently Dutch brand Windmolen produced a unique dual-side printed range, but many Pakistani, Indian, Chinese and other Asian replicas have entered the market since 2000.

In the African cloth trade, competitors such as Pakistan, India and China copy fabric and usurp the market, not least in variants of *isishweshwe*. Several problems have arisen for Da Gama in this kind of direct infringement. Fake blueprint is also an issue. Some of Da Gama's current employees previously worked on fake *isishweshwe* design in Durban. All the company's workers are now subject to contracts protecting copyright and the skills they acquire *in situ*. Restraint of trade agreements prevent knowledge migrating to other companies, but even so this is problematic to control and monitor.[29] Such is the demand for authentic *isishweshwe*, however, that there is little chance of fake variants being marketed in most areas. As noted earlier, Neil Cowie has a cheaper polycotton variant produced in China for sale to the lower end of the market. The designs are often very detailed and smaller than Three Cats variants and, although they are somewhat different, in effect they resemble Da Gama *isishweshwe* design conventions.

The notion of authentic *isishweshwe* is complex. It is located in the origins of the product, in the logos used for decades – Toto, Three Cats, Three Leopards – in the starch and its salty taste on the cloth. Local wearers are very conscious that *isishweshwe* is a porous cotton that washes well, becomes soft and flowing and wears and hangs well.

Over the last century *isishweshwe* has been associated with South African production and its authenticity has assigned it an added status, which is vested in the logo and now also in the cloth's local manufacture. Thus, despite the increased cost of Da Gama's *isishweshwe*, it remains desirable and even de rigeur in many areas. In my ongoing fieldwork I have established that in places such as Lesotho and Botswana fake *isishweshwe* is seldom to be found and is mostly disliked. Traders in Maseru and Maun confirm that they have difficulty selling fake variants, even though they are less costly. In the Eastern Cape, KwaZulu-Natal and the Free State, on the other hand, fake *isishweshwe* has occurred since the late 1980s and its usage has increased since 2012. Its spread is ascribable to the economic downturn in these regions particularly and in South Africa as a whole. The ascendance of fake *isishweshwe* is also attributable to extensive local and Indian, Pakistani and Chinese production and marketing. This inferior and cheaper cloth meets the needs of the rural poor who simply cannot afford the more costly Da Gama *isishweshwe*. Informants in the Eastern Cape, KwaZulu-Natal and Gauteng confirm that they will only use fake *isishweshwe* when economically obliged to do so. On special occasions they revert to the authentic Da Gama product.

Da Gama blueprint is mass-produced, but its authenticating taste, smell, touch and illusionary sheen remain highly desirable. Kirsten Nieser (2005) observes that the sheen on German *Blaudruck* (through calendering) imparts greater value and beauty to the fabric. Sheen is also an integral part of the authentication of some of the South African product, she continues, as in Da Gama's Three Leopards lustre finish, where dots amplify a shimmering appearance.

The sales representative is important in the selection process of *isishweshwe*. He or she has to be intimately aware of trade preferences, which in turn reflect the preferences of the indigenous market. In addition, sales representatives have to recognise the need for innovation when necessary. Da Gama sales representatives

Da Gama Textiles and *isiShweshwe*

also plied the ABC designers with postcards, photographs and books from South Africa. This resulted in innovative motifs and images, but often instilled a flawed perspective of South Africa, its peoples and their aspirations.

◆ ◆ ◆

John Cowie recalled Fleur Rourke's design input at Da Gama Textiles when the company first began to produce *isishweshwe*.[30] Rourke hails from a family of missionaries who worked in Lesotho and later owned trading stores in Pitseng and Leribe. She not only helped her parents to market *isishweshwe* in their stores, but together with her husband managed several outlets for other owners after her marriage. She had an uncanny awareness of local preferences and was at times invited by Cowie and Da Gama Textiles to help develop new designs. To source ideas she drew on the murals of Sotho houses she had seen for decades, reducing her representations to potential repeat patterns. Da Gama reproduced

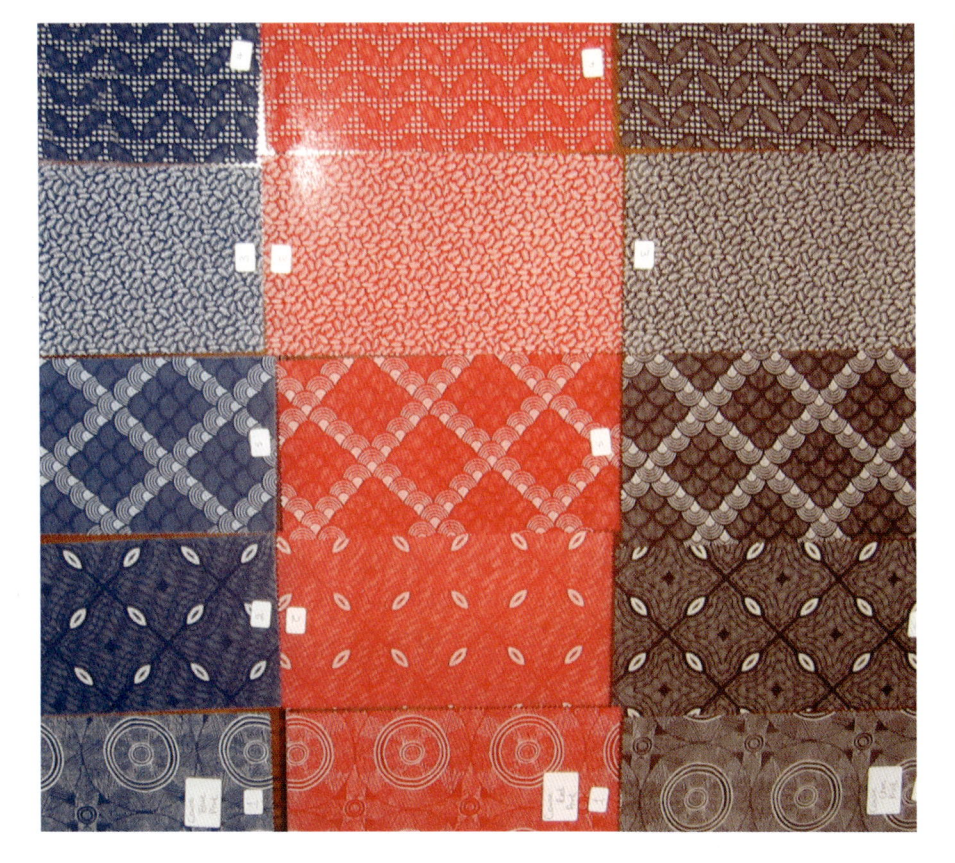

Designs by Fleur Rourke, c.1980s for Da Gama Textiles and John Cowie. Photograph © J. Leeb-du Toit.

many of her designs and retained some until 2005. The sourcing of the designs in indigenous murals reinforced their popularity among the *baSotho*. Rourke also designed blankets for Frasers and these motifs were also reproduced for decades. She traded extensively in Lesotho and her input is discussed further in Chapter 8.

By the late 1970s Da Gama employed a body of designers – mostly women – in its studios. There was an ebb and flow of designers over the years and I was initially unable to trace those who worked on *isishweshwe* at Da Gama and elsewhere in South Africa. They had married and moved on, or simply disappeared. I had a serendipitous encounter near my home in KwaZulu-Natal with Alison Auld, however, a retired designer from Da Gama, whose input proved invaluable.

As a schoolgirl of seventeen, Auld was deeply interested in art and design. Having completed her schooling in 1969 – she attended King's College Convent in King William's Town – she heard that Da Gama Textiles was accepting interns for the school holidays.[31] She visited the printworks, scanned their pattern books and decided to accept a position in the trainee designer programme. Da Gama had also attracted a number of graduates from the East London Technical College, several of whom had studied art. Auld's colleagues at the Da Gama studio were fellow designers Lynn and Mary Elender, Hillary Nolan, John McGregor and a student from Holland. The head of the internship programme was Jean Wyllie, the production manager, who was assisted by Allan Linneker, who was in charge of the studio. Linneker was from Britain and had qualifications in art. Auld's internship and exposure to Da Gama's rich archive of pattern books made her determined to become a textile designer. Da Gama was pleased with her proficiency and accepted her as a permanent employee. Her job was to develop existing designs and to create colourways for them. Like the ABC designers she used Winsor & Newton designers' gouache for her colour matching on 8-gram card.

Auld worked for Da Gama for three years from 1969 to 1971 and subsequently gained considerable experience with other textile manufacturers in South Africa. She rejoined Da Gama in 1984, as head designer, which coincided with the efflorescence of *isishweshwe* on the company's rollers. Her co-designers at the time were Sheila Rasmussen, Jenny Heath and Sherry Land.

Auld began designing *isishweshwe* for the first time when she rejoined Da Gama in 1984. She also produced motifs for Da Gama's popular Cottage range. While working on *isishweshwe*, Auld realised the intricacy of the mark-making on the cloth. Her appreciation of *isishweshwe* grew accordingly. Every year she and the other studio designers would work towards a new range. She recalls that Da Gama seldom asked for specific design types, but sought variety above all else. She enjoyed considerable freedom in creating her designs and was under no pressure to produce specific motifs. As a designer, however, like Hickson at ABC, she received no real recognition: 'We were just machines.'[32]

Da Gama Textiles and *isiShweshwe*

Da Gama's producers selected designs and employees such as Breetzke and Bell vetted new ranges. The new ranges were commonly required at a specific time of year – usually before Christmas or Easter – but preparation continued throughout the year, involving a range of designs over a long period of selection.

Julia Nosipho Funda in the Da Gama Textiles factory, 2012. Photograph © J. Leeb-du Toit.

One needed a 'particular eye' to realise *isishweshwe* designs, Auld recalls, and the process called for patience and meticulous care. At the time, the designs were made in black on white card, which obliged the designers to do the more intricate work by hand: 'We could not do designs in white on black as the paint would bleed and the entire process was more complex.'[33] If designers were required to do a colourway, for example, they did a small section – about 4 × 4 centimetres – in blue, brown or red to get a sense of what the final product would look like.

The pinpoint or dotted design was done with a Unipen. This tool comprised a reservoir that held the paint and a funnel ending in a pointed nib. The Unipen came in different sizes, which facilitated the creation of various sizes of pinpoint

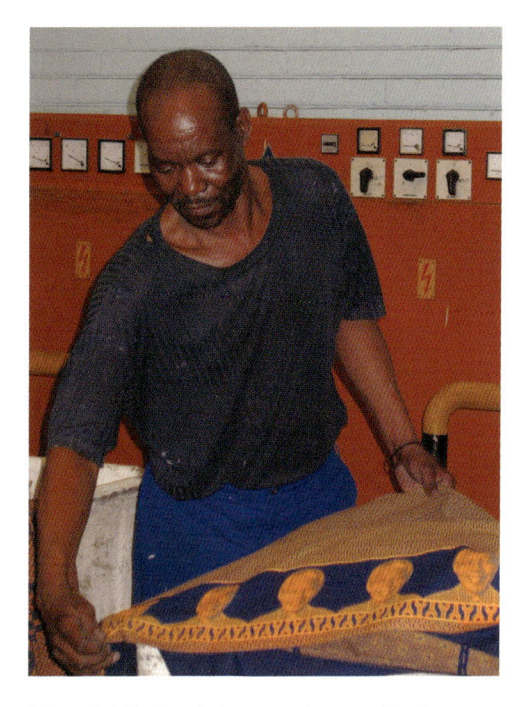

Mncedisi Gobhozi, former printer at Da Gama Textiles (since retired) with indigo-discharged cloth (after removal from the printing machine, before steaming and washing). Photograph © Kirsten Nieser.

marks. The finest details could be achieved, as in 'smokies', but the abrush (a form of colour gradation) could only be realised by the careful application of equidistant dots. Auld never worked with a magnifying glass, saying that her eyes were better years ago. She added that some designers were good at spacing and that others struggled with *isishweshwe* techniques.

Once a design was approved, it was prepared for cylinder engraving. The engravers affixed the inverted design to the roller. Then they dipped the roller into nitric acid and the design became the depressed motif that held the discharge liquid. This liquid would eliminate the dyestuff on the indigo cloth when the rollers were in place on the large printing machines.

Auld sourced her designs in the field at times, recalling that she often travelled through the Transkei on her way from Durban to King William's Town.[34] She would visit local shops to look at the pottery and other crafts. As she lived and worked in King William's Town, she saw many rural *amaXhosa* and *amaThembu*. They gravitated to the town wearing traditional dress and *isishweshwe*, which further inspired her. Auld was aware that local Africans had worn *isishweshwe* for decades, but she knew nothing about the naming of the cloth locally. She recalls that the indigenous people at the time appeared to wear only blue *isishweshwe* and not the red or brown variants that were available. In the late 1970s and again in the 1980s, she said, she and her daughters wore *isishweshwe* often. Like many other white women and children in the King William's Town area, they regarded it as popular wear. Auld remembered the cloth in particular as the fabric for long skirts 'with the navel showing, hippy style'. She also noted that wearing *isishweshwe* was associated with preferences for 'anything ethnic', including Indian textiles and clothing.

One of the designs Auld modified was the rice (*libete*) or shield design (*isitebe*), which she developed with three dots in the centre. But in 2015 it was noted that this design had emerged decades earlier in the Three Cats and other pattern books. This is a typical example of how a designer sourced designs in earlier pattern books and then made them her own. Auld regularly revisited older designs and would modify them. In her experiments she recalls using motifs from other fabric – for example, floral designs that she interpreted and stylised as *isishweshwe*. She added geometric patterns at times. Auld and the other designers at Da Gama were also involved in marketing *isishweshwe* at trade and career shows in the region. This contributed to popularising design as a profession and to foregrounding Da Gama Textiles and the *isishweshwe* manufactured there. Auld produced some skirt panels and worked on sangoma cloth, which was typified in red, white and black motifs, often of fauna. Some of these motifs were shared by *isishweshwe*.

Auld left Da Gama in 1990 and became a freelance designer, working subsequently for a number of textile producers. She created 'granny prints' (detailed stylised floriate designs) where her expertise in *isishweshwe* translated well into desirable patterns. She was subject to restraint of trade, however, which disallowed her from working in *isishweshwe* for any competitors. The restraint applies to this day.

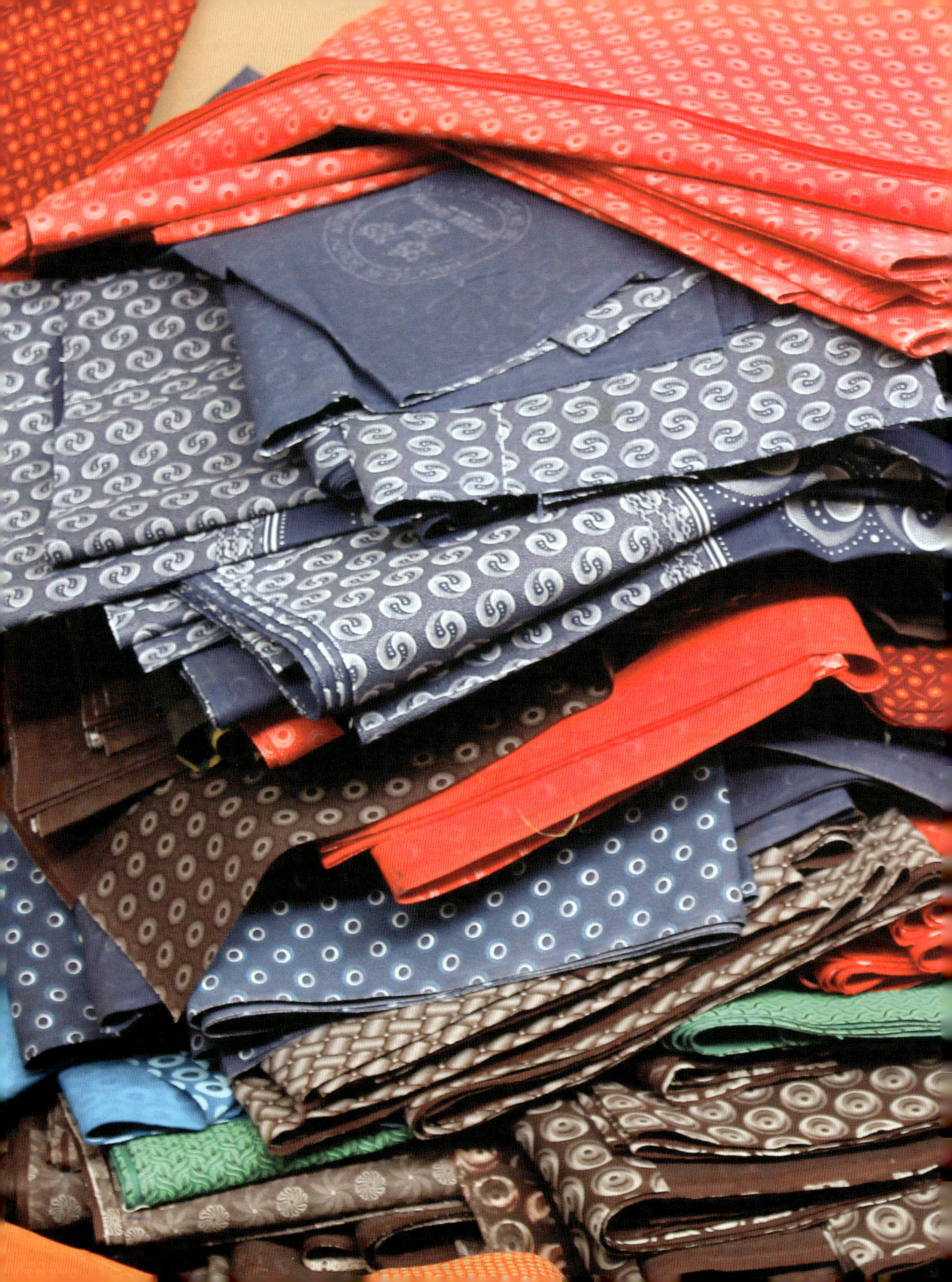

8
Traders and *isiShweshwe*

The 1800s heralded an era of unprecedented scientific and industrial creativity in Europe and Britain. The cloth trade in South Africa proliferated, in blueprint in particular, as major changes in production took place abroad. These innovations sprang from the growth of industrialisation in Britain, which promised wealth for entrepreneurs who created new markets for indigo and for cloth in the colonies. Ordinary people, however, faced overwhelming hardship in the face of these developments as machine-made goods supplanted the handmade items they had once produced. Industrialisation rendered thousands of workers redundant and resulted in widespread German, Dutch and British emigration. Many of these people turned to South Africa for hope and relief, bringing their dress codes with them.

At first, the Vereenigde Oostindische Compagnie – the VOC – strictly controlled the dissemination of Western goods at the Cape, as shown in Chapter 2. Later, however, new laws permitted freer movement of goods under British hegemony, prompting the growth of trade. Many settlers soon migrated to the interior, then predominantly an African domain, where they functioned as farmers, traders and missionaries. Trade was initially based on the exchange of ivory, livestock, skins or produce. Cash was only realised as payment for goods in the nineteenth century.

By the end of the eighteenth century, block-printed indigo cloth had become more mechanised in Europe and 'calico', 'patterned materials' or 'prints' – as blueprint and its derivatives were widely known – were commonly available in South Africa at a reasonable price. Cotton prints in small patterns remained 'the choice of the farmer's wife and daughters though the demands of mourning kept them, like many of their peers in the Western world, in black for long periods' (Strutt 1975: 347). The prevailing dress code also began to influence the indigenous peoples and their economic emergence at this time.

From 1850 to 1900 South Africa, according to S.W. Whitham's 1903 report, had become a significant economic hub for Britain and Europe, notably in the blueprint trade. South Africa was no longer an isolated colonial centre, especially as the hated system of migrancy, driven by the discovery of diamonds and gold from 1866 to 1886, had promoted the absorption of local people into a colonial capitalist economy as expendable labour. This process created a cash flow and a paradoxical decrease in financial restraint among black rural women. They not only controlled the purse-strings – migrancy kept their husbands on the mines for months on end – but assumed growing importance in the rural economy as domestic workers, seamstresses and traders. Daphne Strutt (1975: 147), referring to their white counterparts, remarks further: 'It was an absolute necessity . . . for every man to keep his womenfolk supplied with the clothing that, by its quality and style, proclaimed his social and financial position.' Thus, with the influx of Western trade items now flooding their life-world, the prevailing colonial dress code, as elucidated by Strutt, soon overtook many of the black women in South Africa's rural areas as well.

There were several types of trader in the rural areas of the early nineteenth century, including the transport rider, who criss-crossed the country by ox-wagon, moving laboriously from one region to another, selling goods called for by a diverse market of indigenous peoples and settlers. By the mid-nineteenth century there was an upsurge in the number of traders, many of whom established outlets or permanent stores at strategic places in the countryside, depending on local demand and potential profitability. Traders had to be discerning and held only goods marketable in their areas. Many a trader was ruined by introducing new bead colours or new cloth for which there was no demand. One had to be attuned to the preferences and aesthetics of one's customers, who in turn provided a stable and highly profitable market.[1]

Traders hailed from diverse backgrounds and Cape Muslims – Malays – and Indians played substantial roles in providing and marketing blueprint. Strutt (1975) records an image of a Muslim pedlar trading with Boer women in the late nineteenth century. Several records in the Cape National Archives include references to Cape Malay traders, many of whom were political exiles, allowed to trade as *smouse* (pedlars) in South Africa. Other traders included Lithuanian and Russian Jews, who fled persecution at home and plied the local trade routes from the coast to the interior. Many settled in small villages in the western Cape and in what is now the Free State and also in small towns throughout the country. Many had immigrated into South Africa in the late nineteenth and early twentieth century, especially after the Russian exclusions, pogroms and recurring anti-Semitism. The *smouse* plied their trade along the west Cape coast, in the eastern Cape and along internal routes and wagon trails. The 'Jew woman' and her store described by Pauline Smith in *The Beadle* (first published in 1926) typify this phenomenon. Many Jewish traders' names have been identified, including Mosal and Rose, Lewis, Myers and Marx, and numerous other trading families have emerged in the Eastern Cape, including the Kolbes in Keiskammashoek.

The main internal and coastal trade routes in South Africa were clearly defined by the late nineteenth century. They represent a web of expansion, exchange and

Jewish *smous* (pedlar) selling his wares to a Boer family, late nineteenth century. National Archives, Bloemfontein.

preference among traders and local people, missionaries, settlers and the emergent Boer republics. One route from the Cape led from Cape Town along the western Atlantic seaboard. There was another route through the Little Karoo, up towards the left flank of Lesotho, through Ladybrand towards Johannesburg. Another flank led to Bloemfontein and into the north-west, Namibia and Botswana. A second route from the Cape wound along the coast from Port Elizabeth and East London up the eastern seaboard to what are now the Eastern Cape and KwaZulu-Natal. These trade routes brought the beginnings of settlement. Waves of Germans, Britons and Lithuanian Jews migrated to the eastern Cape – and to the western Cape and what is now the Free State – promoting the expansion of trade and the establishment of a vast network of trading stores. Missionaries in Natal, which had for some time been a fertile site for evangelism, constructed numerous trading stores to supplement their income and to accommodate mission-dwellers and the local peoples.

The increased use of Western-derived trade items, including cloth, by indigenous people in the nineteenth century proclaimed their entry into the settler economy. Black wearers of Western dress items implicitly disclosed their economic power in the guise of their control over surplus wealth and goods – a surplus usually managed by patriarchal order in traditional societies – and industrious women became adept at marketing the fruits of their labour. They acquired Western-sourced items, often innovated their use and then sought the approval of their peers. Their selections would be emulated by large groups of other women who scrutinised and approved their choices. Commercial activity was no longer the exclusive domain of itinerant traders in South Africa. The impetus of this new trend was greatly increased in 1860 by the construction of railways, which spread communication and growth right across the country (Strutt 1975: 291).

Another major factor that contributed to the cloth trade and to early blueprint, in particular, was the rapid emergence of a home-sewing industry, which persists to this day. Major developments in sewing occurred from 1860 to 1890, following the construction of the rail network and the discovery of gold and diamonds. From as early as the 1840s, machine-made garments increasingly replaced handmade items, the sewing machine having become common in most Western homes and locales in the 1850s. Chain stitch and lock stitch were realised for decorative embellishment from 1855 to 1860 (Strutt 1975: 147). Sewing machines were relatively cheap and widely obtainable in South Africa by 1865 – a Singer's Patent or a Britannica cost as little as R3 – and by 1870 most rural dressmakers had a sewing machine. Their handiwork reflected what was done at trading stores for individual clients, as described later in this chapter by Fleur Rourke, and became an integral part of the Westernised training of 'schooled' indigenous women who learnt to sew on the missions. As a result of the availability of sewing machines and imported cloth, almost all clothing in South Africa was machine-made by the 1870s, some of it designed and sewn by men. Several categories of African workwear were developed at this stage, identifying styles in specific cloth and in current African dress, but not always with African preferences. Payne Brothers catalogues from Durban in the 1880s, for example, refer to the 'piccanin suit' and the 'houseboy suit' as current wear for African males employed in urban centres. The use of blueprint as working wear, imported in large quantities from Holland, Germany and Britain at this time, appealed to African women in particular, as also to rural Boer women (Whitham 1903).

Strutt (1975: 291) notes that colour preferences for South African whites changed after the 1870s as the soft pastel shades of the mid-Victorian era began to disappear in urban areas: 'The new aniline dyes brought a fashion for bright colours which, with an increase in tasteless ornament and in combination with shoddy workmanship, rendered much clothing positively tawdry.' One need hardly add that the accessibility of bright aniline-dyed cloth – arguably European *indiennes* – also impacted on black South African women's choices and preferences, as did the designs of the time. White women in the 1890s, for example, wore large, puffed mutton sleeves with capes and mantles. These garments, and many others from the time, showed ample pleats, gathers and tucks, the latter often at the hemline and elsewhere on their garments (Strutt 1975: 360). Many features of these codes – notably sleeves, tucks and braid – were emulated among the *amaXhosa*, *baSotho*, *amaZulu* and *baTswana* in their blueprint preferences.

Despite the adaptations displayed by white South African women in Western dress, however, the local African market derived much of its wear from bales of second-hand clothing shipped to South Africa by donation from benevolent societies and religious groups abroad. This clothing was either used as it was, or it was partly modified, as among the *baPedi*, who wore shortened blouses or undergarments and converted them into the *diele*, an early forerunner of a loose pinafore that was later made of *isishweshwe*, which has become part of Pedi cultural dress.

Traders also helped to produce garments for the clientele in their stores, especially in the late 1900s, when cloth was highly desirable. Indeed, for most of the twentieth century, traders' wives and daughters, their sons and assistants continued to make garments for their clientele, ensuring that their preferences were met and their continuities maintained.[2] This in-house manufacture was often supplemented, from the early 1900s, by industrious Malawian tailors, who came from far afield to machine-stitch garments for customers outside trading stores as they waited.[3] Indian traders also established backroom sewing industries for their customers (such as those at Kwa Keshwa outlets in Durban), some of which function to this day as important sources of *isishweshwe* at urban and rural outlets such as Diagonal Street, Johannesburg, and outlets near Grey Street in Durban, where I have identified Sudanese and Senegalese tailors more recently.

❖ ❖ ❖

Apart from the German settlers of 1858, the eastern Cape earlier attracted Trekboers of mixed nationality and a large influx of British settlers as well, as noted in Chapter 4. Many eastern Cape families sprang from these settlers and from the stream of traders that followed them. This is reflected in surnames such as Marx and Van Niekerk, Baxter, Cowie, Sparg and Wendler, all of whom traded in areas such as Butterworth, Idutywa and Ngcobo. Spargs is a large group of former eastern Cape traders, as are RNE Holdings from East London. The largest remaining *isishweshwe* wholesalers in South Africa today include, among a few others, Cowie's (East London), Fayco (Durban), Waddee's and Dadabhay's (Johannesburg). All these traders have extensive knowledge of *isishweshwe* and have built up a network of mediators in the field. The Cowies still maintain direct contact with their late father's market and regularly visit the family's far-flung stores and outlying trading stores to establish desirable preferences.

Blaudruck was the German farm woman's peasant dress. Her counterparts in the eastern Cape must have used this wear, for some of the second-wave German immigrants there, as noted in Chapter 4, were tradesmen from working-class or agricultural backgrounds. They would have been familiar with the *Blaudruck*, indigo cloth and calico mass-produced in Germany at the time. These dress categories and their variants would also have been well known among the indigenous peoples. The discovery of aniline indigo by Adolf von Baeyer in 1895 had made the mass production of *Blaudruck* much cheaper. Traders marketed this cloth to German settlers, Boers and local Africans. *Blaudruck* imported into South Africa, moreover, was made into clothing locally by settler women and African seamstresses schooled on the missions.[4]

One of the most important Eastern Cape wholesalers and traders in *isishweshwe* was John Cowie.[5] The Cowies initially traded in the Transkei and Ciskei, in Lesotho, the Free State, Botswana and what used to be known as the Transvaal. They are perhaps the biggest traders from the original group who cornered the *isishweshwe* market in South Africa. Others in this group were Randall Brothers and Hudson and W.G. Brown, both from Durban, Elephant Trading Company in Johannesburg and Frasers from Wepener, who at one time were the biggest *isishweshwe* merchants in Lesotho with 56 stores.[6] Frasers, who also sold *isishweshwe* in the old Transvaal and Bloemfontein, have now been absorbed by the Lesotho government or have sold out to other individuals. By 2016 their remaining stores had all closed.

John Cowie's father, Scottish immigrant Frank Hamilton Cowie, bought the business from the second-generation Myers in 1945.[7] He was familiar with the cloth trade conducted by his father in Zambia. According to John Cowie, indigo cloth similar to blueprint was traded there c.1930, but he was unsure of its continuity. Such cloth was variously termed 'print', *ujeremani, ujalmani* or *ujamani* in what is now the Eastern Cape. The Cowies were concerned that about 24 merchants in East London were trading in competition with them in the 1930s. To distinguish themselves they changed their name to Cowie and Wendler. Wendler, like many eastern Cape settlers, had come from Germany after the Depression in the 1930s. The Vidges, also large *isishweshwe* traders, were stationed at Vidgeville and owned some 40 stores south of Mthatha. Anton Vidge, a German national, had come to South Africa in response to a newspaper advertisement asking for traders. Other main wholesalers in the King William's Town area in the 1950s were Radue and James Weir, who both imported directly from Europe before Da Gama Textiles began to produce *isishweshwe*.

The Cowies imported *isishweshwe* from Britain in the late 1950s and earlier, but in the 1930s – when John's father ran the business – their cloth was sourced in Hungary and what was then Czechoslovakia, coinciding with the importation of beads from Czechoslovakia through German intermediaries. Cowie was adamant that during his time as a trader there were no imports of *Blaudruck* and that all German trade with South Africa ended with the Second World War.[8] Thus, while vast amounts of *Blaudruck* entered South Africa in the 1890s, continued references to the cloth arise from association rather than from accurate sourcing. Cowie also confirmed the American link in the importation of blueprint. When he was 'on the road' in 1948, he said, Stifel was the best-known cloth in South Africa. It was always backstamped with a boot and the logo became essential to buyers of *mericani*, as the import was known locally to some traders.

The primary role of *isishweshwe* traders was to provide cloth for their customers. They also played a vital role as mediators of preferred designs and colours, which were conveyed to and from ABC at Hyde in Manchester. When Da Gama Textiles obtained the Three Cats copyright from ABC in 1961, it inherited some of ABC's main customers in Johannesburg, Durban, Cape Town and the Eastern Cape. Da Gama retained these customers without expanding its own trade links, since it was reluctant to flood the market with *isishweshwe*. Exclusivity has been an important strategy in Da Gama Textiles' marketing policy.

Sales representatives – or mediators – regularly consulted traders. Cowie noted that even as a main wholesaler his task was akin to a 'rep's' – he had to be knowledgeable about users' preferences and requirements.[9] Many cloth representatives came from the Eastern Cape or hailed from local trading families. A significant figure at Da Gama Textiles was Rodney Breetzke, who was associated with the manufacturer from his high-school days. He started his apprenticeship at Da Gama Textiles in 1957 when GHT, the parent company, was still printing mainly bleached and dyed calico. Breetzke's parents had been traders and he had seen the vast quantities of *isishweshwe* sold in their stores in the farming areas of Izeli near King William's Town.

◆ ◆ ◆

In Natal various traders functioned as itinerant merchants or were attached to rural localities or mission settlements. Jock Morrison founded one of the most important long-standing trading stores in the province. The store, which was established in the 1920s, still has retail outlets to this day in Mtubatuba and elsewhere in Natal. In 2005, Hugh Morrison, Jock's grandson, invited Kirsten Nieser and me to visit the store. It is located at Makakatana, on Lake St Lucia, an area named after an early Zulu chieftain. In its heyday it was known simply as Morrisons and was initially run by Jock himself and later by his sons. The store was intended to stock basic foodstuff for the local African people who lived across Lake St Lucia near Cape Vidal.

Morrisons is a mine of information with a vast repository of ledgers and other items from a century of trade. Jock Morrison left the store in the 1970s. The building and its contents, with a nearby lodge, still belong to the Morrisons, but are now part of the greater iSimangaliso Wetland Park.

The shop was initially the only outlet between Makakatana and Sodwana. Locals crossed the lake at low tide, having collected fish, mussels and crayfish, which they sold or traded to customers at the shop. They travelled on foot, braving a sand reef across the lake at low tide, a pathway hardened over centuries by elephants searching for pasturage and fresh water. Local Africans also operated a ferry, which still crosses the lake from time to time.

Morrisons' customers bought mainly food, especially sugar and *mntombo*, a sprouted sorghum used for brewing beer. *Blaudruck – ujalmani* to the locals – was one of the main cloth types bought, as were brightly decorated scarves. Women were the principal clients and sales took place in spring, after the winter harvest and just before Christmas. All trade was cash-based, most of the cash deriving from barter with the locals.[10]

Father Edwin Kinch, a Servite missionary who lived and worked in nearby Hlabisa for decades, remembered Jock Morrison discussing the specific needs of his women customers with regard to *isishweshwe*.[11] Morrison had to be certain to hold specific designs and colours in particular areas and at particular times, otherwise his cloth would not sell.

In 2005 I spoke to Ursula and Jimmy Morrison, formerly of Jock Morrison Ltd.[12] Jimmy, Jock's son, remembers how popular *isishweshwe* was. The company bought their cloth in Durban at W.G. Brown Wholesalers and, according to Jimmy, it was imported from Germany. They also bought *isishweshwe* from other wholesalers such as Nelson and Miles Gadden in Zululand, S.S. Butcher and Son and W. Jagger and Company. Jimmy took over the Morrisons' shops in 1948, having served in the airforce during the war. At one stage he went to Holland with Guy Boffer in search of an *isishweshwe* equivalent, but as he remembered it, they did not buy much. Ursula, however, recalls that Jimmy bought some *blauwdruk* in Holland.

As in most trading stores, the Morrisons chose their 'blueprint fabric', as they called *isishweshwe*, from samples brought by travellers. Their decisions about what patterns to choose were based on various opinions and contributions. They relied above all on their African staff – the managers and their wives. Blueprint fabric always sold well and was bought by men for their wives and by women with surplus money. As for the cloth they sold, Ursula recalled: 'German print was "working cloth" and older women would buy it for working clothes not for "Sunday meeting clothing."'[13] In the post-war period, she added, many women went bare-breasted and wore the traditional *isidwaba* (a pleated leather skirt used by Zulu married women) and always *ibhaye* (a shoulder wrap). In her view, a lot of the *isishweshwe* fabric used by local African women at the time came from what was then Czechoslovakia.

Ursula Morrison also remembered that in 1948 ready-made clothes were not widely available locally. Making one's own clothes was the norm, especially in the

Traders and *isiShweshwe*

rural areas. Affordable clothing for the African market was extremely rare, she said, and, situated outside trading stores, 'there was always a "sewing boy", a Malawian, who wore an Arab skullcap. They did most of the sewing for the women, but not all, and their presence continued into the 1950s.'[14] She added that every shop had a 'sewing boy' and that such 'foreigners' regularly set themselves up on Morrisons' verandah.

The Malawian tailor had his own portable sewing machine and would ask the storeowner if he could set up his table on the verandah of the shop to ply his trade. Permission was always given and the tailor's presence was welcomed: it meant that quantities of cloth would sell. Women bought the cloth and within hours the tailor made a garment from it to their specifications. Ursula Morrison recalled: 'They made simple shirtwaister garments with no elastic in the waist and the women wore a wrap of any cloth.'[15] The *Blaudruck* purchased at Jimmy Morrison's stores – he called it *ujeremani* – was always blue and white or brown and white. He was adamant that no other colours were desirable while he ran the store. This coincides with Father Kinch's contentions cited earlier.

The presence of Malawian tailors at local outlets has been attested by traders and storeowners. They were excellent tailors and are still sought after. In Johannesburg I identified a group of Malawian tailors in 2007, sewing garments at an astonishing rate in a Diagonal Street outlet. One claimed that he came to South Africa regularly to make garments at these stores. At the same store I saw a tailor from Burundi and another from Mozambique. The extent of these people's influence on the style and design of local clothing is becoming increasingly identifiable, but most of the

Malawian tailor in Diagonal Street, Johannesburg, 2007. Photograph © J. Leeb-du Toit.

isishweshwe they made at the time, it seems, followed established traditions like the pinafore (*isipinifa*), the wraparound skirt (*jikiza*) and the more ample dress with gigot sleeves, pockets and a trim of *liteke* or tucks.

Until very recently the Kala family from Pretoria Textile Wholesalers employed a Malawian tailor who made dress items for sale, including patchwork pants.

Given the prominence of Malawian tailors in the region – with their Ghanaian, Sudanese and Senegalese counterparts – one can assume that some of the *isishweshwe* they worked on would have been taken back to Malawi with them. One informant indicated that the cloth was used in Zambia and Zimbabwe, but that it probably got there through migrant labourers who worked on the gold mines in Johannesburg. A pale-blue variant popular in Zimbabwe in the 1950s has been identified in Da Gama catalogues. Initially I had assumed that the reference to a pale-blue *isishweshwe* was based on faded or 'washed out' variants, but the catalogues (located in 2015) clearly indicate that this paler *isishweshwe* was intended for specific markets and preferences.

Ursula Morrison commented that large amounts of *isishweshwe* were always on their store's shelves, especially at seasonal times, and she identified the cloth as 'full of starch and [with] a distinctive smell'.[16] She added that there was a change in quality towards the end of the 1970s. This coincides with Da Gama Textiles' initial production when they struggled to match ABC's quality. She was unaware of whites buying or wearing *isishweshwe* at the time. Nor would this have happened in their neighbourhood, she said, as the cloth was seen as 'African wear'. The Morrisons also sold ric-rac binding and beads, the former as an accessory on *isishweshwe* dress.[17]

❖ ❖ ❖

Indian traders are particularly significant in the marketing and continuity of *isishweshwe* throughout South Africa. In what is now KwaZulu-Natal, passenger Indians or 'Arabs', as they were known, were allowed, in preference to indentured Indians, to trade in central Durban when they arrived at the end of the nineteenth century. Many passenger Indians had some trade expertise and capital. At first they imported goods from India that were desirable in their own communities. These items included rice, spices and Indian cloth and apparel (Vahed and Bhana 2015). However, they soon added other goods and had a large white clientele as well. The Indian trader was prepared to make a small markup on his goods and between 1870 and 1885 there was a considerable growth in the number of stores they owned (from two to 40). As a result, they posed a real threat to white urban shopowners and small traders in the countryside.

By 1890 the Indian traders began to cater for the 'kaffir truck' trade, as it was known, importing much of their goods directly from India. Several types of Indian cloth such as *salempore*, *palo* and *injeti* are in fact indigenised Indian cloth types. By 1898 'kaffir truck' was almost exclusively in the hands of Indian traders. Since they were in competiton with whites, they were subject to various restrictions and were eventually refused new licences to operate in Durban's West Street (Vahed and Bhana 2015).[18] Many of the traders were Muslims and they cornered the African cloth trade in the 1950s. Families such as the Gokals, Rawats, Bassas and Kajees of Kwa Keshwa in Durban were known for their consistent supplies and the variety of cloth they held. By the 1960s their intervention in the blueprint trade had increased in importance. They not only provided suppliers such as Da Gama Textiles with clientele preferences, but also helped to develop designs. The panel prints, which when cut to size made individual skirts, for example, were held to be the invention of one of these trading families and of one family member in particular, who showed that this technique would facilitate sewing and allow for a variety of designs on the borders of the panels.

The mediation of Indian traders continues nationally to this day. Since the late 1990s, when the cost of *isishweshwe* rose sharply, they have sought cheaper variants in polycotton and other synthetic fabrics. These versions are often designed locally, in Durban or Johannesburg, and many of the patterns resemble examples from Manchester or Da Gama Textiles. The designs have always been modified, however, to avoid copyright infringement. More recently, variants have been produced in Pakistan and India. They replicate the originals and as variants are affordable to poorer buyers. While the market for this type of *isishweshwe* remains, it has by no means supplanted Da Gama's discharge-printed *isishweshwe*. Helen Bester concedes that even someone on the Three Cats panel, for example, could obtain their sources elsewhere, apply their own stamp and produce their own variants.[19] Big wholesalers can also develop their own brand, provided that they do not copy their designs from Three Cats or from other Da Gama ranges.

Mr Rawat, manager of Fabric Splendour in Pietermaritzburg, 2005. Photograph © J. Leeb-du Toit.

One of the largest interprovincial traders in *isishweshwe* is Salim Kajee, who owns KwaKeshwa Textrim. The consortium is based in Johannesburg, but has additional outlets in Durban and elsewhere. Kajee now almost exclusively holds variants in polycotton or a better cotton mix, some of it produced locally and some in India. KwaKeshwa previously ordered in bulk from Da Gama, in particular specific designs and brands such as Three Cats, as called for by their customers. But by 2015 it was noted that the bulk of their holdings comprised the cheaper polycotton variants. As this cloth is 'hot and airless', either too thin or too thick, informants indicate that they only choose it when funds are limited.

Furthermore, as none of this cloth is discharge-printed, the designs soon rub thin and often disappear entirely in areas subject to friction. One informant indicated that buying this cheaper variant would only be for workwear, as it was actually 'a waste of money' buying it.

Mr Naren Kala has owned Pretoria Textile Wholesalers, located in the former Marabastad – a mainly African trading area in Pretoria – since he took over the business from his father as a young man. His grandfather, who came from a Gujarat family, arrived in South Africa c.1890 to trade in Louis Trichardt when gold was discovered in the Transvaal Republic.[20] The South African government wished to repatriate Indians, but President Paul Kruger allowed them to remain in the Transvaal where he acknowledged that they rendered an important service to whites and blacks alike. Kala's grandfather was a pedlar, selling all kinds of goods, but he soon centred on textiles. Kala's father travelled to India regularly and imported textiles that perpetuated the use of Indian fabrics such as *injeti* and *palo* among local Africans. Most of Kala's *isishweshwe* comes from Da Gama Textiles and his former contacts included Rodney Breetzke and John Cowie. However, by 2015, he also had holdings of other local and imported variants.

The Kalas' immediate competitors were Jewish wholesalers, such as Greenstein and Rosen, M. Bloch, D. Myers and Orwall Distributors. Naren Kala believes that Pretoria Textile Wholesalers cornered a share of the African market in the 1970s because their prices were fair and they realised low markups because they sold huge volumes of cloth. By the late 1970s they also sold increasingly to white customers, coincident with the fashionability of their supplies in dress and handicrafts.

Besides sourcing *isishweshwe* from Britain and later from Da Gama, Kala recalls additional sources for the cloth.[21] One was Four Boots, which, he presumed, came from America, though he could not recall the source. The cloth may well have been from Stifel, but there is no record that they ever used four boots as a logo. Another indigo print was by Hungarotex – it was called Noma – and yet another was by T.H. Faulkner. Kala indicated that Hungarotex had pale-blue designs on a dark-blue ground rather than white designs on a dark-blue ground. Kala discontinued the sourcing, since his clientele found the cloth too narrow, too thin and semi-transparent after washing. Still

Naren Kala, owner of Pretoria Textile Wholesalers, 2005. Photograph © J. Leeb-du Toit.

Traders and *isiShweshwe* 173

Top: Mr Waddee at his store, Johannesburg, 2016. Photograph © J. Leeb-du Toit.
Bottom: Mr Waddee's store with *isishweshwe*, Johannesburg, 2016. Photographs © J. Leeb-du Toit.

another source was a Portuguese-derived blueprint, remnants of which were sold to me by the Kalas, which resembled *Blaudruck* and *isishweshwe*. It was identified by a linen-like texture and loose weave, but was also narrow with border patterns at one end and bold designs. It sold in modest amounts and was discontinued in the 1980s. There was no indication of its manufacturer on the bolts I purchased.

After returning to Pretoria Textile Wholesalers in 2010 and again in 2012, I purchased the last few bolts of Hungarian and Portuguese cloth, which lay at the back of the shop. The Kalas also located large numbers of outdated pattern books from Spruce, ABC and Da Gama, which they kindly gave to my project. Some of the books were donated to the Iziko Social History Collections and others are destined for other national archives once my proposed run of exhibitions has ended.

H.K. Gokal, a wholesale textile store at 43A Market Street, Johannesburg, close to Diagonal Street, is one of many outlets catering for the passing African trade. Gokals used to be one of the largest suppliers of *isishweshwe* in the area. Currently headed by Nipun Gokal, the business stopped holding *isishweshwe* in 2008. The surplus stock was taken over by Nipun's uncle, Viru Gokal. The family decided to relinquish trade in *isishweshwe* as the stock required a huge outlay and the profit margin was low. Gokal also believes that there is currently too much competition from manufacturers who produce cheaper variants.

Mini Mark, another shop with vast holdings of Da Gama (and also variant) *isishweshwe*, is situated down the road from Gokals at 33 Market Street. It was run for decades by the late Sayed Nawab, whose sister-in-law Fatima Akhalwaya recalls that he was highly influential in the *isishweshwe* trade.[22] He not only ensured the availability of a wide variety of designs for his clientele, but also developed new designs, which he conveyed to Da Gama's Rodney Breetzke. The full extent of Nawab's input has yet to be ascertained.

Around every corner in Diagonal Street are readymade *isishweshwe* dresses for sale at low prices – about R250 each in 2009. They were made *in situ* by Malawian and Senegalese tailors employed by the surrounding storeowners to turn out as many dresses as possible. Another major wholesaler of Da Gama-derived *isishweshwe* in Gauteng – and the second-largest retailer of the cloth in South Africa – is Dadabhay's, also near Diagonal Street, Johannesburg. Clientele are obliged to buy a certain amount of the fabric, ensuring a vast turnover at the outlet. Dadabhay's also employs informed African saleswomen who advise on the designs in their holdings and know design names and clientele preferences. They assisted me invaluably with identifying current design names in 2011 and again in 2012.

Muhamed Dadabhay at his store in Johannesburg, 2016. Photograph © J. Leeb-du Toit.

Traders and *isiShweshwe*

isiShweshwe for sale in Lesotho near Ficksburg, 2010. Photographs © J. Leeb-du Toit.

In Lesotho there are several trading families with commercial outlets across the region. Frasers is one of the oldest trading companies and until recently had a string of outlets. They are best known for developing the market for the well-known Sotho blanket, but they also keep a wide range of *isishweshwe*. They developed a trade in the cloth throughout Lesotho, which was initiated at mission stations and small subsistence trading stores. Many independent traders still function in Lesotho today, where authentic Three Cats *isishweshwe* is de rigeur for most wearers.

◆ ◆ ◆

A South African trader who contributed to textile design in South Africa, before and after Da Gama Textiles captured the rights to its production, was Fleur Rourke. She was from a missionary background and her grandfather came to South Africa from Mauge in Switzerland. He was in Lesotho during the Gun War (1879–83), traded at Thabana Morena while he was a pastor of the Paris Evangelical Church and was later stationed at Morija, where Fleur was born.

Fleur and her husband Eddie were the first members of their missionary family to become traders. They both worked in Bloemfontein at *The Friend* newspaper and later returned to Lesotho as traders. At one time they worked for Johnny Wessels at George Stewart's trading store from 1954 to 1955 – in competition with Frasers – and then in Mohale's Hoek for the Jandrells, who owned several stores and had been traders for three generations. After leaving Jandrells, the Rourkes continued to manage various stores throughout Lesotho until 1976.[23]

The Rourkes traded in mohair wool, the Lesotho variety being among the best in the world. The wool would be traded at the stores for cloth and provisions. Before she was aware of *isishweshwe*, Rourke recalls, the *khoreit* that Sotho women wore cost ninepence a yard: 'It was a very cheap cloth patterned with coloured checks of all kinds of tartan.'[24] When *khoreit* was no longer available, Sotho women wore unbleached calico under blankets and other garments, the calico always hidden. Sotho men would buy this calico after they had brought in wool to sell.

In Fleur Rourke's grandfather's time, most *baSotho* still wore karosses, or hide cloaks, but she notes: 'Missionaries found it very important for their converts to wear European clothes to be a sign of civilisation, resulting in a change in dress.'[25] Rourke knew *isishweshwe* merely as 'prints'. There were various grades available to the trader, based on quality and origin, and in her view Cowie and Wendler supplied the best quality. Others tried to print on less stiff material, she claims, but their efforts were unsuccessful, as the cloth had to be stiff and tightly woven. Chops Gasovsky had a wholesale outlet in Bloemfontein and his sales representative sold material to the Rourkes, as well as print salvaged from burnt-out warehouses, which was regarded as 'spoilt stock' and was therefore cheap.

To give the *isishweshwe* skirt weight and to protect the edge and the ric-rac, women used to do rows of tight tucks or *liteke*. Fleur Rourke had several Sotho seamstresses attached to the various trading stores where she and her husband worked. The women used what Rourke termed 'traditional patterns', but were often unwilling to share their expertise.[26] These seamstresses were untrained, but learnt from each other. Rourke notes: 'We used to have one, Maliako, who used to sit in the yard and sew endlessly. She got her four-year-old to thread the needle and she made a good living from her sewing.'

Rourke observes that before the development of panel print, there was a special way of folding the 27-inch cloth for a skirt so that a panel could be made.[27]

Traders and *isiShweshwe*

The tapered panels could then be used to create the distinctive 'gored skirt', with a narrow top and a broad edge below. One would cut as many panels as were needed, depending on one's girth. This was doubtless one of the precedents for the panel prints that made the design of the gored skirt so much easier. To fasten the skirt and fit into it, Rourke adds, 'they would leave a split and then one would use a safety pin to close it'. An apron was worn in front of the skirt and was made with fewer panels. The aprons were sometimes lined and tied at the back. Rourke maintains that the name of the skirt was *isishweshwe* – or *sishoeshoe* – and this was not a reference to the print itself. She called the skirts *dishoeshoe*, in the plural. In her view, the term *isishweshwe* may derive from Moshoeshoe I. She recalls that the king's name meant 'cut' – *shoeshoe* – for instead of killing his enemies, Moshoeshoe I allegedly cut off their beards, both as a warning and a token of compassion. The name could also be onomatopoeic, suggesting the sound of a knife cutting through beards, which Rourke extended literally to the sound of cutting cloth in celebration of Moshoeshoe I's rule.

The third item in the dress ensemble was a matching top, 'which was more or less a square with sleeves (not always used) like a T-shirt . . . but the body part was quite wide, as was the wide round neck lined with a piece of print inside-out'.[28] This was seen as attractive and very 'traditional' and was also made with a pocket. If the neck on the blouse was narrower, it had a split in the front that could open, making it easier to nurse an infant if needed. Although she can no longer recall Sotho names for particular designs, Rourke noted that at one stage there was a zigzag design, which Sotho customers declined to buy. This perhaps refers to something similar to the saw design (*isage*), which later became so popular. When Rourke started trading in 1957, most people in Lesotho – and most of her domestic workers – wore *isishweshwe* in the rural areas. The cloth became increasingly popular in the 1960s and was one of the most profitable items sold in their stores.

Jackson's store, Matatiele, 2008. Photograph © J. Leeb-du Toit.

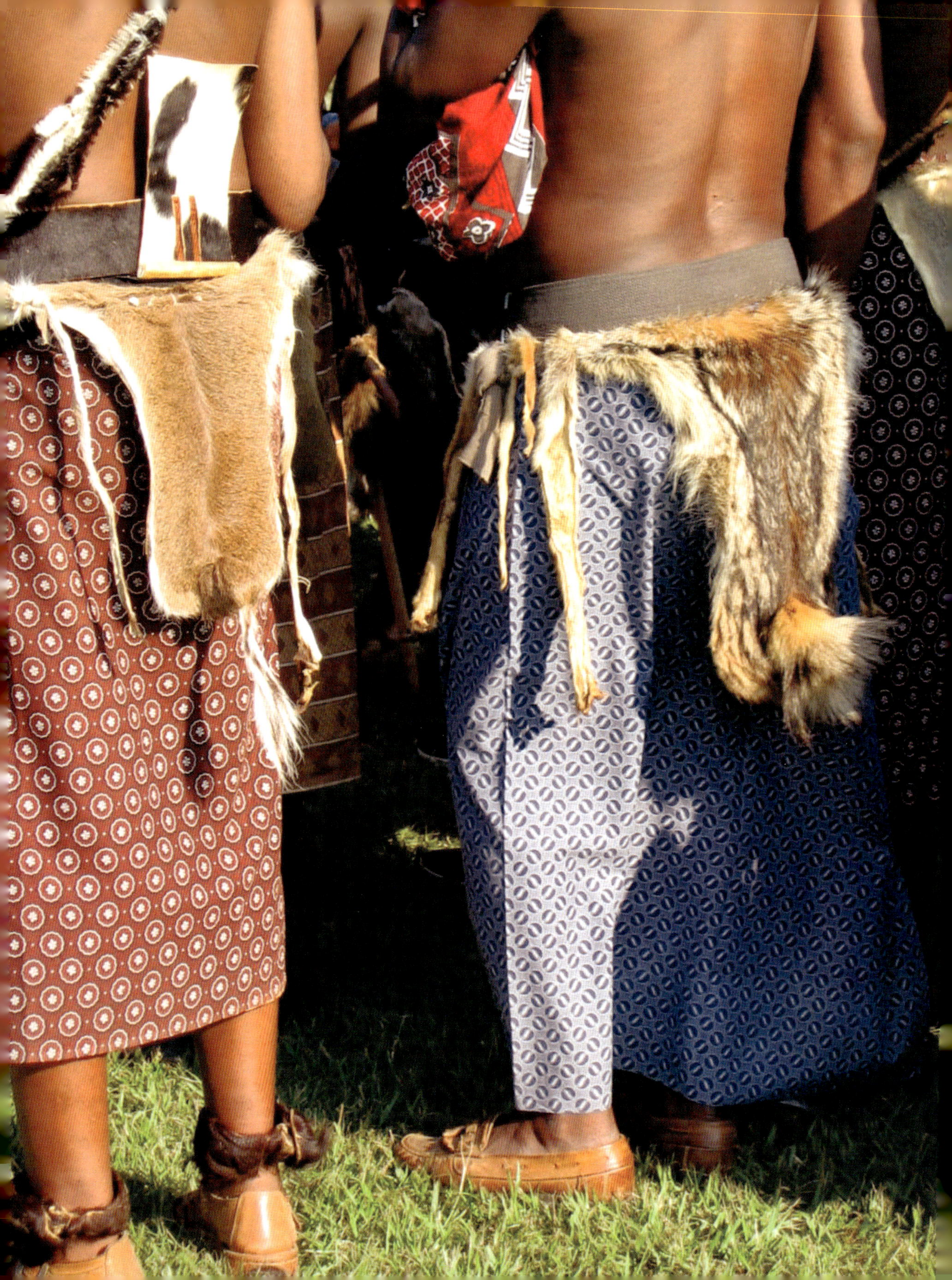

9
Cultural Usage of *isiShweshwe* in Lesotho and Swaziland

It is difficult to separate users of *isishweshwe* in terms of their cultural or racial distinctiveness. In some cases, however, the acquired differences between them may certainly be upheld as distinctive. This is true of Lesotho and Swaziland and of independent states such as Botswana and Namibia. The creation of racial and geographical boundaries and divisions in South Africa, as defined originally by the colonial principle of 'divide and rule', has overlooked the natural blurring of boundaries and cross-cultural links between people.

The British have long since abandoned South Africa's shores, retaining substantial economic vestiges of control and leaving the scars of their empire behind them, but *isishweshwe* continues to exert a unifying cultural influence, however tenuously, over its disparate users at the heart of democratic South Africa.

Structure and emergent identity, as Clifton Crais (1992: 11) observes, arise from the ways in which shared practices and common outlook bind local people together. Daily social practice conferred meaning on the land around them as they engaged, wittingly or unwittingly, in the definition of self and community. In so doing, distinctions arose between them and boundaries were created. Specific ethnic classifications, moreover, defined the groups attached to regions and clans, enabling the British to locate, demarcate and restrict peoples and their access to land and to one another. In what follows, however, I explore the cultural usage and localised meaning of *isishweshwe* among specific peoples in terms of their own self-definition.

In contemporary southern Africa the use of *isishweshwe* is widespread. The cloth has long transcended its original African, international and local origins and is worn throughout rural and urban areas by people from different ethnic and cultural backgrounds. In each region, particular cultures use *isishweshwe* by attaching it to rites of passage and, in particular, to rites associated with women upon marriage, childbearing and mourning. More recently, especially since 2000, *isishweshwe* has become part of high fashion and is used by modern designers in South Africa such as Bongiwe Walaza and Amanda Laird-Cherry, among many others.

The shift in dress and cloth usage reflects the incorporation of African populations in the global economy coupled with colonial capitalism, domination and dependency. As participants in the construction of an 'unequal and racially divided colonial society' (Crais 1992: 1), all cross-cultural and interactive processes between indigene and colonist shift between the affirmation of cross-cultural encounter as a reflection of 'interaction and modernization' and economic coercion in capitalist development (Crais 1992: 2). Within the context of missionisation and cultural imposition, I draw on Crais's suggestion that 'colonizations of the body' are invariably associated with an 'entwined history of the colonizations of the mind' (Crais 1992: 3). In addition, I try to address how changes in dress conventions, where appropriate, are also inevitably associated with emergent nineteenth-century creations, race, thought-patterns, the imposition of social boundaries and with shifting South African economics and ideology.

❖ ❖ ❖

In each region of southern Africa people have developed specific associations and culturally based determinants in their use of *isishweshwe*. In some areas there is a tendency to use specific names for the cloth and its associated garments. These contexts have accrued in the twentieth century and, with each accrual, have been further defined by cultural, religious and personal preferences. For the sake of continuity, I use the name *isishweshwe* for blueprint throughout this discussion, although I point out vernacular terms for the cloth in specific regional and cultural localities.

Besides slave usage, one of the earliest missionary and national associations of *isishweshwe* occurs in Lesotho, a kingdom in the Maluti Mountains. Lesotho was probably among the first regions to claim – justifiably – that its national dress included *isishweshwe* for women, as well as the prescribed Sotho blanket. Several informants indicated that they see *isishweshwe* as culturally specific. The cloth is known as *seshoeshoe* in Lesotho. I have already mentioned its associations but, to reiterate, some informants have indicated that *seshoeshoe* is rooted in the name of Moshoeshoe I, the leader and founder of the *baSotho*. Most *seSotho*- and *seTswana*-speaking informants in the northern regions of South Africa refer to the cloth as *isishoeshoe*, a clear sourcing in the king's name. Some even assert that *isishoeshoe* is onomatopoeia for the scraping of the knife in one of Moshoeshoe's beneficent gestures – he severed his enemies' beards and not their heads. Whatever the case, *isishoeshoe* links blueprint to the *baSotho* nation, to Tswana and Sotho culture and to the mountain kingdom and its dress conventions.

Moshoeshoe I, a member of the *baKoena*, gathered refugees around him. They had fled their homes as a result of the *lifaqane* (*mfecane*) and the associated wars from 1818 to 1830. They were also escaping the Voortrekkers and the British occupation of Thaba Bosigo, a natural fortress. Moshoeshoe's people were further threatened by settler encroachment and ongoing skirmishes with other indigenous groups. Moshoeshoe sought protection from the British Crown and his country became the British Protectorate of Basotholand in 1868 and a British Crown Colony in 1884 (Dieterlen et al. 1912: 465). At the time there were at least ten mission stations in the region – its main contact with Europeans – which Moshoeshoe had welcomed. They provided an important observer body and a protective buffer against marauders, including the Voortrekkers. From 1868 traders had gravitated to Lesotho and were made welcome. The brightly coloured woollen blankets they sold to the *baSotho* reflect an early change in Sotho dress. I have heard it said that a Mr Howell first introduced blankets (rough, light-blue variants) to the newly formed nation and he may well have been among those who first presented blueprint to Moshoeshoe I.

Herman Dieterlen (1912: 468), a missionary to the *baSotho*, termed the hide clothing peculiar to Sotho dress 'picturesque', adding that it was supplanted by garments subscribing to Western tenets of decency, comfort, sanitation and health.[1] According to Mabokang Pheto-Moeti (2005: 1), Sotho women previously wore a knee-length skirt known as a *thetana ea tsikitlane*. The skirt was made from strands of the *tsikitlane* plant and was worn by prepubescent girls.[2] Mature women would also wear an oxhide kaross, or cloak, known as a *mose oa khomo*. In the cold winter climate and summer heat, this item was essential. It also proclaimed a woman's nubility, marriage and maturity. Justinus Sechefo (n.d.) notes that women's dress also included a *morepo*, an outer garment traditionally worn during the day. It was once made from hide, but has been replaced by the Sotho blanket, which is currently worn by men and women. Pheto-Moeti notes that the *mose* (oxhide kaross) is today often interpreted in imitation leather and is used at cultural festivals. Besides the imitation *mose* variant, Pheto-Moeti adds, the concept of the mature woman's covering embodied in the *mose* has been replaced by *isishweshwe* as a signifier of decorum and cultural identity (Pheto-Moeti 2005: 2). In addition, *isishweshwe* as traditional dress is used during established festivals, on royal occasions, at weddings and at international events.

There are several reasons for the decline of hide items among the *baSotho* in the late nineteenth and early twentieth century. This change in dress, brought about over some 60 years, rendered the use of hide items rare by 1912 (Dieterlen et al. 1912: 468). On the one hand, preference for European-derived cloth and blankets was precipitated by need, Basotholand having experienced a drastic loss of cattle after a severe drought and an outbreak of rinderpest in 1897

(Dieterlen et al. 1912: 466). Cattle numbers were gradually restored after the Second Anglo-Boer War (1899–1902), but by this stage European blankets and other items were widely available. Dieterlen states that the *baSotho* found European blankets and cloth more comfortable (1912: 468). The decline in hide production was also due to the cost of producing hide clothing, which exceeded that of imported equivalents (Eldredge 2002: 95). The loss of expertise in hide preparation and garment-making – the domain of men – was also affected by the imposition of tax on all males from the age of twenty (Dieterlen et al. 1912). By the late nineteenth century, this burden had driven most young males to the gold and diamond mines in search of employment to pay their tax. In addition, work on the mines enabled them to afford bride price, which included the woman's clothing and that of her female entourage. The total cost, paid in cloth and blankets, 'was at least 400 francs' – a large sum, even in 1912 (Dieterlen et al. 1912: 468).

Lesotho was a major source of labour for the diamond fields in Kimberley from the 1870s onwards. *baSotho* males were among the earliest to be drawn into a migrant-labour economy by the 1880s, which enabled them to obtain trade goods exceeding their neighbours' acquisitions. In forging nationhood, Moshoeshoe I was at pains to retain his *baKoena* background, language and customs. He ensured that close kinsmen were appointed as governors of territorial areas with different

Left: Young girls from Morija in Lesotho. Morija Museum and Archives, Lesotho.

Right: Mantsaba or Mantsebo (right), later to become a great chieftainess in Lesotho. Morija Museum and Archives, Lesotho.

Cultural Usage of *isiShweshwe* in Lesotho and Swaziland

dialects and customs. Oral tradition has it that in 1835 or later, however, he was given several blankets and metres of cloth for his entourage by the Paris Evangelical Missionary Society, which he had invited to stay in 1833 (Gill 1993: 75). Many of these missionaries were from French-speaking Switzerland and the cloth may have come from that region, which has a long tradition of blueprint production and usage. In addition, the cloth might have been sourced in French blueprint, which

Top: Sotho women grinding maize, late nineteenth century. H. Dieterlen et al. *Livre d'Or de la Mission du Lessouto: Soixante-quinze Ans de l'Histoire d'une Tribu Sud-Africaine, 1833–1908.* Paris: Maison des Missions Évangéliques, 1912.

Bottom: Sotho children on their way to church, 1900s. Morija Museum and Archives, Lesotho.

was widely known, although German and Dutch blueprint were also marketed in France. By the late nineteenth century children and matrons in Lesotho wore blueprint and blankets, as shown in images from the Morija Museum and Archives. German-derived *Blaudruck*, moreover, was widely available in South Africa at the time, as noted in Chapter 2, and was used by Africans and Boer women in particular.

To date only one source confirms French exports of indigo cloth to South Africa (Whitham 1903), which may have included trade cloth and blueprint. But S.W. Whitham also mentions blueprint imports to South Africa emanating from Belgium. Significantly, the French were one of the main European markets for *indiennes*, the printed or painted European cottons that were widely imported and used at the Cape. It has also been established that indigo cloth with white-printed, resist or discharge designs had long been known in France, especially in Provence, Marseilles and regions close to the Pyrenees. Thus the cloth presented to Moshoeshoe I could have been French, Belgian, German or Swiss blueprint. The Paris Evangelical Missionary Society missions also received bales of second-hand clothing from Europe, thus setting important precedents for styles emulated by African seamstresses in Basotholand (Dieterlen et al. 1912: 468).

Writing of Lesotho, however, Dieterlen (1912: 468) notes: 'The cotton covering, the *indienne* skirt, was imposed on women, yet this dress form was agreeable to wear and suited their natural coquetry.'[3] The reference to *indiennes* or Indian-derived cloth provides possible confirmation of the perceived origin of the cloth donated to Moshoeshoe I – in 1912 or before – and earlier variants may have been *indiennes* marketed by traders to the interior of Lesotho from the nineteenth century. Dieterlen may also have been referring to calico prints traded by Muslim pedlars.

In a letter (1998) to Mrs Lineo Lethompa, Stephen Gill, director of the Morija Museum and Archives in Lesotho, points out that the earliest prints that entered Lesotho from the Cape may have been Indian calico (in Pheto-Moeti 2005). These calicoes were paste-prints of simple designs in one or more colours on plain cotton weave. Gill notes further that the *jupe indienne* – Indian skirt – was a calico skirt or *calicot*, but incorrectly assumes that *indienne* refers to indigo dyestuff and not to the cotton prints called *indiennes*. He adds that in the *Dictionary of South African English* the term *voerschitz* (cheap cotton or chintz lining) is explained as 'sis [from chintz], kaffir print and Duitse sis'. He thus concludes that calico entered Lesotho from the early nineteenth century as one of many trade cloths, which included chintz, and that it was sold in lengths of 4–5 metres.

As many *baSotho* worked in the Free State and Gauteng, they also conveyed their identity in these regions, asserting their preferences and differences, their distinctiveness and nationhood. Farmers in towns adjacent to Lesotho have long provided bolts of blueprint to their farmworkers as a Christmas gift.[4] This initially sustained the *baSotho*'s covering in Western- or Eastern-sourced cloth and contributed to the development of workwear made of *isishweshwe*. A picture shows a young Else Schreiner and her caregiver Liesa on the farm Hammonia near Ficksburg. Liesa wears an ankle-length skirt with large *liteke* (tucks) near the hem, emulating Victorian preferences. Significantly, the full length of the skirt is still copied by dance troupes in Lesotho. I saw them in 2005, 2008 and 2010 and the length of their skirts, in keeping with Dieterlen et al.'s observations in 1912, was similar to the leather *mose oa khomo* worn by former traditionalists.

Dieterlen (1912: 468) remarks that the making of clothing shifted from being a male occupation to a female one when all young girls in church schools learnt to use a sewing needle. The making of clothing by women, the choice of fabric and acquired sewing skills, meant that Sotho women came to control and develop the clothing they wore. This marked a creative and economic shift, which not only saw women making their own clothes, but also sewing for others and for trading stores. Fleur Rourke provided an account of the seamstresses who worked in her stores, as noted in Chapter 8.[5]

A young Else Schreiner (right), her brother (left) and their caregiver Liesa on the farm Hammonia near Ficksburg, Orange Free State, c.1925. Else Schreiner collection, Pietermaritzburg.

Over the years, Sotho seamstresses, who design and make among the best-sewn *isishweshwe* dresses and garments in southern Africa, have been widely acknowledged. Full dresses sell today for R1 500 or more – as noted from 2005 to 2015 – and their creators contribute substantially to their own livelihoods. For the last two decades at least, and perhaps for much longer, Sotho seamstresses have exported their ready-made dresses as far afield as Gauteng and Swaziland. Several dressmakers in Maseru are widely supported for their exceptional skills. On several visits to Swaziland, for example, I saw Lesotho-made *isishweshwe* dresses for sale in the central market.

The entry into a European-based economy had significant repercussions for the *baSotho*. The purchase of clothing by the Sotho male came to betoken his economic capacity and authority and his control over the propriety he found desirable for his wife. This included the purchase of *isishweshwe* cloth as well as ready-made dresses in this cloth, sourced both in Lesotho as well as further afield.

Several trading concerns in Lesotho have contributed substantially to the promotion and availability of *isishweshwe*. One of the earliest established traders was Frasers, but many of their stores were bought out by local government concerns. Several smaller traders also sustained and contributed to the distinctiveness of Lesotho *isishweshwe* usage and to particular designs in relation to the mountain kingdom. Gill (1993: 44–5) suggests that preferred designs among the *baSotho*

> are generally called *litema,* a word derived from *ho lema*, meaning to cultivate. *Litema* can resemble furrows made in the earth when planting. They were found on the inner walls of houses (and later on the exterior as well) and on pottery, which was also made by women. Later still, such designs were used in beadwork, and then transferred to 'Basotho' blankets and women's braided hairstyles.

The circle as a preferred design represents 'life, the cycle of the seasons, wholeness, fertility and the community . . . set within the circle is movement, not usually in the form of an unbroken straight line, but rather in the zigzag line (like the *isage* pattern on *isishweshwe*) which symbolises the polarities or oppositional features of life' (Gill 1993: 44-5). It is suggested, therefore, that certain motifs and designs that are reflected in Sotho material culture (beadwork, blankets and hairstyles) are also reflected in *isishweshwe* preferences.

Initially the wearing of *isishweshwe* in Lesotho was associated with missions, with obtaining a Western education and with conversion to Christianity. Conversion was the salient marker of a shift in cultural practice and many *baSotho* were Christianised by the early twentieth century. The donning of Western clothing or cloth, however, may have signified more than a religious shift for women. Men, for their part, wore the rudiments of Western dress in trousers, shirts and jackets.

Pheto-Moeti (2005) identifies several reasons for the retention and proliferation of *isishweshwe* in Lesotho. Gill provided her with valuable information from three elderly male informants: A.B. Thoahlane, L. Moteetee and B.N. Motsetsela. They note that one of the early versions of the Christian-associated covering in which *isishweshwe* was used is the *terantala*, a voluminous skirt gathered at the waist with elastic (in Pheto-Moeti 2005: 39). Recent forms of this dress, identified from 2005 to 2014, show young girls wearing a white shirt as well. Pheto-Moeti suggests that the name of the skirt may be sourced in the Afrikaans word *tarentaal* (*khaka* or *dikhaka* in *seSotho*), with reference to the guineafowl's white spots on grey-blue feathers. For Gill, however, the word *terantala* derives from *traan* (meaning style or manner) and *taal* (language). But he was corrected by another of his informants, Mamongoli Pitso, who confirmed the association with the guineafowl's spots. Most of the troupes seen wearing this skirt at recent festivals in Maseru and Morija have

baSotho attending the cultural festival associated with the 11 March birthday celebrations in commemoration of King Moshoeshoe I in Maseru, Lesotho, 2005. Photograph © Kirsten Nieser.

worn dot-patterned *isishweshwe* or very minute-patterned variants. They perform a slow, shoulder-and-arm gesticulating dance that commences in a squatting position on the ground as the dancer rhythmically raises and lowers her torso and increases the pace. The dance, too, is termed *terantala*.

This dance was enculturated by its association with marriage, a defining rite of passage in a young woman's life. Upon reaching nubility, the Sotho woman was expected to acquire knowledge about her role as wife and mother in various rituals. As among the Nguni peoples, who subscribe to an appropriate system of female and male behaviour associated with *ukuhlonipha*, or showing respect, the Sotho woman also learns about appropriate behaviour, which includes respect and even subservience to her male counterparts.

The wearing of *isishweshwe* has also come to be seen as a manifestation of national dress in Lesotho. This applies to women and children and more recently to men as well. A more widespread association of the term *isishweshwe* with Moshoeshoe I indicates an early pan-Africanism, in which regional and ethnic divisions are blurred to shape and encompass an overarching southern African identity and distinctiveness. Motsetsela, one of Gill's informants, maintained that *isishweshwe* first became associated with national dress in the 1950s following a meeting of the Homemakers' Association at the Morija Training College in Thabeng (in Pheto-Moeti 2005: 39). A large contingent of teachers from the Transkei were invited to the gathering. They were resplendent in their 'national dress' – terracotta-red and ochre sheeting – and 'provoked the Basotho by asking why they had no national outfit'. Thoahlane confirmed that the term *seshoeshoe* coincided with a revival of 'nationalist sentiment' in the 1950s. After ongoing deliberations, Motsetsela claimed that the *terantala* garment, although widely regarded as 'old-fashioned' by the younger generation, was adopted to 'fill the cultural dress vacuum'. This skirt was later replaced by full-dress *isishweshwe*.

As noted earlier, the term *isishoeshoe* (*isishweshwe*) appears to have emerged in the 1950s, coincident with the fact that the *baSotho* are called *Bashoeshoe*, after their founder, Moshoeshoe I (Pheto-Moeti 2005: 39). Today, the *baSotho* inhabit two regions, the one being Gauteng and Limpopo and the other the independent mountain kingdom of Lesotho itself. They are accordingly distinguished as the 'Transvaal Basotho' and the 'Moshoeshoe Basotho' (Rosenthal 1967: 45).

Most of Pheto-Moeti's informants regarded the terms *terantala* and *seshoeshoe* as the same thing (Pheto-Moeti 2005: 49). This information from Motsetsela is significant in that, on the one hand, it acknowledges a long-standing tradition in the *terantala* skirt and, on the other hand, links the renewed emphasis on *isishweshwe* dress conventions with emergent nationalism both in Lesotho and the Transkei. In the 1950s renewed attempts were made in the Transkei to gain a degree of independence from South Africa, resulting in the adoption of the Transkeian Territorial Authority in 1957, followed by self-government in 1963 to 1964. The region was dominated by four paramount chiefs, a Legislative Assembly, territorial franchise and other independent authorities. The construction of a 'Transkeian identity', represented by Xhosa cultural symbols, was cultivated by the introduction of national and regional signifiers, such as the flag, a national anthem and *isiXhosa* as an official language, with *seSotho* for some official occasions (Rosenthal 1967: 565).

The Transkei government, via the Xhosa Development Corporation (XDC), encouraged the foregrounding of Xhosa and Thembu dress in XDC-sponsored workshops and co-operatives. For a time the dress form extended into popular ethnic dress among a range of black and white South Africans as representing both a regional and national dress form. The fact that Xhosa women prompted the consolidating of Sotho national dress is significant in that several informants have suggested that German settlers and missionaries inspired the use of cloth and *isishweshwe* among Transkeian women. As Lesotho borders on the Transkei for several hundred kilometres and has harboured and incorporated *isiXhosa*-

Cultural Usage of *isiShweshwe* in Lesotho and Swaziland

speakers since the nineteenth century – they settled in areas on the southern and western borders of Lesotho – it is not surprising that this link was fostered in Transkeian aspirations for autonomy from colonial systems of governance. Even today, dance troupes in Xhosa dress can be identified at the Morija Cultural Festival, celebrating the long-standing presence of *isiXhosa* speakers in Lesotho.

The 1950s saw increasing political pressure in what was then Basotholand for greater independence from Britain. This was realised in 1966 when Lesotho became an independent kingdom, with its own flag, and a part of the Commonwealth. The movement to independence grew from a revival of nationalist sentiment, according to Gill, 'elevating certain objects of popular culture like the Basotho hat (*mokorotlo*), blanket and *terantala*, to the status of national dress by which Basotho should be distinguished by others and from others' (in Pheto-Moeti 2005: 39).

Gill's informants also foreground support by the state for *isishweshwe* dress, educational and cultural bodies and the church in Lesotho. Dress designs and selection in the 1950s were made by teachers and concerned women. They issued a challenge to consider ethnicity and distinctiveness.

In urban and rural Lesotho the wearing of *isishweshwe* abounds and garments are made predominantly from the Da Gama version of the cloth. Besides this

Pupils in Lesotho, late nineteenth century. Morija Museum and Archives, Lesotho.

baSotho attending the 11 March birthday celebrations in commemoration of King Moshoeshoe I in Maseru, Lesotho, 2005. Photographs © J. Leeb-du Toit.

Cultural Usage of *isiShweshwe* in Lesotho and Swaziland

Above and right: Sotho women attending the Princess Diana competition in Maseru, Lesotho, 2005. Photographs © J. Leeb-du Toit.

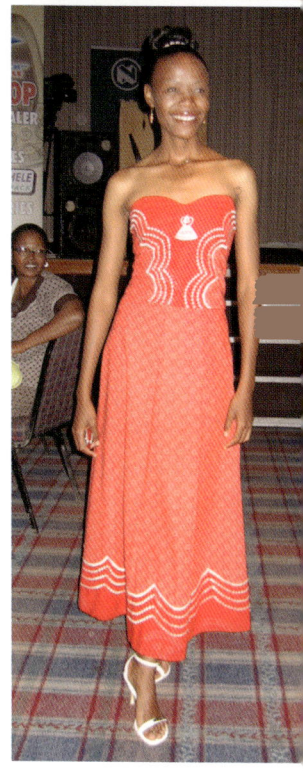

usage, the distinctiveness of *isishweshwe* became particularly apparent when I first attended the celebration of King Moshoeshoe I's birthday in Maseru on 11 March 2005. Most women and several men at the gathering wore *isishweshwe*, as did dignitaries from the government and a few foreign ambassadors. In particular, Queen Masenate Mohato Bereng Seeiso, wife of King Letsie III, wore an exceptionally well-made *isishweshwe* dress and headscarf, both in keeping with the dress conventions widely observed in Lesotho at the time.

Later in the day, at a competitive cultural gathering at a local hotel, attended by at least 400 guests, about 30 women paraded in *isishweshwe* dresses and Sotho blankets, competing for the position of 'the ideal Basotho woman'. This display had been arranged by Princess Diana Dressmakers. The founder of the venture, the dressmaker to King Letsie III's late mother, remarked how her patroness had been at pains to foster a sewing industry and to retain *isishweshwe* in terms of Sotho womanly ideals and cultural encoding. This sanctioning of *isishweshwe* by the royal family, and especially by the king's mother, contributes to the role and meaning attached to the wearing of *isishweshwe*. In several rounds of display that included posturing and strutting the catwalk to rhythmical music and ululation by the audience, the competitors at the 2005 competition appeared. They wore *isishweshwe* dresses and the de rigeur Sotho blanket pinned at the front, with the red fault line aligned. Then they removed the blankets to reveal the dresses alone. The association between *isishweshwe* and being an ideal Sotho woman is integrated in the wearer of the dress. The women were judged on their outfits, but primarily on their posture and mediation of ideal Sotho womanhood. This was conveyed in a conversation I had in 2008 with a Lesotho radio personality, who indicated that women should be conservatively dressed in high necklines, long sleeves and hems below the knee. He was unsure whether the new 'slim bodies' accepted into the competition were desirable. To him a woman wearing *isishweshwe* must ideally have a full figure, reflecting her husband's ability to provide for her. He added that women were regarded as decorous when wearing *isishweshwe*: they defined themselves as *baSotho* and promoted the cloth in Lesotho. He confirmed a tendency reflected in the views of many male informants – that wearing *isishweshwe* conveyed respect and was culturally symbolic.

The Sotho queen wears a newly designed dress to the official ceremony at the statue of Moshoeshoe I in Maseru each year on 11 March. In 2011 she donned a garment different from those worn to celebrations such as the Princess Diana competition in 2005. The queen selects an *isishweshwe* design of her own choice, drawn from a new or prevailing Da Gama range for the year. In 2005 she wore an *isage* (saw) design in blue and white and in 2004 the red print known as *libete* (rice or shield). The fabric she chooses in a particular year usually becomes the main cloth preference for that year. Traders make sure that they stock large amounts of this cloth. In her opening address at the evening award ceremony in 2005, the queen delivered a speech in which she announced her admiration for the tradition of wearing *isishweshwe*. She encouraged designers and seamstresses and invited more males to wear the cloth. She extolled the female wearers as 'cultural icons' who embodied the ideals of womanhood, motherhood and Sotho cultural identity.

Virtually the entire audience at the Princess Diana competition in 2005 wore *isishweshwe* in a range of inventive designs. All the dresses, however, were sourced in traditional prototypes – gigot sleeves, *liteke*, an apron or *foskoti* (*voorskoot*), a hemline below the knee and an inverse Da Gama logo, such as Three Cats, as embellishment at the neck, pockets and sleeves. Many aspects of these dress

Top: Queen Masenate Mohato Bereng Seeiso of Lesotho at the Morija Cultural Festival, Lesotho, August 2011. Photograph © J. Leeb-du Toit.

Bottom: The Queen at the Princess Diana competition, Maseru, Lesotho, 2005. Photograph © J. Leeb-du Toit.

Cultural Usage of *isiShweshwe* in Lesotho and Swaziland

Top: Sotho woman, near QwaQwa, 2015. Photograph © J. Leeb-du Toit.

Bottom left: Sotho woman in patchwork *seshoeshoe* skirt, Maseru, Lesotho, 2011. Photograph © Kirsten Nieser.

Bottom right: *baSotho* man at the 11 March birthday celebration in commemoration of King Moshoeshoe I in Maseru, Lesotho, 2005. Photograph © Kirsten Nieser.

preferences have prevailed among Sotho women for decades. The widely used *liteke*, for example, like the overall demureness and amplitude of design, remain located in an early Victorian source. This includes the mutton-gigot sleeve with its gathered top and ample size. The full dress is known in Lesotho as *seshoeshoe* and the pinafore and under-dress are the *mohlolohadi*. Some informants indicate that this represents the dress of a widow.[6]

After the 2005 official celebrations, we were invited to a competitive cultural festival on a nearby sportsfield just outside Maseru's city centre. Teachers and vast numbers of children from schools throughout Lesotho formed dance troupes and executed traditional dances competitively. Some of the boys and girls wore hide and grass garments, but most of the girl troupes wore *isishweshwe*. The event was sponsored by local and regional businesses. From 2010, it appears, a similar event – the Morija Cultural Festival – has been held in September each year. At the 2005 Maseru cultural competition, I first noted the use of ankle-length, gathered *isishweshwe* skirts for some female troupes that danced the *terantala*. Wearing white shirts and sheep-wool crowns, they danced the gesticulating movements associated with nubility and respect.

In addition, several dances were associated with the harvest. They featured performers in full *isishweshwe* dress, but not in the dress of the *makoti* or older woman. The female teachers who had trained the pupils in the cultural dances wore intricately decorated *isishweshwe* garments in the latest fashions and designs. Teachers interviewed over the last decade indicate that they are intent on preserving and inculcating the traditional dance associated with Sotho culture. These routines also foster the decorum associated with Sotho women.

My former students from Lesotho, Matsooana Sekokotoana and Thakane Lerotholi, assisted me with research in Lesotho several times, acting as translators and informants. Lerotholi mentioned that *isishweshwe* fabric was cool, durable and suited ample figures.[7] As young Sotho women, the two students elected to wear *isishweshwe* on several occasions of cultural importance, including university functions when in KwaZulu-Natal, and regarded the fabric as central to their culture. They also noted that the cloth was often provided by a future bride's in-laws, denoting the decorum and respect required in her new domestic role.[8] Thus *isishweshwe* further demonstrates the terms of the new bride's acceptance into her husband's clan. Pheto-Moeti (2005: 63, 66) confirms this practice, noting that the donning of *isishweshwe* still represents 'the change from one status to another'. She also notes that it betokens the acceptance of the bride and her marriage by her spouse's family and emphasises the 'culture of the bridegroom' (Pheto-Moeti 2005: 64), especially in instances when there is an intercultural marriage. Pheto-Moeti's informants concurred that in this context the dress should be traditional and modest. Her informants added that when wearing an *isishweshwe* dress, women saw themselves as 'more noticeable, well-dressed, comfortable, confident, attractive . . . unique, respected, presentable . . . they feel proud and perfect'.

Sotho women have devised names for a number of *isishweshwe* designs over the years. Many of these designs have been discontinued and their names are lost or forgotten. The naming of *isishweshwe* designs reflects a further degree of indigenisation. *seSotho* speakers are the main group who developed a substantial vernacular for *isishweshwe* designs. Their naming identifies a collective association with the designs and with their cultural significance. In Phuthaditjhaba, the capital of the former QuaQua homeland, for example, female *seSotho* speakers at the craft development centre called the *impangele* or guineafowl-spot design *dikgaka* and the wave-like motif *diphororo* (rippling river). They called the small lozenge-design *thebe* (shield) and the circular motif with floral insert (sourced in China and Japan) *lehlogkhomo* (eye of the cow).[9] A comprehensive list of names is located in an appendix to this book.

Many *isishweshwe* designs have become associated with Sotho wearers and have been created with them in mind. This means that many designs – such as the Sotho hat, the Sotho rider on a pony and the zigzag design (*maloti* or *moloti*) named after the Maluti Mountains – have developed geographical and cultural associations. As noted earlier, designers at ABC, such as Margaret Hickson, were plied with photographs of Sotho scenes by sales representatives from Da Gama Textiles and often created these culturally specific motifs.

Dress styles have been modified or developed over the years, but well-known idioms remain. According to one informant, the *isishweshwe* dress worn as one of the garments at weddings was known as a *tibiti*.[10] The prevailing tradition of a wraparound skirt (*jikiza*), with a loose apron, is another example, as is the full dress with a mock apron attached, a high neck, *liteke* at the hemline, gigot sleeves and deep pockets. These idioms have more recently been amplified with widespread machine embroidery at the neckline and pockets. The embroidery is in satin stitch or chain stitch, both of which have been available to seamstresses for decades, but have only become prominent since 2000. In 2011 there was an increasing use of new styles, such as a two-piece outfit with mandarin collar and trim and ankle-length dresses combined with imitation shantung or silk trim. Besides the preferred blue, red or brown *isishweshwe*, a wide variety of new colour combinations marketed by Da Gama has been embraced. It includes ochre, red and black; brown and turquoise; turquoise, blue and black; and the blue, black and ochre of Fancy Prints.

Some Sotho informants agree that recent trends have been influenced by the attire of West Africans, which shows preferences for machine-embroidered detail, and by the widespread development of new idioms in local fashion. On many Maseru-based dressmakers' walls I saw designs, taken from popular South African media, by Bongiwe Walaza, Amanda Laird-Cherry, Stoned Cherrie and many others. There is a considerable amount of cross-cultural borrowing in these styles. The multiple black-braid trim, for example, typical of Xhosa and Thembu wraparound skirts, is used in many *isishweshwe* variants.

The headwear of *isishweshwe* users in Lesotho from 2005 to 2013 included a Sotho hat or simple headscarf. More recently, headscarves have assumed a conical shape with the tied ends protruding at the sides and back, as seen in images of Queen Masenate. Her two-piece outfit on this occasion was typical of a Western-style garment widely used in Lesotho and South Africa.

Pheto-Moeti (2005: 61) includes valuable statistics in her research. Most of her Christian, urban-based informants concurred that the wearing of *isishweshwe* was no longer associated mainly with mature married women. Many younger women, as well as children and men, were opting to wear the cloth. Most of her informants were opposed to wearing *isishweshwe* as mourning attire and preferred black. One informant noted that they avoided *isishweshwe* when in mourning for fear that its use might make the youth disdainful. In addition, many informants were displeased with new idioms, with fake variants of *isishweshwe* and with the undignified dress of some users who exposed parts of the body and wore seductive skirts (Pheto-Moeti 2005: 50). The use of *isishweshwe* was widely regarded as signifying Sotho national identity and, in particular, as distinguishing Sotho women (Pheto-Moeti 2005: 52).

Most Sotho women know at least a few *isishweshwe* design names. Dressmakers interviewed over the years have become better informed of these names. *isiXhosa* speakers seldom name or know prevailing terms for *isishweshwe*, but many *isiZulu* speakers have an idiom for a few cloth designs. Pheto-Moeti asked informants whether they were familiar with the symbolism behind *isishweshwe* designs. More than half said they were, but she did not test the question in her research (Pheto-Moeti 2005: 53). Most names derive from literal, visual

Mosala Design dressmaker, Maseru, 2008.
Photograph © Kirsten Nieser.

associations with the design motif. A.M. Zaverdinos (1997) notes that the *baSotho* have a long-standing tradition of clan totems, however, and some of their animal motifs – the crocodile, the gazelle, the lion and the rooster – may be reinforced by that association.

The wearer of *isishweshwe* in Lesotho has very specific demands regarding design and fabric usage and wholesalers such as Neil Cowie are careful to meet these demands. In 2010 I visited a trading store known as Gateway Fabrics at Maputsoe on the Lesotho side of the Ficksburg border. With the help of Ismail and Arif Osman and their staff, I obtained the names of most designs held in the store.[11] The list has been amplified over the years by contributors such as Pretoria Textile Wholesalers, Dadabhay's in Johannesburg, Fabric Splendour in Pietermaritzburg, Fayco in Durban and many others.

Many dressmakers of *isishweshwe* in Lesotho indicate that they have been in business for at least a decade or more and describe themselves as self-taught. They purchase *isishweshwe* either in Lesotho, or preferably in South Africa, claiming they find more variety at a cheaper cost in the South African shops. They travel widely to trading outlets in Ficksburg, Matatiele and Johannesburg, Pretoria, Ladysmith, Pietermaritzburg and Durban in search of variety. Most dressmakers continue to produce desirable traditional styles, but are always prepared to devise new styles based on customer preferences. This means that new *isishweshwe* styles are dynamic, but preserve the traditional ideals of modesty. However, there is also a burgeoning demand for 'modern attire' in which *isishweshwe* is used in a range of modern clothing designs that range from strapless gowns to elegant dresses with a combination of other fabric types. Pheto-Moeti (2005: 84) indicates that respondents refer to any *isishweshwe* dress without tucks simply as a *seshoeshoe* dress, while my informants indicated that such dresses were simply regarded as modern.

❖ ❖ ❖

The wearing of *isishweshwe* with cultural and regional associations is also found among the *baSwazi*. These Nguni people reside in the kingdom of Swaziland, a former British protectorate nestled in north-eastern South Africa. They originated in a migrant people who lived in southern Tongaland where they amalgamated under Mswazi in the sixteenth century (Rosenthal 1967: 547; Kuper 1986) and then settled near Bremersdorp. To protect his group from increasing Zulu militancy and encroachment from the south, the Swazi leader Sobhuza I sought protection from Queen Victoria. Swaziland thus became a British protectorate upon the intervention of Sir Theophilus Shepstone.

Early twentieth-century Swazi male wearing a *sidvwashi*. Prince Tshekedi Dlamini collection, Mbabane.

As a result of Swaziland's proximity to northern Zululand, many Swazi customs reflect those of their Nguni neighbours. After the Second Anglo-Boer War (1899–1902), Swaziland became a high commission territory. It was supplied by traders en route to or from Delagoa Bay, many of whom settled in Swaziland from the nineteenth century onwards. Thus trader holdings there resemble those in northern Zululand and KwaZulu-Natal.

Distinctive dress emerged among Swazi men and women in the form of a cotton wrap. The use by Mozambicans of a similar wrap, popularly termed a kanga, might have been a precedent for this wear. So too with the *ibhaye*, worn over the shoulders as a sign of respect among *isiZulu* speakers. This is still used by traditionalist rural women in KwaZulu-Natal and is often made from the more diaphanous plain dark-blue or black *salempore*. Images of Swazi males wearing printed cotton cloth from waist to knee, wraps and shoulder shawls, have been located from the early twentieth century. This cloth is multicoloured and is distinguished by large geometric or floral patterns. The cloth used after the 1930s has smaller designs. It was not *isishweshwe*, but was doubtless a precursor.

The development of a distinctive dress code, a shoulder and lower torso wrap, among Swazi males has accrued over the last 100 years, but the use of *isishweshwe* for the lower wrap seems to have emerged in the 1950s. Swazi women wear *isishweshwe*, the indigo and brown variants in particular, and use the red, black and white shoulder covering, the *umhelwane*. They know the term *isishweshwe* for the Da Gama-derived cloth (or fake variants) as do their Nguni counterparts in KwaZulu-Natal. Swazi men, however, have chosen to use specific variants and colours of *isishweshwe* to uphold their cultural distinctiveness and don these items on personal or official occasions. The Swazi traditionalist male wears only authentic Da Gama-produced cotton *isishweshwe* (if possible) for his waist-to-knee wrap (the *sidvwashi*). This is not surprising as the cloth is cool, washes well and hangs well. Some *sidvwashi* cloth in ochre, brown and maroon has been identified among Swazi men. It is not recognised at Da Gama as *isishweshwe*, but Da Gama produces it for the Swazi market and its use is exceptional. Its sourcing in local trading stores as ready-made wraps has been identified in Mbabane and other parts of rural Swaziland.

Cultural Usage of *isiShweshwe* in Lesotho and Swaziland

Swazi men of the king's regiment, the *amabutho*, at King Mswati III's birthday celebrations in Manzini, Swaziland, 2005. Photographs © J. Leeb-du Toit.

By the late 1960s Swazi males increasingly wore *isishweshwe* cloth as their *sidvwashi* and it became a sign of their cultural identity and affiliation with the monarchy and traditionalism. Nel (1983: 12) observed that such dress first occurred particularly among males between the ages of 17 and 27. The young Swazi male was now entitled to begin courting and took special pride in his dress. He was a *lijaha* or *libungu* and, when he was a mature married man, would become an *indvodza*. Nel adds that the pubescent female between the ages of fifteen and seventeen – the *lichikiza* (at times spelt *lidjikiza*) – gradually assumed the reponsibilities of womanhood and took increasing pride in her dress. She was allowed to wear cloth over the shoulders – *emahiya* – and the lower torso wrap also known as a *sidvwashi* (Nel 1983: 14, 25). Nel points out that the cloth was imported from Japan, Holland and Germany, adding that the Oriental manufacturers sent designers to assess preferences in colour and taste (1983: 25–6). It is not certain where Nel derived this information from, as no sources are cited. Red, orange and maroon with white and black motifs were perceived as 'traditional' Swazi colours at the time of his writing.

Primarily, it is adult males who wear *isishweshwe*, as a wraparound from the waist to below the knees (*sidvwashi*). Worn after puberty, the *sidvwashi* is accompanied by a second cloth over the shoulders, *umhelwane*. The latter is in red, white and black. Nel (1983: 28) adds that the *sidvwashi* was also called *sijalimane*. The name recalls terms for *isishweshwe* used by other groups, such as *isijalmani* and *ujeremani* – names that reinforce the cloth's German associations – and is similar to the *isiZulu* terminology for the cloth, *ijeremani* or *ijalmani*. Nel observes that mature men can wear up to eight *sidvwashi* at a time, especially on ceremonial occasions, but after puberty as a rule they wear only two. When attending King Mswati III's birthday celebrations in 2005, none of the *amabutho* (the members of the adult male regiment who protect and uphold the king's authority) at the ceremonies wore more than one or two *sidvwashi*. This might be a result of the increasing cost of Da Gama *isishweshwe* – or it could merely reflect current preferences.

Swazi males, as the main wearers of the *isishweshwe sidvwashi*, rarely don blue and white *isishweshwe*. In 2005 I noted only one exception. The coloured variants, predominantly in maroon or deep red, black and white, brown and white or brown and ochre, persist today. When a combination of two or three variants is worn, one over the other, it is allegedly to 'prevent transparency'.[12] The cloth is also worn by the *amabutho*. They also dress to honour the authority of the king's mother, the custodian of rain-making, who occupies a prominent role in government. According to Prince Tshekedi Dlamini, the multilayered *sidvwashi* 'must have skin' as an accompaniment and a skin sporran known as *ijobo* or *injobo* is worn in front of the *sidvwashi* wearers' groin area. It was originally of leopard skin, but has been replaced by duiker, reedbuck or even baboon or monkey skin (*ingobiyane*) (Nel 1983: 29). The entire pelt is fashioned into this *ijobo* or sporran, with a small round tuft or knot projecting. In traditional celebrations, the regiment dances the *umgubho* in slow movements, raising and lowering their legs, shields, axes and sticks, reflecting in song and gesture their sacred role as the king's protectors. Formerly, only the Swazi male who had been trained in the royal barracks was entitled to wear beads known as the *simohlwane* (Nel 1983: 38).[13] However, my informants were unsure if this is still enforced today. In the 1960s the use of a large pink bead was still exclusive to the *amabutho* (Tyrrell 1968: 137). In addition, men wear a beaded neckpiece, comprising two squares on a string of beads, mostly red, black and yellow on a white ground, although new variants have been identified since 2005. The *amabutho* also take part in the *incwala*, a bucolic rite, which tests their manhood before the king's authority.

Some of the *isishweshwe* worn as the *sidvwashi* differs from that marketed in other regions. According to Neil Cowie, specifically desirable designs and colours are currently identified by Da Gama Textiles as catering exclusively for Swazi usage.[14] Preferences are for spots and variants of round motifs — such as the *lehlogkhomo* (eye of the cow) design — and for small, repeat patterns, stripes and large ochre, white, black and brown paisley shapes. Maroon with black and white circular or floriate patterns is also popular. Some of these designs have acquired specific names, but the consistent use of two types, the floral circular motif (*lehlogkhomo*) and the brown, gold and white snake-like floriate design (*libululu*), seem to have persisted for some time. Prince Tshekedi Dlamini informed us that design preferences had only shifted fairly recently. An example is the lozenge motif in black and white on a red ground known as *injika* or *indutwane*: the ant. This was one of the designs preferred by Swazi males in 2005 and was also worn by the Lesotho queen in 2004.

In 2005 Kirsten Nieser and I met a group of young unmarried men in a fabric shop in central Mbabane. After

Swazi men of the king's regiment, the *amabutho*, at King Mswati III's birthday celebrations in Manzini, Swaziland, 2005. Photograph © J. Leeb-du Toit.

much discussion, having mulled over the *isishweshwe* on offer for the *sidvwashi*, the men settled on a few patterns. One of them informed me that they would be attending a wedding the following weekend and had decided to wear the same cloth combinations for their *sidvwashi* apparel to reinforce the fact that they were from the same region and of the same age grade. They chose two brown *isishweshwe* designs, one to be worn over the other. They stressed that the doublet prevented transparency and reflected their aesthetic preference. Worn for cultural display at weddings and in the official sphere, the *sidvwashi* signifies the wearer's age grade and his national and cultural identity. At the graduation ceremony at the University of KwaZulu-Natal in Pietermaritzburg in 2006, I saw a young graduate from Swaziland who wore his traditional *sidvwashi* and shoulder wrap to proudly proclaim his cultural origins.

Young girls wear similar overlaid cloth as a lower torso wrap, also termed *sidvwashi*, and over this, suspended from the shoulder, the red, white and black *emahiya*, also termed 'Swazi cloth'. The *emahiya* may at times include a portrait of the current monarch, King Mswati III. The same red, white and black *emahiya* is also worn by virgins as a lower or upper torso wrap at the Swazi reed ceremony, the *incwala*, where maidens celebrate their heritage (and until recently their virginity) and their hope to be chosen as the king's new wife or at least to be identified by a suitor. This ceremony was once associated with AIDS prevention in promoting celibacy, especially among the youth, but the association had ceased by 2005.

Mature women in Swaziland wear *isishweshwe* to denote age grade and cultural or ceremonial associations as found throughout South Africa. They refer to their all-in-one dress as an 'attire' and describe the cloth as *isishweshwe*.

Top: *Libululu* design, Da Gama Textiles *isishweshwe* preferred by the Swazi king for *sidvwashi* in 2005. Photograph © J. Leeb-du Toit.

Bottom: Woman selling thatching-grass at the Mbabane market, Swaziland, 2005. Photograph © Kirsten Nieser.

The use of blue, red and brown *isishweshwe* (with white motifs) is widespread, seemingly without specific preferences. The supervisor of the marketers at the municipal market in Manzini wore brown and ochre *isishwshwe*, while the nearby grass-sellers and weavers were dressed in well-worn blue *isishweshwe*.

Garments with innovative designs are locally made and some are imported from Lesotho for sale in Maseru. But there is also a considerable industry in the making of *isishweshwe* dresses in Mbabane and smaller towns in Swaziland. A particular design of a plaited, open-sleeve dress was identified at Melusha's Fashion, headed by Mrs Maimuna Dlamini, but it was made of synthetic *isishweshwe*. Several dressmakers in the region were using fake *isishweshwe* because the cost of the Da Gama variant was beyond their reach. But men almost exclusively wore original Da Gama *isishweshwe*, which is clearly identifiable.

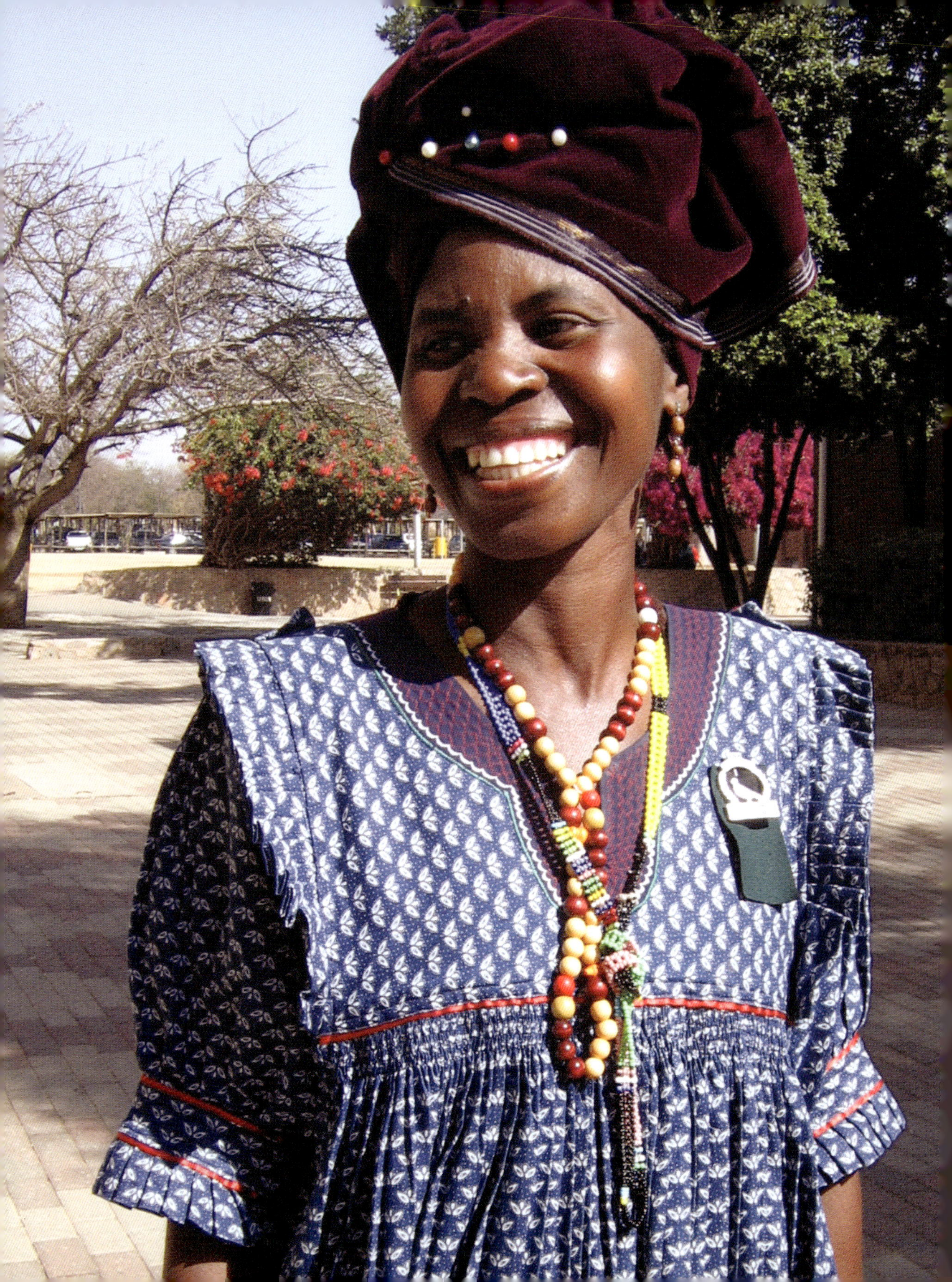

10
Cultural Usage of *isiShweshwe* in South Africa, Botswana and Namibia

In the 1830s complex intercultural events brought about change in Natal and Zululand. The Zulu peoples dominated after internecine conflict and power struggles led to widespread clan dispersal. The Zulu clan rose to power as a formidable military force, many groups with distinct cultural identities were incorporated into their ranks and their authority extended over the territory north of the Tugela River, which the colonial powers called Zululand.

King Dingane of the Zulu Kingdom in his dancing dress and cloak (centre). Frontispiece to A. Gardiner's *Narrative of a Journey to the Zoolu Country in South Africa*, 1836.

Dutch and British traders and adventurers had settled at Port Natal under King Shaka's patronage by 1824. But the impact of settlement was not fully realised until later and was preceded by an influx of missionaries who originated from the United States, Germany, Norway, Sweden and Britain, the area becoming known as the most missionised region in the world. Many references to missionary activity in Natal reiterate the need to clothe mission adherents, a practice that resulted in prescriptive changes to dress. The desire to clothe converts is a process of moral encoding, but was balanced by preferences for cloth, which were not associated with conversion.

It is possible that blueprint was worn by some of the early missionaries in Natal, all of whom hailed from areas where block-printed variants of blueprint were produced and used mainly as workwear. Missionaries not only evangelised the *amaZulu*, but also gave refuge to Zulu outcasts and women who, for various reasons, were disenchanted with the Zulu centre because of broken familial bonds or abuse. These people may have donned their new dress or covering in the hopes of protection, inclusion and with the intention of eventual conversion. I located several images to support these contentions in Lutheran and American Board sources in KwaZulu-Natal. They show that young African women at mission stations wore cotton prints, calico and blueprint. Such images are to be found from Hermannsburg near Greytown to the Inanda Seminary outside Durban. This association between blueprint and missions is also supported by informants' recent recollections. Victoria Francis remembers clearly that in the 1970s blueprint was known as 'mission print' in trading stores in Hillcrest and other outlying areas of Durban.[1]

Mission dress persisted in Natal and was eventually promulgated into law by Lieutenant-Governor Sir Benjamin Chilley Pine in 1854. The legislation applied in particular to the entry of local people into the economy. He decreed that Africans residing in or passing through Pietermaritzburg, Durban or Ladysmith had to be covered. This provoked an acute need for cloth and second-hand clothes, particularly when indigenous people entered the economy as labourers.

Early accounts of the cloth trade in KwaZulu-Natal refer to calico, cottons (which would have included blueprint) and blue *salempore*. Henrietta Robertson notes that a blue-striped cloth was preferred and was in great demand (Robertson 1866: 98; Mitford 1883: 129, 135). Catherine Barter, the sister of a Natal trader whose business she ran while he was ill, provided invaluable information about her stock and about indigenous preferences in the region. When alerted to the fact that a wedding or a feast or dance was approaching, she noted that the local women 'clamoured for blue stuff to make cloaks' (Barter 1866: 88–9). Barter was referring either to *salempore* or plain indigo cloth for shoulder wraps (*ibhaye*). These cloaks, she adds, were 'de rigeur at dances and all occasions

Cultural Usage of *isiShweshwe* in South Africa, Botswana and Namibia   207

of ceremony'. In particular, the cloaks would have been sanctioned by males, who allowed women to barter with traders, reinforcing the significance of indigo cloth as culturally condoned and desirable. Barter's account shows that plain indigo cloth, as used at the Cape and worn by slaves and Khoisan such as Sarah Baartman, functioned as partial covering for women from diverse cultural backgrounds and regional areas.

The significance of various colours in Zulu cosmogony might also have informed the preferences identified by Barter. In her important account of colour in Zulu beadwork preferences, Princess Magogo, the mother of Inkatha leader Mangosuthu Buthelezi, notes that blue is associated with the divine realm (Grossert 1967). This is the realm in which *uNkulunkulu* or *uMvelinqangi* resides. Both these names refer to the divinity – and as the Zulu monarch is divinely appointed and is allied to this realm, wearing blue, whether in cloth or beadwork, reinforces the association. Furthermore, blue is also associated with aspirational concepts of well-being, calm, spirituality and coolness (and related wellness), not only as qualities attached to the divine, but also as desirable attributes associated with womanhood. Although there is speculation about cross-cultural influence in these interpretations of blue, they are ratified by many current users of beadwork and *isishweshwe* in KwaZulu-Natal.

That indigo cloth, and probably blueprint, were favoured by Zulu royalty is indicated by Hildemarie Grünewald (1998: 64). With reference to Ferdinand Krauss's *Travel Journal / Cape to Zululand* (1973), she mentions King Mpande's wives as being privileged to wear 'a particular, strong blue' trade cloth. An early photograph of three of King Dinuzulu's wives shows them wearing print dresses, possibly with blue and white motifs, in the distinctive Victorian style with puffed gigot sleeves, narrow waists and full-length skirts.

Krauss notes that from the nineteenth century, Westphalian cloth production, including linen from Bielefeld – predominantly blueprint – was marketed in Lisbon. From there, Portuguese traders brought it to Mozambique, from where it is said to have reached Zululand (in Grünewald 1998: 64). This significant reference reinforces a later Portuguese role

Dinuzulu's wives. *Ilanga Lase Centenary Supplement*, 7 April 2003, p. 8.

in disseminating German-derived and locally produced *Blaudruck*. As noted in Chapter 8, I located several metres of Portuguese-derived blueprint, said to have been manufactured in Portugal, at the Kala's store, Pretoria Textile Wholesalers. But the fact that German *Blaudruck* was exported from Portugal to southern

Africa is significant as it reinforces the fact that during the nineteenth century trade routes other than the Cape for African-designated goods from continental Europe could only have entered through Delagoa Bay and other parts of East Africa.

The demand for indigo and cotton production worldwide in the early nineteenth century was such that cotton production in Natal was mooted by several entrepreneurs. Attempts were made to cultivate it alongside indigo. One of the central figures in this venture was Jonas Bergtheil, a German from Bavaria who had interests in cotton production for Manchester. He and his associates had already experimented with cotton production on the farm Wandsbeck (now part of the suburb of Westville) outside Durban. Believing cotton to be a viable crop in this humid area, Bergtheil set about attracting 600 German settlers to the region. They later came to be known as the 'Cotton Germans'. The *Natal Mercury* of 16 June 1981 noted that he and his colleagues established the Natal Cotton Company in order to purchase land for the envisioned settlers. As Natal was a Crown Colony, neither Lieutenant-Governor Martin West nor the Colonial Secretary in London favoured official sponsorship of German immigration to Natal. The *Natal Mercury* reported that Bergtheil therefore established a private immigration scheme, which received official British sanction – provided that the immigrants were naturalised, subject to British law and to a host of other regulations. German settlers came to Natal in 1848 and again in 1858. Bergtheil proposed to retain the land offered to them and to appropriate a large share of their cotton production and the right to market it. Initially he aimed to entice his fellow Jewish Bavarians to emigrate, but the local rabbi dissuaded them. Bergtheil's schemes led to his expulsion from Bavaria where he had obtained his first batch of immigrants. He then enticed potential settlers from parts of northern Germany – mainly Bremen and Osnabrück – which were flax-growing and linen-weaving areas. Both groups of settlers were drawn to South Africa by worsening economic conditions in Europe, political unrest in France and growing militarism and unemployment in Germany. Their first three cotton crops in Natal failed and cotton production in the region ceased in the late nineteenth century.

Attempts to grow indigo were also made on the Wandsbeck farm. The crop flourished and two large vats were built to ferment the dye in what is now Paradise Valley near Pinetown. These vats were last used in the nineteenth century and are now national monuments.

The German presence in Natal precipitated trade with Germany and set precedents for German wear, which were reinforced on the many German missions in rural Natal and Zululand. Numerous informants, whose ancestors were among these 'Cotton Germans', recall the use of *Blaudruck* as workwear used by settler women. The German associations of the cloth are further reflected in its indigenous names, which are still used by Zulu women in 2017 (such as *isijalmani* and *ujeremani*), often in preference to the popular name *isishweshwe*.

Most women wearers of blueprint interviewed in KwaZulu-Natal from 1993 to 2016 reinforced the Sotho origin of blueprint, associated with the name Moshoeshoe I – as reflected in the names *isishweshwe* or *seshoeshoe* – and linked its use to marriage or at least betrothal. They also noted that maturity and childbearing were significant rites of passage that enabled them to wear *isishweshwe*. Some stated that they were expected to wear *isishweshwe* at home and especially after marriage. Bolts of the cloth and even ready-made *isishweshwe* garments are usually part of a marriage gift (*umabo*) and are presented to the bride by the groom's family. I noted this rite at a marriage procession in Bulwer in 1996 and at another in Ndwedwe in 2003. In Bulwer a large bolt of *isishweshwe* was carried to the bridegroom's home, together with blankets, grass mats and enamel dishes. In Ndwedwe the bride changed into an *isishweshwe* pinafore at the close of the first day of her marriage celebrations when she was accepted into her husband's family. In this custom *isishweshwe* is associated with desirable respect, nubility, domesticity and maturity. Some women have also identified the cloth with the coming-out ceremony for young women, the *umemula*. Women who attend either a marriage or the *umemula* often elect to wear *isishweshwe*. Informants note that wearing *isishweshwe* is so ingrained in traditional usage and defines them so clearly as *isiZulu* speakers that they express its usage thus: 'It is my culture.'[2] The predominant associations of the cloth, however, remain marriage and maturity, although many young women and men, and even children, wear it today, in keeping with *isishweshwe*'s ascendance into mainstream fashion.

At Zulu weddings today, the bride commonly elects to marry in a Christian church or community hall in a white Western-derived dress. She then returns to her husband's home where she changes into traditional beadwork, *isidwaba* (a pleated leather skirt) and *ischolo* (a conical or fluted removable headpiece) and only then into a dress or pinafore (*isipinifa*) made of *isishweshwe*. In this rite the bride is accepted into the control of her parents-in-law, her husband and his line, where she remains for up to a year in respectful submission. Her wearing of *isishweshwe* dress or at least *isispinifa* in this cloth conveys her submission to *ukuhlonipha* or traditions of respect.[3] These traditions are associated with the bride's subservience and domesticity, her willingness to serve and be accommodating as she adapts to the conventions of her new family. Usually about a year later, the couple move to their own home with an *umabo* and ritual slaughter, bringing the husband's ancestral blessing with them. The attire on this occasion is at times dominated by the wearing of *isishweshwe* by guests as well as by the bride.

Yvonne Winters (2015) notes that wearing *isishweshwe* is also a Christianised variant of domesticity and marriage. Her informant, Sandile Mbanjwa, was a

Below and top right: Ntlangwini women at the home of Nomandla Nodolo near Harding, KwaZulu-Natal, 2008. Photographs © Kirsten Nieser.

Opposite: Zulu woman near KwaDukuza, KwaZulu-Natal, 2016. Photograph © J. Leeb-du Toit.

Catholic who dressed according to the traditional age sets around St Faiths and Highflats and attended church so dressed. But in 1987, when she married an Mkhize *Mbo* from Umlazi township south of Durban, she gave up her traditional dress for an *isishweshwe isipinifa* with a black cashmere headscarf as correct wear for a newly married Catholic.

Among the many African independent churches that have been founded throughout South Africa, KwaZulu-Natal boasts one with a significant history of sustaining traditional dress, namely iBandla lama Nazaretha or Shembe (founded in 1910), named after its founder Isaiah Shembe. Male and female followers commonly wear a version of traditional Zulu dress, but research by Phyllis Zungu at eBuhleni reveals that for many Shembe women *isishweshwe* dress is also a sign of mourning, especially after the death of a spouse, and is typically worn in the rural areas.[4] Recent Shembe informants at ekuPhakameni, another Shembe sacred site, indicated that *isishweshwe* is worn only when a woman's husband has died and not with other deaths in the family.[5] The dress, consisting of an ankle-length garment, fitted shoulder cape and headscarf, is worn for a year. It is washed daily and is said to be the ultimate token of respect (*ukuhlonipha*) for the deceased and his family.

Many minor groups in KwaZulu-Natal, which were previously embraced as part of the extended Zulu nation, have developed distinctive dress. One such group is the *amaNtlangwini* from the Harding area, near Port Shepstone. On several visits there I noted women wearing *isishweshwe* during ceremonies at the home of Nomandla Nodolo, a cultural custodian, historian and museum curator. She confirmed that the wearing of the *isishweshwe isipinifa* was de rigeur among her people. Winters (2015) suggests that wearing *isishweshwe* among the *amaNtlangwini* has become a distinctive 'intermediary code' (a term I used for the cloth as a whole in 1995) in the region. The dress modes are similar to those in other parts of KwaZulu-Natal although the *isipinifa* predominates in Harding.[6]

In the late 1960s *isishweshwe* began again to span cultural divides in KwaZulu-Natal when many white women elected to wear kaftans, skirts, dresses and quilted jackets, all made of *isishweshwe*, in a usage associated with widespread international trends in cross-cultural dressing. Attached to these trends in

Cultural Usage of *isiShweshwe* in South Africa, Botswana and Namibia

South Africa was a resistance to Western hegemony. To some, the wearing of *isishweshwe* was also regarded as partly subversive in a challenge to the taint of apartheid and its draconian segregationist policies. The latter were entrenched in the 1960s when the Bantustans came into being.

In the mid- and late 1980s there was an enormous increase in the marketing of *isishweshwe* in Natal, with a noticeable surge in dressmaking. At the time, this increase in the wearing of the cloth was identified as being associated with immanent political and social change, such dress denoting Africanness and pending independence in a new democratic order.

◆ ◆ ◆

As noted in Chapter 4, Coloured people's usage of *isishweshwe* probably originated in the context of worship. Until 1780 the Reform Church was the only church allowed at the Cape (Newton-King 1999: 6). The widespread occurrence of Coloured communities in South Africa has resulted in diverse cultural practices and dress conventions – many of which have been identified only recently and have long associations with *isishweshwe*. The early Khoisan community at Genadendal was arguably among the first to use *isishweshwe* in this country; the Moravian missions and their outstations in the western and eastern Cape, which embraced followers of mixed race, used *isishweshwe* extensively. In 2005

I visited a 98-year-old woman at Genadendal who claimed that *isishweshwe* was widely used there at least until the late 1960s. Thereafter its association with 'black persons' gradually led to its discontinuation among Coloureds on the mission. Mrs Taljaard also indicated that *isishweshwe* usage, especially by 'older people', continued throughout the 1940s while she still worked in the mission shop at Genadendal. Although Mrs Taljaard did not personally wear the cloth, she shared the other informants' views that *inheemse mense veral dra dit nou* (local people above all wear it now), referring to black South African wearers.[7] Informants concurred that the cloth was linked to Moravian or German usage from earliest times, an association stemming from the Moravian usage of *isishweshwe* as workwear on their missions and in the regions from which they hailed from the eighteenth century onwards.

In the town of Greyton, not far from Genadendal, Ms Blignaut – the daughter of a former white *bywoner* or tenant farmer – indicated in a conversation with me that she wore *isishweshwe* as a young girl, but had discontinued its usage. Blignaut's information, however, confirmed that for a time in the early twentieth century both poor whites (*bywoners*) and Coloureds wore *isishweshwe* concurrently. An image discovered in the Muslim trading store in Greyton (which has since changed hands) was particularly helpful. The photograph showed the current owner's grandfather as a child, *c*.1910, his Coloured caregiver wearing a printed cotton dress. The owner recalled distinctly that the dress was in fact blueprint: cloth they had sold for decades at their store.

When doing research in the Parliamentary Archives in Cape Town, guided by Rayda Becker, former curator of the Parliamentary Collection, I came across an image of Sarah Baartman, the much-exploited Khoisan woman, who in the late nineteenth century was taken to Europe as a living display of Khoisan anatomy, culture and difference. Her only covering, apart from some beads, was a long swathe of plain, deep-blue indigo cloth over her right shoulder, descending to the floor and partly hoisted over one arm. Whether this anonymous image depicts her in the Cape or abroad, it supports Khoisan and earlier slave preferences for indigo cloth. The cloth was in all probability diaphanous *salempore*, but could well have been a heavier indigo-dyed cloth type.

On the advice of Lalou Melzer and Gerald Klinghardt, from the Iziko Museums of South Africa, I accessed the Lucy Lloyd and Wilhelm Bleek photographs of Damara people from 1905. The images were made around Prieska in the north-western Cape. The Damara mostly wore variants of Western clothing, but Lloyd was known to have them wear hide clothing in order to photograph them in their 'authentic' dress. Among the black and white images were excellent examples taken by Lloyd of women wearing cotton prints, the dress style typically Edwardian-Victorian, with some of the sleeves gathered at the shoulder and others somewhat

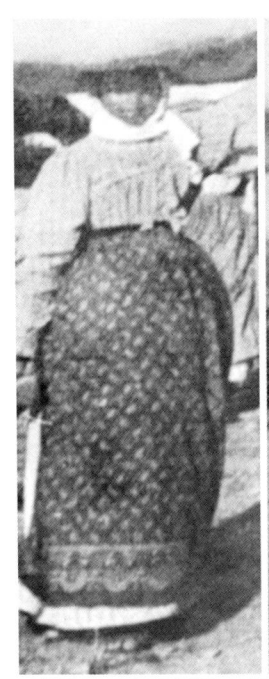

Cultural Usage of *isiShweshwe* in South Africa, Botswana and Namibia 213

Top left: Woman at municipal wash-house, Platteklip, c.1910. © National Archives, Cape Town.

Top right: Woman with digging stick, Prieska, Northern Cape. Iziko Museums of South Africa.

Bottom left: Namaqualand !Xam and Damara, c.1920s. Iziko Museums of South Africa.

Bottom right: Bushmen or Khoisan from Prieska district, c.1910. Photograph by Dorothea Bleek. Iziko Museums of South Africa.

shapeless. All the garments were from neck to ankle, often with a headscarf in printed cloth. These clothes may have been second-hand, but many of them were in fair condition and only some were tattered and threadbare. The cloth and dress suggest that in all likelihood the wearers were converts and were perhaps subject to the preferred attire under mission and state auspices.

Top left:
Bushman family, possibly from Prieska area, c.1950. Katesa Schlosser collection, Kiel.

Top right:
Bushman, possibly from Prieska area, c.1950. Katesa Schlosser collection, Kiel.

Almost 50 years after Lloyd's photographs, the German anthropologist Katesa Schlosser visited Pella and Kimberley. She took a number of colour photographs of Damara women dressed in virtually the same style of garment. With few exceptions, their dresses were clearly of blueprint. In 2009 very few of the women of Garies in Namaqualand wore pinafores, dresses and *kappies* of *isishweshwe*. To them the dress represented a familiar continuity and reinforced a burgeoning tourist market before which they wished to appear in 'authentic wear'. The aged songstress and poet (since deceased), Tante Grietjie, interviewed shortly before her death, referred to a strong German presence in the region. She recalled surnames such as Pachter, Klug, Boiskind and Rosenberg.[8] Many other local white families in the region were of Russian or Lithuanian origin, who had originally come to the area as pedlars and had settled there as farmers or shopowners. Many were Jewish, reinforcing the fact that numerous *smouse* were Jews familiar with the rural peasant associations of blueprint and probably with its many Jewish manufacturers in Eastern Europe.

Other people in the Northern Cape who inhabit the Namibian border, like the Nama and Damara peoples, provide a significant source for wearing *isishweshwe*. At the Catholic mission of Pella, established in the late nineteenth century, the wearing of blueprint prevailed for decades among converts. In writings presented to me by historian Gerald Klinghardt about the Salesian missionary presence, I identified an image of the first Damara novice of the Oblate Sisters of St Francis de Sales (Salesians) who entered the order *c.*1890. The daughter of a local headman, she became Sister Lydia. Her habit and surplice were entirely of blueprint. Sister Leonie of Vredendal told me that Sister Lydia was obliged by her

Cultural Usage of *isiShweshwe* in South Africa, Botswana and Namibia

superiors to wear blueprint, as it was regarded as proximate to 'typical Damara Christian dress'.[9] All future Damara novices wore this attire and, I was told, the differentiation of dress was decided by the mother house in France. Only in the 1920s, several decades later, was it agreed to allow Damara novices to wear the order's white garments, like those worn by their white peers.

One could interpret this dress differentiation as rooted in racial prejudice, but other factors, such as acknowledgement of local preferences, dress prescriptions for the order's novices and the practicality of blueprint, may also have prompted the decision. There may also have been some input from Sister Lydia herself, but no record has been found. Images from Pella and other missions in the region, located at the Oblate Sisters' mother house in Paris, show several women in blueprint and reinforce the cloth's widespread presence among the Damara and Nama. When I visited Pella in 2011, there were no wearers of blueprint, but informants in nearby Riemvasmaak showed me some of their blueprint garments, which they called *sis*. Most of these were of a cheap

Top left: Sister Lydia of the Oblate Sisters of St Francis de Sales, Pella, Northern Cape, 1920s. Collection of Piet van Heerde, Springbok.

Top right: Sister Lydia with fellow Oblate Sisters of St Francis de Sales, Pella, Northern Cape, 1920s. Collection of Piet van Heerde, Springbok.

Bottom: Namaqua mission family at Pella, Namaqualand. University of Cape Town Library.

polycotton. They also recalled their own parents wearing *kappies* and garments of blueprint. I ordered a *kappie* of the type still worn and made by women in the district. Several informants in Riemvasmaak indicated that they no longer wore blueprint, since it was scarce and had become expensive over the years. Other inhabitants indicated that they would continue to use it if it were still available at local trading stores and especially if it were reasonably priced.

Another large body of Coloured people of Griqua origin reside in the Eastern Cape-KwaZulu-Natal towns of Kokstad and Matatiele to this day.[10] The area is still popularly known as Griqualand, a region once dominated by Adam Kok and ceded to him eventually after years of dispute with British and Natal ruling authorities. The remnant 'Griqua Coloureds', as some informants called themselves, have since intermarried with neighbouring white, Khoisan and African peoples. While conducting research in the Kokstad and Matatiele area between 2005 and 2012, I observed no Coloured people wearing *isishweshwe*, though many former residents such as Eric Kopman and his aunt Hilda, *née* Kopman, indicated that their mothers and grandmothers wore *isishweshwe*, if only as workwear.[11] The Kopmans were of German origin and other members of the community were of Creole and mixed German-English descent. The Griqua Coloureds appear to have ceased wearing *isishweshwe* in the 1960s when local Africans began to use it predominantly. This shift could be ascribed to several factors, but was probably linked to changing social and economic conditions. The Coloured population and many Africans, as they became economically secure, aspired to Western predilections in fashion to suit their improved education and prospects in the urban areas to which they gravitated. The African market in *isishweshwe* persisted, however, and a member of the Sparg family – they are still well-known traders in 'African truck' (goods intended for African usage) in Kokstad and the Eastern Cape today – recalled that he helped his mother over weekends and school holidays by sewing braid onto sheeting as well as onto *isishweshwe* skirts, which his parents sold in their local store. In areas where there are extensive Coloured communities, such as Port Elizabeth, East London and smaller inland villages, I have ascertained similar patterns of usage.

❖ ❖ ❖

In 1806, when the Cape fell under British rule for the second time, the *amaXhosa* were still a major political and cultural force across the Fish River – the border between the Colony and the eastern hinterland, where they had lived **for centuries. They** often assimilated weaker groups into their ranks to increase their military and political strength at this time. The *amaThembu*, who often complained to

Cultural Usage of *isiShweshwe* in South Africa, Botswana and Namibia

the Colony about Xhosa aggression, were one such group. Another was the *amaMfengu*, whom the *amaXhosa* scorned. Many *amaThembu* continued to work assiduously on the surrounding missions and adapted themselves – and their dress – to the Christian norms prevailing in their new milieu.

The *amaXhosa* were distinguished by anthropologists as either 'red', *amabhinca*, or 'schooled', *amagqoboka*. Christian *amaXhosa* had received a measure of Western education, but the 'red' *amaXhosa* stuck to their traditional beliefs. Unschooled Xhosa women were subordinate to their menfolk at this time, in keeping with Nguni custom, but were allowed to carry out certain legal acts befitting their status in colonial

Top left: Young women from the Eastern Cape collecting wood. Main Library, Port Elizabeth.

Top right: Xhosa Christian converts. Amathole Museum Archive, King William's Town, Eastern Cape.

Bottom left: Lovedale basketmaker's class. Cory Library for Humanities Research, Rhodes University, Grahamstown.

Bottom right: Woman from the Eastern Cape, c.1920. Amathole Museum Archive, King William's Town, Eastern Cape.

society (Peires 1982: 41). They worked for settler farmers, for example, and sold their produce, baskets and clay vessels. They not only made blueprint garments – *ujamani* or *ujeremani* – from imported German *Blaudruck* or British and Dutch blueprint, but also repaired or modified Western dress donated to local missions from abroad.[12] The burden of their involvement in labour and economic transactions increased with time (Beinart and Bundy 1987: 3). Numbers of unschooled Xhosa men survived as pastoralists or subsistence farmers, while others became wealthy cattle traders, who sold produce and cattle to the Colony, but farming for subsistence remained the rule (Davenport 1987: 485).

Cultural Usage of *isiShweshwe* in South Africa, Botswana and Namibia

Opposite page: On the main road between Mackay's Nek and Queenstown: two Xhosa women in traditional clothing, 1959. Photograph © Katesa Schlosser. In K. Schlosser, *Der Wahrsager Njajula: Historische Farbphotographien von den Xhosa in Sudafrika 1959.* Kriel: Museum fur Volkerkunder der Universitat Kriel, 2009.

Above left: Xhosa members of the Uhadi cultural group, Grahamstown, 2005. Photograph © Kirsten Nieser.

Above right: *isiXhosa*-speaking widow in Stutterheim, Eastern Cape. Photograph © Kirsten Nieser.

Bottom left: Xhosa woman attending a wedding at the Feather Market Hall, Port Elizabeth, 2008. Photograph © Kirsten Nieser.

Bottom right: Xhosa woman carrying wood, near Stutterheim, Eastern Cape, 2014. Photograph © J. Leeb-du Toit.

The *amaXhosa*'s circumstances in 1806 indicate how extensively their early colonial dress – especially the Christianised wear of the *amaMfengu* and the attire of men and women schooled on the missions – was linked to the Colony, to second-hand clothing donated from abroad and to British, Dutch and German textile production where their blueprint, which also served as Sunday finery, was sourced (Nieser 2005).

Long-standing attempts to dispossess the *amaXhosa* of their land continued at this juncture, pursued by British settlers, disaffected free burghers and Trekboers, who crossed the Fish River in 1836 to initiate the Great Trek. Many of these colonial groups were intent on settling in the hinterland, where sheep-farming had proliferated to such an extent by 1830 that it aroused the interest of the London stock market (Oakes 1988: 130–8). Archaeological evidence suggests that sheep existed at the Cape from the first century AD. The Dutch had introduced new strains to the Cape, which interbred with Khoisan fat-tailed sheep, and they introduced other sheep from New Zealand in 1789. The flocks thrived and British wool merchants acknowledged the importance of eastern Cape wool in 1830 when home supplies failed to meet the demand for the product in England.

Conflict with the *amaXhosa* over land before 1836, when the Great Trek was initiated, had provoked three Frontier Wars between 1811 and 1836. Further wars, similarly caused, followed from 1846 to 1879. These confrontations involved Khoisan and *amaXhosa*, free burghers, Trekboers, settlers and British soldiers. They ranged from skirmishes to fierce engagements – the *amaXhosa* obtained arms illegally from itinerant traders – caused stock and crop losses, razed the surrounding countryside and posed a real threat to agriculture and food security. Land ownership thus became crucial in the eastern Cape after 1836 – not only for pasturage, but also for the provision of food and the future viability of stock and crop farming (Davenport 1987: 41).

The *amaXhosa* suffered defeat after defeat in the Frontier Wars – the pioneers, the settlers, the Colony and even the *amaMfengu* united against them – and they finally sealed their own fate with the Xhosa cattle-killing of 1856, two years before their rout in the succession of Frontier Wars. Their infamous act of 'national suicide', combined with their ongoing defeats, finally deprived them of their livelihood and independence as subsistence farmers and cattle traders with their own rural culture (Oakes 1988: 137).

The European-derived clothing, which the *amaXhosa* had discarded during the cattle-killing – they perceived European dress as an affront to their ancestors – they now begged for again. Ladings of second-hand garments were shipped to them from Europe, and, as the surviving remnant of the cattle-killing and their overlords' predations, the *amaXhosa* conceivably began to associate Western dress with a spirit of accommodation and sympathy. Many Christianised *amaMfengu*, meanwhile, wearing the very attire the *amaXhosa* longed for, pursued their role as servants, farm labourers and subsistence farmers on mission land. They enjoyed a measure of political prestige besides, acquired from their pastoral guardians, who mediated regularly with the Colony on their behalf.

The unschooled *amaXhosa*, after 1856, suddenly found themselves irrevocably attached to a money economy – they had eradicated their cattle-based wealth entirely – and initially shrank from a system that exacerbated their oppression. They feared the prospect of indentured labour on settler sheep farms for three years – wool had made up 65 per cent of British revenue from the Cape in 1850 and sheep farmers were desperate for labour – and the strictures of migrancy posed a dreaded alternative. The colonial centre, again, fearing a local economic slump in the aftermath of the 1856 cattle-killing, promoted the advantages of capitalism at every turn, while Ngqika, a prominent Xhosa leader, is recorded as having called for 'clothes, cattle and brandy' in his people's hour of need (Peires 1982: 60).

The British had introduced trade fairs in the eastern Cape around 1820 to stimulate the local economy, to promote exchange among the settlers and local people and to impress colonialist ideas about money on the *amaXhosa*. Beads, imported from Czechoslovakia via Germany, possibly together with *Blaudruck*, became prized items (they served as personal adornment and for blueprint dress), sold for more than they cost and were widely used even to purchase livestock. The Colony insisted that every Xhosa transaction in beads should include a 'useful item' such as cotton print or a cooking pot (Peires 1982: 100). Thus the British authorities continued to promote the interests of Manchester and Sheffield so that, in the long term, it was not the *amaXhosa* who benefited from the Colony's economic policy, but itinerant and local traders and sheep farmers, who continued to penetrate the hinterland, especially after the 1856 cattle-killing. These classes thrived on the wool boom, hired impoverished settlers and missionaries as political and financial agents and replenished their own cattle stocks indiscriminately. The unschooled *amaXhosa* hated them and their wretchedness culminated in the rout of the last Frontier War in 1877.

The *amaXhosa*'s plight in the bind of colonial capitalism was impressed on them insistently by the Colony. Colonel Harry Smith, a militarist who was governor of the Cape from 1847 to 1852, told the Xhosa chieftains in 1848 that they had to trade, teach their people to sell, learn the art of money and buy goods for themselves. Money made people rich, he claimed – it would make the *amaXhosa* rich too if they helped to build roads – and honest, industrious work would not only clothe the *amaXhosa*, but would also turn their people into Christians (Peires 1982: 166). Sir George Grey, later governor of the Cape from 1854 to 1859, told the *amaXhosa* to share the Christian faith, serve the settlers usefully, consume British goods and contribute to the fiscus to enrich and strengthen the Colony as God had ordained (Peires 1982: 57). A crippled people, their social structures broken, the *amaXhosa* finally bowed under the colonialists' yoke. A great many of them turned to the missions for hope and relief and many converted to Christianity. Thus new forms of consciousness and resistance – national, ethnic, racial, work-based – arose from their predicament. The flood of conversions among the *amaMfengu*, for example, drew unschooled *amaXhosa* under the mission aegis where, of all their needs, clothing was 'the first in both time and importance' (Peires 1982: 107). Western attire and mission-based education now signified a new social respectability, which, hand in hand with British commerce and capitalism, came to designate a new class of *amaXhosa* – 'a progressive peasantry . . . an educated elite' – a rejuvenated people who functioned at the centre of a mixture of colonial imperialism and African aspirations (Beinart and Bundy 1987: 9).

While traders prospered in this situation, they were not well received everywhere and opposition against them has been identified. In 1922, for example, during a trade boycott in Herschel, the Herschel Women's Movement, which arose from the dissent, threatened to boycott local mission schools (Beinart and Bundy 1987: 246). The protest was caused by rural barter and indebtedness – families sold their grain to meet trading store debts and cover their immediate needs after the harvest, even if they had not produced enough for their subsistence (Beinart and Bundy 1987: 233). Traders bought this grain, sold it later at higher prices and began to control the local people through their indebtedness. Interestingly, the Women's Movement began among better-dressed women who suffered most under rural poverty (Beinart and Bundy 1987: 237). They complained that they now wore blankets instead of dress.

Migrancy, again, a salient aspect of the *amaXhosa*'s subjugation, had ironically lent their women greater independence. They traded freely in their menfolk's absence, learnt dressmaking on the missions or from their peers and used their surplus money to dress themselves. The most traders ever in eastern Cape history – some 2 300 in 1885 – stood by to satisfy their needs.

The use of *isishweshwe* among the *amaXhosa* in the eastern Cape, then, may be linked to British and European settlement of the area, to the European textile trade, to Christian missionary endeavour and to the interaction with colonial hegemony. Stefania Victor, from the Amathole Museum in King William's Town, noted that the *amaMfengu*, who were among the earliest local converts to Christianity, adopted Western clothing as a visible symbol of their new religion and education.[13] Many Xhosa informants and traders from the former Ciskei provided valuable perceptions about wearing *isishweshwe*. Most of these informants associated the cloth with 'schooled' *amaXhosa*, *amaThembu* and *amaMfengu*, whose dress and economic capacity reflected their education and standing. Their attire and concomitant acculturation showed not only that they were converts, but also that their status had considerably improved.

Also at the Amathole Museum, anthropologist Dr Manton Hirs mentioned the recollections of a local Mfengu, Kwa Themi, who grew up in a rural Christian home near King William's Town.[14] Themi allegedly became a designer at Da Gama Textiles and afterwards, while working at the East London Museum, wrote an account of his adolescence as a Christian Mfengu growing up in a household where his mother always wore *isishweshwe*.

The *amaXhosa* asked English traders among the 1820 settlers in Grahamstown and in the Keiskamma area to stock blankets. These the traders imported from Britain – and with them large quantities of 'cotton print', that is, British blueprint – making Britain and Germany the main traders in cloth and affiliated goods for the *amaXhosa* and *amaMfengu* in the eastern Cape c.1850.[15] These facts are borne out by S.W. Whitham's 1903 report.

In the mid-1850s German missions and settlements, some of them shared with Christianised *amaXhosa*, functioned as a frontier defence of the eastern Cape. This compromise created a close association between the German, Christian and Xhosa communities. There was also cultural exchange between the German settlers and the *amaXhosa*, which the anthropologist Hirs observed in 1978 when he joined the Amathole Museum.[16] He visited a local German settler homestead made of wattle and daub, with dung floors and crude wooden windows. He found it almost identical to a 'Transkei hut' and recalled his informants' assurances that German settlers were so poor that the unschooled *amaXhosa* considered themselves better off. The German settlers ate wild sorghum, for example, which even the unschooled *amaXhosa* would never touch.

The German association with *Blaudruck*, discussed in Chapters 3 and 4, predominated in the eastern Cape. By 1903 all the blueprint there, Whitham points out, derived from Germany, although much of the cloth had come from Britain and Holland, even Belgium before that. The association of *Blaudruck* with Germans also stemmed from Xhosa usage: they often emulated the German settler woman's industriousness and piety (Jikelo 1995). German informants such as Frau Schuch from East London, moreover, emphasise that *Blaudruck* was extensively worn by German settler women in the eastern Cape.[17] Schuch adds that as late as the 1950s it was not uncommon for a German farmer's wife to come to market wearing *Blaudruck*, with her domestic worker similarly clad at her side. Schuch also testifies that many German women ceased wearing *Blaudruck* for workwear after the 1960s when it became associated with 'an African identity'. However, they continued to wear similar cloth for festive German cultural wear, as noted in the 1908 *German Settlers' Jubilee Souvenir Booklet*, continuing a well-established expatriate convention in South Africa.

In the Amathole Museum a display from 1958, erected to celebrate the German settlers' arrival in 1858, shows a German settler woman in a *Blaudruck* dress. Surprisingly, in the displays of local African peoples, none of them is shown wearing *isishweshwe*, although the archive at the Amathole Museum is an invaluable source of photographs showing blueprint dress. One image portrays a local white settler woman in Victorian-style blueprint with a *kappie* to match. One cannot be certain that her apparel was indeed blueprint – the image is black and white – but the contrast suggests that the floral pattern was on blue or brown cloth. In the museum holdings I located a typical German settler *kappie*, probably dating from the early twentieth century, made of imported German *Blaudruck*.

Marius Bester regards the proliferation of trade and the demand for *isishweshwe* in the eastern Cape c.1900 as directly linked to major historical events affecting the indigenous peoples.[18] Only a fraction of the *amaXhosa* survived the *mfecane* and subsequent decimation by the British. Their traditions remained, but their culture was fragmented by drives to draw them into farming, urban labour and the mines. Many *amaMfengu*, in particular, have remained in the Eastern Cape near King William's Town and present-day Bhisho (formerly Bisho) and many *amaMfengu* still work for Da Gama to this day. The devastating rinderpest in the 1930s caused further economic hardship for local people. Numerous *amaMfengu* recall being offered cattle if they sent their sons to the mines. Many underclass whites and farmers also went to the mines and relinquished their economic potential by becoming labourers. Johannesburg – the City of Gold – established in 1886, offered economic and employment prospects to rural Africans, whose entry into the market stimulated cash flow and a burgeoning demand for Western goods. As noted earlier, homebound women gained more economic choice and freedom in their menfolk's absence. Many traders recognised harvest time as a period of surplus when grain was exchanged or sold for goods such as *isishweshwe*.

Even today, many informants indicate that wearing and receiving *isishweshwe* fabric or garments are still associated with specific ceremonies connected to Xhosa cultural rites such as marriage. After payment of bride-price, the wedding plans are accelerated. The bride's peers support her by attending to her at the *umbholoro*, a gathering at her parent's home that may last for several days. When the pre-wedding feast is held, gifts (*amabhaso*) are provided for the bride. They may include functional items for the home as well as cloth and clothing. The bride is expected to provide dresses (*abakhapi*) for her maids of honour that are often of *isishweshwe* (Pauw 1969: 97). The handing over of the wife (*umtshakazi*) takes place after that. At a church wedding the bride initially wears white, but after the ceremony she and the bridegroom change their clothing (*ukutshintsha*) and wear 'change dresses' (Pauw 1969: 95). This might occur twice. One of the more recent 'change dresses' I saw was a panel- or wide *isishweshwe* skirt with a white blouse and

Cultural Usage of *isiShweshwe* in South Africa, Botswana and Namibia

doek or headscarf. B.A. Pauw cites an instance where the bride's mother had two dresses made for her daughter by a white dressmaker: 'a blue dress for admonition . . . a dark brown costume for afternoon tea' (Pauw 1969: 98). It is very probable that the dress colours mentioned refer to blue and brown *isishweshwe* wear, but this cannot be proved. The idea of admonition attached to blue, however, is a significant association. Admonition suggests disapproval and the need to uphold respect and submission. This may attach to the new bride's pending entry into her husband's clan and home, where she is initially an outsider. In a custom typical of Nguni culture, she must remain subservient to her parents-in-law, often for a year, although in recent times this period is far shorter. Pauw also refers to 'speeches of admonition' given at the wedding. The bride is admonished by both families about her pending role: 'You are now a married woman . . . Do not disgrace us in your [spouse's] family. Let us not hear any bad things about you . . . Go then . . . and create friendship with your [spouse's] family' (Pauw 1969: 99).

In a description of a young woman in an urban setting, Pauw (1969: 74) refers directly to the use of *isishweshwe*: 'On one occasion she wore a clean German-print dress buttoned up at the neck.' In this instance, the clothing might have reflected both modesty and modernity. In 2008 I observed a marriage in the Feather Market Hall in central Port Elizabeth where many of the guests wore contemporary *isishweshwe* garments. In popular texts on peoples in South Africa by Alice Mertens (1987) and Aubrey Elliott (1978), there are several images of Xhosa women in traditional skirts of yellow or red ochre sheeting with panel *isishweshwe* skirts underneath. These images were made in the late 1960s or early 1970s when panel skirts were commonly worn.

In parts of the Eastern Cape, such as Matatiele, which borders on the former Transkei, KwaZulu-Natal and Lesotho, the occurrence of *isishweshwe* is marked among residents. On any given day, women in Matatiele wear elaborate, well-made *isishweshwe* dresses and skirts. There are thriving dressmaking businesses in the centre of town and the Da Gama outlet – now Jacksons – is owned by Neil Cowie. The demand for *isishweshwe* in Matatiele and its outskirts is considerable. Informants indicate that many users visit from Lesotho and that others are rooted in local groups (such as *isiXhosa*- and *isiZulu*-speaking groups) after years of intermarriage. Most locals recognise *isishweshwe* as designating respect, married status and decorum. Given that Matatiele was in dispute about inclusion in the Eastern Cape or in KwaZulu-Natal – the townsfolk elected to settle the matter in a referendum and chose the former – the display of ethnicity as Sotho, Zulu and Xhosa is particularly striking. Many women of Sotho origin don a grass Sotho hat and as many of Xhosa origin wear a headscarf.[19]

Several Xhosa groups continue to wear *isishweshwe* in a cultural context. In the performing arts, the Uhadi, initiated and led by Nosipho Makwetu, performed at the Grahamstown Festival in 2008 and continue to perform locally. They don traditional white Xhosa dress with blue *isishweshwe* panel skirts and aprons. Some live in King William's Town near Zwelitsha and the Da Gama factory and travel throughout the region.

◆ ◆ ◆

In Limpopo province the main context that prompted intercultural dress exchange or imposition was a large body of German missionaries who influenced the *sePedi* speakers in the region. My correspondence in the late 1980s with Frau Schnell indicates that 'church women' – implicitly converts – were expected to wear *Blaudruck*. Barbara Tyrrell's images from the 1950s indicate blueprint's early usage as a small ill-fitting smock, or *diele*, worn just below the bosom by mature women, suggesting that they were not necessarily converts, but that aspects of *isishweshwe* had been assimilated and indigenised by the *baPedi*. An image located in the Iziko Museums of South Africa collection c.1967 shows two mature married women in the longer, more modest *diele*, although the researcher had initially photographed them to show their grass baskets.

In 2005 I interviewed a number of women who lived in the environs of Polokwane in Limpopo. Describing themselves as *baTswana* or *baPedi*, they provided significant accounts of their motivation for using *isishweshwe*. All had elected to wear the *diele*, though they believed that it was not Tswana 'traditional attire'. All used the term *motoishi* to describe the *isishweshwe* cloth they used, the term clearly sourced in a phoneticisation of *modeutsche(i)*. The *diele* was worn over a wraparound ankle-length skirt made of *isishweshwe*, usually of the same design or in a combination of two or more patterns. Other cloth was also sometimes used for the wrap. The *motoishi diele* was variously illustrated by Barbara Tyrrell (1968) as a short smock ending just below the breast, or as a longer smock with a contrasting border ending mid-thigh. In all instances the smock had short, puffed sleeves and ample gathering at the bib, below which the gathers hung. The origins of this smock may have been located in second-hand garments, even nightgowns or smocks, used by settler women and adapted for Pedi wear. Karen Tranberg-Hansen (2004) indicates the extent to which second-hand clothing in parts of southern Africa has affected borrowings and adaptations over the years.

The women I interviewed informed me that all their garments were locally made of cloth carefully selected by themselves. One of them, wearing her original marriage *diele*, noted that many women in the region chose a special *isishweshwe* cloth, based on individual preference, for their marriage garment. She now keeps

Cultural Usage of *isiShweshwe* in South Africa, Botswana and Namibia

Top left: Pedi women, with *diele* (*semabajane*) and woven under-skirts (*ndepa*), Polokwane, Limpopo, 1973. Photograph by John Kramer. Iziko Museums of South Africa.

Top right: Pedi woman's marriage *diele* (or *semabajane*), Polokwane, Limpopo, 2005. Photograph © J. Leeb-du Toit.

Bottom: Group of Pedi married women each in their own variants of the *diele* marriage garment, Polokwane, Limpopo, 2005. Photograph © J. Leeb-du Toit.

Top left: Pedi woman healer in her *diele* smock. Painting by Barbara Tyrrell, *c.*1950. Campbell Collections, Durban.

Top right: Pedi women in their *diele* (*semabajane*) smocks. Painting by Barbara Tyrrell, *c.*1950. Campbell Collections, Durban.

the garment for special occasions only. Her *diele* has red, yellow and green embellishments in the form of bias binding, machine-embroidered decorative rows in different colours and ric-rac braid. The women noted that the *motoishi diele* was highly desirable as a garment that showed respect and was culturally imbued.

Traders in Mpumalanga and Limpopo confirmed the long-standing tradition of *isishweshwe* in the region. None of the wearers was aware of *isishweshwe*'s European origins, although they identified its German roots by calling it *motoishi*. German missionaries dominated the eastern Transvaal in the late nineteenth century. Frau Höhne indicated that the use of blueprint was widespread on local Lutheran missions from the late nineteenth century, where it was used by missionaries' wives and by locals.[20] She also intimated that African women were encouraged to acquire sewing skills at the Lutheran missions in order to clothe themselves and to earn an income from sewing or mending clothes for others. *Blaudruck* predominated in this activity.

◆ ◆ ◆

Cultural Usage of *isiShweshwe* in South Africa, Botswana and Namibia

Late in 2005 a research visit to Botswana to identify patterns of *isishweshwe* usage proved particularly rewarding. The wearing of *isishweshwe* is widespread there, not only among rural Tswana women, but also in contemporary outfits in urban centres such as Gaborone. Fashion magazines at the time showed images of young Tswana women in contemporary garments, which attached *isishweshwe* to modernity and cultural pride.

In all the areas I visited in Botswana, informants reinforced the association between *isishweshwe* and Tswana cultural identity. Botswana comprises different cultural groups, not least those of Herero and Khoisan origin. When travelling into the Botswana interior in search of wearers and potential informants, I was advised to seek permission from the local chieftain, Joanda Meroro, before I spoke to women in Mahalapye. Girlie Kakuyarukua Chezuba assisted me there and was my main informant. The women were alerted to our visit and a group of ten came out to meet us. They all wore Herero dress, predominantly in blue *isishweshwe*. In our lengthy discussions they noted that *isishweshwe* was worn by married women and to them represented a unique fusion of both Herero and Botswana cultures and preferences. They were preparing for a wedding the following week where they would wear these garments. In the main the patterns worn were relatively small on a dark indigo ground. The women's distinctive Herero hat

Top: Women in Botswana, *c.*1900s. National Archives, Bloemfontein.

(*otjikeriva*) and dress (*ombanda*) were of the same fabric and design. The shawl, however, was often a commercial white shawl. The *isishweshwe* was known as *ndoeitji* (phonetically *ndeutsche*), a name clearly denoting its German roots.

Asked when they wore *ndoeitji ombanda*, the group indicated its usage at funerals and weddings, adding: 'Sometimes when we come to *khotla* meetings, when the chief has called us we put on our attire – on special occasions'.[21] The dress therefore denoted authority, respect and cultural propriety. They encouraged other women to wear the attire, especially the youth, albeit in modern versions. They also referred to the cloth as *mateis* (sourced in *madeutsch*), further locating

Cultural Usage of *isiShweshwe* in South Africa, Botswana and Namibia

Left and far left: *ovaHerero* women, Botswana, c.1955. Katesa Schlosser collection, Kiel.

Left: Herero women in Maun, Botswana, 2005. Photographs © Kirsten Nieser.

its orgins in German cloth, German dress or mission precedents. Wearing the cloth was also

> a way of showing off our tradition . . . we are proud of being a Herero woman . . . we can see from generations – of my age, I'm in the youth group – but, you know, we feel so proud when wearing this attire. Even where I am working at FNB – but on weekends I put on this attire to go to work with it.[22]

The cloth is also regarded as forging significant links with their ancestry: 'In Namibia, that's where our forefathers lived, that's where we originate, all of us here – our great-grandmothers were born here, but we were trained to keep that tradition to go on in the new generation'.[23] When asked if they used any other form of *isishweshwe* besides the Da Gama-produced variety, Chezuba said:

> Normally we use this one, the one that has got a name – we just call it *ndoeitji* – it means German, we translate it *ndoeitji*, that's how we pronounce it, that's how we call it, that's how we differentiate it from nylon or other material – just say *ndoeitji* – when you say, 'Go and get my *ndoeitji*', then you know she's going to get this type of dress.[24]

One of the informants chose to wear green polycotton *ndoeitji*, which was explained as: 'Just a colour she has chosen, but we found that most of us prefer blue. If you put it into percentage wise, it has got a higher percentage than other colours, but we just choose a cotton [*ndoeitji*].'[25] All their blue *ndoeitji* was the Three Cats variant and most of the garments were designed and made by one of the wearers, Patrina Zeriuaa. Most wearers also regarded themselves as 'spiritual' and belonged to the local Apostolic Church, further reinforcing independent Christian church associations with the cloth.

In 2013 Mrs Basha Motsomi, from Francistown, Botswana, expounded the Tswana usage of *isishweshwe*.[26] She noted that for Tswana women the wearing of *isishweshwe* apparel is associated with respect and marriage. She also noted that it distinguished her Tswana heritage and associated it with particular styles, such as the full dress with tucks and a wraparound skirt, much like that of South African Tswana and Sotho women.

The *ovaHerero* in Botswana are a minority group, many having gravitated to the region after encounters in Namibia with German colonial forces in the late nineteenth century, which culminated in the Herero War of 1904. They retain vestiges of Victorian dress in their garments. Hildi Hendrickson (1996) suggests that this dress in effect signified the absorption of German mission attire. Thus it functioned as a form of cross-cultural assimilation and authority, which, in its indigenisation, expressed resistance to erstwhile German control.

Cultural Usage of *isiShweshwe* in South Africa, Botswana and Namibia

ovaHerero women near Mahalapye, Botswana, 2005. Photographs © Kirsten Nieser.

Chippy Bruce, Cowie Trading's travelling salesman at the time, now a shareholder, notes that he could only sell Three Cats in Botswana and not Toto, as locals saw a difference in quality and attached status to the Three Cats range.[27] Bruce also noted that in the swampy areas of Botswana proximate to Maun and surrounds, the crocodile motif on the panels was preferred. The choice was doubtless supported by association, as the swamps were full of crocodiles, which were a clan totem in the region. Asked if he provided what locals want, Bruce replied by recounting an instance when he sold some print in Maun with a distinctive elephant motif. The print was poor and had come through on the inverse. Although it was flawed, the print proved to be one of the most popular versions of *isishweshwe*. When Bruce later went back to Maun, the locals wanted more of the flawed cloth and rejected the better print, which he returned to Da Gama.

The borders between Botswana and the North West province were originally imposed by British partition. This means that many *baTswana* today actually reside in South Africa. Their preferences for *isishweshwe* extend into this country. Most wearers in Limpopo province, such as those in Polokwane and towns such as Modimolle, share similar preferences.

When I visited Botswana in 2005 I found that a rudimentary but well-researched exhibition had been curated at Mahalapye Museum by a German exchange student earlier that year. Sonja Petersen, who was from the University of Giessen, had identified the *Blaudruck* roots of *isishweshwe* while working at the museum. She had conducted several interviews with local women, done research on the German roots of the cloth – assisted by colleagues in Germany – and had mentioned mission-based and historical links with the cloth in Botswana. She presented photographs and a short text on her findings and included images located in Germany of old women wearing *Blaudruck*.

❖ ❖ ❖

In 1884 Germany assumed colonial control over South-West Africa (now Namibia). This took place as a result of the late nineteenth-century partition of Africa in which European countries literally divided Africa into desirable parts for colonisation. As occurred in most colonial ventures, the boundaries between South-West Africa and Bechuanaland (now Botswana) were artificially constructed, resulting in the presence of *ovaHerero* on both sides of the border.

In German South-West Africa, the use of German *Blaudruck* saw European settler women and indigenous Herero women wearing the cloth from as early as the 1850s. Herero women elected to wear Western dress for several reasons

(Hendrickson 1996: 226). John Comaroff and Jean Comaroff (1997a, 1997b) would no doubt see this as manipulating indigenous peoples into acquiring Western goods, but Hildi Hendrickson (1996) and Joanne Eicher (1995) also regard the wearing of European dress as desirable emulation and indigenisation, which transposes colonial attachments to the cloth. Hendrickson proposes that the wearing of dress and cloth in emulation of the German settlers, who were known to have perpetrated genocide against the *ovaHerero*, suggests that the *ovaHerero* were emulating the German centre and were acquiring and indigenising its erstwhile authority as an act of defiance.

The dress of the Namibian *ovaHerero*, directly sourced as a variant of Victorian colonial dress, is distinguished by its headpiece comprising a rolled transverse cloth above a wrapped lower headpiece of the same cloth or a variant. The dress typically has pronounced gigot sleeves, tucked pleats at the hem, a high neck with buttoned bib and a detailed, body-fitting top. The Herero woman's long dress is known as the *ohorokweva onde*, the bodice is called *otjari*, the sleeves are termed *omaoko*, the skirt midsection is the *oina* and the skirt length the *orema*. Below the skirt are several petticoats known as the *ozondoroko* – compare the Afrikaans *onderrok*, or petticoat – while the headscarf is known as the *otjikaiva* (plural *ovikaiva*). At times a jacket, the *eyaki*, is worn (compare Afrikaans *jakkie:* a small jacket) (Hendrickson 1996: 223). In using *isishweshwe* for their dress, and referring to it as *ndoeitji*, the *ovaHerero* attach the function of dress to the cloth in an individual and collective statement of personal choice and what has come to be regarded as traditional attire. The cloth thus acquires added value and significance. Herero cloth usage has recently given way to the use of synthetic fibre and sateen cloth in bright colours and bold prints, said to reflect an increasing East Asian presence and market. But in places there are still women who prefer cotton (or even fake) *isishweshwe*. This applies particularly in the eastern regions of Namibia bordering Botswana.

Hendrickson points to the significance of colour in the *erapi* or body flags used by women and men in Namibia (1996). The flags reflect personal, political and cultural associations. It has been suggested that blue, the preferred colour of Namibian Herero *isishweshwe*, may have some significance as it is the ground colour of the Namibian flag, but I have yet to find any support for this assertion. As noted earlier, the Herero women I visited in Botswana in 2005 still elected to use blue *isishweshwe* as the preferred cloth for their dress.

ovaHerero women near Mahalapye, Botswana, 2005. Photograph © Kirsten Nieser.

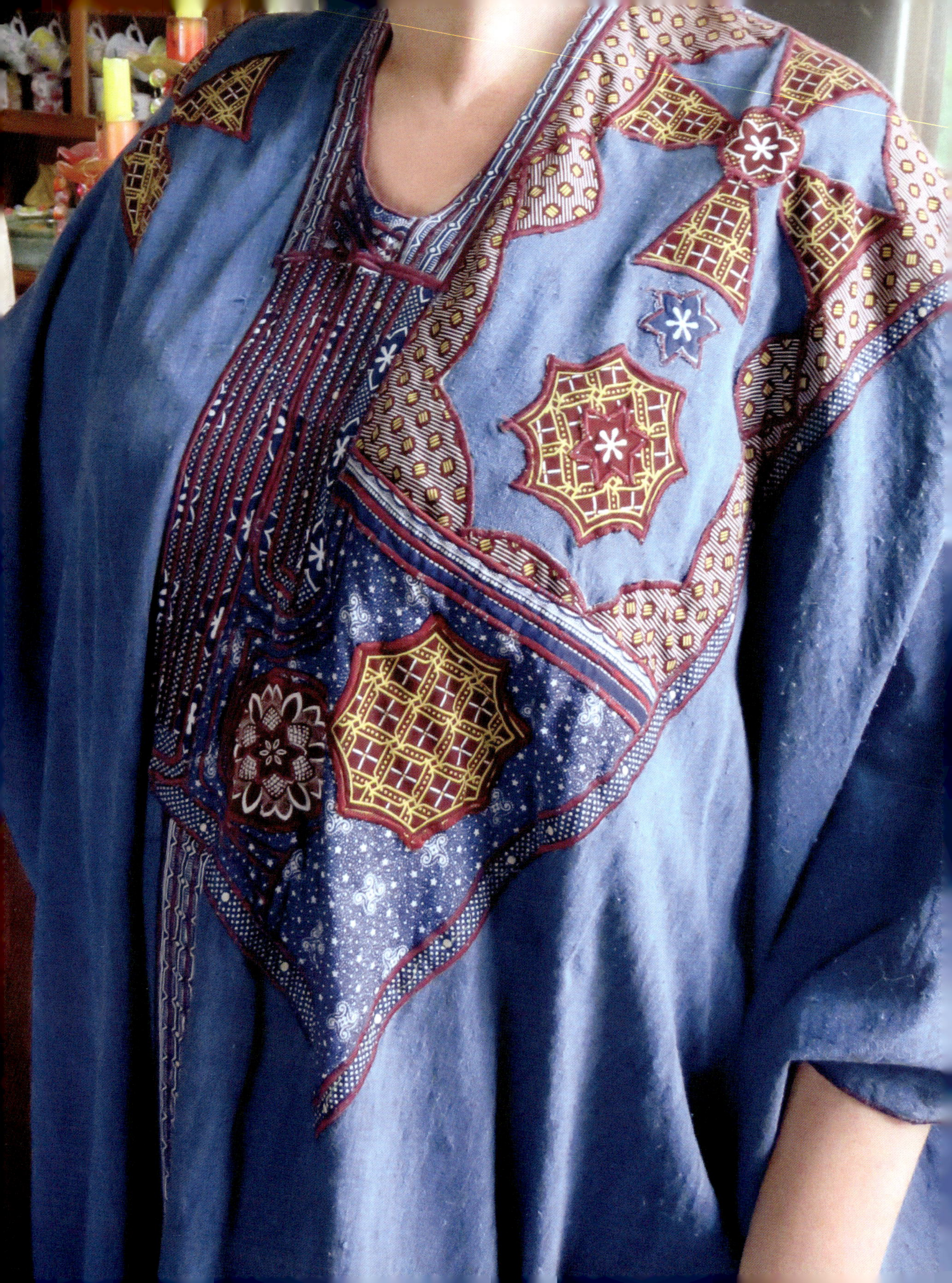

11
isiShweshwe Dress and Its Modernities

The extensive marketing of British cloth in South Africa – produced by Tootal and Sasscord, Tobralco, Star Toto and Robia – was endorsed by groups of select African users who preferred the well-known brands. Their tastes were widely exploited by home seamstresses, especially when Da Gama Textiles began to produce blueprint in 1975. At this point, *isishweshwe* acquired an added South Africanness, in that it was locally manufactured.

An advertisement in *Drum Magazine* in June 1955 refers to Star Toto 'printed cotton cloth' as preferred by black female dressmakers. It was 27 inches wide and had two perfect selvages. Star Toto cloth was described as 'of small cost and long wearing quality' and was endorsed by an image of Miss Priscilla Mtimkulu, a 21-year-old beauty queen, the 'Toast of the Transvaal'. A professional dressmaker, she was 'most particular' in obtaining genuine Star Toto material for her everyday dresses. She exclaimed: 'Such lovely designs . . . and they wear so well!' The advertisement went on: 'These good-value materials have been popular in South Africa for over twenty years. And now they are being made in a great variety of the very newest colourful designs which will thrill any woman who loves pretty dresses at a price she can afford.' It concluded: 'Smart women insist on genuine *Star Toto*.' At the time the cloth cost 4s/6d per yard, one could make a dress for less than £1 and an apron cost less than 5 shillings. The cloth targeted the home dressmaker, with the assurance that it would cost her less to make a dress than to buy one in a store. The cloth could be washed, the advertisement claimed, 'over and over' without fading or shrinking. Designers and dressmakers also advertised garments for the 'not so slim figure'. Star Toto cotton, the advertisement implied, was clearly desirable because it was reasonable, attractive and durable.

Black South African women soon established their idiosyncratic traditions in *isishweshwe* when Da Gama Textiles began to produce the cloth in 1975. White women at first reinforced and then relinquished their usage of *isishweshwe*. By the late 1800s the rural Boer woman, and her later Afrikaner counterpart, had upheld their ideals of womanhood and domesticity, propriety and religiosity. They championed these beliefs in the symbolic wear of their Voortrekker predecessors. In post-Trek communities – the members are today called 'pioneers' by some cultural historians – the Boer woman in her *kappie* and serviceable dress, often of *bloudruk*, epitomised the indomitable and steadfast spirit of the Second Anglo-Boer War of 1899–1902. Her iconic image, shown on the front pages of *L'Assiette au Beurre* and *Le Petit Journal*, the French pro-Boer journals, internationalised her portrayal, in identifiable but worn dress, as the victim of Queen Victoria's indifference, Kitchener's intransigence and Britain's ruthless imperialism.

The Boer woman's dress also heralded the roots of a national – and later a nationalist – paradigm that was reinforced from the 1920s onwards as the epitome of resistance and indigenisation. Positioned culturally in direct opposition to imperialism and Anglophile liberalism – as reflected in the tenets of the South African Party led by Jan Smuts – the opening of the Voortrekker Monument in 1949 saw thousands of men and women gather in what was identified as Afrikaner traditional wear originating in Voortrekker and pioneer dress codes. Attached to political entrenchment by the National Party, this dress soon became racially sanitised by its Afrikaner ethos and National Party associations.

Both pre- and post-Trek pioneer women often wore *bloudruk* or *blou sis*, a usage they shared with black South African women and other marginalised groups. This commonality of blueprint and *bloudruk* was discarded in the selective and conceptual reconstruction of Voortrekker and pioneer identity. In Chapter 10, for example, I observed that Coloured communities at Genadendal and in the greater Kokstad area abandoned their usage of *isishweshwe* in the 1940s – rather than in the 1960s – when their status improved and black communities wore the cloth predominantly. Perhaps this abandonment of *isishweshwe* stemmed from class, racial and political tensions, which were increasingly foregrounded in the post-war period. Some informants suggest that the shift occurred in the 1940s in conjunction with improvements, economic and educational, in the lives of Afrikaner and, for that matter, Coloured communities.

Voortrekker and pioneer dress reflected a minority status. But it was increasingly, albeit problematically, foregrounded by the state in the public and international domain as typical of white South African identity, especially from 1938 to 1980.[1] The construction and sanitising (and dehistoricising) of a popular Voortrekker dress code soon emerged, associated with *volkspele* or dance groups and other cultural activities. As pioneer dress, it was translated into new fabrics, which around 1930 to 1960 saw the emergence of variants in plain and pastel colours on modern synthetic cloth.

White South African women's wearing of dress identified as black or African, however complex its sourcing and origins might be, has emerged at salient periods in South Africa's history. Aspects of what was perceived as indigenous African dress became a desirable source of emulation for some white South African women from at least the 1940s. The motivation for this dress choice varied and was located in a sense of self and place, in a desired affinity with Africa and in the construction of a perceived Africanness. It was also attached to emergent, perhaps flawed, associations with patriotism and nationalism.

❖ ❖ ❖

Cross-cultural dress in South Africa is the outcome of a number of intersecting factors, including desirable individuation, overtures to exotic modernities and ostensible partisanship and liberalism. It conveys alterity as well as presumed interracial affinity. By the late 1960s such dressing was seen by some as a subversive appendage to white liberalism and partisan sympathy for the oppressed majority and their struggle for independence. Some white South African wearers of African dress were conscious of what their dress might convey; others were partly oblivious to the implications of their preferences. One must therefore situate this phenomenon between intentionality and reception. The wearing of *isishweshwe* is subject to scrutiny in situations where intercultural dressing is questioned and condemned as naive, liberalist rapprochement or as othering or appropriation. I am aware too that academic scrutiny might deconstruct cross-cultural dressing cynically. But I believe, nevertheless, that the wearer's intentions must be taken into account. The construction of self, however flawed, is a process of interrogation and necessary incompleteness. Cross-cultural dressing marks the renegotiation of self precisely in a context of cultural self-interrogation. As a part of historical events, shifting ideologies and inclusivity – under the impetus of modernity, globalisation and nationalist strategies – cross-cultural dress challenges the specifics of exclusivity in a multicultural context, upholding the porosity of traditional boundaries ostensibly demarcating race, ethnicity and nationhood.

Thus cross-cultural dress cannot simply be set in an anthropological, ethnographic or social context, or laid down in a political or historical framework. This would be too restrictive since many elusive factors, such as emergent Africanness, South Africanness and indigeneity, reinforced the process of cross-cultural dress after 1950. This trend was reflected in the performing and visual arts and was attached further to the globalisation of Africa and its presumed 'exotic' ethos. A local and international tourist market also contributed to the demand for indigenous dress and for items deemed vernacular, including beadwork, basketry and carving.

The embracing of cross-cultural dress was mooted as early as 1947 when the Afrikaans women's journal *Fleur* suggested that indigenous African design located in the beadwork and grass-weaving of the *amaZulu* and *amaXhosa* was desirable for white South African women. Using examples from the collection of Dr Maria Stein-Lessing, an art historian from the University of the Witwatersrand in Johannesburg, the magazine proposed that indigenous designs were highly appropriate for Afrikaner women and were of such high quality that they should replace 'inferior imports' from abroad. The sanctioning of cross-cultural referencing coincided with cross-cultural hybridity in design and the visual arts, shaped earlier by the efflorescence of ethnography and anthropology in the early twentieth century when a romanticised affinity for African culture resulted in conceptualisation and syncretism. Ironically, indigenous African material culture was viewed nostalgically as a creation with which white South Africans could identify. Fears about emerging African modernity, however, and black political aspirations continued to disconcert many white South Africans. But the attachment of Africanness to modernity prevailed for decades, fostered too by many diasporic Europeans who settled in South Africa before and after the Second World War.

Stein-Lessing was part of this European diaspora and moved to South Africa after the war. She opened her shop l'Afrique to market the beadwork and other items she collected. Her prominent role and perceptions of Africa and its cultural resources played a crucial part in foregrounding African design, which was being gradually assimilated into local material culture. Many white South African women had already responded to *Fleur* and examples of beadwork shown in the magazine became fashionable in the 1950s.

In the 1960s many white South Africans felt estranged from everything associated with the segregationist regime. Electing to renounce their colonial past and their status as a culturally exclusive white minority, they chose to align themselves with an African identity and context. At the time political dissidents were often subject to banning and restriction. White partisanship thus expressed itself in bona fide organisations associated with the alleviation of poverty, social upliftment, political freedom and redress. Many of these bodies, such as the Black Sash and various church groups, were led or initiated by women of all races.

Indicative of new intercultural support and engagement, cross-cultural dress came to signify a new alterity to the white mainstream in all spheres. Couched within popular cultural trends and marked since the 1960s by anti-establishment dissidence and protest, alternate ethnic dress was less noticeable at first, for African and Indian cloth and other dress forms were widely worn. The embrace of perceived 'local' black South African clothing by white women, however, implied a clear partisanship, which saw the appearance of Sotho-blanket ponchos, *isishweshwe* garments and traditional or tourist African beadwork.[2]

But at the same time *isishweshwe* usage also entered peripheral fashion, albeit on a limited scale. Penny le Roy, a well-known local designer in what is now the Gauteng region, used *isishweshwe* in designs identified as both African and modern, representing one of the first expressions of such design in a South African context. Similarly, Helen de Leeuw (of the Craftsman's Market

isiShweshwe Dress and Its Modernities

Top left and clockwise: Devcraft catalogue. Devcraft was a commercial outlet for 'ethnic' clothing and objects in South Africa c.1972. Photographs © J. Leeb-du Toit. **Bottom left:** A young Natal family, c.1970. Jenny Aitchison collection.

and Helen de Leeuw Gallery in Gauteng) promoted both Finnish and local cloth usage – for example, using cloth designed at Rorke's Drift (KwaZulu-Natal), as well as *isishweshwe*, in her many locally designed kaftans and mandarin-collared creations. To her, such dress reflected indigeneity, alterity and a shared modernity that transcended national, international and cultural boundaries. For many, the wearing of *isishweshwe* was associated with an emergent South African modernity and with the embrace of the exotic as a desirable alternative to mainstream fashion. Interviewed in 2005, Jutta Faulds, nationally and internationally known textile artist, spoke at length about cross-cultural *isishweshwe* usage in her dress:

My relationship with *isishweshwe* began in the 1970s hippy era. It was a comfortable alternative fabric to work with. It wasn't phoney; it wasn't sophisticated; it was wonderfully free. In those days *isishweshwe* just lent itself to hippy clothes. I can remember when I first saw *isishweshwe* on an exhibition at the Old Mill [an outlet of the African Art Centre] in Printing Office Lane, Pietermaritzburg, in 1971. Cheryl Alessandri used the stuff. I started making kaftans and shirts with it. At the time I paid 25 cents per metre. Now you pay R25 per metre! [In 2016 the cost was about R58 per metre.] The indigo is very special. At that time I thought it didn't need decoration. It was beautiful in itself.

The motivation for making clothes was because I am big. I made for myself and got carried away. I crept into embellishing clothes I made and expanded into wearable art. The style of the hippy clothes fitted into the local climate and lifestyle; beautiful to make and comfortable to wear. I am anti-commercial, anti-fashion and yet fashionable. People were finding the cloth terribly comfortable – basic and at the time unpretentious – which also makes it non-fashion. In the '70s I had done tiny hand-stitched art. It was time-consuming and that pushed me into decorative clothes and wearable art. It is an extension of decorative clothes. Wearable art is a protective art you can hide behind. If you wear an extreme garment, people will only see the clothes. People are bowled over by what you are wearing. That's what clothes do and now I have moved back into the decorative.

Top: Top made and worn by Jutta Faulds, textile artist, Pietermaritzburg, 2005. Photograph © Kirsten Nieser.

Above: Kaftan made by Else Schreiner, *c*.1975. Iziko Museums of South Africa. Photograph © Kirsten Nieser.

When I begin a piece I look at the fabric, start intuitively and claw my way to the finished product. I just collect things. Things get washed up on the waves and I just keep them, even fabric. I have used *isishweshwe* pieces for quilting. I still have dishcloths I made 30 years ago. My clients were friends: friends from the university and crafters. I don't know my client base in the craft boutique shops in Ramsgate and the Cape. I made what I felt like without trying to anticipate fashion trends. There was a time I made specific political statements about South Africa in my art. Around the time of the death of Steve Biko I embroidered a statement about the killings. Probably I have been, and still am, more environmentally motivated than political. So there are also recurring themes of environment in what I do.[3]

Cross-cultural dress was mostly the domain of women. Most women I interviewed on the topic were from educated backgrounds and many were also part of the political left. Jenny Aitchison, for example, initially wore and collected Indian prints, then 'African dress' after she started teaching in the 1970s. Later, she met

Lawrence and Carol Gilley (centre and far right) and family, *c.*1973 with Steve Hayes (far left). Congregational Missionaries of the United Reformed Church, Natal.

Maternity dress worn by Jenny Aitchison, 1980s. Photograph © J. Leeb-du Toit.

and married John, an activist member of the Liberal Party who was subject to several banning orders by the state, restricting his movements, public communication and social interaction. In this context, Aitchison's electing to wear African-sourced dress assumed a subversive dimension, in that it showed her support of the political beliefs to which her husband was aligned.

Many items of Aitchison's clothing were of *isishweshwe*, which, at the time, was associated with the dress of black South African women. She notes:

> Not only did I like the designs on the cloth, but by wearing items I'd made from it I could align myself with the black majority who were marginalised and oppressed by apartheid, and show respect for them. Although the clothing I made was not exactly like that blacks would have made, wearing this cloth differentiated me from other members of the white minority who either supported the National Party or did nothing to resist it. It was a way of making a political statement without opening my mouth.[4]

Aitchison's wearing of *isishweshwe* for pregnancy clothing also subscribed to a propriety of which she was initially unaware. Many married or pregnant African women are expected to wear *isishweshwe* at some stage of their lives, mostly when they are mature, to signify their status and authority as childbearers, respected mothers or matriarchs. Aitchison's material support of African women resulted in her ordering more traditional dress items from her aunt, a nurse who worked in the rural Eastern Cape and who commissioned local women to make clothing and beadwork for her.

Gertrude Strauss, a publisher and author from KwaZulu-Natal, claims that she wore dress across ethnic lines as part of her appreciation of its functional qualities and beauty.[5] Her mother-in-law, on the other hand, wore it in a politicised context, as she was a member of the Black Sash, a liberal resistance movement of white women who challenged apartheid on a number of fronts. Many members of the Black Sash aligned themselves with the cause of black resistance by wearing clothing that distinguished them from other white people, signifying their empathy with African women. Else Schreiner also came to regard the wearing of *isishweshwe* as a reflection of her partisanship and South Africanness.[6]

For women such as Aitchison and Strauss, the wearing of African dress, in particular *isishweshwe*, reflected alterity and a distinctive modernity oppositional and challenging to mainstream dress, culture and hegemony, rendering the wearer's action mildly subversive. In adopting this kind of dress, white women confronted inequalities of race, gender and class and, in effect, tested their independence and anti-establishment support of other women under dominance. This was also the perspective of Sandra Klopper, who, as an exchange student in America, wore items of *isishweshwe* as a signifier of her South Africanness.[7]

isiShweshwe Dress and Its Modernities

I took several *isishweshwe* panel-based skirts with me as my version of South African dress, but also as daily student wear, when I studied abroad in Italy from 1972 to 1974 and in France from 1974 to 1975. I wore these items to denote my nationality and to reflect my self-perception as a dissident South African. At South African Embassy functions in Paris, where my sister was a translator, I made certain that I wore the terracotta Xhosa skirt I had brought with me. I believed my dress choice and *isishweshwe* would dissociate me from the enclave of South African officials abroad. I was very well aware, however, that 'ethnic dress' was highly fashionable at home, not least in ostensibly enlightened academic and artistic circles. My clothing in South Africa might have been designated as 'arty', doubtless as pseudo-liberal or intellectual, and ultimately as modern and partisan.

I perhaps failed to realise that in my dress I was also invoking difference and separateness, especially with reference to the newly formed Transkei homeland, where clothing like mine was produced by women's groups and then marketed widely in South Africa and abroad. The homelands – areas demarcated and isolated politically and economically – were intended for tribally specific black South Africans, but were tainted by exclusionary racism. Thus, while ethnicity celebrated 'white women' wearing ostensible 'black clothing' such as *isishweshwe*, an ambiguous and complicit reading also applied. Did this cross-cultural dressing suggest a sanctioning of separation and difference, or was it a tacit sign of empathy for subject peoples against policies imposed by the state? While celebrating my appreciation for and interest in traditional cultural groups and ethnicity, was I unwittingly aligning my display of self with an appropriation of the 'stereotypical African' as a fixed entity with ethnically specific dress encoding?

While intercultural dress had an implicit reading in a liberal and oppositional sphere in the 1960s, the state also sanctioned ethnic expression in dress, art and culture. In 1960 South Africa celebrated 50 years of union, followed in 1961 by the declaration of a republic and independence from Britain. The outcome of this important development in nation-state formation was that ethnic identity and dress from the 'ethnic periphery' again became an object of interest and celebration as an 'apparent counter-current' (Chapman 1995: 20). Malcom Chapman maintains that this can only occur when a group is no longer a threat to the centre and

Top: Malin Sellman at Rorke's Drift, *c*.1970, wearing an *isishweshwe* garment she made. Photograph album, Malin Sellman, Sweden.

Bottom: Former Rorke's Drift teachers, *c*.1975, woman wearing a homemade *isishweshwe* skirt. Photograph album, Malin Sellman, Sweden.

consequently becomes 'an object of romantic interest'. This similarly reflects the situation in Australia and New Zealand where first-nation minority culture has been appropriated as an adjunct to, or a definition of, national and even white settler identity.

Ironically, in the 1960s, within a markedly different cultural and political sphere, dress was used by the South African state to suggest an idealised co-operation between the races. In the state-sponsored publication *Panorama* (1973) I saw several images of the sanctioning of ethnic dress in vogue. They showed a white mother and child in Xhosa-based ethnic skirts of white and printed calico sheeting. Produced in the Transkei homeland, such dress reinforced difference. Yet within the confines of segregation, with its implicit tensions and mutual suspicion, such suggested inclusivity was flawed. Implementing its ominous strategy of exclusion, the state launched its homelands policy in 1961. Several areas with assumed ethnic exclusivity were demarcated for 'independence' in segregated areas – homelands – administered by local black authorities.[8] In the process the state's celebration of its regional and ethnic distinctiveness, reinforced by independence celebrations, was widely publicised in official, local and international sources.

Top left: Helen de Leeuw wearing an *isishweshwe* kaftan at an opening at the Craftsman's Market gallery, c.1970. Marieke de Leeuw collection, Cape Town.

Bottom left: Hat and dress in blueprint from the Craftsman's Market, owned by Helen de Leeuw, c.1970. Press cutting in Helen de Leeuw's collection.

Far right: Jo Thorpe, head of the African Art Centre, with a group of artists. She is wearing an *isishweshwe* skirt, c.1975. African Art Centre, Jo Thorpe Collection, Campbell Collections, Durban.

The development of a quasi-ethnic dress code also occurred in the peripheral fashion industry. Entrepreneurs such as Helen de Leeuw in Johannesburg, Pretoria and Cape Town – she founded the Craftsman's Market – and Jo Thorpe in Durban – she was a founding member of the African Art Centre – developed a dress code of loose-fitting, ethnically sourced kaftans, which drew on local and imported cotton and woollen textiles. De Leeuw also favoured the use of indigo *isishweshwe* and was among the first to launch a range of *isishweshwe* dress for men, women and children. She set a widely emulated trend in the 1970s.

It is important to repeat that the performing arts were another significant factor in the wearing of African dress by white women in a changing political framework. The visibility of African traditional dress became prominent in the 1960s when several major theatrical productions contributed to its renewed foregrounding. *King Kong* (1959), for example, a highly popular musical, prompted widespread demand for Zulu beadwork. This was followed in 1970 by *uMabatha: The Zulu Macbeth* and *Ipi Tombi* in 1974. The impact of these productions was tremendous, both in South Africa and abroad, and they contributed to a growing appreciation of African music and dance and to aspects of African dress. The dress of cast members was a rudimentary interpretation of indigenous attire and these variants were adapted to the local white and tourist markets.

The wearing of cross-cultural dress remains fraught with historical and situational issues and with complex perceptions and intentions. It is also subject to approbation and criticism. Veronica Baxter, the daughter of traders in the former Transkei, recalls that she wore *isishweshwe* dresses from an early age.[9] Within a trader context, this dress was perhaps not unusual. The cloth was carried in the family store and her mother, who made clothing for the rural community, naturally used *isishweshwe* remnants for her daughter. In her white-school context, however, Baxter was ridiculed by her peers in racist language for wearing blueprint dresses, no doubt because this was regarded as African wear or reflected relative poverty.

Victoria Francis, mentioned in Chapter 10, whose Canadian-born mother was a member of the Black Sash, recalls that she wore many Indian-made garments in the 1970s, but also used *isishweshwe* extensively.[10] The cloth was bought at Elangeni, a local trading store in Hillcrest, and she made her own clothes – kaftans and especially wraparound skirts – out of the fabric. At the time she termed the cloth 'mission print', aptly reinforcing its earlier associations. The trading store owner used the same term. Francis was aware that her use of this fabric reflected a partisanship with black South Africans and was associated with her political opposition to apartheid.

My own experience of wearing *isishweshwe* reminds me of a response to my usage that remains with me to this day. I had begun to use the cloth from the early 1970s, especially the traditional *jikiza*, or wraparound skirt, with pockets and a gathered lower section with a series of tucks as worn by *seSotho-* and *seTswana*-speaking women in Pretoria. I bought my skirt via my mother's domestic worker, Eva Mokgoko, inspired by the beautiful skirts she wore and by the prominence of the cloth at outlets such as Helen de Leeuw's. Wearing the skirt in 1972, I met some *seSotho*-speaking women on my way to work. They stopped me, complimented me on my traditional *isishweshwe* skirt and thanked me for wearing 'their' clothing. Their thanks seemed to suggest that, in using their clothing, I was identifying with them and with their cultural preferences and personal significance. Given the year, 1972, this affirmation and support of my dress seemed auspicious. Not only did the women's comments show me the impact of wearing *isishweshwe*, but they also made me resolve to continue wearing it in future. For the first time I gained an insider's perspective on what contemporary African women thought of my use of their clothing. The views of the black domestic workers inspired me, but the opinions of my peers were less supportive. My colleagues at the University of South Africa (UNISA), where I worked for a time, were bemused but tolerant. They saw me as a naive, politicised leftist who relentlessly engaged in debates about the plight of the country and the pressing need for change.

The *isishweshwe* panel skirts I took with me to Italy and France, for me represented my national referencing and I wore them to classes and to local functions. In Paris, where I donned the skirts, I found myself under critical scrutiny by some conservative officials at the South African Embassy. Dress across ethnic lines certainly has a problematic history. There are cases where people who wore local clothing, befriended nationalists or sided with advocates of protest, were branded traitors by their countrymen (Chapman 1995: 20). It would be wrong to suggest that my usage of *isishweshwe* elicited such responses, however, even though it signalled overtures to a multicultural dress code and inclusive multicultural identity.

Heather Schreiner, originally from Britain, but married to a South African, believed cross-cultural dressing was pretentious.[11] A member of Amnesty International and the Anti-Apartheid Movement, she regarded her political task as 'real work' as opposed to the white posturing by pseudo-liberals in South Africa who believed that their dress conveyed political partisanship. But, as Hildi Hendrickson (1996: 14–15) reminds us: 'Bodily signifiers present an ever-present semiotic possibility for expressing identity and intention, for asserting the legitimacy of the status quo or subverting it . . . [and] treatments of the body's surface allude to linkages between oneself and people, power and knowledge beyond the immediate, local context.'

In 2003 academic Elizabeth Ralfe, from KwaZulu-Natal, decided to purchase *isishweshwe* cloth for her daughter to take to the United States as part of the 'national costume or traditional dress' she was expected to bring with her (Ralfe 2004: 212). Faced with the question of national dress in a post-democratic South Africa, Ralfe senior realised that all previous dress traditions, at least under apartheid, were tinged with histories of white settlement, supremacism and colonial enterprise. In deciding to use *isishweshwe*, she believed she was choosing who and what she identified with in 2003. *isiShweshwe* was used by rural African women, Ralfe knew, and was associated with German settlement in the eastern Cape in 1858. Straddling both whiteness and blackness, Ralfe seniors' wearing of her own *isishweshwe* when lecturing in South Africa was greeted by ululation by her African peers as a sign of approbation (Ralfe 2004: 216). She was no doubt unaware at the time that its history also straddled Boer or pioneer preferences and associations that long preceded her choice.

In recent years, in the course of nation-state formation in South Africa, local ethnic identity has again become an object of interest and celebration – but also of contestation. Xhosa and Zulu ethnic dress and associated traditionalism have been politicised and then depoliticised in the wake of internecine conflict. This occurred particularly in the early 1990s, when the wearing of traditional Zulu dress was attached to party-political affiliation and was consequently adjudged either suspect or regressive. In the later 1990s, for a time at least, in the interests of national reconciliation and reconstruction, cross-cultural dress re-emerged. Currently, fashion designers have reclaimed traditional dress codes and fabric and have incorporated South African dress from all racial groups into mainstream design. They have reinforced a national encoding vested in the cloth types and idioms used in the process, which has emerged after a century of complex interactions initiated by colonialism.

My own assumptions about the role of dress in cross-cultural borrowings are probably flawed. I was perhaps mistaken about the presumed partisan readings and shared nationalisms located in dress. I, too, was prone to discredit white borrowers as co-opting ethnicity, as making empty socio-political gestures of affirmation and empathetic partisanship. My research has unearthed some ambiguities that require further scrutiny. Ultimately dress and the self can constantly advance and recede in terms of who we are and who we want to be in a changing frame of reference.

At a symposium on transformation at the University of the Witwatersrand in 2016 (the site of violent demonstrations in the #FeesMustFall campaign demanding free tertiary education), a colleague wearing a dress in one of the latest purple and pink *isishweshwe* variants was reminded by a black participant that she was wearing what her challenger saw as 'our African dress'. My colleague reminded her critic that *isishweshwe* derived from a long history of trade and intercultural borrowings and was sourced in complex design exchange and development, and, ultimately, in European and American mass-production.

isiShweshwe smock made by Jutta Faulds, late 1970s. Iziko Museums of South Africa. Photograph © Kirsten Nieser.

This response failed to appease the commentator who typified the widespread lack of knowledge among many *isishweshwe* wearers about its history, indigenisation and cross-cultural usage.

◆ ◆ ◆

The entry of *isishweshwe* into mainstream fashion was initiated in the late 1970s when designers such as Jutta Faulds, Helen de Leeuw, Penny le Roy and many others opted to use *isishweshwe* in their work. Wearing *isishweshwe* in the 1960s was fraught with partisan and political affinities. Mrs Chaskalson, wife of the country's former Chief Justice, wore Rorke's Drift prints and *isishweshwe* garments, as did Black Sash member Else Schreiner, a prominent activist. Their wearing of such clothing was clearly located, in part, in their roots and political gestures.

Marianne Fassler, a well-known fashion designer and owner of the label Leopard Frock, was in the vanguard of *isishweshwe* design usage after the 'alternative' period from 1960 to 1980. She reintroduced the cloth into mainstream fashion *c.*1990. Although she used *isishweshwe* purchased from commercial outlets, she subsequently modified the cloth by stressing or 'stonewashing' it and dyeing it, and was given permission by Da Gama to print *isishweshwe* design-patterns on tulle, which was then embellished with beads. One of the patterns was the Sotho hat motif.

Fassler claims that her tendency to absorb and adapt African fashion was spearheaded both by her own political persuasions and by her attachment to the changing political dynamics after 1990.[12] For Fassler, there were also earlier precedents, however, and she acknowledged her interest in ethnic dress, which emerged in the late 1950s coincident with a range of theatrical performances.

Fassler noted that she had grown up with *isishweshwe*, that for her it was one of her main associations with Africa. Her use of the cloth in mainstream fashion was initiated when it was seen as an overture to inclusivity and a distinctive South African identity in dress. As noted earlier, black South Africans, in particular, started to use more of this fabric during the pre-election euphoria of the late 1980s. Fassler's use of *isishweshwe* found an immediate echo on the international market. A woman based in the United Kingdom, for example, started a range there, as did another producing children's clothing in France. More recently, a Japanese woman living in South Africa – her company is known as Le Mouflon Toqué – began to export children's garments to Japan, where

isiShweshwe Dress and Its Modernities

the fabric is particularly admired.¹³ There was also an increasing amount of *isishweshwe* for children's and adults' clothing for sale at craft markets in South Africa – with *isishweshwe* dress regarded as alternate, but above all as indigenous. More recently, innumerable products in *isishweshwe* have entered the market, with shoes and bags, such as those in the new Da Gama colour ranges by Helge Janssen from KwaZulu-Natal.

In more recent usage Fassler has continued to modify the cloth. In 2005, for the South African Fashion Week (SAFW) in Johannesburg, she had the familiar Sotho hat design in blue screen-printed onto tulle, with Da Gama's permission, and made it up into a gathered skirt. Her usage today tends to obscure the obvious referencing to the cloth, as she regards its impact as 'expired' in terms of immediacy, difference and fashionability.¹⁴

By the 1990s designers such as Amanda Laird-Cherry and Bongiwe Walaza had increasingly incorporated *isishweshwe* into their clothing designs. For Laird-Cherry the incorporation was intended to be a major reference to, and reflection on, something distinctively South African. By 2005 her designs had become quasi-African with layered skirts in a range of *isishweshwe* fabric designs. She also developed a range of flowing robes for men made of the cloth as well as shirts suited to urban wear. Her clothing for males drew loosely on Japanese crossover garments similar to a kimono and other oriental sources with long, open-collared tunics for males and females. Her own garment worn at the opening of her show at the

Top: Tulle skirt with Sotho hat motif, Marianne Fassler, owner-designer of Leopard Frock, Johannesburg, 2010. Photograph © J. Leeb-du Toit.

Bottom: Mixed textiles with *isishweshwe*, Marianne Fassler, owner designer of Leopard Frock, Johannesburg, 2010. Photograph © J. Leeb-du Toit.

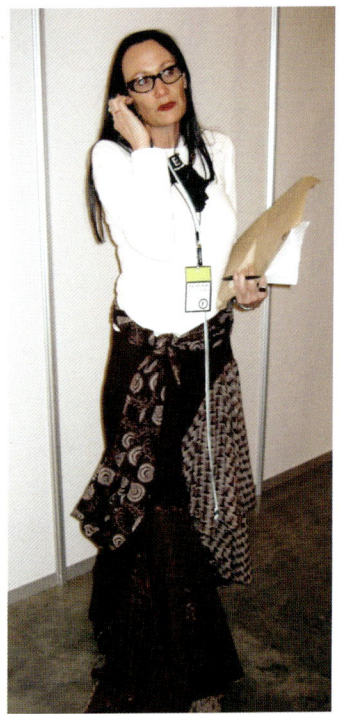

2005 SAFW consisted of a few torn bits of *isishweshwe* randomly sewn and tied together.

Laird-Cherry has risen to international prominence in recent years. Trained at the former Natal Technikon as a designer, she elected to use *isishweshwe* in the late 1990s when she was searching for something that reflected a distinctive South African idiom. This derives from her ideas on 'creative research' – constructively seeking new idioms – a diligent quest in which she carefully investigates particular usage and interpretations.[15] Laird-Cherry continues to use *isishweshwe* and has produced garments in the cloth that are dyed, combined with other fabrics such as silk, and obscure the immediate identification of *isishweshwe*.

Bongiwe Walaza trained at the Natal Technikon as a civil engineer and had never worn *isishweshwe* as a youngster. Born to Xhosa parents, she soon gravitated to the fashion world and has developed elegant variants of *isishweshwe* dress with 'traditional' trimmings, such as flared skirts, emphatic sleeves and overlaid strip skirts. By 2008 she had added a mixture of silk and shantung to her *isishweshwe* in a trend that is now widely followed. Significantly, in her downtown studio in Johannesburg's Fashion District, Walaza employs a Sudanese and a Ghanaian tailor, regarding their sewing skills as far superior to those of local seamstresses.[16] She merely does a drawing and presents it to them – they develop the pattern and finish the garment.

Designers who function under labels such as Sun Godd'ess (founded by Thando and Vanya Mangaliso) and Stoned Cherrie (Nkhensani Nkosi) also developed *isishweshwe* ranges and innovated designer garments with an African traditionalist aspect. Sun Godd'ess adapted them, developing the essential lines of Xhosa dress in skirts of *isishweshwe* and other fabric (such as shantung) and in rows of braid at the hem and a tight-fitting upper half. Stoned Cherrie was more innovative with a range of *isishweshwe* designs that were quasi-African, Victorian and modern. This can perhaps be identified as 'African sartorial', in which a chic urban variant of traditional African dress has found currency in an Afropolitan context.

Amanda Laird-Cherry (top) at South African Fashion Week with one of her designs, Johannesburg, 2005. Photograph © J. Leeb-du Toit.

isiShweshwe Dress and Its Modernities

Bongiwe Walaza (top left) at South African Fashion Week with her designs, Johannesburg, 2005. Photographs © Kirsten Nieser.

Da Gama Textiles, the sole producer of authentic discharge-printed cotton *isishweshwe* in South Africa, first became associated with SAFW in 2003 when Laird-Cherry and Helen Bester, the latter then marketing manager at Da Gama Textiles, met for the first time. Laird-Cherry was enquiring about the bulk purchase of *isishweshwe* and from then on used Da Gama's fabric consistently in her work. Da Gama sponsored Laird-Cherry and two other designers – Walaza and a newcomer named Ruby – to maximise its publicity at SAFW in Johannesburg in 2005. Da Gama bore the three designers' forum costs, which were considerable, and provided them with free bolts of *isishweshwe* for use in showcasing their productions. The designers were expected to reproduce their most popular interpretations, which they could sell, but not keep, after the show. Laird-Cherry, who had worked with *isishweshwe* for nearly ten years by this time, no longer enjoys sponsorship from Da Gama. Currently no designers are sponsored, but Da Gama still supports emerging designers when they are engaged in marketing and publicity drives.

The presence of *isishweshwe* in quilts has a long history in South Africa. As noted earlier, a *Blaudruck* fragment on linen was identified as part of a Boer-pioneer quilt in Bloemfontein and several quilts in Pretoria contain remnants of machine-made *isishweshwe*. In the 1960s the incidence of *isishweshwe* was widespread when handwork of all kinds, including quilting, increased in popularity and began to use the cloth. By the 1970s quilted garments were particularly fashionable and quilting skills and handwork had become highly desirable. This continued into the 1980s, after which the popularity of handwork declined somewhat, as did the traditions associated with it. Since then, there has been an upsurge in the production of machine-made quilts produced at home and a women's guild recently made a quilt to celebrate the arrival of the German settlers at the Cape in 1858. In 2015 at the National Quilt Festival held at Kearsney College outside Durban, there were numerous quilts that included *isishweshwe*. However, these were eclipsed by a series of quilts in Hungarian *kékfestö* that had been included in the show and were brought to South Africa by Anna Dolanyi.

As a result of extensive marketing and word-of-mouth exchange, quilters from across the world have come to hear of Da Gama Textiles' discharge-printed *isishweshwe*. Large amounts of the cloth are now exported to Europe and the United States for use in quilting. Several American quilters are using the cloth and there are even intimations of a new market for the cloth in the United Kingdom.

◆ ◆ ◆

isiShweshwe has become widely recognised as a distinctive South African cloth. It is rooted in a complex historical matrix associated with trade, colonial economies, missions and cultural appropriation. Thus it represents a major historical remnant of an intercultural past, with both Eastern and Western dimensions, and it testifies to a history of interaction and exchange permeating human association across the globe. In its production and consumption *isishsweshwe* is linked to the East, to the United States and Europe, and has recently begun to turn full circle back to China and Japan.

isiShweshwe retains its historical references, but has been indigenised and appropriated to the extent that its earlier roots have all but receded. Its production has become centred in South Africa, where cultural usage has associated it with specific practices and rituals. It has assumed iconic status here and its continuity seems assured. As a cloth type, it continues to fulfil many of the functional and cultural needs of the country's various inhabitants. The extent to which it is associated with a South African identity is revealed by the continuities of its cultural usage in interior design, high fashion and the tourist market.

isiShweshwe usage in South Africa assumed complex origins, allegiances and associations at an early stage. The cloth often brought about deprivation and coercion or was aspirational and stood for conversion, education or Westernisation. Among the *baSwazi* and *baSotho*, *isishweshwe* denoted aspirations to new or emergent nationhood. In its use as a signifier of economic capacity and male dominance – in the propriety and decorum expected of traditional wives – it reinforced patriarchal authority and the subservience of many women from African communities. Conversely, however, an increase in autonomy and wealth has suggested the wearing of *isishweshwe* as a challenge to the traditional control of women's labour and expenditure. This crucial development has contradicted the place of women as an underclass in a society where they now function far more freely in vital roles, which they celebrate in their cultural usage of *isishweshwe*.

As South Africa enters a counter-revolutionary phase, new claims of exclusivity and ownership emerge, as advocates of postcolonialism and decolonisation aspire to reposition and rewrite history. In this context, *isishweshwe* incorporates significant facets of history, contextualised within a number of racial and economic perspectives. It is deeply embedded in the South African psyche, for example, where – regardless of race – it remains steeped in a complex system of shifting values. Having perused *isishweshwe* as a significant marker of intercultural encounter, however, I am reminded of how rapidly assumptions about its history, accessibility and associations can shift and become contentious. Perhaps that perspective will provide new material for later study by other researchers.

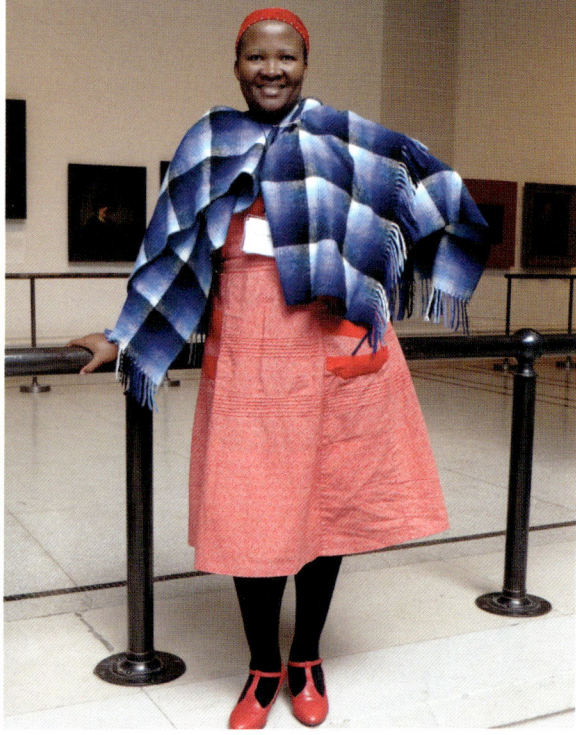

Top: Zanele Mbeki (right), wife of former president Thabo Mbeki, wearing an *isishweshwe* suit at the funeral of former South African president P.W. Botha in 2006. Photograph © Esa Alexander.

Bottom left: The Bhaca king, iNkosi uMadzikane II, in green *isishweshwe* shirt at the Barbara Tyrrell memorial service at the Campbell Collections, University of KwaZulu-Natal, 2015. Photograph © J. Leeb-du Toit.

Bottom right: Senzeni Marasela, performance and installation artist in one of her many married woman's *isishweshwe* outfits (*ipinifa* with *foskoti*), New York, 2012. Photograph © J. Leeb-du Toit.

isiShweshwe Dress and Its Modernities

Top left and middle: Jacket designed by Marie Peacey, c.1975. Leeb-du Toit collection, Iziko Museums of South Africa.

Bottom left: Dresses by Senegalese designer Elijah Ciss in Bloemfontein, 2007. Photograph © Kirsten Nieser.

Top right: Lulu Xingwana, then deputy minister of Arts and Culture, at a National Heritage Council presentation, 2009. Photograph © J. Leeb-du Toit.

Bottom right: Wedding guest at the Port Elizabeth Feather Market Hall, 2008. Photograph © Kirsten Nieser.

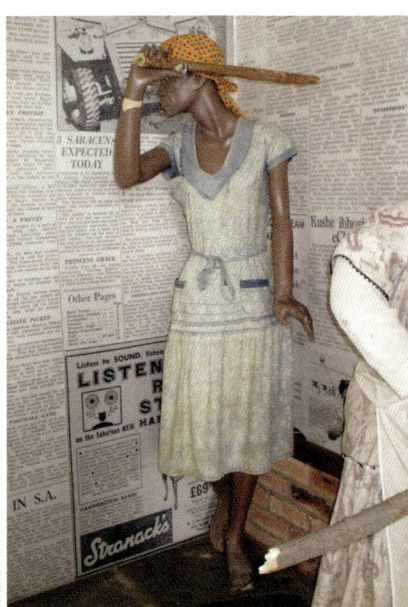

Top left: Seamstress in Matatiele at the local co-operative outlet, 2008. Photograph © Kirsten Nieser.

Top centre: Noni Gaza, model, wearing an outfit by Bongiwe Walaza, South African Fashion Week, Johannesburg, 2005. Photograph © J. Leeb-du Toit.

Top right: Protestor at strikes in Durban, c.1970. KwaMuhle Museum, Durban, KwaZulu-Natal. Photograph © J. Leeb-du Toit.

Bottom right: Unidentified model in a dress designed by Amanda Laird-Cherry c.2006.

isiShweshwe Dress and Its Modernities

Top left: Owner of The Brewery inoculating his goats, Nieu Bethesda, Eastern Cape, 2011. Photograph © J. Leeb-du Toit.

Top right: Woman photographed near Queenstown, Eastern Cape, 2011. Photograph © J. Leeb-du Toit.

Centre and bottom left: *isiShweshwe* at Becker Street Wholesalers, Johannesburg, 2016. Photograph © J. Leeb-du Toit.

Below: *isiShweshwe* dress with embroidered mirrorwork bodice. Made and purchased in Cape Town, 1979. Owned by Saskia van Oosterhout. Photograph © Kirsten Nieser.

Appendix
Naming *isiShweshwe* Designs

Naming *isishweshwe* designs is a significant aspect of their indigenisation over time. Owners of textile outlets throughout southern Africa have contributed largely to this naming, thereby facilitating their ordering and identification of particular *isishweshwe* designs for customers, although many designs still remain unnamed. As a result, however, some design names differ. In what follows I have retained the most commonly used names identified in the field.

In the main, design names have been created by Sotho-speakers, perhaps not surprisingly, as the Southern Sotho (in Lesotho) were among the first to identify *seshoeshoe* (*isishweshwe*) as part of their national dress.

The names of specific patterns appear to have developed by association. So the dot pattern is likened to the spots of the guinea fowl, the rounded floriate shape to the cabbage and jagged lines to a saw. Other designs have been closely based on local Sotho mural traditions, for example those created by Fleur Rorke.

More recently, specific traders have developed their own exclusive *isishweshwe* designs produced for them by Da Gama Textiles. At Fayco Wholesalers, for example, a Durban based outlet, the designs especially made for the owner, Mohamed Patel, are based on his ideas communicated to Da Gama, and are named uniquely by him.

Select *isishweshwe* motifs have been retained for decades, and are often based on popular demand by customers. Some designs are released again in keeping with the originals, or are modified according to Da Gama's marketing strategies. This might see a design reappear in the new colourways of Da Gama's Fancy Prints range like a brand new creation.

Named *isishweshwe* designs appear only to be used for Da Gama-produced discharge-printed cloth at present. To date I have not located any names used for the thousands of other *isishweshwe* designs on the market today.

As shown in this appendix, many designs were produced in tonal ranges for specific regions. One such tonal range was Southern Rhodesia (Zimbabwe) blue, also known as 'blue down' by Wigan Printworks (England), in which the deep indigo-blue ground was retained but the patterns were lightly discharged, resulting in pale-blue motifs rather than white ones. This cloth type has since been discontinued, and the usage of *isishweshwe* in present-day Zimbabwe is virtually non-existent.

In this appendix I have also included some of the Portuguese blueprint cloth located at Pretoria Textile Wholesalers, which is identical to that worn by some Angolan peoples, suggesting that the trade in this cloth extended to this country.

The nature and extent of *isishweshwe* usage in Namibia and Angola, Zimbabwe, Zambia, Botswana and Malawi will be the focus of later research. My funding constraints only allowed for research in South Africa, and my forays further afield were largely self-funded or coincided with conferences in these locales.

Mozambican sculptures, c.1980. Mario Pissarra collection

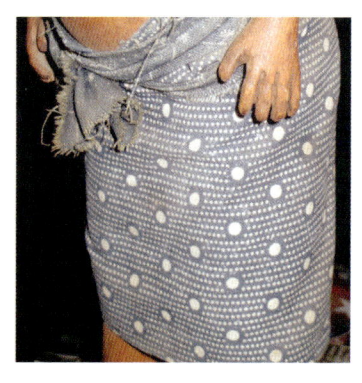

Mozambican sculpture (detail). Mario Pissarra collection

Mucuval celebration near Virei, Angola. Pinterest

Appendix

261

Bonbons, buttons or sweets

Bonbons, buttons or sweets

Bones (*masapo lesapo*)

Bones (*masapo lesapo*)

Brains

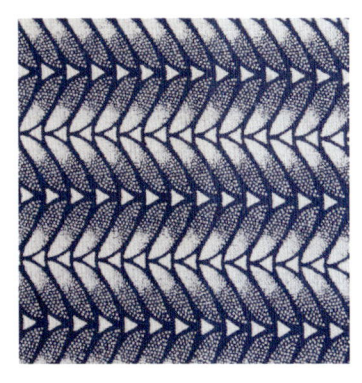

Butterflies

Butterflies

Cabbages (*moroko*)

Canoes, rice (*libete*), spears (*lerumo*), big Chinese eyes or sorghum (*mabele*)

262   *isiShweshwe*

Canoes, rice (*libete*), spears (*lerumo*), big Chinese eyes or sorghum (*mabele*)

CDs (compact discs)

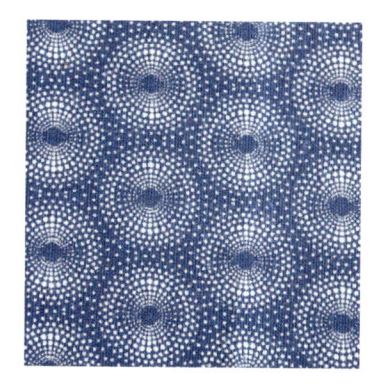

CDs (compact discs)

Chains

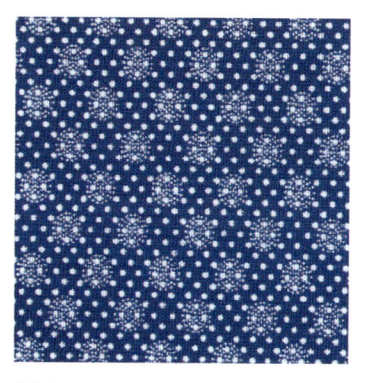

Chicken pox (or *tsitlili*)

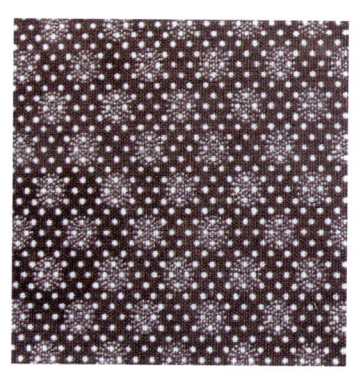

Chicken pox (or *tsitlili*)

Chicken pox (or *tsitlili*)

Chicken's eyes (*leihlo lo khoko*)

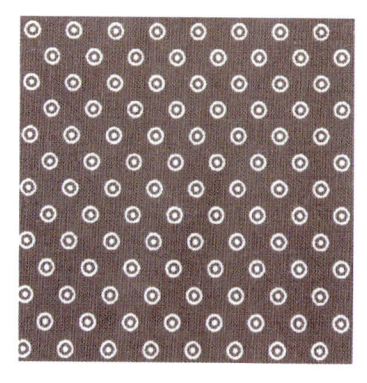

Chicken's eyes (*leihlo lo khoko*)

Appendix

263

Chinese eyes

Clams, windows or scales

Clams, windows or scales

Cow's eye (*lehlolakgomo*) (detail)

Crocodile's eyes (*leihlo la koena*) or small Chinese eyes

Diamonds (*litaemene*)

Diamonds (*litaemene*)

Diamonds (*litaemene*)

Diamonds (*litaemene*)

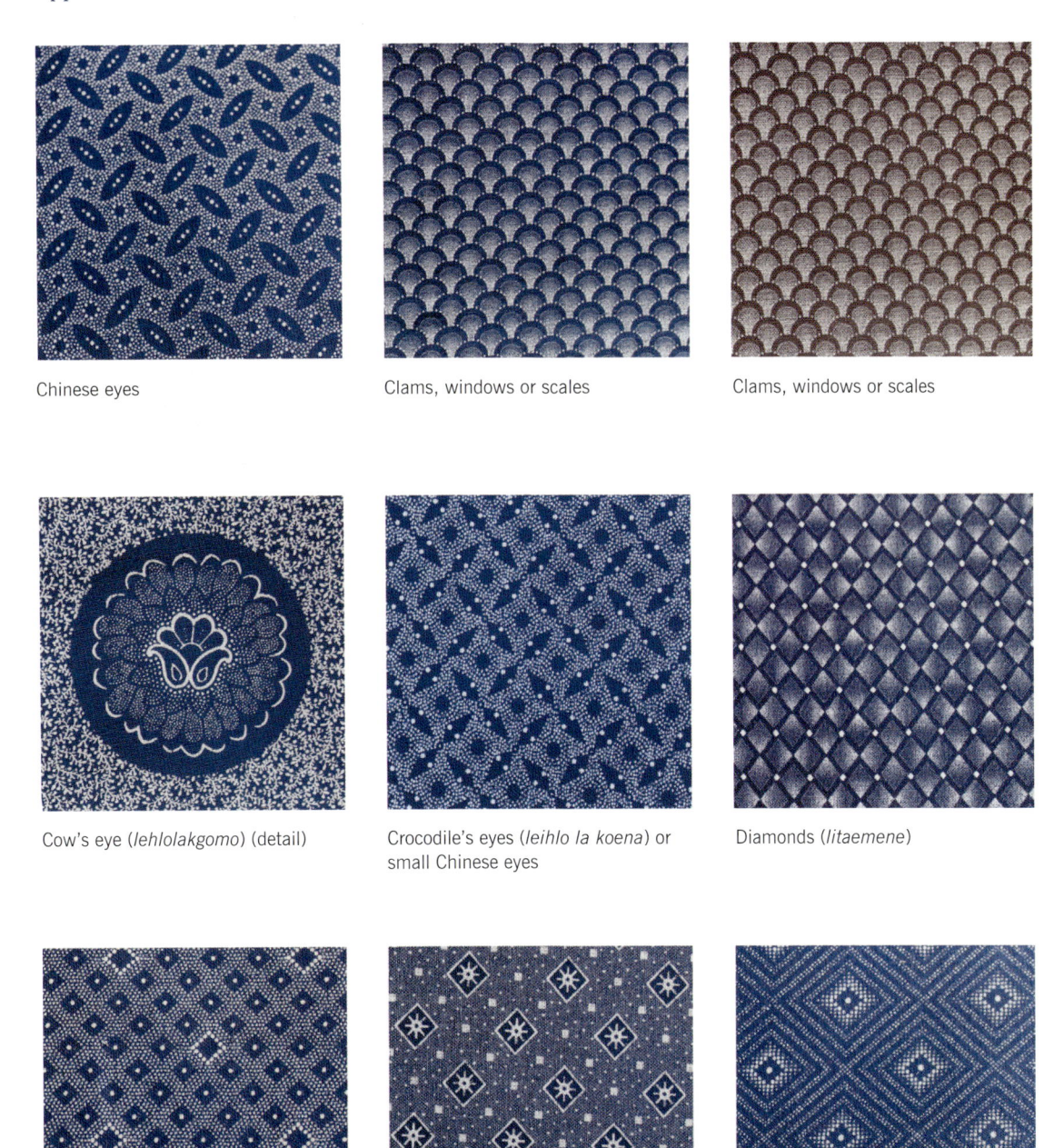

264 *isiShweshwe*

Double diamonds

Earrings (*lesale* or *manyenenyene*)

Earrings (*lesale* or *manyenenyene*)

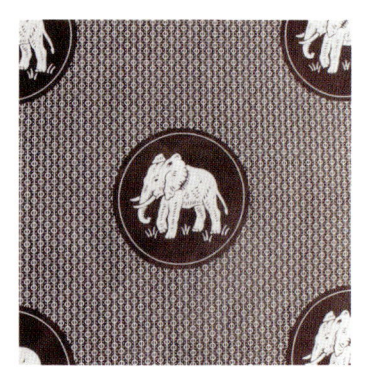

Elephants (*tlou* or *indlovu*)

Elephants (*tlou* or *indlovu*) (detail)

Eyes (*billu* or *leihlo*)

Eyes (*billu* or *leihlo*)

Eyes

Fans (*sefehla moea*) or bananas

Appendix

Fans (*sefehla moea*) or bananas

Fans (*fene*) or peacocks (*pikoko*)

Fans (*fene*) or peacocks (*pikoko*)

Fans (*fene*) or peacocks (*pikoko*)

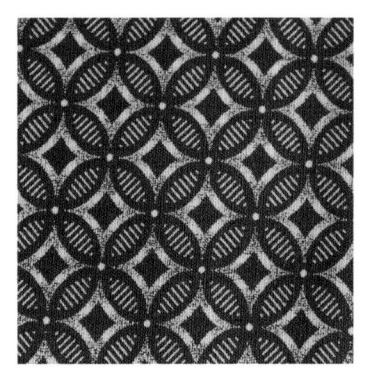

Fayco design

Feathers (*lesiba*) or leaves

Feathers (*lesiba*) or leaves

Fencing

Fishbones (*khopo tsa tlhapi*)

266 *isiShweshwe*

Fishbones (*khopo tsa tlhapi*)

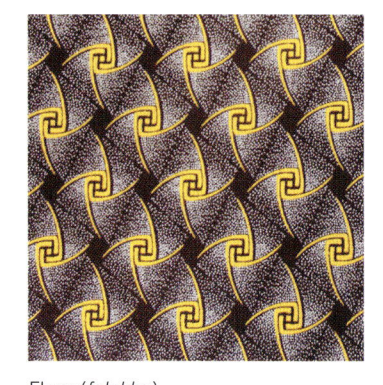

Flags (*folokha*)

Flames (*lelakhapo*)

Flames (*lelakhapo*)

Flowers

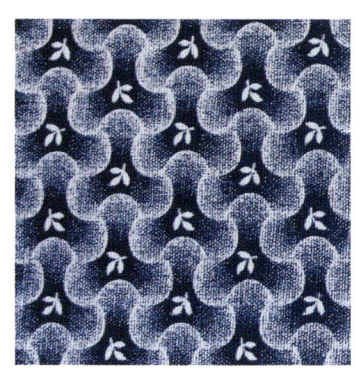

Flies

Ginger

Ginger

Goat's eyes (*seSotho*) or crocodile's eyes (*leihlo la koena*)

Appendix

267

Grass (*mokhoa* or *mohloa* or *mokhova* or *boeia*)

Grass

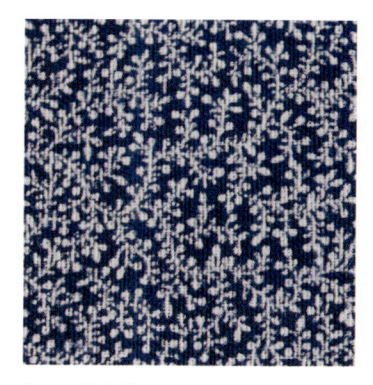

Grass (detail)

Guinea fowl's spots (*khaka dikgaka* or *impangele*)

Guinea fowl's spots (*khaka dikgaka* or *impangele*)

Hairy caterpillars (*thithiboeia*) or porcupines

Hairy caterpillars (*thithiboeia*) or porcupines

Hitler (*hitlerare*)

Hitler (*hitlerare*)

268 *isiShweshwe*

Hitler (*hitlerare*)

Honeycomb

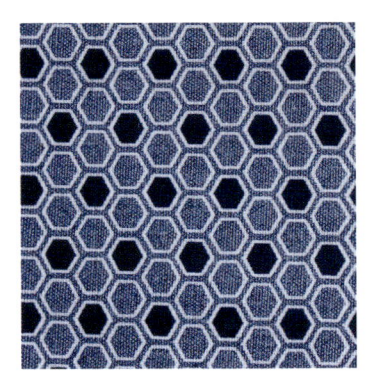

Honeycomb

Honeycomb

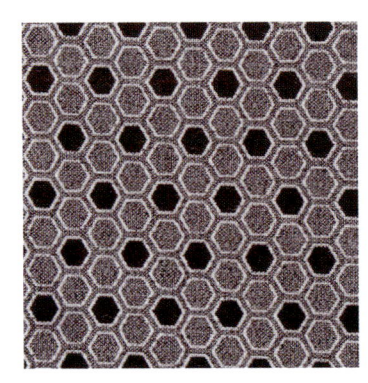

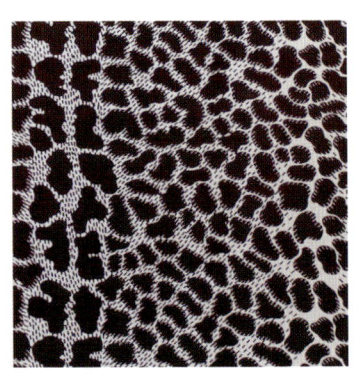

Honeycomb

Ingwe (feline pelt)

Iscor (named after the steel manufacturing company)

Jellyfish or mushrooms

Koro (wheat)

Appendix   269

Leaves (or *muthlaba*)    Leaves (or *muthlaba*)    Leopards (*ingwe*)

Leopard (*ingwe*)    Lightning 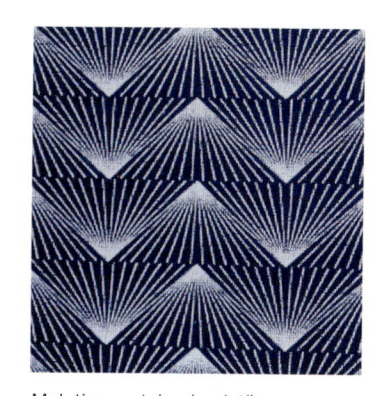   Maluti mountains (*moloti*)

Maluti mountains (*moloti*)    Mangoes, paisley    Minora (razor blades)

isiShweshwe

Mixed masala

Mixed masala

Mugabe's hair (named after President Robert Mugabe of Zimbabwe) or *moriri*

Mugabe's hair (named after President Robert Mugabe of Zimbabwe) or *moriri*

Mushrooms, brains or *mlungu* (European) hair

Mushrooms, brains or *mlungu* (European) hair

New mushrooms

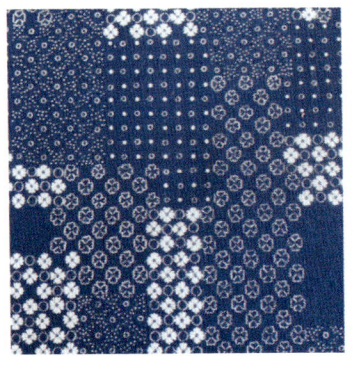

Patchwork (patch)

Peacocks (*pikoko*)

Appendix

271

Peacock's feathers (*lesiba la pikoko*) (detail)

Peanuts (cousin, *makhoto mane*)

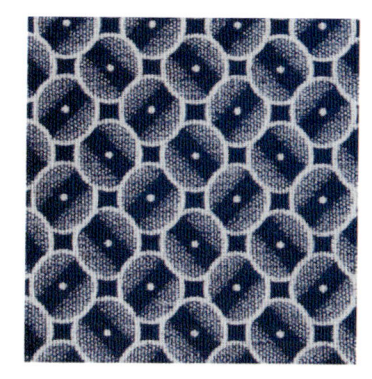

Peanuts (*makhoto mane*)

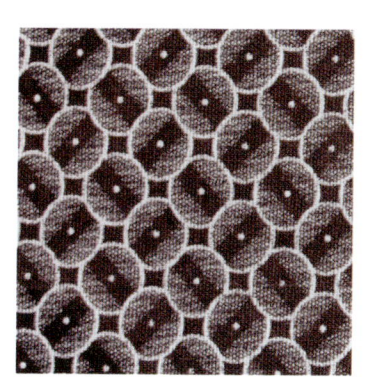

Peanuts (*makhoto mane*)

Peas (*ertjies*)

Pegs (*ipegs*)

Pegs (*ipegs*)

Pegs (*ipegs*)

Pimville (part of Soweto, a township near Johannesburg in Gauteng)

272 isiShweshwe

Pineapples

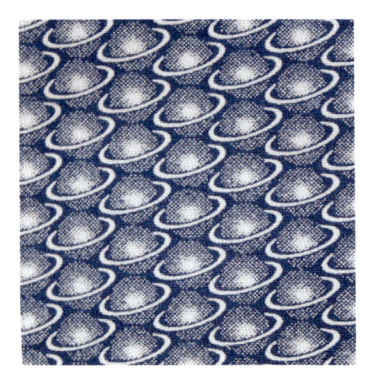

Planets

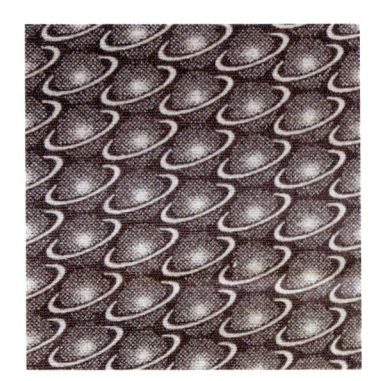

Planets

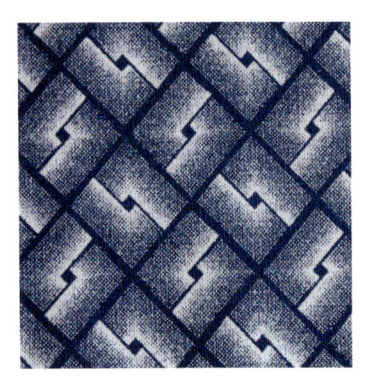

Planks (*lepolanka*)

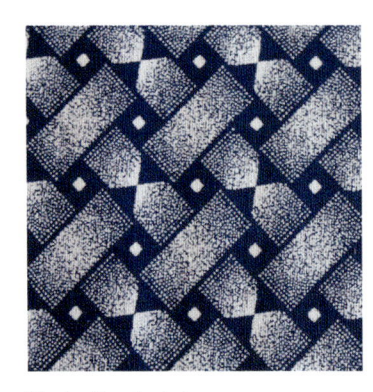

Planks (*lepolanka*)

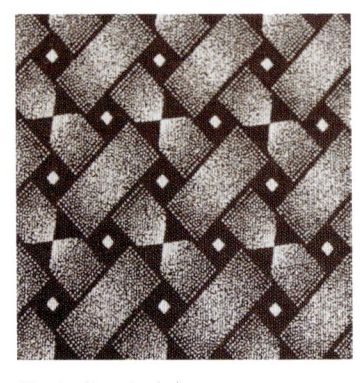

Planks (*lepolanka*)

Post Office

Post Office

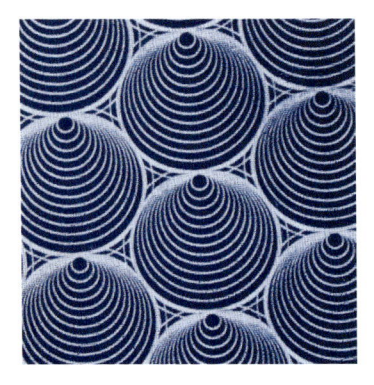

Pyramids, Sotho hats (*mokorotlo* or *khetla*)

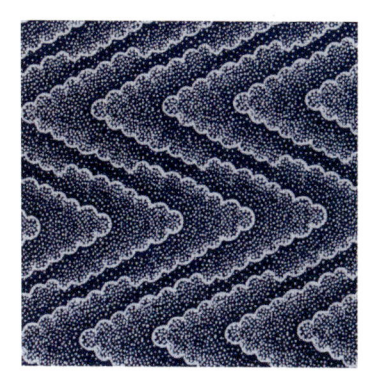

Appendix

Rippling or wavy river (*diphororo* or *moloti*) or *maru a matso* (thunder clouds)

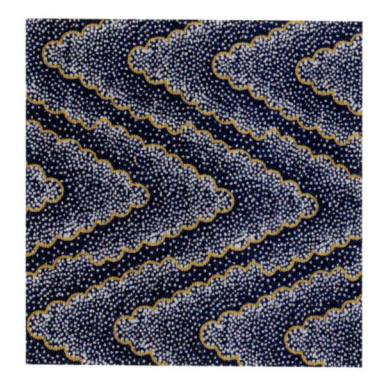

Rippling or wavy river (*diphororo* or *moloti*) or *maru a matso* (thunder clouds)

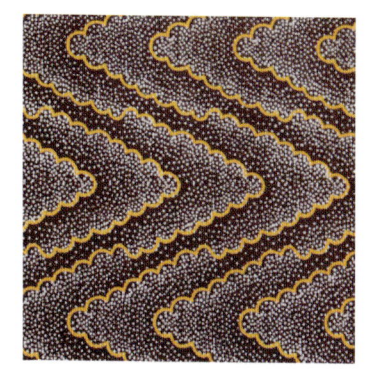

Rippling or wavy river (*diphororo* or *moloti*) or *maru a matso* (thunder clouds)

Ropes (*ropo*)

Saws (*isage*, *sakha*) or combs (*kama*)

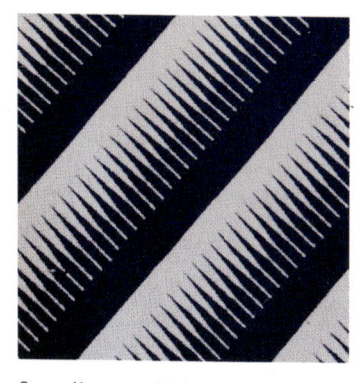

Saws (*isage*, *sakha*) or combs (*kama*)

Saws (*isage*, *sakha*) or combs (*kama*)

Skirt panel – aloes in flower (winter)

Skirt panel – praying hands (from Albrecht Dürer's praying hands)

274 *isiShweshwe*

Skirt panel- soccer design

Soccer balls (spliced)

Sotho hats (*mokorotlo*)

Sotho horsemen (*pere*)

Sotho horseman (*pere*) (detail)

Spears (*lerumo*)

Spear circles or wheels

Spiders

Strelitzia (Wigan Printworks blue down range)

Appendix

Strelitzia (Wigan Printworks blue down range)

Suns

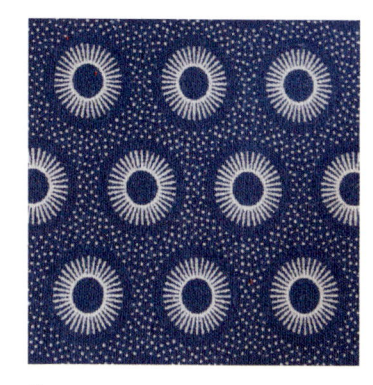

Suns

Suns or stars (*naledi*)

Swazi cloth

Swazi cloth (diamonds)

Swazi cloth (diamonds)

Swazi cloth (*libulu* or *marabe*)

Swazi cloth (smart partnership)

isiShweshwe

Swazi cloth stripes

Swazi cloth stripes (*livundla*)

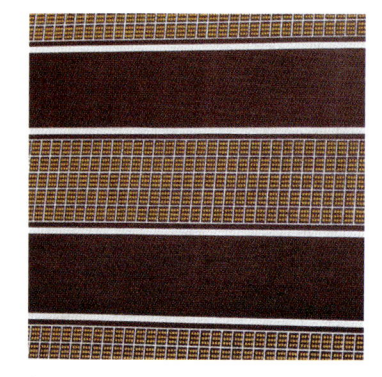

Swazi cloth stripes (*livundla*)

Swazi dots (*indlobu*)

Tennis balls (*itenis*)

Ticks (*bosoleisi*, from the Afrikaans *bosluis*)

Trees, windows or clams

Watermelons

Zigzags

Notes

INTRODUCTION

1. *Salempore* is a coloured cotton cloth widely used in Africa and the West Indies as trade cloth. Originally made in Nellore in India (in the Godavari and Visakhapatnam districts), it was known locally as *salembari gudda* (Swarnalatha 2005: 23–4). It was largely exported as undyed cloth to Britain and Europe for printing. A dyed variant, mostly indigo and known as *allegars*, from the Masulipatnam factory area, emerged in the mid-eighteenth century. Other variants, known as *callowpores*, included multicoloured stripes at regular intervals that were woven at the loom into the cloth. This cloth was later widely copied (for example, in Portugal) for trade with Africa. The latter name also applied to cheap checked-plaid cotton cloth. *Callowpore* cloth (known locally in South Africa merely as *salempore*) has become widely used in various dress forms in the region, even acquiring religio-cultural associations in Mpumalanga and elsewhere.
2. Elizabeth Melville, e-mail to J.C. Leeb-du Toit, 2016.

CHAPTER 1: Indigo Textiles in Context

1. The earliest references to the presence of dyed cloth include the writings of Herodotus (c.450 BC) who mentions a Scythian tribe 'who painted their garments in indelible colours' (probably henna or indigo) (*HOCP* n.d.: 7).
2. Records of early pre-Christian trade between Rome and India indicate that India had a long-standing trade relationship with Phoenicians, Arabs, Persians and Chinese. There is increasing evidence to show that India traded in East Africa and along the eastern seaboard and it has been established that at a far earlier date, possibly 2500 BC, Indian textiles were traded in Africa. If recently discovered Chinese documents and maps are taken into account, it is also evident that the Chinese were aware of the route around the Cape and may well have been among the first to circumnavigate the Cape, possibly to conduct trade in Africa (Rayda Becker, interview by Juliette Leeb-du Toit, Cape Town, 2005; see also the map exhibited in the South African Parliament c.2005, which was a copy of a map of Africa sourced in China). Chinese activites may have included cloth exchange and dyeing, but that must remain speculative for the present.
3. Alex Campbell, interview by F. Bell, J.C. Leeb-du Toit and K. Nieser, Gaborone, Botswana, 2005.
4. Campbell, interview, 2005.
5. Thomas Huffman, pers. comm., 2005.
6. Indigo is required for creating most colours of the spectrum such as greens, reds and browns (Balfour-Paul 1998: 5).
7. In Indian indigo dyeing, the freeing of the cloth of all astringents is achieved by steeping it in goats' dung and additional continuous washing. The parts not to be coloured are protected by a coating of wax and the cloth is dipped into the indigo vat. It is then washed and dyed with a madder or *chaya* root. Only the Sindh and Multan areas in Pakistan use natural indigo (*HOCP* n.d.: 14).
8. 'The process of extracting the dye from the [woad] plant was unbelievably long, complicated, labour intensive, and smelly, as it included many weeks of fermenting in manure, which had to be constantly stirred.' Apparently, such was the stench that Queen Elizabeth I forbade woad-dyeing

within a five-mile radius of any royal estates. An entire barrel of woad would only dye about three pieces of cloth. As a result, the cost of a blue woad-dyed garment might exceed the cost of a small house (http://renaissancedancewear.com/fabric_colors_in_the_renaissance.html).

9. Bartolomeu Dias in 1487, Vasco da Gama in 1498 and later Pedro Álvares Cabral in 1500 established links in India, but they were initially not well received. At the time, the Mamluks of Egypt and Syria controlled the Mediterranean and the overland routes to Mecca and spices and goods from the east reached Venice via Mamluk territory. The explorations made in the Indian Ocean were an attempt to disturb the Venetian trade with the Mamluks, the Venetians supporting the Mamluks in the fray (Lunde 2005a).

10. John Vogt (1975) notes that cloth has, to date, received little attention and that only 10–15 per cent of the records from this period have survived. Other trade items were glass beads, slaves, wine and foodstuffs. Vogt notes further that the availability of foreign textiles so depressed the local Portuguese textile producers that they eventually only made woollen and linen products for those who could not afford the foreign cloth.

11. The Portuguese were the first to import indigo with agents in Lahore, Agra, Ahmedabad and Multan via Surat. Portuguese control and military intervention challenged the increasing opposition in the Indian Ocean principalities. The Portuguese, under Alfonso de Albuquerque, established a military base in Goa on the Malabar coast in 1510 to protect their interests, Goa remaining the capital of the Portuguese seaborne empire, the 'Estado da India' until as late as 1961 (Lunde 2005c: 3). In addition, Albuquerque occupied Malacca in 1511, expelling Gujurati, Bengali and Muslim-Tamil merchants. In 1513 he laid siege to Aden and in 1514 to the island of Hormuz. Many years later, the Portuguese increasingly established themselves on the west coast of Africa, seizing Luanda in 1641, as it was an important source for slaves (Lunde 2005d: 4).

12. Jenny Balfour-Paul, pers. comm., 2016.

13. Balfour-Paul, pers. comm., 2016.

14. In furthering their intentions of controlling the maritime trade with the East, the Portuguese took over several important Indian Ocean ports by force, resulting in the sacking of Mombasa, where among the spoils taken by the Portuguese were 'great quantities of cotton cloth, silk and gold-embroidered textiles as well as valuable carpets' (Lunde 2005a), the cloth in all probability from India.

15. https://www.kimonoboy.com/short_history.html. The Portuguese introduced Indian-patterned calico to Japan in the sixteenth century, with floral, scallop and geometric designs. The Japanese copied these and produced their own cheaper variants in shades of madder, red and brown which were widely used in kimono *obis* (sashes), futon covers and cloths. Even discarded indigo cotton cloth 'was acquired in Western Japan and then sold into the poorer Northern rural and seaboard communities. Japanese farm women purchased these used fabrics and gave them new life by remaking them into *boro* field clothing (*noragi*), futon covers (*futongawa*) and other useful household textiles.'

16. The Portuguese were believed to be cannibals and their trade goods were regarded as inferior. Hence, they initially had little success in the Far East. However, this improved as 'they brought silver, ivory, ebony and sandalwood from Goa and Malacca to Macao, took Chinese silks and other goods to Nagasaki in exchange for silver, exchanged the silver for gold with Chinese merchants in Macao, and returned to Malacca and Goa with gold, silk, camphor, copper, mercury and porcelain, all in great demand in the Indian Ocean trading network' (Lunde 2005a). The Dutch also imported silk cloth from Japan (Jacobs 2000: 117). Elisabeth Jacobs describes a loosely fitting *Japonse rok* with wide sleeves, resembling a gown that typified the Oriental style (*habitu asiatico*) imported into Europe. However, imitations of these gaments were soon made in India as the originals were too costly (50–70 guilders).

Notes to Chapter 1

17 The Portuguese mediated trade between China and Japan from Macau, near Canton, where they had been granted a 'trading factory' in 1556 (Lunde 2005a). Cotton cultivation was introduced into western Japan via China in the sixteenth century and resulted in widespread handspun cotton and weaving there. Japanese cottons were costly and highly valued and, in the 1870s, a few commercial mills for weaving and spinning cotton emerged (https://www.kimonoboy.com/short_history.html). But the rural cottage industry and weaving of cotton by farm women still dominated this production. Indigo was the preferred dyestuff since it grew in Japan. Indigo cotton fabrics were widely used for clothing by peasants and were known as *noragi*. Their peasant use and production stems from the Edo period (1603–1867) when peasants, restricted by law from wearing silk, could only wear coarse hemp. Japanese farm women mostly made jackets, pants, covers and other household items, such as curtains, indigo being the primary dyestuff used (https://www.kimonoboy.com/short_history.html). Other Japanese dyeing techniques were incorporated in their designs and required additional skills. Most Japanese items were too costly even for the European market, however, and so cheaper copies were made in India. This is a significant early instance where designs located in Japan were copied in India for cheaper production and dissemination to other markets. As will be shown later, this tendency problematised attempts to initiate and enforce design copyright by subsequent manufacturers throughout the world. Some design modifications have been patented in the West and in Africa, but the origins of a design are often from eclectic sources where copyright did not initially apply. Centuries of repeated copying and interpretation and modification in various parts of the world make it virtually impossible to determine and locate the origins of most designs, except by identifying their parallels with continuities still existing in the East. Plain and printed indigo cloth from India and Batavia (Java) was linked in part to process and design in China and Japan and was widely traded internally. Thus, patterned and plain indigo cloth reaching the Cape in the mid-1550s may have come from two or three communities in the East, but was implicitly linked to many sources.

18 By 1622 the Dutch had some 83 vessels on their inter-Asiatic trade routes alone, as well as several other agent's vessels. In 1641 they conquered Malacca, in the process assuming control from the Portuguese and taking over the textile trade in Makasser from the Indians in 1668 (Abbott 1999). In India, the VOC sold Japanese lacquer, African ivory, luxury European goods as well as American cochineal (Jacobs 2000: 81). They also traded with Ceylon (now Sri Lanka). The Dutch negotiated agreements via brokers, who in turn traded with individual weavers (Jacobs 2000: 76). Gold traded in India came from Persia and Japan and copper from Japan was highly desirable in India and in the Moluccas. The VOC again had a virtual monopoly in these metals.

19 The VOC established four offices on the Indian subcontinent: in Surat in the north-west, in Coromandel on the lower east coast, in Bengal on the north-east and in Cambay in Gujerat. So did other East India traders (for example, the French, British, Portuguese, Danes, and Swedes-North Germans), but these did not pose a threat to the Dutch. The greatest market for textiles was in the Indonesian archipelago (Jacobs 2000: 78), in particular Bengal cloth (cotton mixed with silk) and other cotton cloths and loosely woven *bafta*. Rougher cloths were *niquanias* and *salempore*. The Dutch established trade offices in Indonesia in Banda, Ternate and elsewhere. While the British had had a post in India at Fort George (Madras), since the seventeenth century, the French had had centres at Pondicherry, the Portuguese at Thome and the Danes at Tranquebar (Tharangambadi). Only the British were eventually to pose a real threat to Dutch control from the early eighteenth century when they negotiated more favourable trade agreements in the region and, instead of paying a percentage interest, paid a fixed annual amount in tax, regardless of the volume of goods traded (Jacobs 2000: 75). This privilege was realised by promising to take pilgrims to Mecca every year. Trade with India and the East was affected by three great events: the war between the French and the British in the eighteenth century, trouble in the Mogul area to the north and the War of the Austrian Succession (1740–8). East coast trade diminished as

costs rose (Jacobs 2000: 85–6). With a weakened Mogul rule, conflict emerged: weavers fled to the cities and the harbour became a production site (Jacobs 2000: 86). By 1730 Bengal, not Coromandel, became the main centre for the textile trade.

20 The importation of indigo was prohibited in France in 1598 until 1737. In Germany the first prohibitions were recorded in 1557 until 1700. In England initial prohibitions were recorded in 1532; in 1581 use of indigo was prohibited without woad; and in 1640 dyers were encouraged to use indigo and in 1660 the ban on indigo was finally lifted in Britain.

21 The dyeing and printing techniques used on the *indiennes* were created through mordant dyeing (fixative chemicals were printed onto cloth then dipped into dye), resist-dyeing (resist paste was coated onto the fabric then cloth-dyed), relief printing (block prints coated with dye were pressed onto fabric) and hand-painting.

22 Kirsten Nieser (2005: 52) notes: 'As printing works for calicoes flourished in Europe, the Hanseatic port city of Hamburg competed with Amsterdam and London as an entrepôt for goods related to the fabric industry in Europe. Rich in waterways necessary for the fabric industry, its first *Kattundruckerei* [calico printworks] was established around 1690 – for multiple colour-printing on cotton (Koch 1984: 8, 22). Augsburg and Hamburg became the largest 'Manufakturen' [manufacturers] for 'modern' textiles, which included *Blaudruck*, while auction houses in Hamburg turned over vast amounts of various textiles. Just under half of the 53 businesses in 1797 were blueprinters (Koch 1984: 52, 119), but – judging by the number of printing tables (*Drucktische*) – these were markedly fewer than those printing multicoloured fabrics with mordant dyes (Koch 1984: 52). Hamburg's fabric industry could not compete with British and French mechanization – begun early in the 18th century. A last attempt to compete was the perrotine, which incorporated hand-made printing blocks – but to no avail.'

23 Ebeltje Hartkamp-Jonxis (1995) notes that of the few examples of early cloth that survive, there are four samples of printed cotton from 1787, possibly from Amsterdam and destined for the West African trade (now housed in the Rijksarchief in The Hague). Some samples for the trade to the East were discovered in the Dutch trade mission to Nagasaki from 1813 to 1829. More examples exist from after the Dutch cession from Belgium and the Industrial Revolution began in 1830. Overtooms is a significant example of a Dutch printworks, which mostly block-printed cloth by hand, but some was perhaps from copper-engraved plates. The 'Dutch manner' described the method of realising designs: to print on a colourless ground in which ground indigo mixed with coppergreen and gum Arabic was printed on the cloth, mostly in blue, sometimes in red or *porceleynrood*. The use of *blauw grond porcelein* meant that a reserve (usually wax) was used for the design or motif, then the cloth was dipped in an indigo bath and the wax removed by heat. The *blauwdrukken* reserve was known as *leminiasdrukken* (China Blue in Britain) or as the 'Dutch manner' (Hartkamp-Jonxis 1995: 195).

24 In 1750 there were about 100 printworks in Holland, of which 80 were in Amsterdam, but by 1772 a mere 21 remained and by 1796 only 12. However, the Flemish had a well-established industry in the eighteenth century. In 1801, in Ghent, where many cotton printers began, J. Wilkens wrote a practical manual for printers titled *Den Volmaekten Katoen-drukker*.

25 The British reacted to constraints imposed on them in Bengal (by other traders) and, as a result, gained even greater control of the Ganges delta, adopting a more colonial approach and control, their adage being 'we are men of power ... and take advantage of it' (*HOCP* n.d.: 10). The British exercised control over the middlemen, who obliged weavers to sell at a specific price and forbade them from working for other consignments, at least until English orders were completed (Jacobs 2000: 106). During the Fourth English War, the British occupied all the Dutch establishments in India in 1781, taking their goods and destroying their buildings. But while these were returned to the Dutch four years later, by then British control was such that the

Notes to Chapter 1

Dutch could not recover their former position of strength. The VOC had lost its creditworthiness and could no longer use its own coinage as previously. The last ship with any considerable cargo traded there in 1788. Between 1730 and 1769 the EIC textile imports rose considerably (Jacobs 2000: 90), with the French Compagnie des Indes importing about half the amount of textiles and the VOC in definite third place. By 1760, many areas of India were under British control.

26 English dyeing was initiated in the twelfth century and a dyers' guild was established in London as early as 1188 (*HOCP* n.d.: 9). Saxony and Thüringen were the main dye-producing districts in the north of Europe. Charlemagne laid down rules for the cultivation of woad, madder and kermes on his estates, products that were exported to England from Erfurt by the Hanse in the fourteenth and fifteenth century. Swiss printers were employed in Richmond in 1675, as was a Swiss national, Jacques Deluye. In 1697 a Frenchman Mauvillian worked at Mitcham and Wandsworth. There were Flemish artisan bleachers in England in the fourteenth century who settled in Lancashire, soon to become one of the major areas of domestic cloth production. The Dutch were, however, still considered to be better finishers, the 'Dutch manner' being highly regarded (*HOCP* n.d.: 12). Not surprisingly, therefore, Dutch printers were responsible for initiating the textile-printing trade in Scotland, establishing a workshop on the banks of the Donear, in Aberdeen, in 1720. By the early seventeenth century, Lancashire was localised as the centre of the dyeing and bleaching industry, with merchants sending their cloth to be bleached, dyed and finished there, then received back for sale (*HOCP* n.d.: 11). Lancashire calico-printing was initiated in 1738 by Messrs Clayton of Bamber Bridge, near Preston, while the first print works was established in 1764. Glasgow produced shawls, bandanas and handkerchiefs for the southern states of America and the West Indies, while Lancashire specialised in dress fabrics and London did block-work for furnishings and silks, with France and Germany the main opposition.

27 The British arranged product exhibitions that resulted in an enormous increase in exports. Few designers were initially keen to expose their designs, especially in view of competition from the export trade. But later the 1851 Great Exhibition of the Works of Industry of All Nations was a major showcase supported by Prince Albert as its president. France had had a National Exhibition as early as 1798 (*HOCP* n.d.: 154). A Manchester exhibition was held in 1846 and 1849. The 1851 exhibition resulted in a huge increase in exports and the British Empire Exhibition in 1924–5 also resulted in expanded markets (*HOCP* n.d.: 170), but there was a lot of competition from French, German and Dutch fabrics.

28 S.W. Whitham (1903: 16) notes that textiles from France and Germany imported into South Africa included 'estamenes, Cashmeres, poplins, nuns . . . veiling and silks'. Foreign textiles were preferred as there was greater intensity and variety of colour. One of the reasons put forward by Whitham for British lack of competitiveness with foreign manufactured and dyed goods was that 'our dyeing interest has been handicapped by the fact that spirit used for dyeing purposes has to pay excise on the basis of spirit for consumption'. One of the wholesalers in Cape Town also reminded Whitham that 'German manufacturers are straining every nerve to secure new business, and never more so than at the present time. I have often four or five different foreign travellers calling upon me in a week, making tempting offers of all kinds' (Whitham 1903: 19).

29 In 1940 the Cotton Board in Manchester launched a new venture, the Colour and Style Centre, to undertake the maintenance and extension of the export trade through advertising and demonstrations. Exhibitions were held displaying products from the United States. The board also established a good library of design samples (*HOCP* n.d.: 177–8). Before the Second World War, the United States used the slogan 'export or die', resulting in a slight decline in home production, but this was not wholly successful (*HOCP* n.d.: 388). In 1944 the Council of Industrial Design was established by the president of the Board of Trade to improve British design, giving rise to the Britain Can Make It Exhibition in 1946 and, among others, the Festival of Britain project in 1951.

CHAPTER 3: Frontier, Voortrekker and Pioneer Dress

1 Annemarie Carelsen, pers. comm., 2005; pers. comm., 2010.

2 'Coloureds' are a multiracial group originating in colonial South Africa. The term Coloured was used by the apartheid government to describe one of the four main racial groups.

3 Erica Erasmus, interview by J.C. Leeb-du Toit, Pretoria, 2012.

CHAPTER 4: German Missionaries, *Blaudruck* and German Settlers

1 Unschooled or 'heathen' *amaXhosa* were referred to as 'red' by missionaries and settlers, with reference to the clay they used to protect their faces from the sun and from insects and to colour their cotton blankets. The red was, in fact, a deep reddish terracotta.

CHAPTER 5: Modern European and American Blueprint in Context

1 Van Rood, interview by J.C. Leeb-du Toit, Helmond, Netherlands, 1995.

2 Van Rood, interview, 1995; Helen Bester, interview by J.C. Leeb-du Toit and K. Nieser, King William's Town, Eastern Cape, 2005.

3 Van Rood, interview, 1995.

4 In Haarlem the Dutch engineer Braam Fleming, Van Rood observed, had developed contacts with West Africa. Fleming was well aware of the existing trade between Manchester and Africa. The Haarlem Cotton Company contacted him to help them market their goods in West Africa, on the east and west coasts of the continent, and especially in Ghana and on the Ivory Coast. Fleming registered the cloth designs in England and obtained the copyright to use Dutch-Java-Africa patterns in England. This manoeuvre involved him in the African and Eastern Company and in the Swansea Company. He established trading posts in West and East Africa and traded with batik in West Africa. Van Rood noted that East Africa was already influenced by Indian and Arab trade. The West Africans in particular were familiar with Indian textiles and the country was well structured, with a good agricultural sector to provide raw goods (Van Rood, interview, 1995).

5 John Cowie, interview with J.C. Leeb-du Toit and K. Nieser, East London, Eastern Cape, 2005.

6 Naren Kala, pers. comm., 2010.

7 Cowie, interview, 2005.

8 Katalin Földi-Dózsa, interview by J.C. Leeb-du Toit and K. Nieser, Budapest, Hungary, 2005.

9 Földi-Dózsa, interview, 2005.

10 Földi-Dózsa, interview, 2005.

11 The marginalisation of Romanians in Eastern Europe remains contentious, even today.

12 Monika Lackner, interview by J.C. Leeb-du Toit and K. Nieser, Budapest, Hungary, 2006.

Notes to Chapter 6

CHAPTER 6: Modern British Blueprint in Context

1. David Bradley, pers. comm., 2006.
2. Despite Glasgow's initial prowess, Lancashire, by the early seventeenth century, was the heart of bleaching and dyeing in Britain. It was soon a specialist centre in dress fabrics, too, and print works were established there in 1764. Even by this early stage, however, Britain, together with France and Germany, had reached the peak of its textile production, but the British cloth industry fell into slow decline in the aftermath of the two world wars and the Great Depression of the 1930s.
3. Bradley, pers. comm., 2006.
4. John Cowie, interview by J.C. Leeb-du Toit and K. Nieser, East London, Eastern Cape, 2005.
5. Craig McCann, pers. comm. to J.C. Leeb-du Toit, 2005; Craig McCann, interview by J.C. Leeb-du Toit, Manchester, England, 2008.
6. Bradley, pers. comm., 2006; McCann, pers. comm., 2005; Margaret Hickson, interview by J.C. Leeb-du Toit, Manchester, England, 1995.
7. Margaret Hickson, interview by J.C. Leeb-du Toit, Manchester, England, 1995.
8. Margaret Hickson and Ann Shaw, interview by J.C. Leeb-du Toit, Manchester, England, 2005.
9. Hickson and Shaw, interview, 2005.
10. Hickson and Shaw, interview, 2005.
11. Hickson and Shaw, interview, 2005.
12. Hickson and Shaw, interview, 2005.
13. Hickson and Shaw, interview, 2005.
14. Hickson, interview, 1995; Hickson and Shaw, interview, 2005.
15. Hickson and Shaw, interview, 2005.
16. Hickson and Shaw, interview, 2005.
17. Hickson and Shaw, interview, 2005.
18. Hickson and Shaw, interview, 2005.
19. Hickson and Shaw, interview, 2005.
20. Jeff Wood, interview by J.C. Leeb-du Toit, Manchester, England, 2005.
21. Peter Barton, interview by J.C. Leeb-du Toit, Manchester, England, 2005.
22. Barton, interview, 2005.
23. Barton, interview, 2005.
24. Barton, interview, 2005.
25. Barton, interview, 2005.
26. Barton, interview, 2005.
27. Barton, interview, 2005.
28. Jennifer Harris, interview by J.C. Leeb-du Toit, Manchester, England, 2006.

CHAPTER 7: Da Gama Textiles and *isiShweshwe*

1   John Cowie, interview by J.C. Leeb-du Toit and K. Nieser, East London, Eastern Cape, 2005.
2   Cowie, interview, 2005.
3   Cowie, interview, 2005; Helen Bester, interview by J.C. Leeb-du Toit and K. Nieser, King William's Town, Eastern Cape, 2005.
4   Cowie, interview, 2005.
5   Cowie, interview, 2005.
6   Cowie, interview, 2005.
7   Naren Kala, pers. comm., 2010.
8   Bester, interview, 2005.
9   Rodney Breetzke, interview by J.C. Leeb-du Toit, Zwelitsha, Eastern Cape, 2005.
10 Breetzke, interview, 2005.
11 Breetzke, interview, 2005.
12 Bester, interview, 2005.
13 Helen Bester, interview by J.C. Leeb-du Toit and K. Nieser, King William's Town, Eastern Cape, 2008.
14 Helen Bester, interview by J.C. Leeb-du Toit, King William's Town, Eastern Cape, 2012.
15 Bester, interview, 2005.
16 Helen Bester, interview by J.C. Leeb-du Toit, King William's Town, Eastern Cape, 2015.
17 Bester, interview, 2012.
18 Bester, interview, 2005.
19 Breetzke, interview, 2005.
20 Bester, interview, 2005.
21 Bester, interview, 2005.
22 Bester, interview, 2005.
23 Cowie, interview, 2005.
24 Cowie, interview, 2005.
25 Bester, interview, 2005.
26 Bongiwe Walaza, interview by J.C. Leeb-du Toit, Johannesburg, Gauteng, 2005; Bongiwe Walaza, interview by J.C. Leeb-du Toit, Johannesburg, Gauteng, 2008; Amanda Laird-Cherry, interview by J.C. Leeb-du Toit, Johannesburg, Gauteng, 2005; Amanda Laird-Cherry, interview by J.C. Leeb-du Toit, Johannesburg, Gauteng, 2008.
27 Bester, interview, 2005.
28 Phil Staunton, interview by J.C. Leeb-du Toit, Zwelitsha, Eastern Cape, 2005.
29 Bester, interview, 2008; Bester, interview, 2012.
30 Cowie, interview, 2005.
31 Alison Auld, interview by J.C. Leeb-du Toit, Pietermaritzburg, KwaZulu-Natal, 2012.
32 Auld, interview, 2012.
33 Auld, interview, 2012.
34 Auld, interview, 2012.

CHAPTER 8: Traders and *isiShweshwe*

1. Father Edwin Kinch, pers. comm., 1994.
2. John Sparg, interview by J.C. Leeb-du Toit and K. Nieser, Kokstad, KwaZulu-Natal, 2005.
3. Naren Kala, pers. comm., 2010; Jimmy Morrison, pers. comm., 2005; Ursula Morrison, pers. comm., 2005.
4. Marius Bester, interview by J.C. Leeb-du Toit and K. Nieser, East London, Eastern Cape, 2005.
5. The Cowie family – John and his two sons Ian and Neil – bought Cowies (later Jacksons) in 1945. John's father, who had run a chain of trading stores in Zambia, brought a wealth of experience and expertise to the business in East London. At the time of my first interview with John in 2005, the family's interests had grown to include six trading stores across the Eastern Cape and the thriving business in East London, which dealt mainly in *isishweshwe*. By this time John had worked for the family for 50 years, Ian for 26 years and Neil for 20 years. John, a graduate of Rhodes University, was, I should add, indisputably the doyen of cloth traders in South Africa. John Cowie died in 2009.
6. John Cowie, interview by J.C. Leeb-du Toit and K. Nieser, East London, Eastern Cape, 2005.
7. Frank Cowie was the youngest surviving Cowie son, one of five: three of his brothers were killed in the First World War in France in 1915, while the fourth was gassed and lost the use of a lung. On appeal to the war tribunal, Frank was recalled from the frontline in France, and served for the remainder of the war as a signals-corps instructor in Bedfordshire, England. Cowie, interview, 2005.
8. Cowie, interview, 2005.
9. Cowie, interview, 2005.
10. Hugh Morrison, pers. comm., 2005.
11. Kinch, pers. comm. 1994.
12. Jimmy Morrison, pers. comm., 2005; Ursula Morrison, pers. comm., 2005.
13. Ursula Morrison, pers. comm., 2005.
14. Ursula Morrison, pers. comm., 2005.
15. Ursula Morrison, pers. comm., 2005.
16. Ursula Morrison, pers. comm., 2005.
17. There were many more traders in the Morrisons' territory, but Jock cornered the rural market in KwaZulu-Natal for decades. Among the many other trader families, the Rutherfords had a shop at Ubombo and Rob Rutherford wrote a book about his experiences there. In Eshowe the Adams family were well-known missionary traders, Charlie Adams being close to the Zulu royal family as an adviser and mediator.
18. As a result of trade restrictions in West Street, many shopowners moved to Grey Street. Between 1905 and 1918 there was additional pressure on Indian shopowners and finally all trading licences to operate in the city centre were terminated. The Indian Immigration Prevention Bill further attempted to stem the mercantile capacities of Indian immigrants.
19. Helen Bester, interview by J.C. Leeb-du Toit and K. Nieser, King William's Town, Eastern Cape, 2005.
20. Kala, pers. comm., 2010.
21. Kala, pers. comm., 2010.
22. Fatima Akhalwaya, interview by J.C. Leeb-du Toit, Johannesburg, Gauteng, 2010.
23. Fleur Rourke, interview by J.C. Leeb-du Toit and K. Nieser, Scottburgh, KwaZulu-Natal, 2006.

24 Rourke, interview, 2006.

25 Rourke, interview, 2006.

26 Rourke, interview, 2006.

27 Rourke, interview, 2006.

28 Rourke, interview, 2006.

CHAPTER 9: Cultural Usage of *isiShweshwe* in Lesotho and Swaziland

1 All translations in this chapter from Dieterlen et al.'s original French to English are my own.

2 Alison Lockhart, editor of this publication, found various sources online for the botanical names of this plant. One site claims it is *Hypoxis argentea* (http://bukantswe.sesotho.org/Shweshwe_%28lebitso%29_%5B8519%5D.html) while others think it is *Gazania krebsiana*, subsp. *Serrulata* (http://www.bgci.org/worldwide/article/0441/). Both sources give the alternative *seSotho* name for the plant as *shweshwe*. This may well provide yet another source for calling blueprint, as substitute for the *thethana ea tsikitlane,* by the name *seshoeshoe*, unless the *seSotho* name of the plant arose from their name for blueprint. It is significant that the author of the site uses the term *shweshwe* (a vernacular used throughout South Africa and incorrectly spelt here: it should be *isishweshwe*) and not *seshoeshoe* (the correct terminology among *seSotho* speakers), suggesting that perhaps this information is speculation.

3 Dieterlen et al.'s use of the term 'natural coquetry' may be problematic, in that it implies a natural flirtatiousness among Sotho women. I have elected to retain this part of his quotation, well aware that postcolonial, revisionist and feminist readings might problematise his choice of words and suggest a stereotyping of *seSotho*-speaking women and women in general in a way typical of the patriarchal gender perspective prevailing at the time.

4 Else Schreiner, pers. comm., 2003.

5 Fleur Rourke, interview by J.C. Leeb-du Toit and K. Nieser, Scottburgh, **KwaZulu-Natal**, 2006.

6 Selina and Samuel Mokoena, interview by J.C. Leeb-du Toit and K. Nieser, Maseru, Lesotho, 2005.

7 Thakane Lerotholi, pers. comm., 2005; pers. comm., 2008.

8 Lerotholi, pers. comm., 2005; pers. comm., 2008 and Matsooana Sekokotoana, pers. comm., 2005; pers. comm., 2008.

9 Mantsebeng Khati, interview by J.C. Leeb-du Toit and K. Nieser, Maseru, Lesotho, 2008.

10 Mokoena, interview, 2005.

11 A combined effort from a designer-seamstress in the store on 22 July 2010, Mankosinathi Basholo (from Mohale's Hoek); from the sewing machine technician and assistant, Tjale Peter Motsoari; from shop assistant Ma Tsidiso (Tsidi); and from assistants Sima Panderkar and Ma Mamphole. They provided me with the names of most designs held in the store. On going through the bolts of cloth on the shelves, they were in no doubt as to the names of the designs, the identity of new designs and preferences for particular designs.

12 Prince Tshekedi Dlamini, pers. comm., 2005.

13 Sometimes a smaller pink bead, the *ihholomu* or *inholomu*, is worn instead. Two crossed *simohlwane* are worn across the shoulders to the waist, comprised of pink, white, red and black beads.

14 Neil Cowie, interview by J.C. Leeb-du Toit, 2012.

Notes to Chapter 10

CHAPTER 10: Cultural Usage of *isiShweshwe* in South Africa, Botswana and Namibia

1   Victoria Francis, interview by J.C. Leeb-du Toit, Hillcrest, KwaZulu-Natal, 2011.

2   Rose Gumede, interview by J.C. Leeb-du Toit, Pietermaritzburg, KwaZulu-Natal, 1994; Quikizana Kate Phungula, pers. comm., 1993.

3   Christina Shange, interview by J.C. Leeb-duToit, KwaNyuswa, KwaZulu-Natal, 2003.

4   Both ekuPhakameni and eBuhleni are in the Inanda valley near KwaMashu, a township near Durban.

5   Phyllis Zungu, interview by J.C. Leeb-du Toit, Durban, KwaZulu-Natal, 2006.

6   Nomandla Nodolo, interview by J.C. Leeb-du Toit, Ntlangwini homestead near Harding, KwaZulu-Natal, 2013; Simon Mtolo, interview by J.C. Leeb-du Toit, Hillcrest, KwaZulu-Natal, 2016.

7   Tante Taljaard, interview by J.C. Leeb-du Toit, Genadendal, Western Cape, 2005.

8   Tante Grietjie, interview by J.C. Leeb-du Toit and K. Nieser, Garies, Northern Cape, 2011.

9   Sister Leonie, interview by J.C. Leeb-du Toit and K. Nieser, Vredendal, Western Cape, 2011.

10 The Griqua were a predominantly Dutch-speaking community of Khoisan and African slaves. They moved from the former Orange Free State to East Griqualand in the 1860s. The British took control of the area in 1874 and Griqua authority ended soon after the death of their leader, Adam Kok.

11 Eric Kopman, interview by J.C. Leeb-du Toit, Pietermaritzburg, KwaZulu-Natal, 2009; Aunt Hilda, interview by J.C.Leeb-du Toit, Pietermaritzburg, KwaZulu-Natal, 2009.

12 The name *jamani* (*ujamani*) may also have other associations. Between 1904 and 1912 a group of about 10 000 men from the Eastern Cape (probably mainly *amaXhosa*) were recruited to work in German South-West Africa, a region then predominantly used for trade and pastoralism. The men were to assist in building and maintaining railways, and to fight against the *ovaHerero*, if need be (Beinart and Bundy 1987:166–7). The men came to be known as 'Jamani'. They were supplied with transport rations and clothes offered by the recruitment company Koppel (Beinart and Bundy 1987: 169). Ethiopian missionaries there helped to mobilise them and they engaged in a strike to improve their lot in 1910 (Beinart and Bundy 1987: 181). Despite the harsh conditions they endured there, they preferred to remain rather than work on farms and mines.

13 Stefania Victor, interview by J.C. Leeb-du Toit and K. Nieser, King William's Town, Eastern Cape, 2005.

14 Manton Hirs, interview by J.C. Leeb-du Toit, King Williams' Town, Eastern Cape, 2005.

15 Hirs, interview, 2005.

16 Hirs, interview, 2005.

17 Frau Schuch, pers. comm., 2008.

18 Marius Bester, interview by J.C. Leeb-du Toit and K. Nieser, East London, Eastern Cape, 2005.

19 In conversation, Euphemia Thembela Mayila, a Xhosa domestic worker in Cape Town, told me that she only began to wear *isishweshwe* when she settled in Cape Town, c.1989. This suggests that the cloth assumed a rural and cultural reference in Cape Town, which she did not associate with her hometown in the Tsolo district of the former Transkei.

20 Frau Höhne, pers comm., 1989

21 Girlie Kakuyarukua Chezuba, interview by J.C. Leeb-du Toit, Kirsten Nieser and Fiona Bell, Mahalapye, 2005.

22 Chezuba, interview, 2005.

23 Chezuba, interview, 2005.

24 Chezuba, interview, 2005.

25 Chezuba, interview, 2005.

26 Mrs Basha Motsomi, pers. comm., 2013.

27 Chippy Bruce, pers. comm., 2006.

CHAPTER 11: *isiShweshwe* Dress and its Modernities

1 By the 1930s this trend was accompanied by a militaristic mode of dress for males and females of the Voortrekker Youth Movement, a counter to British prototypes in the Scouts and Girl Guides. The construction of Voortrekker and pioneer wear and its assimilation as national dress after 1948 manifest the coercion of dress as an emblem of particularising ideas of national aspirations. Such was the national profiling of these variants that by the 1950s this dress code, given its sourcing in settler and generalised military wear, was regarded as representing white South African national dress. Many cultural representatives from South Africa wore it – a problematic signifier for most South Africans – ridiculously perhaps when worn at Miss World competitions in the 1960s.

2 Included in this repertoire was silk-screened cloth from the Evangelical Lutheran Church Arts and Crafts Centre at Rorke's Drift. It was made by African women and was located in an amalgam of Swedish, Finnish and indigenous design produced for export to the Nordic countries and for the more exclusive interior design outlets such as Afro-Art in Stockholm. Locally it went to Craftsman's Market in Hyde Park, Johannesburg, and to Klaus Wasserthal's stores in Pretoria.

3 Jutta Faulds, interview by J.C. Leeb-du Toit, Pietermaritzburg, KwaZulu-Natal, 2005.

4 Jenny Aitchison, interview by J.C. Leeb-du Toit, Pietermaritzburg, KwaZulu-Natal, 2004.

5 Gertrude Strauss, interview by J.C. Leeb-du Toit and K. Nieser, Kloof, KwaZulu-Natal, 2007.

6 Else Schreiner, pers. comm., 2003.

7 Sandra Klopper, interview by J.C. Leeb-du Toit, Cape Town, Western Cape, 2012.

8 The homelands policy has been justifiably maligned from all quarters. For many African and white nationalists, however, this crypto-independence represented at least some autonomy. Bantustans received preferential development grants that sought to retain production and labour within their geographical confines. Migration to urban centres beyond their borders was curbed by legislation, resulting in the development of localised entrepreneurial ventures, including the manufacture of traditional clothing. The flagship of the Bantustan policy was the Transkei – now part of the Eastern Cape – which gained self-government from 1972 to 1976 (Davenport 1987: 374). Xhosa selfhood and ethnicity, foregrounded as the prevailing culturally specific identity in the 1970s, marginalised other regional groups such as the *amaThembu* and *amaMfengu*. As noted in Chapter 9, the *baSotho* were well aware of the Xhosa efflorescence in self-identification and dress, but endeavoured to emulate the process in their use of *isishweshwe*. In the Transkei, however, Xhosa skirts in particular were widely marketed in tourist centres, ethnic boutiques and craft outlets, and even today have been foregrounded again in designs by fashion houses such as Sun Godd'ess.

Notes to Chapter 11

9   Veronica Baxter, pers. comm., 2002.
10 Victoria Francis, interview by J.C. Leeb-du Toit, Hillcrest, KwaZulu-Natal, 2011.
11 Heather Schreiner, pers. comm., 2003.
12 Marianne Fassler, pers. comm., 2009.
13 See http://www.hikarunoguchi.com/mouflon/index.html.
14 Fassler, pers. comm., 2009.
15 Amanda Laird-Cherry, interview by J.C. Leeb-du Toit, Johannesburg, Gauteng, 2005; Amanda Laird-Cherry, interview by J.C. Leeb-du Toit, Johannesburg, Gauteng, 2008.
16 Bongiwe Walaza, interview by J.C. Leeb-du Toit, Johannesburg, Gauteng, 2005; Bongiwe Walaza, interview by J.C. Leeb-du Toit, Johannesburg, Gauteng, 2008.

Select Bibliography

INTERVIEWS

Unless otherwise indicated, all interviews were conducted by Juliette Leeb-duToit.

Aitchison, Jenny, Pietermaritzburg, KwaZulu-Natal, 2004.

Akhalwaya, Fatima, Johannesburg, Gauteng, 2010.

Auld, Alison, Pietermaritzburg, KwaZulu-Natal, 2012.

Barton, Peter, Manchester, England, 2005.

Becker, Rayda, Cape Town, Western Cape, 2005.

Bester, Helen, King William's Town, Eastern Cape, 2005 (with Kirsten Nieser).

Bester, Helen, King William's Town, Eastern Cape, 2008 (with Kirsten Nieser).

Bester, Helen, King William's Town, Eastern Cape, 2012.

Bester, Helen, King William's Town, Eastern Cape, 2015.

Bester, Marius, East London, Eastern Cape, 2005 (with Kirsten Nieser).

Breetzke, Rodney, Zwelitsha, Eastern Cape, 2005.

Campbell, Alex, Gaborone, Botswana, 2005 (with Fiona Bell and Kirsten Nieser).

Chezuba, Girlie Kakuyarukua, Mahalapye, Botswana, 2005 (with Kirsten Nieser and Fiona Bell).

Cowie, John, East London, Eastern Cape, 2005 (with Kirsten Nieser).

Cowie, Neil, Zwelitsha, Eastern Cape, 2012.

Erasmus, Erica, Pretoria, Gauteng, 2012.

Faulds, Jutta, Pietermaritzburg, KwaZulu-Natal, 2005.

Földi-Dózsa, Katalin, Budapest, Hungary, 2005 (with Kirsten Nieser).

Francis, Victoria, Hillcrest, KwaZulu-Natal, 2011.

Grietjie, Tante, Garies, Northern Cape, 2011 (with Kirsten Nieser).

Gumede, Rose, Pietermaritzburg, KwaZulu-Natal, 1994.

Harris, Jennifer, Manchester, England, 2006.

Hickson, Margaret, Manchester, England, 1995.

Hickson, Margaret and Ann Shaw, Manchester, England, 2005.

Hirs, Manton, King William's Town, Eastern Cape, 2005.

Khati, Mantsebeng, Maseru, Lesotho, 2008 (with Kirsten Nieser).

Klopper, Sandra, Cape Town, Western Cape, 2012.

Kopman, Eric, Pietermaritzburg, KwaZulu-Natal, 2009.

Kopman, Hilda, Pietermaritzburg, KwaZulu-Natal, 2009.

Lackner, Monika, Budapest, Hungary, 2006 (with Kirsten Nieser).

Select Bibliography

Laird-Cherry, Amanda, Johannesburg, Gauteng, 2005.

Laird-Cherry, Amanda, Johannesburg, Gauteng, 2008.

Leonie, Sister, Vredendal, Western Cape, 2011 (with Kirsten Nieser).

McCann, Craig, Manchester, England, 2008.

Mokoena, Selina and Samuel, Maseru, Lesotho, 2005 (with Kirsten Nieser).

Mtolo, Simon, Hillcrest, KwaZulu-Natal, 2016.

Nodolo, Nomandla, Ntlangwini homestead near Harding, KwaZulu-Natal, 2013.

Rourke, Fleur, Scottburgh, KwaZulu-Natal, 2006 (with Kirsten Nieser).

Shange, Christina, KwaNyuswa, KwaZulu-Natal, 2003.

Sparg, John, Kokstad, KwaZulu-Natal, 2005 (with Kirsten Nieser).

Staunton, Phil, Zwelitsha, Eastern Cape, 2005.

Strauss, Gertrude, Kloof, KwaZulu-Natal, 2007 (with Kirsten Nieser).

Taljaard, Mrs, Genadendal, Western Cape, 2005.

Van Rood, Frans, Helmond, Netherlands, 1995.

Victor, Stefania, King William's Town, Eastern Cape, 2005 (with Kirsten Nieser).

Walaza, Bongiwe, Johannesburg, Gauteng, 2005.

Walaza, Bongiwe, Johannesburg, Gauteng, 2008.

Wood, Jeff, Manchester, England, 2005.

Zungu, Phyllis, Durban, KwaZulu-Natal, 2006.

OTHER SOURCES

Abbott, M. 1999. 'Indian Trade Textiles'. Speech delivered to the Asia Society, Sydney.

Balfour-Paul, J. 1998. *Indigo*. London: British Museum Press.

Barnard, Lady A.L. 1999 [1799]. *The Cape Diaries of Lady Anne Barnard, 1799–1800*. Two volumes. Edited by M. Lenta and B. le Cordeur. Cape Town: Van Riebeeck Society.

Barter, C. 1866. *Alone among the Zulus: The Narrative of a Journey through the Zulu Country, South Africa*. London: Society for Promoting Christian Knowledge.

Bate, S.C. 2000. 'Points of Contradiction: Money, the Catholic Church and the Settler Culture in Southern Africa (1837–1920) – Part 1: The Role of Religious Institutes'. *Studia Historiae Ecclesiasticae* 26(1): 165–88.

Beinart, W. and C. Bundy. 1987. *Hidden Struggles in Rural South Africa: Politics and Popular Movements in the Transkei and Eastern Cape 1890–1931*. Berkeley: University of California Press.

Bell, C. 1993. 'Die Geschichte des Blaudrucks: Zur Geschichte des Zeugdrucks in Mitteleuropa'. In H. Walravens (ed.) *Ein Blaues Wunder: Blaudruck in Europa und Japan*, edited by H. Walravens. Berlin: Akademie Verlag GmbH.

Bindewald, E. and K. Kasper. 1950. *Bunter Traum auf gewebtem Grund: Aus der Wunderwelt des Stoffdrucks*. Braunschweig: Georg Westermann.

Blaut, J.M. 1995. *The Colonizer's Model for the World: Geographical Diffusionism and Eurocentric History*. New York: Guildford Press.

Botha, C.G. 1970. *Social Life in the Cape Colony during the 18th Century*. Cape Town: Struik.

Boyajian, J.C. 2008. *Portuguese Trade in Asia under the Habsburgs, 1580–1640*. Baltimore: Johns Hopkins University Press.

Buntman, B. 1996. 'Bushman Images in South African Tourist Advertising: The Case of the Kagga Kamma'. In *Miscast: Negotiating the Presence of the Bushmen*, edited by P. Skotnes, Cape Town: University of Cape Town Press.

Burchell, W.J. 1953 [1822]. *Travels in the Interior of Southern Africa*. London: Batchworth Press.

Chapman, M. 1995. 'Freezing the Frame: Dress and Ethnicity in Brittany and Gaelic Scotland'. In *Dress and Ethnicity*, edited by J.B. Eicher. Oxford: Berg.

Comaroff, J. and J. Comaroff. 1997a. *Of Revelation and Revolution Vol. 1: Christianity, Colonialism and Consciousness in South Africa*. Chicago: Chicago University Press.

———. 1997b. *Of Revelation and Revolution Vol. 2: The Dialectics of Modernity on a South African Frontier*. Chicago: Chicago University Press.

CPA (Calico Printers' Association) 1949. *Fifty Years of Calico Printing: A Jubilee History of the C.P.A.* Manchester: Calico Printers' Association.

Crais, C.C. 1992. *White Supremacy and Black Resistance in Pre-industrial South Africa: The Making of the Colonial Order in the Eastern Cape, 1770–1865*. Cambridge: Cambridge University Press.

Davenport, T.R.H. 1987. *South Africa: A Modern History*. Cape Town: Southern Books.

Dieterlen, H., F. Kohler and E. Jacottet. 1912. *Livre d'Or de la Mission du Lessouto: Soixante-quinze Ans de l'Histoire d'une Tribu Sud-Africaine, 1833–1908*. Préface by M.A. Boegner. Paris: Maison des Missions Évangéliques.

Eicher, J.B., ed. 1995. *Dress and Ethnicity*. Oxford: Berg.

Eicher, J.B. and D.B. Ross, eds. 2010. *Berg Encyclopedia of World Dress and Fashion, Volume 1: Africa*. Oxford: Berg.

Eldredge, E.A. 2002. *The Pursuit of Security in Nineteenth-century Lesotho*. Cambridge: Cambridge University Press.

Elliott, A. 1978. *Sons of Zulu*. Johannesburg: Collins.

Farber, L. 2010. 'Africanising Hybridity: Towards an Afropolitan Aesthetic in Contemporary South African Fashion Design'. *Critical Arts* 24(1): 128–67.

German Settlers' Jubilee Souvenir Booklet. 1908. East London.

Gill, S.J. 1993. *A Short History of Lesotho, from the Late Stone Age until the 1993 Elections*. Morija Museum and Archives, Lesotho.

Grossert, J.W. 1967. 'Zulu Bead Love Letters: Princess Magogo Talking of Bead Colours and Meanings. In *Art and Craft in Education*, Vol. 2. Pietermaritzburg: Shuter & Shooter.

Grünewald, H. 1998. *Die Geschichte der Deutschen in Südafrika*. Cape Town: Ulrich Naumann Verlag.

Guest, B. and J.M. Sellers, eds. 1985. *Enterprise and Exploitation in a Victorian Colony: Aspects of the Economic and Social History of Colonial Natal*. Pietermaritzburg: University of Natal Press.

Hammond-Tooke, W.D., ed. 1974. *The Bantu-speaking Peoples of Southern Africa*. London: Routledge and Kegan Paul.

Hansen, K. Tranberg, 2004. 'The World in Dress: Anthropological Perspectives on Clothing, Fashion and Culture'. *Annual Review of Anthropology* 33: 369–92.

Select Bibliography

Hartkamp-Jonxis, E. 1995. 'Wat Overbleef van Een Achttiende-eeuwse Amsterdamse Katoendrukkerij'. In *Voor Nederland Bewaard: De Verzamelingen van het Koninklijk Oudheidkundig Genootschap in het Rijksmuseum*, edited by J.F. Heijbroek and R. Meijer. Baarn: De Prom.

Hendrickson, H. 1996. 'Bodies and Flags: The Representation of Herero Identity in Colonial Namibia'. In *Clothing and Difference: Embodied Identities in Colonial and Post-colonial Africa*, edited by H. Hendrickson. Durham: Duke University Press.

Hobhouse, E. 1984. *Emily Hobhouse: Boer War Letters 1860–1926*. Edited by R. van Reenen. Cape Town: Human & Rousseau.

HOCP (*History of Calico Printing*) (undated and no author identified). ABC archives, Hyde, near Manchester.

Howe, A. 1984. *The Cotton Masters*, 1830–1860. Oxford: Clarendon Press.

Jacobs, E.M. 2000. 'Koopman in Azië. De Handel van de Verenigde Oost-Indische Compagnie tijdens de 18de Eeuw'. Ph.D. diss., University of Leiden.

Jikelo, C. 1995. Written account of her fieldwork in the Eastern Cape.

Keegan, T., ed. 2004. *Moravians in the Eastern Cape*. Cape Town: Van Riebeeck Society.

Kiplinger, J. 2011. 'The Indian Head Connection of Indigo, Calico and Bulldog: The J.L. Stifel Co'. http://info.fabrics.net/the-indian-head-connection-of-indigo-calico-and-bulldog/.

Klopper, S. 2005 ' "Civilized Garments": The Missionary Origins of Traditionalist Dress Styles in Southern Africa'. Unpublished paper presented at the Dress in Southern Africa Conference, Centre for Visual Art, University of KwaZulu-Natal, 5–7 August.

Koch, J.H. 1984. *Mit Model, Krapp und Indigo*. Hamburg: Hans Christians Verlag.

Kok, D. 2014. *Kleurrijk Gedrukt: Oorsprong en Ontwikkeling van het Staphorster Stipwerk*. Staphorst: LK Mediasupport.

Koopman, A. 2005a. 'Crossing Cultural Boundaries: The Attire of KwaZulu-Natal Politicians'. Unpublished paper presented at the Dress in Southern Africa Conference, Centre for Visual Art, University of KwaZulu-Natal, 5–7 August.

———. 2005b. 'Sartorial Style in Contemporary South African Dress'. Unpublished paper presented at the Dress in Southern Africa Conference, Centre for Visual Art, University of KwaZulu-Natal, 5–7 August.

Krauss, F. 1973. *Travel Journal / Cape to Zululand; Observations by a Collector and Naturalist, 1838–40*. Cape Town: A.A. Balkema.

Krostewitz, W. 1938. 'Hohenlimburger Heimatblätter für den Raum Hagen und Iserlohn'. *Heft* 7(2005): 225–50.

Kuper, H. 1986 [1963]. *The Swazi: A South African Kingdom*. New York: Holt, Rinehart & Winston.

Leeb-du Toit, J.C. 1989. 'Diversity and Interaction: Sr. Pientia of Mariannhill'. Paper presented at the South African Association of Art Historians Conference, University of Natal, Pietermaritzburg.

———. 1994. '*isiShweshwe*: On Black Women's Identity in Commercial Cloth'. Unpublished paper presented at the Gender Studies Conference, University of Natal.

———. 1995. '*isiShweshwe*: The Forging of Black Women's Identity in Commercial Cloth. Paper presented at the American College African Studies Association Conference, New York University.

———. 2003. 'Sangoma Cloth Usage in Context'. Paper for online publication for the Campbell Collections (no longer available online).

———. 2005a. '*isiShweshwe/uJamani*: British Sources of Indigo Cloth in South Africa'. Paper presented at the Design History Society Conference, London Metropolitan University.

———. 2005b. 'Sourcing *amaJamani/isiShweshwe* and its Indigenisation in South Africa'. Unpublished paper presented at the Dress in Southern Africa Conference, Centre for Visual Art, University of KwaZulu-Natal, 5–7 August.

Lunde, P. 2005a. 'The Coming of the Portuguese'. *Saudi Aramco World*. 56(4): 54–61. http://archive.aramcoworld.com/issue/200504/the.coming.of.the.portuguese.htm.

———. 2005b. 'The Explorer Marco Polo'. *Saudi Aramco World* 56(4): 37–40. http://archive.aramcoworld.com/issue/200504/the.explorer.marco.polo.htm.

———. 2005c. 'The Fable of the Rat'. *Saudi Aramco World* 56(4): 2–3. http://archive.aramcoworld.com/issue/200504/the.fable.of.the.rat.htm.

———. 2005d. 'Monsoons, Mude & Gold'. *Saudi Aramco World* 56(4): 4–11. http://archive.aramcoworld.com/issue/200504/monsoons.i.mude.i.and.gold.htm.

Maclennan, B. 1986. *A Proper Degree of Terror: John Graham and the Cape's Eastern Frontier*. Johannesburg: Ravan Press.

Maree, J. 1995. *An Industrial Strategy for the Textile Sector.* Cape Town: UCT Press.

Mattson, A. 2005. 'Indigo in the Early Modern World'. https://www.lib.umn.edu/bell/tradeproducts/indigo.

Mertens, A. 1987. *African Elegance*. Cape Town: C. Struik.

Mitford, B. 1883. *The Induna's Wife*. London: Kegan Paul, Trench & Co.

Moodie, J.W.D. 1835. *Ten Years in South Africa*. London: Richard Bentley.

Mukuka, G.S. 2008. *The Other Side of the Story: The Silent Experience of the Black Clergy in the Catholic Church in South Africa (1898–1976)*. Pietermaritzburg: Cluster Publications.

Nel. 1983. Untitled document. Current location unknown.

Newton-King, S. 1999 *Masters and Servants on the Eastern Cape Frontier, 1760–1805*. Cambridge: Cambridge University Press.

Nieser, K. 2005. ' "German Wear" in Africa: European Sources of Indigo Dress'. Unpublished paper presented at the Dress in Southern Africa Conference, Centre for Visual Art, University of KwaZulu-Natal, 5–7 August.

Oakes, D., ed. 1988. *Reader's Digest Illustrated History of South Africa: The Real Story*. Cape Town: Reader's Digest Association of South Africa.

Ovens, C. 1954. *A Commercial Traveller in Zululand in the 1950s: A Catalogue of My Experiences As a Commercial Traveller whilst Employed by Marshall Industrials and J.W. Jagger and Co. (Pty) Ltd*. Bloemfontein: C. Ovens.

Pauw, B.A. 1969. *Xhosa in Town: The Second Generation*. Cape Town: Oxford University Press.

Peires, J.B. 1982. *The House of Phalo: A History of the Xhosa People in the Days of Their Independence*. Berkeley: University of California Press.

Pheto-Moeti, M.B. 2005. 'An Assessment of *seShoeshoe* Dress As a Cultural Identity for baSotho Women of Lesotho'. M.Sc. thesis, University of the Free State.

Ralfe, E. 2004. 'Love Affair with My *isiShweshwe*: Theorizing Dress Stories'. In *Not Just Any Dress: Narratives of Memory, Body and Identity*, edited by S. Weber and C. Mitchell. New York: Peter Lang.

Rivett-Carnac, D.E. 1961. *Thus Came the English* in 1820. Cape Town: Howard Timmins.

Select Bibliography

Robertson, H. 1866. *Mission-life among the Zulu-Kafirs: Memorials of Henrietta Robertson Compiled Chiefly from Letters and Journals Written to the Late Bishop Mackenzie and His Sisters*. Edited by A. Mackenzie. Cambridge: Deighton, Bell & Co.

Rosenthal E. 1967. *Encyclopedia of Southern Africa*. 4th edition. London: Frederick Warne & Co.

Rovine, V.L. 2015. *African Fashion, Global Style: Histories, Innovations, and Ideas You Can Wear*. Bloomington: Indiana University Press.

Sandberg, G. 1989. *Indigo Textiles: Technique and History*. London: A & C Black.

Schnell, E.L.G. 1954. *For Men Must Work: An Account of German Immigration to the Cape with Special Reference to the German Military Settlers of 1857 and the German Immigrants of 1858*. Cape Town: Maskew Miller.

Sechefo, J. n.d. *The Old Clothing of the Basotho*. Mazenod: Catholic Centre.

Strutt, D.H. 1975. *Fashion in South Africa 1652–1900: An Illustrated History of Styles and Materials for Men, Women and Children, with Notes on Footwear, Hairdressing, Accessories and Jewellery*. Cape Town: A.A. Balkema.

Swarnalatha, P. 2005. *The World of the Weaver in Northern Coromandel, c.1750–c.1850*. New Delhi: Orient Blackswan.

Telford, A.A. 1972. *Yesterday's Dress: A History of Costume in South Africa*. London: Purnell.

Thomas, H. 1997. *The Slave Trade: The Story of the Atlantic Slave Trade, 1440–1870*. New York: Simon & Schuster.

Tippett, L.H.C. 1969. *A Portrait of the Lancashire Textile Industry*. London and New York: Oxford University Press.

Tyrrell, B. 1968. *Tribal Peoples of Southern Africa*. Cape Town: Books of Africa.

Vahed, G. and S. Bhana. 2015. *Crossing Space and Time in the Indian Ocean: Early Indian Traders in Natal – A Biographical Study*. Pretoria: UNISA Press.

Vilakazi, B.W. 1973. *Zulu Horizons:* Johannesburg: Wits University Press.

Vogt, J. 1975. 'Notes on the Portuguese Cloth Trade in West Africa, 1480–1540'. *International Journal of African Historical Studies* 8(4): 623–51.

———. 1979. *Portuguese Rule on the Gold Coast, 1469–1682*. Athens: University of Georgia Press.

Weiner, A.B. and J. Schneider, eds. 1989. *Cloth and Human Experience*. Washington and London: Smithsonian Institution Press.

Whitham, S.W. 1903. *Report on the Textile and Soft Goods Trades of South Africa*. London: P.S. King.

Winters, Y.A. 2015. 'Review of the Visual Symbolic Language of Southern KwaZulu-Natal's Beadwork and Dress Held in the Campbell Collections, University of KwaZulu-Natal in the Light of Sociocultural Theories'. Ph.D. diss., University of KwaZulu-Natal.

Zaverdinos, A.M. 1997. 'Assessment of a Collection of Basotho Artefacts in the Natal Museum'. Master's thesis, University of Natal.

Zungu, P. 2005. 'Aspects of Shembe Dress'. Unpublished paper presented at the Dress in Southern Africa Conference, Centre for Visual Art, University of KwaZulu-Natal, 5–7 August.

Index

ABC (company)
    designers 116–26, 151, 155
    origins and ownership 115–16, 131
    relationship to Da Gama 136, 137, 138, 139
    technical expertise 126–30
    see also skirt panels
African Art Centre 247
African National Congress 87 see also Madiba range; MaSisulu
Africanness 151, 211, 239, 240 see also South Africanness
Aitchison, Jenny 243–4
amatoishi (sePedi) 1 see also names and naming
American Board of Missionaries 110
Anderson, Margie 151
Anglo-Boer War Museum 53, 57, 58
Ashton, Benjamin 115
associations with *isishweshwe* dress
    'African wear' 98, 170, 223, 247
    ancestral link 209, 232
    empathy with oppressed 97, 151, 244, 245
    Christianity 186, 189, 209–10, 222, 232, 255
    confidence/pride 195, 232
    cultural 191–2, 195, 200, 202, 209, 255
    geographical 195
    inclusivity 250
    married status 196, 210, 229, 232, 244
    maturity 202, 209, 226, 244
    modernity 225, 252
    modesty 225
    pan-Africanism 187
    partisanship 244, 245, 247, 250
    patriotic nationalism 97, 98–9, 151, 187–8, 189, 196, 248, 249, 251
    respect 192, 194, 195, 200, 209, 210, 225, 232
    rurality 96, 151
    subservience 9, 209
    subversion 211, 233, 235, 244
Auld, Alison 156, 157–9

Baartman, Sarah 212
bafta 18
barter 20, 38, 51, 161, 176, 221, 222, 224 see also trade cloth
Barton, Peter 127–31
Baviaanskloof 67 see also Genadendal
Baxter, Veronica 247
beads 83, 87, 102, 221
Bergtheil, Jonas 82, 208

Berlin Mission Society 67
Bester, Helen 138, 140, 144, 151, 152
blanket production and sales 51, 62, 181
blankets 8, 181, 182, 184, 222, 223
Blaudruck (German) 1, 76
    aprons 27, 80
    Boer usage 184
    calendering process 26–7
    ceremonial use 90
    German settler usage 1, 78, 80, 82, 90, 93, 208, 223–4
    in Germany 25, 26–7, 87–91, 165
    importation to South Africa 28, 33, 63, 87, 88, 166–7, 207–8
    kappie 224
    links to Britain 65, 115
    marketing 166
    amaMfengu usage 71
    monopoly in colony 62–4
    name 1, 22, 26, 64
    pattern books 27
    production, rise and fall 26, 87–88, 90
    quality 87, 90
    traders and 166, 168, 169
    amaXhosa usage 218, 223
    see also names and naming; mission, influence on dress
Blaut, James 75–6
blauwdruk (Dutch) 1, 2–4, 26, 76
    designs 86, 87
    export to South Africa 86
    headscarves 86
    pattern technique 24, 86
    production 85
    see also names and naming; Vlisco Cotton Company
blockprinting 24, 25, 29 see also perrotine
bloudruk (Afrikaans) 1, 6, 77
    Boer usage 58, 61, 62, 238
    cross-cultural use 57, 58
    kappie 58
    at Moravian Mission (Genadendal) 75, 78
    pioneer usage 238
    quilts 53
    see also names and naming
blou sis 6, 58, 91
iblu (isiXhosa, isiZulu) 1 see also names and naming
blue (colour) associations 207, 235
blue dye see indigo dye
Blue Land Folklor 95

Index

blueprint (English) 1, 4, 6
  Boer usage 62, 65, 164
  characteristics 5, 57, 76, 107, 137
  Coloured usage 57
  competition for markets 32, 33, 64, 65
  Damara 214–16
  design 113, 115, 116–26, 127, 130, 131, 155
  designers 116–26, 154, 155
  early Cape 39, 40, 44, 47, 50, 51, 76
  exchange of knowledge and skills 26, 29, 115, 135
  Far East influence on design 18, 130, 131
  guilds 26, 31
  importation to South Africa 32, 33, 44, 65, 69, 83, 110, 135, 167
  kappies 56, 57, 58
  large-scale production 29, 31
  amaMfengu 223
  modern European manufacture 85–107
  Nordic countries 110–11
  origin and spread 6, 23, 31, 32, 35
  baPedi 226–8
  Portugese-derived 174, 207–8
  production 64, 88, 107, 109, 110, 114–16, 135–7
  quality, for export to colonies 32
  quilts 53
  techniques 24, 26, 29, 31, 114, 116, 119, 126–31, 135
  use in Britain 113
  use in Lesotho 184
  use in Spain and Portugal 20
  use in USA 107–9
  Voortrekker 52, 53, 56, 58
  workshops European 23, 24, 25
  amaXhosa 6, 223
  see also indigo cloth; *isishweshwe*; names and naming; Da Gama Textiles; skirt panels; mission, influence on dress
Boer 57
  cloth preferences 62, 63, 65, 164, 166, 184
  dress preferences 58, 61, 238
  see also pioneers; Trekboer; Voortrekkers
Bradley, David 114, 131
Breetzke, Rodney 123, 126, 138, 167, 174
British East India Company (EIC) 20, 27, 28, 31, 44
British settlers 49–52
  dress preferences 50, 51
  as traders 51–2
Brotherton 115, 141
Bruce, Chippy 149, 234
Brunnschweiler, Alfred 115
Bryant, A.T. 8

CHA Group 116, 131
calico 6
  use of 135, 176, 206, 246

Calico Printers' Association 114–15, 119, 122
Calico Printers' Association of Glasgow 62, 64
Calico Printers' Association of Manchester 62, 64
calico production in SA 134–5, 167
Campbell, Killie 8
Cape Town Fashion Week 152
Cape Verde islands
  and indigo trade 16, 17, 21
Cha Chi Ming 115, 116, 131
Chang, Dion 152
chintz 18, 184 *see also indiennes*
cloth names *see Blaudruck*; *blauwdruk*; blueprint; *indiennes*; indigo cloth; *isishweshwe*; *kékfestö*; *modrotisk*; names and naming
cloth types favoured
  Africans 62, 63, 65, 164
  Boers 62, 63, 164, 166, 184
  British settlers 50
  Coloured people 57, 211–12, 216, 238
  Damara people 212–15
  free burghers 43, 44–5
  German settlers 78, 80, 82, 83, 90, 223, 224
  ovaHerero 229, 230, 232, 234, 235
  Indigenous/Khoisan people 22, 37, 69, 207, 211, 212
  baPedi 9, 226
  shared preferences 62, 65, 83, 90, 223, 228, 234, 238
  baSotho 6, 176, 182, 185, 186, 189, 191
  baSwazi 200, 201, 201–2, 203
  trekboers 47
  baTswana 226, 232, 234
  VOC employees 37–8
  Voortrekkers 52, 56
  'working class' 24, 27, 33, 37, 38, 42, 43, 164, 168
  amaXhosa 6, 65, 158, 223
  amaZulu 83, 206–7
  see also slaves and slavery
Coloured people
  cloth preference 57, 211–12, 216, 238
Comaroff, Jean 75, 76, 77, 78
Comaroff, John 75, 76, 77, 78
copyright on design 153
cotton-growing industry 82, 138, 208
Cowie, Frank Hamilton 166
Cowie, John 122, 149, 166
Cowie, Neil 143, 144, 149, 154
Cowie and Wendler 166, 176
Cowie Trading 149
cross-cultural contact 3, 8, 36, 57, 70–1, 180, 223, 232
cross-cultural dress 75–8, 239–50
  as co-operation between races 246
  fashion/design 242, 243, 250
  nation-state formation 249

performing arts 247
  in practice 158, 164, 210–11, 239–45, 247–8, 250
  significance 232, 239–40, 242, 244–5, 246–50
  state sanctioned 245, 246
  theoretical underpinnings 239–40
cultural and ceremonial use of *isishweshwe* 148, 159, 210
  childbearing 209, 244
  coming-out ceremony 209
  festivals 181, 194
  marriage 98, 181, 187, 194, 202, 209–10, 224, 225, 226, 230, 232
  mourning 194, 196, 210, 230
  official occasions 98, 146, 192, 194, 198, 200, 202, 206–7, 230
  rejection 170, 248, 249–50
  see also isishweshwe, cultural usage
Cyril Lord (firm) 135
Czechoslovakian blueprint *see modrotisk*

Dadabhay's 143, 174
Da Gama Textiles
  and ABC 125, 136, 137, 138, 139, 140
  and authenticity of *isishweshwe* 137, 138, 142, 152, 154
  competition 139–40, 143, 152, 153, 171,
  continuities with *blauwdruk* 87
  continuities with blueprint 75, 125, 133, 137, 141
  continuities with *modrotisk* 104, 106
  copyright 153
  design process 140–1, 144, 156, 157–8
  design ranges 98, 143–8, 153, 156, 157
  designers 140–1, 144, 154–6, 157–9, 223
  and fashion designers 151–2, 251, 254
  feedback on design 100, 148–9, 150, 152, 155, 171, 174
  markets and marketing 143–6, 151–2, 154–5, 159, 167, 201, 254
  location of 133
  origins of 65, 134–5
  ownership change 140, 144
  preference for textiles from 143, 152, 154, 189, 190, 192, 203
  production techniques and technology 130, 136, 137, 138–9, 140–1, 146
  restraint of trade agreements 154, 159
  stockists (retail and wholesale) 140, 143, 170, 171, 172, 174, 175
  and Vlisco Cotton Company 86, 87, 136, 146
  see also copyright on design; logos; Good Hope Textile Corporation; traders and pedlars
Damara people
  dress 212–15

Danziger family (blueprinters Czech) 103
idark (*isiXhosa*, *isiZulu*) 1 *see also* names and naming
David Whitehead 131
De Leeuw, Helen 240–2, 247
diele 226–8
diffusion theory 75, 76, 77
discharge printing *see* pattern printing
Dlamini, Maimuna 203
dress
  early Cape 37–47
  'ethnic' 188, 245, 249, 250
  preferences
    Boer 58, 61, 237–8
    British settler 50, 51
    company officials 37
    Damara people 212–15
    free burgher 37, 44–6
    German settler 78, 80–1
    ovaHerero 230, 232
    indigenous peoples/Khoisan 2, 4, 8, 51–2
    baPedi 6, 165, 226–8
    baSotho 164, 176–7, 181–2, 185, 186–7, 188, 189, 192–4, 197
    baSwazi 198, 200, 201, 202, 203
    Trekboers 47
    baTswana 164, 226, 229
    Voortrekkers 52–3, 56–7
    'working class' 37, 42, 80
    amaXhosa 51–2, 65, 77, 78, 164, 218, 220, 222
    amaZulu 51–2, 164, 168, 198, 206–7, 209–10
  see also cross-cultural contact; cross-cultural dress; slaves and slavery
dresses, ready-made 174, 185, 203
Duitse sis 1, 6 *see also* names and naming
dye, blue *see* indigo dye

Elender, Lynn 156
Elender, Mary 156
Elliott, Aubrey 8
exiles to Cape from India and Indonesia 41–2

F.W. Ashton and Company 115
Fancy Prints 2, 97, 136
Farber, L. 9
Fassler, Marianne 250–1
Faulds, Jutta 242
Firma Harbig (firm) 90
Földi-Dózsa, Katalin 93, 96
Four Boots 172
Francis, Victoria 247
Frasers 156, 166, 175, 186
free burghers 35
  cloth preference 43, 44–5
  dress preference 37, 44–6

Index

Gateway Fabrics 197
Gaylard 9
Genadendal 67, 212
German missions 208, 223, 226, 228 *see also* Moravian missionaries
German National Museum 90
German print 1, 63 *see also* names and naming
German settlers 67, 78–9, 82, 166, 208
    cloth preference 78, 80, 82, 83, 90, 223, 224
    dress preference 80–1
    see also Moravian missionaries
Gokal, Nipun 174
Goldberger, Ernst 101–2
Goldberger Museum 101
Good Hope Textile Corporation 134
Good Hope Textiles 133, 135, 137
guinea 18

H.K. Gokal 174
Hanoverian Free Church Missions 67
ovaHerero
    cloth preference 229, 230, 232, 234, 235
    dress preference 230, 232,
Hickson, Margaret 116–26, 143, 151
home-sewing 164, 165 *see also* seamstresses
Horvath (family) 94, 95
Hungarian blueprint *see kékfestö*
Hungarotex 93, 106, 172

India
    textile production 13–15, 17–18
indiennes
    definition 5, 16
    design 24
    in early Cape 38, 39, 42, 43, 44, 47, 52
    Lesotho 184
    popularity of in Europe 22, 23, 26
    production in Europe 23, 24
    trade in 16, 22, 23, 28, 44
indigenous peoples
    cloth preference 6, 45, 158, 166
    dress preference 2, 3, 4, 8, 36, 51–2, 83, 102, 206
    see also Khoisan
indigo cloth
    characteristics 22
    design 5, 6, 24
    early Cape 23, 37, 38, 41, 45, 46, 47, 207
    preference for 5, 22, 23, 24, 33, 51, 138, 146, 206, 207, 212
    production in Europe and Britain 23, 24, 26, 29, 31, 88, 90, 91, 113
    production in India 13–14, 17–18, 29, 32
    variants 6, 17
    see also indigo trade; pattern printing techniques

indigo dye (chemical) 32, 78, 88, 127
indigo dye (natural)
    African (*Indigofera frutescens*) 12
    alternatives to Indian organic 14–15, 26
    Asia (*Indigofera tinctoria*) 14
    Latin America (*Indigofera suffruticosa*) 14
indigo dyeing
    technique 14, 26
indigo farming 14, 208
indigo trade 11–13, 21, 31
    African 12–13, 17
    British 21, 28, 31, 36
    Dutch 20–3, 36
    French 36, 184
    Indian 14, 17
    Indonesian 21
    Portugese 15, 16, 17, 18
    routes 11, 12–13, 15, 16, 17, 18, 20, 36
    and slavery 16, 18
    see also indiennes; traders and pedlars
intercultural dress *see* cross-cultural dress
Iziko Museums 9, 22

Jacksons 143, 225
isijalmani (isiXhosa, isiZulu) 1 *see also* names and naming
ujamani (isiXhosa, isiZulu) 1, 166 *see also* names and naming
Janssen, Helge 251
ujeremani (isiXhosa, isiZulu) 1, 166, 169 *see also* names and naming
Joch brothers 104–5
Jock Morrison and Sons (Morrisons) 122

Kajee, Saleem 171
Kala, Naren 92, 122, 137 169, 172
kappies (bonnets) 53, 56, 57, 58–9, 216, 224 *see also isishweshwe*, headwear
kékfestö (Hungary) 1
    continuities with *isishweshwe* 93, 95, 97, 98, 99, 100–2
    design 92, 93, 94–5, 97, 99, 100, 102
    importation to South Africa 92, 102
    mass production 92, 101
    pattern books, value and influence of 100
    printing techniques 92–3
    quilt 254
    rural associations 96–7
    usage 97, 98, 100–1
    workshops 92, 93
    see also names and naming
Kékfestö Muzeum 102
Khoisan 35, 37, 43, 68
    cloth preferences 22, 37, 69, 207, 211, 212

khoreit 176
King, Vernon 133
Klopper, Sandra 9, 244
Knotts, *Mr* 120, 123
Kohler, Max 8
Kolora 105, 106
Koopman, A. 9
Krige, Eileen 8
KwaKeshwa Textrim 171

Laird-Cherry, Amanda 152, 251–2, 254
Landsman, Adrie 140–1
Le Roy, Penny 240
Leeb-du Toit, J. 9, 245, 247
logos 75, 109, 127, 139, 141–2, 145, 154 *see also under* individual names
London Missionary Society 35, 68, 77
Lowe, Ted 121, 123, 125, 126
Lutheran Church 67

Madiba range 98, 146–8
Mahalapye Museum (Botswana) 234
Manchester Art Gallery 131
Manchester textile mills *see* textile industry, British
Mandela, Nelson Rolihlahla *see* Madiba range
Mangaliso, Thando 252
Mangaliso, Vanya 252
market research 63, 65
marriage dress 187, 195, 202, 209, 224–5, 226, 229
MaSisulu 148
mateis 1, 230 (*seTswana*, *otjiHerero*) *see also* names and naming
media and advertising 237, 238, 239, 246
Melusha's Fashion 203
mericani cloth *see* Stifel
Mertens, Alice 8
amaMfengu 6, 71, 217, 221, 222, 224
Mini Mark 174
mission
 influence on dress 69, 71, 75, 76, 78, 206, 211, 214–15, 222, 228, 232 *see also* Shembe Church
mission print 206 *see also* names and naming
missionaries *see under* names of individual missions
modrotisk (Czech) 1
 association with rural life 106
 design 104, 106
 family-owned businesses 103, 104
 imports to South Africa 92, 102–3, 105
 mass production 105, 106–7
 pattern books 105–6
 production techniques 103, 104
 uses 103
 see also names and naming
Moravian missionaries 36, 67–9, 70–4, 212

Moravian Missionary Society *see* Moravian missionaries
Morrison, Hugh 167
Morris, Jean 8
Morrison, Jimmy 168
Morrison, Jock 167, 168
Morrison, Ursula 168, 170
Moshoeshoe I 180, 181, 184, 191
motifs, popular
 crocodile 197, 234
 Hindu swastika 150
 soccer 125, 151
motoishi 226
mouri 18, 37
Msunduzi Museum 53, 57, 58
Mukuka, George 74–5, 76
Museum of Science and Industry (Manchester) 131
Museum für Thüringer Volkskunde 88

Nama 215
names and naming 1, 5, 77, 114, 158, 176, 180, 195, 196, 206
 vernacular 1, 166, 177, 180, 195, 200, 209, 215, 226, 230
National Cultural History Museum 56, 57, 58
national dress 187–9, 196, 249
National Museum (Budapest) 93
Nawab, Sayed 174
ndoeitji (*seTswana*) 1, 230, 232, 235 *see also* names and naming
Neprajzi Muzeum 99
Nettleton, Anitra 9
Nieser, Kirsten 9, 87–91, 167
niquania 18
Nkosi, Nkhensani 252
noragi 18
North Sotho
 reflected in design 125
nostalgia 9, 90, 91, 137, 240

oppositional dress 71, 98, 244, 245, 247 *see also* cross-cultural dress
Osman, Arif 197
Osman, Ismail 197
Ovens, Cyril 92

pattern books 27, 100, 104, 105, 106, 115, 131, 144, 158, 174
pattern printing techniques
 discharge-print 24, 31, 114, 127, 137, 139, 146
 hand/block 24, 25, 94, 103
 resist-print 23, 24, 31, 86, 99, 103
 roller 6, 109, 114, 128, 137
 roller engraving 127–30, 158
 roller-screen printing 130, 158

Index

rotary-screen 130, 139, 140
see also perrotine
peasant dress (Europe) 24–5, 87, 88–9
baPedi
   cloth preference 226
   dress preference 165, 226–8
Peers Brothers 122
Pella mission 214–15
performing arts 225–6, 247
perrotine 25, 31, 88, 90, 114
pioneers 57, 237
political figures in design 146–8
Pretoria Textile Wholesalers 92, 100, 169, 172

quilts and quilting 53, 110, 138, 254

Rainbow range 153
Ralfe, Elizabeth 248–9
Reform Church 67
research on textiles and dress in southern Africa
   ethnographic and anthropological 7–8
   need for further 8–9
   see also market research
Rhenish Mission Society 67
Rorke's Drift cloth 242
Ross, Doran 9
Rourke, Eddie 176
Rourke, Fleur 122, 155–6, 176
Rovine, Victoria 9
Rudolph, Mandy 144, 151

salempore 6, 18, 83, 198, 206
Schreiner, Else 185, 244, 250
Schreiner, Heather 248
Schulze, Margrit 9
seamstresses 149, 165, 176, 184, 185, 191, 203, 222, 225, 226, 228 see also tailors
second-hand clothing 42, 61, 83, 165, 184, 206, 218, 220
Shanghai Printing and Finishing Works 133–4
Shaw, Ann 116–26
Shembe church 210
isishoeshoe (seSotho) 180, 188 see also names and naming
seShoeshoe (seSotho) 177, 180 see also names and naming
isishweshwe 1
   authentic 110, 137, 138, 142, 152, 154
   colour preferences 138, 149, 151, 158, 170
   cost 96, 102, 154, 171, 200, 203, 216, 237, 242
   cross-cultural use 158, 170, 210–11, 212, 239–45, 247–9, 250
   cultural usage (Botswana) 229–32
   cultural usage (Lesotho) 181, 186–95, 196
   cultural usage (Namibia) 234–5
   cultural usage (South Africa) 194, 206–11, 209–11, 224–8, 255
   cultural usage (Swaziland) 197, 198, 200–3
   design copying 153, 171
   design sources 136, 143, 144, 149, 153, 155, 197
   design trends 149–51, 152, 176–7, 195–6, 197, 250–2
   distinguishing characteristics 137–8, 154, 170, 176, 194, 198
   fashion design (contemporary) 152, 197, 229, 240–2, 247, 249, 250–4
   finish 137–8, 153, 154
   headwear 191, 196, 210, 229
   international ranges developed 250–1
   marketing 148, 151–2, 155, 159, 166, 168, 170
   production techniques 138–40, 152
   and royalty 148, 181, 192
   skirt panels 123–5, 171
   sources for sale in trading stores 166–7, 168, 172, 174, 176
   South Africanness 237, 244, 250, 255
   spread to neighbouring countries 6, 7, 170
   traders and wholesalers 148, 165, 166–77
   usage by Coloureds 216
   variants of traditional colours 2, 93, 97, 146, 148, 151, 152, 153, 198
   variants of traditional (or fake) 139–40, 143, 152, 153–4, 171–2, 195, 203
   see also cross-cultural use; Da Gama Textiles; Good Hope Textiles; individual group names; names and naming; national dress; traders and pedlars
sis 215
skirt panels 123–5, 171
slaves and slavery 17, 20, 21, 38–42
   dress 22, 37, 39–42, 47, 207
   emancipated 42
   see also indigo trade
smous see traders and pedlars
Somhlahlo, Lizo 141, 144, 148, 151
baSotho
   cloth preference 6, 176, 182, 185, 186, 192, 197
   dress preference 176–7, 181–2, 185, 186–7, 188, 189, 192–4, 197
   reflected in design 125, 195
Sotho hat motif 125, 195, 250, 251
South African Fashion Week 151, 251, 252
South Africanness 6, 237, 239, 244, 245, 250, 251
   see also Africanness
Spruce 115, 141, 145, 149
Staphorster doekjes 24
Stein-Lessing, Maria 239–40
Stifel 75, 76, 100, 109–10, 167
Stifel, Johann L. (Johan Louis) 109

Strauss, Gertrude 244
Strines 115
Strutt, Daphne 8
baSwazi
   cloth preference 200, 201, 201–2, 203
   dress preference 198–200, 202, 203
Swedish Evangelical Lutheran Church (mission) 110–11

T.H. Faulkner 172
tailors 165, 169–70, 174 see also seamstresses
Telford, A. A. 8
terantala 186–7, 188
textile industry
   American 107
   British 107, 113–16, 133, 135, 137
   local 51, 82, 133–7, 138 see also Da Gama Textiles
Textile Museum, Česká Skalice 105
amaThembu 6, 9, 188, 196, 216–17
Thorpe, Jo 247
Three Cats range 109–110, 116, 135, 136, 137, 140, 141, 143, 144, 175, 232, 234
Three Fish range 86, 136, 145–6
Three Leopards range 144–5, 154
Tootal 131, 135, 137
Toto logo 116, 135, 145, 150, 234
trade cloth 18, 20, 21, 23, 37, 207 see also barter
trade routes 2, 11, 13, 15, 16, 17, 18, 20, 36, 82, 208
   see also indigo trade; individual cloth names
traders and pedlars 36, 42, 45, 49, 51, 57, 122, 162–77, 221, 222
   backgrounds of early 162, 165, 170
   and design 123–4, 125, 144, 148, 149, 150, 167, 174, 176
   Eastern Cape 165, 166, 167
   German settlers as 79
   Indian 170–4
   influence on dress preference 4, 167
   Jewish 162, 172
   Lesotho 175–7, 186, 197
   Natal 167–72
   and needs of customers 4, 5, 122, 123, 138, 167, 168, 171, 206
   number 222
   own production of garments 165, 169, 176
   routes (internal) 162–3
   see also barter; trade cloth
trading stores 175
   Lesotho 175–6
   mission 163, 175
   Moravian 69
   Natal 167–8
Trekboers 44, 47

baTswana
   cloth usage 6, 229, 232, 234
   dress usage 164, 226, 229
Tyrrell, Barbara 8

Van Rood, Frans 85, 86
Van Warmelo, N.J. 8
Vereenigde Oostindische Compagnie (VOC) 20, 23, 27, 36–7, 42, 43, 44 see also free burghers
vernacular names (of cloth) see names and naming; see under individual names
Vidge, Anton 166
Vilakazi, A. 8
Vlisco Cotton Company 85–7, 136, 146
voerschitz (chintz lining) definition 50, 184
Von Baeyer, Adolf 32, 78, 88
Voortrekkers
   dress preferences 52–3, 56–7
   origins 52, 57
   quilts 53–5
   see also Boer

Walaza, Bongiwe 152, 251, 252
Whitham, S.W. 32–3, 62–5, 76, 78, 79, 81, 90
Windmolen 153
Winters, Yvonne 9
woad (*Isatis tinctoria*) 15, 21, 23, 26
women, autonomy 163, 222, 224, 255
Wood, Jeff 126–7

amaXhosa 216–26
   cloth preference 6, 65, 158, 223
   dress preference 51–2, 65, 77, 78, 164, 218, 220, 222
   reflected in design 125
   see also amaMfengu; amaThembu

amaZulu 205–7
   cloth preference 83, 206–7
   dress preference 51–2, 164, 168, 198, 206–7, 209, 210
   reflected in design 125